THE FALL

THE FALL

The End of
Fox News
and the
Murdoch Dynasty

Michael Wolff

Henry Holt and Company

New York

Henry Holt and Company
Publishers since 1866
120 Broadway
New York, New York 10271
www.henryholt.com

Henry Holt® and ⒽⒸ® are registered trademarks of Macmillan Publishing
Group, LLC.

Back cover photographs courtesy of Getty Images and Dia
Dipasupil (Rupert Murdoch), Drew Angerer (Lachlan Murdoch),
Bryan Bedder (James Murdoch), Dave M. Benett (Elisabeth Murdoch),
Jason Koerner (Tucker Carlson), Roy Rochlin (Sean Hannity),
SOPA Images (Laura Ingraham), Stephanie Keith (Donald Trump),
Stephen Lovekin (Roger Ailes), Larry Busacca (Suzanne Scott),
and Karwai Tang (Rebekah Brooks).

Library of Congress Cataloging-in-Publication Data is available.

ISBN: 9781250879271

Our books may be purchased in bulk for promotional, educational,
or business use. Please contact your local bookseller or the Macmillan
Corporate and Premium Sales Department at (800) 221-7945, extension
5442, or by e-mail at MacmillanSpecialMarkets@macmillan.com.

First Edition 2023

Designed by Meryl Sussman Levavi

Printed in the United States of America

1   3   5   7   9   10   8   6   4   2

For Louise and Jack

"Let's face it, Tom, with all due respect, the Don, may he rest in peace, was slipping."

Sollozzo,
who has ordered the Godfather's death,
to Tom Hagen

"Let me wipe it first; it smells of mortality."

King Lear to Gloucester,
who has asked to kiss his hand

Contents

Introduction

Yes, yes, here is quite a bit of the raw inspiration for *Succession*, that roman à clef soap opera about you-know-who and his family and their empire. But this could be, too, the stuff of a TV newsroom sitcom. Breathing new life into an old genre, here is a conservative station and its upstairs-downstairs shenanigans and broadside characters. The aged patriarch lost in conversations with himself; the get-me-out-of-here son; the know-it-all brother; the smarter-than-the-rest of-them daughter; the paranoid anchor running for president; the dumb-as-brick anchor loved by all; the mocked-and-traduced woman anchor; and the dead evil-genius founder whose ghost continues to haunt the place.

To appear to take the *real* Fox News and, in the mind of the left, its almost-war-criminal-stature owners, less than seriously, to treat the Fox phenomenon and the Murdoch family as a cultural confection ripe for comedy, may be dangerously close to liberal sacrilege.

The sentinels of liberal propriety and right thinking aren't wrong. Fox News is agitprop (among the most successful ever employed) in the service of ever more extreme views, responsible as much as any agent for the election of Donald Trump and for animating right-wing certainties, very often utterly fake ones. Fox has helped bring the forces of reaction and racism pushed to the margins during the decades of liberal dominance out of the shadows and given new pride to the illiberal impulse. It is understandably difficult to see Fox News beyond its political heart and mission.

On the other hand, its *foremost* mission is not, by any practical measure, politics. It is television. More than conservative politics, Fox is ruled by all of the unique considerations that keep something on the air, and, behind that, the internecine battles of power, personality, money, not necessarily in that order, that go with fighting for airtime. Were a reconstituted age of liberal ambition, aspiration, and fashion to sweep a new generation, it would be an ultimate television test to see how Fox would try to hold an audience (or drift into irrelevance). The opposite television point is also true: having found its surefire formula, one still working at the highest ratings levels seemingly possible, why would it give it up? Has television, no matter how low, ever been ambivalent about success?

Many books, of greater and lesser rage and recrimination, have been written by crusaders against Fox News, its founding executive, Roger Ailes, and its insidious owners, the Murdochs. These books, not unfairly, take Fox at face value. They are the product of literally watching Fox and judging it for what it says and reacting with appropriate and reflexive umbrage. "It is not enough that conservatives like us," Roger Ailes often pronounced as part of his winning formula, "but that liberals hate us." The liberal commentary about Fox is part of that counterintuitive ecosystem—attack it and it grows. In all of these treatments, Fox is not just a subject, it is the enemy. Journalists have spent decades ably writing behind-the-scenes stories about the snake pit of traditional network and cable television, exposing the Faustian bargain that has been made to be on the air and the merciless backstabbing that gleefully goes with it. This makes sense; the majority of journalists exist in a professional community with the mainstream media—they understand its pain and comedy.

They have not covered conservative media with a similar professional understanding. These worlds, mainstream media and conservative media, really don't cross. Conservative media has remained "the other." The journalist, Gabriel Sherman, in his 2014 biography of Roger Ailes, *The Loudest Voice in the Room*, widely intimated that Ailes's refusal to speak to him for his book was both a sign of the Fox chief's contempt for real journalism and a de facto indication that he was hiding something (this seemed supported when, several years after the book's publication, Ailes's long history—never too well hidden—of his mistreatment of women was revealed). As it happened, Ailes was a willing and useful source during the years when I was covering the media business for *New York* magazine and *Vanity Fair*. I knew that Ailes would talk to almost anyone—you really couldn't shut him up—and offered to arrange an introduction to Ailes for Sherman, who I also knew. Sherman, in the interest of his own virtue, I suppose, failed to take me up on my offer.

As I was completing this book, I happened to attend a dinner with various heads of mainstream news channels and several notables from the *New York Times*. One of the *Times* people, stressing the dinner party's collective virtue, interrupted the rather sonorous discussion about the various crises in the journalism world (as well as its important, or self-important, personalities) to ask whether anyone at the table could even *imagine* a similar discussion taking place among people on "the other side." Well, yes, in fact. The discussion would be different only in quality, not kind. Everybody in the news business, right or left, is in a crisis in which they are at the center.

For myself, I have always found the people at Fox, including Ailes and its various stars, easy to engage beyond politics and willing to share their stories of working there—they, too, are conscious of the fickleness of media fate, including their own. This has allowed me to write a different kind of book about Fox, less about what is on the air, than what is in its heart, or churning in its stomach. Here is a television story of ego, money, power, and the unnatural obsession to be on the air. That it happens to be far-right air, rather than television's more familiar middle of the road, changes the story less, I believe, than you might think.

All television news operations, with zero-sum airtime (*if I get it, you don't*), are riven by envy and bitter rivalries, some more murderous than others. Fox under Ailes, a micromanager paying outsize salaries and turning nobodies into stars, was in fact less fraught than most, with a large portion of its employees—at least the men among them—grateful for their positions there. But then, after Ailes's defenestration from Fox in 2016, and with a sudden leadership vacuum, Fox began to revert to the power struggles and standard acrimony of other television news operations. But, of course, Fox isn't just television, or mere backstage story. Its prime-time anchors have become among the most dominant political figures of our time. Trump is a Fox manifestation. Arguably, the nation's bitter divide is a Fox divide. What happens to Fox happens to . . . the nation.

I got here, with an interest in, tolerance for, and access to the "other side," out of a set of mostly happenstance factors going back to the network's early years.

In 2001, I went to town on Ailes in the weekly column I was then writing about the media business for *New York* magazine. Shortly thereafter, he called me up, both to violently disagree with everything I had said about him, but also to invite me to lunch. Such, I suppose, is how devil's bargains are made. But beyond his evilness as Fox chief and as a key political operative in the Nixon, Reagan, and Bush campaigns, evil with which I now willingly dined, he was also incredibly incisive about the business of media and politics and a raconteur with wellsprings of gossip. This was the beginning of our regular lunches over the next fifteen years.

In 2008, Fox's owner and Ailes's boss, Rupert Murdoch, in his excitement about taking over the *Wall Street Journal*, one of his career dreams, agreed to cooperate in a biography I proposed to write about him. Over the course of a year, Murdoch sat for countless hours of interviews with me. That may make me the journalist not in his employ who knows him best. What's more, I had carte blanche to interview every member of his family, including his mother (a visit memorable for the hot-rod golf-cart tour of her rose garden at Cruden Farm outside of Melbourne, Australia, with ninety-nine-year-old Dame Elisabeth Murdoch at the wheel) and all his executives, past and present. The only stipulation was that I *not* speak to Ailes. Murdoch was jealous of the Fox chief, and Murdoch's lieutenants were trying to block off another venue in which Ailes might hog the credit (fairly hog the credit, I'd say) for what was fast becoming the most profitable and influential piece of the Murdoch empire, Fox News. I accepted this singular ground rule and ignored Ailes, a wound, albeit temporary, to our relationship. But Murdoch hated my book about him, which pleased Ailes, and as Ailes's troubles with the Murdoch family intensified, I was welcomed back to lunch.

As a further step into this story, my relationship with Ailes, and the friendly things he said about me to Trump and his people, helped grease my way into an observer status in the first year of the Trump White House, resulting in my book *Fire and Fury* and my books *Siege* and *Landslide* thereafter. Trump and his relationship with Fox is of course central to this tale. I have been a silent witness to various of its highs and lows.

What I have tried to do here is to bring to life the contradictory forces that now tear at the network. Based on conversations specifically for this book, and other conversations that have taken place over many years, and on scenes and events that I have personally witnessed or that I have re-created with the help of participants in them, my effort is to write something much closer to the private life than the public position of Fox News. As a writer, perhaps more so than as strictly a journalist, I see this as a story of human flaws and folly—ever magnified by the power and poison of being on the air—and of the doubts and fears keeping everyone at Fox up at night.

THE FALL

Prologue 1

Keith Rupert Murdoch

1931–202_

*In newsrooms around the world—and Rupert Murdoch con-
trolled more of them than anyone else ever has—the common
practice is to write advance obituaries for the great and good
and the notably mendacious and vile. The obit is put in the
"can," all but finished save for a last-minute update and the
final details. While this one would likely not be among those
under lock and key and special passwords at Murdoch's own
newspapers, here is a summation of one of the most consequential lives, for better or worse, of our time—with its end
presaging one more of the kind of dramatic business and political developments that he caused throughout his long career.*

Keith Rupert Murdoch, who revolutionized the media industry in
his seventy-year career, has died at the age of __ after a brief illness,
a spokesperson for his family confirmed.

It was a life of stark contradictions, an example of will and denial,
purpose over nature, for this heir to generations of Calvinist clergymen.

The sharpest negation of self might be that the mogul's paramount legacy was a business, Fox News, he had little to do with and often contempt for, and a president, Donald J. Trump, who he regarded as a "fucking idiot," who his news network had been instrumental in electing.

He was an Australian princeling, a child of one of the most vaunted and privileged families in his country, who became a publisher of working-class, down-market newspapers. He was a personal prude, an upright Presbyterian, who blew up the British publishing world with his pictures of bare-breasted girls on Page 3 of the *Sun* newspaper, transforming it into Britain's largest-selling paper. He was a dedicated newspaperman, perhaps the last on earth, in love with his newsrooms and his presses, whose real fortune would be made from television that he didn't watch and movies that he didn't see, in a Hollywood that he disdained (and that disdained him). He was the consummate tabloid newspaper publisher—the rougher, tougher, crueler, more sneering his papers were, the better—who believed there was no reason he could not also run the world's most respected newspapers, acquiring the London *Times* in 1981, and the *Wall Street Journal* in 2007. He was among the men who defined the model of modern business ruthlessness and unsentimental bottom-line sensibility, but his biggest dream was to pass his company to his children, no matter how unprepared or unworthy or fractious they might be.

He was born in 1931 into a near-Victorian world. His parents, Sir Keith Murdoch and Dame Elisabeth Murdoch, both children of upper-class nineteenth-century Scottish immigrants, were of an elite circle more attached to high British culture than egalitarian Australia. His father, by temperament cold and withholding, and Rupert, resentful and rebellious, remained at continuous odds. Keith Murdoch sent a series of emissaries to his son at Oxford, where he was in school after the end of the second World War, to reprimand him for his spending, idleness, and flirtation with left-wing ideas. Nor was his relationship with his mother, who lived to 103, all that much more congenial. He faulted her for poorly handling the estate when his father died in 1952 and hobbling his inheritance.

Perhaps it was the disdain he harbored toward his own father's business acumen that explained the ferocity and single-mindedness that would make him among the most transformative global business minds of the era. Keith Murdoch was the chairman of the Herald and Weekly Times, one of Australia's largest media concerns, but not its owner and was ultimately kicked out of the company he built by men with greater ownership stakes. Lesson learned: control is everything. (The son would later buy the company that had fired his father.) Another lesson he learned growing up in Australia's small circle of power that often gathered at his parents' table: power is an insider's game. To gain it, he learned from his own days as an interloper publisher, beginning with the single paper his father left him in Adelaide, an outsider must replace the insiders.

His goal was clear: global power. His method, without much capital, hardly any organization, nor significant connections beyond Australia, he had to invent. Newspapers he understood were a sure route to influence and power—many newspapers meant more influence and power. Here began his historic arc of often predatory acquisitions. He expanded his business from Australia to the UK by astutely playing, if not tricking, the family that owned the down-on-its-heels British tabloid the *News of the World*, followed shortly by using similar backdoor tactics to acquire the beleaguered *Sun*. With a down-market plunge to new levels of tabloid scandal and outrage, he turned both papers into industry phenomena. He was promptly nicknamed by the British satirical publication *Private Eye*, with arch disparagement, "the Dirty Digger," for his Australian roots, his Page 3 girls, and the scandals his papers unearthed. The name stuck for quite some decades. After his move into London, there followed his acquisition in the US of a paper in San Antonio, Texas (for no clear reason, other than that he could afford it), then the *New York Post*, the bottom-rung paper in New York, and simply because they were available, *New York* magazine and the *Village Voice*, and then the down-market papers in Boston and Chicago.

He sought always to turn his business power into political power. He was responsible for a succession of Australian prime ministers. In Britain, he was a pivotal supporter of Margaret Thatcher; the *Sun's* switch to supporting Labour was among the significant factors in the election of Tony Blair. Within months of his takeover of the *New York Post*, he made it the paper's mission to elect Ed Koch the mayor of New York in 1978, and succeeded, a precursor to his dream of electing an American president.

But the real transformation for him and for the media world, and ultimately for American politics, came in 1985 with his agreement to buy the movie studio, Twentieth Century Fox. Up until this moment, the media business was firmly compartmentalized: publishing, television, movies, radio, books, and the nascent home video and cable business, all finely—vertically—segmented by different corporate owners. But, suddenly, Murdoch was a publisher with a movie studio. Then, vastly overextending himself, Murdoch became not just the only publisher with a movie studio but, in a further deal, his movie studio became the only one that owned television stations. Following Murdoch's example, Time Inc. shortly merged with Warner Communications; Viacom bought Paramount, adding on CBS a few years later; and Disney snapped up ABC. Hundreds of independent media companies were soon reduced to a handful.

Next, Murdoch decided to try to break through another media wall: he would launch a fourth US television network. Using his television stations, and with Barry Diller, an upstart television and movie executive running the company—and with the hit show *Married . . . with Children*, a breakthrough sitcom on the biliousness, rather than television's usual idealization, of American family life—the Fox Network was soon a ratings competitor against ABC, NBC, and CBS. Murdoch was now the most important figure in the American media business, and, aggressive in his conservative views, a political power in the land.

His personal center of gravity stayed in the newspaper business. He was at home in a newsroom in a way that he could never settle into on a movie lot, where executives strove to keep him out of meetings with directors and stars whose costs and conceits he had little patience for. As he created the modern, cross-platform, media megalith, he remained, for the ever-cooler media kids, the scowling old guy, his singlet visible under his white shirt, only truly happy studying a front page.

In the late 1980s, like much of the business community Murdoch, too, was in a state of financial delirium. Making acquisitions in Australia, Britain, and the US, he was in an almost constant state of flight and jet lag. By the end of the decade, he had added to his publishing-movie-and-television empire, two book publishers, Harper in the US, and Collins in the UK, creating one of the world's largest publishing houses, assembled a major magazine publishing group, acquired a controlling interest in Britain's vast and money-losing satellite television company, BSkyB, and for no clear purposes, an airline in Australia.

But then the financial crisis in the media business of the early 1990s all but bankrupted him. At any point in a six-month period of negotiating with his creditors, he was days or hours away from losing his business. It is certainly among his greatest achievements—one of stamina, and humility—that he did not.

He regrouped in California. These were unhappy, wilderness years. He was ill-suited to a daily dose of the entertainment business. He had promised his wife—his second wife, Anna, the mother of three of his children, who he had married in 1967—that, if his company survived his financial undoing, he would turn it over to others to run and, as he approached sixty-five, start to wind down for their retirement together. But he chafed under this pledge, as his wife sourly tried to hold him to it. Evenings found him buttonholing his executives as he sought company for lonely dinners in the Fox commissary.

He wanted to get back to news and away from entertainment. He wanted a 24/7 cable news network. He wanted CNN. But his move was rebuffed—he was still looked down on as "the Dirty Digger"—and CNN was sold to Time Warner, the five-year-old conglomerate that was now the biggest power in media. His response was simple: he'd start his own around-the-clock cable news station.

Roger Ailes, a television executive, and former Republican political operative, unhappily employed at NBC, to whom Murdoch offered the job of starting a cable news station from the ground up, was firm in his conviction that he could create an upstart news channel and do it within the bounds of the money Murdoch was willing to spend.

Fox News launched in 1996. Staying within budget, and then beating early projections, meant Ailes encountered little oversight from his boss.

Murdoch had more pressing concerns: he was in love. At the age of sixty-five, this most cold and impersonal of men, married for three decades, with four adult children, met a junior staffer—an intern on a work break from business school—at his company's outpost in Hong Kong. Wendi Deng, daughter of a provincial couple in post–Cultural Revolution China, was twenty-nine when she met Murdoch.

Murdoch's natural and careful outward countenance was formal and puritanical. He took great pains to publicly end his marriage with his wife Anna before revealing any hint that his affair with Wendi had begun. The announcement of the split startled the Murdoch world. But not even his closest circle suspected that he might have a girlfriend. Two months after the split, he called his daughter Prudence in Australia and said he had met "a nice Chinese lady." Making a whooping sound of astonishment, she ran upstairs in her family's home in Sydney, shouting to her husband, "You won't believe it!"

The Murdochs were residents of California, a community property state. A division of his assets might easily have sundered his company, or at least his control over it. But Anna hobbled him in a different way. Instead of the billions she might have extracted, she agreed to a settlement of $100 million, conditioned on freezing his assets in a trust for his four children, with each receiving one vote, and precluding any "issue" that might follow from any new relationship from participating in the trust. Such was the structure that would dog him until his death—and after.

The early years of his marriage to Wendi, with, in quick succession, the birth of two daughters, Grace and Chloe, were something of a constant negotiation between his new life and old. With his daughter Elisabeth furious about his divorce, not speaking to him, he bound his sons to him with outsize authority in his company. His older son, Lachlan, was installed in the office next to him in New York. His younger son, James, became the company's de facto transformation agent, overseeing News Corp's manic pace of digital investments.

Murdoch was negotiating between old family and new, but also negotiating between his executives and his children.

Fox News had quite unexpectedly, and on the cheap, with its big blondes, and emphasis on talk radio–type broadcasters, become the number one and most profitable cable news station in America. By 2005, Fox was a brand name greater than Murdoch's own. Ailes had achieved a success in the company great enough and specific enough to make him one of the few executives in Murdoch's long history that would cost Murdoch too much to replace. A schemer and plotter, Ailes focused much of his ever-boiling resentments on Murdoch's children and the power Murdoch was extending to them. Elisabeth (Vassar), Lachlan (Princeton), and James (Harvard), he correctly saw as East Coast Ivy yuppies. Lachlan and James were gay, he whispered—this became nearly gospel within Fox News—and Elisabeth, a drug addict who hosted sex parties. He had proof, he maintained. In 2005, in a showdown with Lachlan over the son's push for more authority, Ailes rushed to Murdoch and issued an ultimatum: him or me. Murdoch chose Ailes. Lachlan, in a huff, packed up and moved his family back to Australia.

This left James as the heir. He had been sent to run the struggling UK satellite television company BSkyB—now known as Sky—and then was elevated to running all Murdoch operations in Europe.

In 2007, in what now appears to be the last moment of belief in a credible future for newspapers, Murdoch realized a near lifelong dream of acquiring one of the world's two most authoritative papers: the *Wall Street Journal* (the *New York Times* remained out of his grasp). Here was, in Murdoch's mind, the capstone of his career. But in many ways the most tempestuous part of it had just begun. Within months the global financial crisis descended, dooming the newspaper business. The election of Barack Obama, supported by all the Murdoch children, and, indeed, a reluctant Rupert, had suddenly turned Fox News from what could yet be regarded as a gadfly, tabloid, right-leaning voice, into something more evidently virulent, truthless, and racist—ever more popular and profitable for it—earning the enmity of his cosmopolitan and elitist children.

Then, just as Murdoch was closing in on his goal of acquiring the 61 percent of Sky that was owned by public shareholders, which would firmly establish both his company's global reach and its status as the world's largest media enterprise, scandal struck.

Reporters at two of Murdoch's London papers, the *News of the World* and the *Sun* had been systematically hacking into the voice mail of celebrities, sports stars, and royals, with at least the tacit awareness of James Murdoch, and, quite likely, his involvement in a subsequent cover-up. Compelled to acknowledge this as the lowest public moment of his career, a befuddled-seeming Murdoch, with James beside him, was forced to testify in a televised hearing before a Parliamentary Select Committee. Barely escaping prosecution, James was secreted out of the UK and back to the US. Murdoch was forced to close the *News of the World.* The Sky deal was scuttled by regulators who formally deemed Murdoch "not a fit person" to own a major British company. And shareholders would soon push Murdoch to sequester his beloved but tainted newspapers into their own entity, divorced from Twenty-First Century Fox. Murdoch still controlled both companies, but the larger statement was clear: nobody wanted the newspapers that Murdoch cherished.

And then, finally, Murdoch's marriage to Wendi Deng, long unwinding, came undone with company sources leaking news of his wife's affair with former UK prime minister Tony Blair.

Nevertheless, the eighty-three-year-old Murdoch, battered by events of his own making, set out with absolute determination not to change direction.

Having sidelined the two executives, Peter Chernin and Chase Carey, most responsible for turning his company into a well-managed, modern enterprise favored by Wall Street, he then issued an ultimatum to his son Lachlan after his nearly ten years of idleness in Australia: if he had any hope of a leadership role in the company, it was now or never, or else James, however recently disgraced, would be appointed CEO. In 2014, Lachlan and his family returned from Australia and he and his brother became co-CEOs in a primal bake-off.

But, if Chernin and Carey had been taken out of the game, Ailes had not. Ailes's toxicity and enmity toward his new nominal bosses was one of the few things the brothers—James largely in New York, Lachlan in LA, hardly talking to each other—could agree on: it was either them or him.

In July 2016, Murdoch was on an extended honeymoon with his new wife, the 1970s top model, longtime former partner of Mick Jagger, and rock-and-roll society fixture Jerry Hall. At that moment, a sexual harassment suit was launched against Ailes by a former anchor, Gretchen Carlson. Ailes believed it was instigated by the brothers, exactly timed for their father's absence. They acted immediately and in concert,

mobilizing the company and its lawyers against Ailes and largely leaving their father in the dark. Two weeks later, the first major takedown in the yet unnamed #MeToo movement was a fait accompli, and
Ailes, after twenty years as the Fox heart and soul, was ignominiously
cast out.

This precipitated a ferocious battle between Lachlan and James
for control of Fox News. Fox's unresolved future, combined with the
wholly unexpected election of Donald Trump and recent notice that
the final effort to buy Sky would not receive the necessary approval in
the UK, left the company in perhaps the greatest existential state it had
ever known.

In 2017, in a deal shepherded by James, and hotly resisted by
Lachlan, Twenty-First Century Fox accepted a $71 billion offer from
Disney for the lion's share of its assets, leaving behind only properties
Disney could not take for regulatory reasons and Fox News, which it
did not want. Each of the six Murdoch children received a $2 billion
disbursement. James walked away from further responsibility for the
company's remaining assets—most notably Fox News. Lachlan's consolation prize was the reins of the diminished enterprise.

Fox had become, since Trump's election, even more successful. It
had not only survived the loss of Ailes—who died in his Palm Beach
exile in the spring of 2017—but the loss of its ratings leader Bill O'Reilly
in a further sexual harassment scandal and of Megyn Kelly, the anchor
who the Murdochs had hoped might lead the network to a not-*so*-
right-wing future. Instead, Trump was now its star. Sean Hannity, the
longtime prime-time ratings laggard revived his career with an unques-
tioning devotion to Trump—making himself, to boot, one of Trump's
leading inner circle advisers. Tucker Carlson, given an anchor slot
because the Murdochs believed he was a more moderate Republican,
overnight became a firebrand of the new Trump order and cable television's ratings winner.

Despite the Murdochs' tentative efforts to moderate their news network's worst excesses, Fox morphed into something close to an arm of the Trump administration. The irony cut deep: Murdoch had long used his media power to make and break politicians, now he was helpless to control the supplication by the most powerful news outlet he had ever owned to the belligerent president. The money was just too great.

This left father and son, Rupert and Lachlan, in their own estimation, as nearly martyrs, bearing the pain of Fox in order to preserve its value. Lachlan found himself all but ostracized in liberal Los Angeles. Rupert found his happy life with his new wife, Jerry Hall, increasingly strained amid her entertainment, art, and fashion social set, and their open antipathy, and often anger, toward Fox and Trump—and him. In 2022, the marriage, his fourth, ended.

Murdoch was more and more encouraged by his daughter Elisabeth to think about his historic legacy and to consider the ways to free himself from Fox, especially as it once again, following the north star of its massive profits, might be the instrument of reelecting Donald Trump. Fox's fate was yet unresolved at the time of his death.

[FINAL GRAPH TK—DEATH CIRCUMSTANCES. ENDIT.]

Prologue 2

Roger Ailes

SUMMER 2016

"The people you know," said Roger Ailes, the founder of Fox News, and for twenty years as chairman and CEO its malevolent, cynical, brilliant, and absolute ruler, "live in this moment, whatever *this* is—" he added with a wave of disdain at the moment's foolishness. "The people who Fox is for live in—" he paused as though to get this calibration as precise as possible "—1965." He thought about this for a second, and then, pulling wings off of a liberal butterfly, added, "before the Voting Rights Act," that is, the moment before civil rights became the political and cultural achievement of the age.

Ailes's legs, too weak to use, seemed to dangle off the side of his couch in the living room of his suburban house. It was an upper-middle-class, ranch-style home, every room cushioned in thick, tufted, wall-to-wall carpet in Cresskill, New Jersey. Forty-five minutes away, in Garrison, New York, on the other side of the Hudson River, Ailes, under whose leadership Fox News had gone from start-up to $1.5 billion in profits, and his wife, Beth, had built themselves a showpiece mansion on a promontory overlooking West Point and the Hudson tributaries.

It is one of the great vistas in the northeast. But, in truth, he was still more at ease in Cresskill, in ordinary suburban comfort, than in his grand redoubt.

An iced tea sat on the coaster on the side table next to him. Ailes was home on a midweek workday because in a spectacular piece of cultural jujitsu, he had gone in the blink of an eye from being the most powerful and prescient voice in American politics to a man without position, status, influence, or future. Accusations of sexual abuse in a surprise lawsuit by a former Fox anchor, Gretchen Carlson, exposed both Ailes's personal cruelties and the not-so-secret culture of sexual humiliation at the network. Compliance was the game; noncompliance a career buster. This public airing of what otherwise so many had privately known became the lever to expel him from television and influence.

Ailes had continued to live in his own 1965, but the world, and the newly enforced rules of sexual behavior, had caught up with him, even at Fox. And the Murdoch sons, who, for so long, had been offended and tormented by Ailes and the license his success had afforded him, seized the moment. With more will and determination than anyone might have credited them, they saw the opportunity to destroy Ailes and grabbed it. There was great social significance in Ailes's downfall. It was a brilliant victory for the liberal cultural majority. It was perhaps less understood that politically Ailes's removal as the leading power on the right now left that job open for Donald Trump to fill. Which he did shortly.

"Donald lives in 1965, though it is more 1965 Vegas than Kansas, but close enough," Ailes said of his friend Trump, who had just, astonishingly, and ridiculously, even to Ailes, secured the Republican nomination for president.

"The boys—" by which he meant the Murdoch boys "—live in the present. They are private school, Ivy League, New York rich kids. Fox News supports them. I make the money, they spend it—" a line from the

Ailes catechism. "But do they want Fox News? No. It's a pile of steaming shit on the table to them. It's a pile of steaming shit to every liberal in America—and the goddamn American hearth to everyone else."

His bitterness was momentarily overshadowed by a near childlike glee. To say the least, Ailes was not an introspective man, but he was a political man, and politics is a constant study of how you might have been bested and of how to game the new field of play that any sudden reversal creates. Ailes, in his years as a canny adviser to presidents and as the vaunted and feared chairman of Fox News, had always kept up a running side commentary, a private (albeit out loud) cynic's diary of winners and losers.

"And Rupert?" his interlocutor prompted about the then eighty-five-year-old Fox chairman.

"He likes the money. For that, he can put everything else out of his mind. I've never had the clear impression he much watches us, in fact."

"What time does he live in?"

"What time does he live in?" Ailes hooted. "He's walking into walls. He doesn't know what time it is. It's old man time. He just wants his kids to love him. And they don't. Rupert is an odd bird. A cold fish, but a fucking wet noodle—it's pathetic—around those kids. They're always stomping off and giving the poor guy the finger."

"And so . . . okay . . . then what happens to Fox?"

If Fox was half television juggernaut and half political movement, it was also for Ailes something higher. It was a sovereign state. Its practices, its culture, its governance, all its own. It was North Korea. Ailes was the Kim in charge. But now the dictator was exiled to his couch in New Jersey.

Of course, just because the dictator was toppled did not mean that the struggle went with him. Not unusually, the time of the dictator might come to be seen as stable and straightforward, and the vacuum without him a far more volatile and frightening situation. Ailes, the great force of disruption in the nation, was the real stability at Fox—its true anchor.

His fingers were together in near prayer.

"Okay. So . . . they'll want to sell it. Right now, I think you could fairly ask for fifty billion dollars. But . . . who would buy it? There isn't a conservative-leaning media operation in the country that has that kind of money. The rich media is entirely liberal. And without our cash flow the economics of all of the Murdoch corporate empire are thrown into disarray—" that is, the other cable channels, the Fox broadcast entertainment network, and the movie and television studio (not to mention the vast, and increasingly weak, publishing side of the Murdoch holdings). "No, they are stuck with it," he laughed demonically. "But they can't run it either. Oh, they'll try. They are both wannabe little kings, the brothers. I think they both really believe they were put on earth to show up their father, rather than the reality, which is that they would be mid-level media executives making a quarter million a year and grateful for it, without their old man. But, honestly, even if they were geniuses . . . television is a beast. A fucking beast. That's why you've got so many television shows *about* television, because everybody is insane. It doesn't matter that it's a conservative network, it's fucking television. Everybody is demented. But at the same time, it *is* conservative. And the boys aren't. The old man is a pole-up-his-ass businessman-round-table conservative. We are no longer talking about ideology or about party affiliation; we are talking about where people live. Fox people have secured their land. You people—" meaning the people who live in the here and now "—want to move them out. But they are dug in. They are not going anywhere. The more you insist, the more they dig in. And they are locked and loaded. You are like missionaries trying to convert the natives—the cannibals. But they end up eating you."

"So *we* are the Christians? And these are the heathens."

He wasn't happy with where this metaphor was going. Ailes and his people were clearly the Christians.

"Well, really," said Ailes, perhaps trying not to go in this direction, but going all the same, "you are the Jews, of course." He tittered at his indiscretion. But then he went on in the schoolteacher voice he sometimes summoned. "Okay, it used to be that time was relatively stable," he said. "Except for weirdos or the Amish or people in the mountains, we all lived in basically the same moment. We all fought in the same wars, we all went to similar churches and schools, we all watched the same television. We all moved forward at a mostly shared pace. Some maybe a little faster. There were those who wanted progress and those who wanted less progress. But progress was pretty slow in any event. And then it speeded up. Progress became about the speed of progress. Some people had more technology. Some people had more money. Some people went to school longer. Some people picked up and moved to cities. And some people didn't. So what your people thought about the military, and religion, and schools, and men and women, became very different . . . one hundred percent different from what my people thought."

"And Trump?"

"Donald? He's Richie Rich. He's richer than you but he's not smarter than you—in fact, he's clearly a dumb motherfucker, I say with all due respect. He is *so* dumb. But smart is what people hate. God, they hate it."

The phone rang—a landline. "It's Rudy," Ailes's wife, Beth, called.

Showing off for his guest and, too, as just general bad boy stuff, Ailes put the former mayor on speakerphone, unaware that he had a larger audience. Ailes had run Rudy Giuliani's first campaign for New York city mayor in 1989. Giuliani was a pro-choice, pro–gun control, New York Republican, and his and Ailes's politics, except for basic law-and-order rhetoric, didn't much cross over. But they were both ambitious and cynical operators in the Republican Party and that was enough to cement them as members of the small Republican circle in New York. Plus, they both liked to go out at night. And although Rudy had social aspirations, he was still, basically, an unreconstructed neighborhood guy. And unreconstructed is the language Ailes spoke best.

After Giuliani's failed bid for president in 2008—a dead-on-arrival campaign—Ailes had diligently supported his friend even in his obvious descent: huge weight gain, drinking problems, bad marriage, and, most difficult of all, no public role. Now Giuliani was Ailes's lawyer, trying to help get Ailes his hundred-million-dollar payout from the Murdochs.

Well, that was not precisely true. Giuliani was part of a vast law firm with lawyers who would do that. Giuliani's real job was commiseration. And now, without prelude, Giuliani launched into a denunciation of the growing list of women at Fox who had turned against Ailes. For a moment, Ailes seemed to be the rational one, indicating for his guest's benefit with a tip of a virtual highball glass that Giuliani, at 11:00 a.m., was already drinking ("all my lawyers are drunks," Ailes would note). But in no time at all Ailes, too, was swept up in this world of disloyal and plotting women. It was a set piece between the two men: this dark world of women whose inner avarice and aggression had been released in this new age.

Each of the boys, the Murdoch boys, had their blood score against Ailes—"They would have done anything," said Ailes, as though for the first time, instead of the thousandth. "They would have done anything to get you," confirmed Giuliani. And, darkly, the boys were at the center of a wider conspiracy against him and their own father, everybody seemingly a mover in some intricate and venal plot.

This was, yes, crazy stuff, but aptly reflecting a parallel world, one in which lots and lots of people, perhaps half the country, lived, a world of rage, recrimination, and conspiracy. No longer an aberration but a baseline. In recent years, Murdoch, who saw himself as a figure, despite the tabloids on which he had built his empire, of straitlaced conservatism and establishment rectitude, had started to pronounce Ailes "crazy," using this as a defense—"Roger is crazy"—as he felt Fox, more and more, get away from him.

Anyway, none of this was what Giuliani had actually called about.

What he really wanted was Ailes to agree to help get Trump, for whom Giuliani had become an informal adviser, ready for his first debate with Hillary Clinton. Giuliani regarded Ailes, not inaccurately, as a puppet master and Trump, deep down in the polls at that point, as ready to take on a puppeteer. Ailes was not so sure. "The problem with Donald is that he doesn't listen. He's incapable of listening."

"He'll listen," said Rudy.

"Rudy, you know he doesn't listen."

"He'll listen to you. Do you want me to have him call you?"

"I can call him. But, yes, have him call me."

For many years, the three men had been a curious trio, united less by politics than by celebrity and media and nightlife. The New York liberal order had only contempt, or, at best, a mocking tolerance, for all of them, but they formed a small network of unique success: Trump with his theoretical billions and clownish celebrity (which the two others could both appreciate and mock him for); Giuliani with his political success, and, despite his failures, continued notoriety; and Ailes with ratings that, year in and year out, kept rising and defining some kind of new power zeitgeist.

"It's a day at the golf course—" said Giuliani about the Trump country club in Bedminster, New Jersey, where the debate prep was scheduled to take place, although neither he nor Ailes was able to walk a golf course.

There was, likely, never any doubt that Ailes would show up—what else did he have to do?—but he wanted to be importuned. Giuliani, not just desperate to be involved, but desperate to pursue the small chance, however far-fetched, that Trump could be helped into the presidency, and Giuliani restored to . . . *something*, was willing to beg Ailes to be his wingman.

"He needs to listen," said Ailes.

"He will, he gets it, he does," said Giuliani.

"Donald is ignorant," expounded Ailes after the call. "What would he *do* if he became president?" Ailes chortled, implying that Trump would have no idea what to do. "But if you are on Fox enough—and good enough on the air—yes, yes, you could certainly become president. Donald, for instance, is barely pro-life, no matter what he says now. Just imagine how many abortions he's paid for. And he thinks guns are for trailer trash. But he's a Fox favorite, so that doesn't matter—he's one of us. Of course, on top of being ignorant, he's incompetent, and it's complicated to run for president, which is why he's twenty points down. Bill O'Reilly once thought that *he* could run for president, but he was too mean. Donald is mean, but it's a different kind of mean—you're not sure he's serious about being mean. Bill is truly mean and you know it. Megyn? Yes, that might have been possible—the first woman president. But now she's dead." When she'd jumped to NBC from Fox a few months before, Ailes, correctly, foresaw that Megyn Kelly's television news career would soon be over. "She made a bet and it's not going to pay off," he said. She's now positioned as "a conservative who liberals think is underneath good people. It never works. You can't leave Fox. You can't switch sides."

Such was the curious trap in ideological television. It was no longer a talent or craft industry. Barbara Walters once could circle the dial as a free agent. But Fox shaded your personality. You weren't you. You were Fox.

Ailes, with his fingers interlaced across his large belly, clearly found some satisfaction in Megyn Kelly—whose accusations against him had been the true silver bullet that finished him off—as a Fox captive. In other words, still his captive.

"What if Trump wins?"

"He's not going to win."

"Hypothetically."

He made a face to say he did not have time for such hypotheticals, although he had all the time in the world.

"Well, how would the Murdochs react if he won?"

"Oh, my fucking God." With a deep laugh, he made an exploding noise. "Poor Rupert. Rupert wanted CNN. I gave him Fox. And then the money followed. He never knew what hit him. He came down—" that is, from the executive floor to Ailes's office on the second floor "—in June and shuffled about and it was '*Trump . . . umm . . . hummm . . . eggg . . .*' said Ailes, delivering a reasonable imitation of the inarticulate Murdoch, "'. . . *what a loser. Okay, Hillary . . . mumble . . . mumble,*' he said and then left."

"So, Fox should be for Hillary, he meant?"

"He meant he was for Hillary. Or James was for Hillary. James was the one who was always needling him. Yab, yab, yab, yab, jab, jab, jab. Pathetic. But Rupert was very bad about giving directions. The idea that he might cost himself money was painful to him. And he never really understood why Fox was making so much money."

"Did he understand that Fox created Trump?"

"If he doesn't, James is telling him. That was the James message, '*You have lost control, old man.*' And, of course, James is right. He's a prick, but he's right."

WINTER 2022

1

Rupert

IN THE SUN

Rupert Murdoch often picks up his conversation in the middle of his thinking, as though the conversation began somewhere else. The line between what he is thinking and saying is a fine one. A thinking Murdoch often seems agitated, eyes, jaw, lips at work back and forth, from iron concentration to sour scowl. Out loud is only to add an ever-so-quiet mumble.

In the winter of 2022, he was having a holiday on St. Barts, in the French West Indies. St. Barts is a resort island for billionaires, the European creative leisure class, and international villains. Money is its highest attribute. It's a notably good place for the very rich and very old with younger wives, a cool place for the wife to get a break from the usual older friends and associates, and where you, being so filthy rich, get a pass for being an old man in a bathing suit. And Murdoch would soon be ninety-one.

He was full-time on the job running the Fox News cable channel, its sister Fox Broadcasting Company, the television stations he owned across the country, newspapers in the US, Britain, and Australia, and the book publisher HarperCollins—the ultimate decision-maker and, when he felt like it, the micromanager of all those businesses. But he lived the life, too, of a wealthy retiree, on his vineyard in California, his ranch in Montana, his sheep station in Australia, and for weeks enjoying the Caribbean in winter and the Mediterranean in the summer, on his boat, *Vertigo*, a sixty-seven-meter schooner.

His wife, Jerry Hall, twenty-five years younger than Murdoch, wanted to sail to Mustique, an island preserve for upper-class British socialites made famous by Princess Margaret. That's where her former partner Mick Jagger had a house, and where their four children might show up. But Murdoch didn't want to go to Mustique. He had been quite enamored with his wife's family and social set when they were first married six years ago but now was tired of them. Or they him.

He seemed to have just gotten off the phone with his conversation continuing from there, or from some other conversation he might have had—or just from somewhere in midthought. Someone was gay, Murdoch was saying to a few friends—really, his wife's friends—who had joined him at the patio table in St. Barts. Someone at Fox News, it seemed. But then with an abrupt segue it might seem that it was Ron DeSantis, who Murdoch was increasingly seeing as a powerful alternative to Trump, who was gay, or that someone was accusing the Florida governor of being gay. Someone at Fox—possibly Tucker Carlson—was saying that Trump was saying that DeSantis was gay. The connections here, even making a supreme effort to follow the low voice and interior mumble, were not necessarily clear.

"Rupert, why are you such a homophobe?" his wife interjected with something more than annoyance. Then she directly accused him: "You're such a homophobe." Then to her friends: "He's such an old man."

Murdoch had sought and achieved greater and greater power and control through his seventy-year career, but had opinionated wives who openly disagreed with him, upbraided him, or insulted him in public.

Wendi Deng, his third wife, thirty-eight years his junior, had a rou-
tine, which became more biting over the years, about his cheapness,
his knowing, obsessive, wrathful, consuming cheapness—the constant
calculation of the money he might have saved, or the small change he
might be losing. On the other hand, it was not clear he was ever listening to his wives.

His hand suddenly hit the table, a hard blow, shaking it. This might
have appeared like sudden fury at his wife's challenge. But, no, it was
directed somewhere else.

At Trump, apparently. Here, nearly under his breath, was a rat-
a-tat-tat of jaw-clenching "fucks." Murdoch was as passionate in his
Trump revulsion as any helpless liberal. He quite appeared to embody
the rage so many people had for a modern politics that appeared to be
absurd, illogical, and beyond their control. The only difference here,
and it brought the table to some moment of confused silence, was
that as the all-powerful chairman and controlling shareholder of Fox
News, the single greatest political voice in the nation, *he* had the control. Didn't he?

"Well, do something, Rupert!" said his wife. For the others, she reiterated his hatred of Trump, their mutual hatred of Trump, adding that
everyone they knew hated Trump. "But he can't," she told the others.
"He'll lose money."

Money. "This lawsuit could cost us fifty million dollars," he said
quietly, but clearly.

His wife was making a greater point: Fox News tolerated, and actually exalted Trump, for the ratings, and the unprecedented sums it produced for a news company. But his point of aggravation was the lawsuit
brought by Dominion, the maker of voting machines, against Fox News
for echoing the Trump camp's nonsense charges that Dominion, as
part of an international left-wing conspiracy, had helped rig the 2020
election. This is what might cost him $50 million!

"But that *was* crazy, right, that voting machine stuff?" ventured one of the people at the table, pinning the fault, it might even seem, directly on Fox.

Crazy. "Trump is crazy, crazy, crazy," sighed Murdoch.

Again, there was the weight at the table of the rude understanding that it was Murdoch's Fox News that had made the crazy man president—that could make him president *again*. "You helped make him president," said Hall, harshly, if there was any doubt.

"We have some idiots," said Murdoch, as though ruefully—but his meaning unclear.

Hall seemed to clarify. "Sean Hannity is such an idiot."

Murdoch did not disagree. But, in fact, for a moment—or two, or three—seemed to phase out of the discussion. "Tucker is a wacko," said Hall.

From wherever he was, Murdoch returned to the discussion: "Lachlan likes Tucker." This seemed begrudging, but who was he begrudging? Tucker Carlson, Fox's leading star, or his son, Lachlan, the CEO of Fox? It wasn't clear. Was it a good thing or a bad thing that his son, who Murdoch had appointed CEO of Fox, liked Carlson? "He's smart," murmured Murdoch, seemingly to mean Carlson.

Although Murdoch could often seem opaque or even incomprehensible in his utterances, there was also a strange feeling of transparency, sitting with him, that the facets of his empire, and the next moves within it, were always open for discussion. In this there was something of a weird feeling of disassociation on his part. His business interest, his empire, might have grown entirely out of his instincts, drives, passions, and calculations, but he could also step back and view this all impersonally—pieces to be moved this way or that, or to be disposed of at will, having no relationship to him.

As 2022 began, it had seemed to some friends that Fox had become a moving piece. Was he suddenly concerned with his legacy—uncharacteristically? At his ninetieth birthday his daughter Elisabeth had produced a hagiographic video tribute and, while usually dismissive about most sentimentality, this sentimentality about himself had moved him. And then there was the *Succession* business—the HBO show modeled at times loosely, other times exquisitely closely, on the Murdoch family. He didn't watch it, or said he didn't watch it, but he scoffed perhaps too many times at the character of Logan Roy, repeating that he himself was nothing like "that asshole."

Sometimes Murdoch regarded Fox as just something he had gotten stuck with. He'd sold his other cable stations and movie studio to Disney in 2018 for a colossal, top-of-the-market, sum; he would have sold Fox News too, but Disney hadn't wanted it. So, now he had a single cable station in a world of cable giants, the opposite of the business strategy of control and dominance he had always pursued. It did keep him in the game, though. That was true. He was still Rupert Murdoch, the owner of the single greatest political force in America. His son James had wanted (smartly) to do the Disney deal; his son Lachlan very much hadn't. So Murdoch, as a consolation prize, had committed to supporting Lachlan as the CEO of Fox News—he would give him that. Again, not a sentimental man, to say the least, but he did feel he owed Lachlan Fox. But his other children hated Fox. Really hated it. And they all hated Trump. Fucking hated him. And it really gnawed at him the $50 million Trump might imminently cost him in this festering Dominion defamation suit because Fox had supported Trump's ludicrous election claims and the wild conspiracy the Trumpers had concocted about Dominion's voting machines. So, yes, it was a question that now seemed always on his mind: what to do with Fox.

On the other hand, could you really tell what was on his mind?

"My other children hate him," said Murdoch, apparently about Carlson.

"For good reason," added Hall.

"What is Carlson's Putin relationship?" asked one of the people at the table. Night after night on his prime-time show, Carlson, like

Trump, had come back again and again to his respect for and fascination with Vladimir Putin—Putin should be our ally; we should be on
Putin's side. Not Ukraine's side. *Ukraine?*

Murdoch seemed to ignore the question, or to be so absorbed by it
he forgot where he was. Putin, Trump, Carlson—was Murdoch responsible for all this?

"Rupert!" said Hall, calling him back.

"They're—yeah . . ." He didn't complete this thought and became
distracted again. But Murdoch, yet a reliable cold warrior Republican,
had told Lachlan to have Carlson cut it out. They weren't going to support Putin, who was crazy. "Crazy, crazy." Dangerous crazy, diabolical
crazy.

"Is he going to invade Ukraine?" Murdoch was asked.

"Never!" Murdoch nearly shouted, his voice for the first time clear
and roused, "*Never!*"

"He hates Putin," said Hall.

Murdoch again focused somewhere else. Then he returned and
wanted to know what his companions thought about the Florida
governor—DeSantis. But no one had a clear opinion.

"He can beat Trump!" Murdoch said, still roused. "He can beat
Trump!" he repeated, banging the table. DeSantis would take the evangelical vote in Iowa. It was going to come out about the abortions Trump
had paid for, Murdoch assured.

"He's becoming a right-to-lifer," said Hall, dismissing her husband.

Murdoch scowled and grumbled. He couldn't be even if he wanted
to, he said. He had two woke college daughters, Grace and Chloe, from
his marriage to Wendi Deng. That was always the reality, no matter how
much it aggravated him: his children.

The theoretical golden years of Murdoch's life, thirty years now, had
been so much about winning the approval of his children. He really
had tried. Lachlan Murdoch reassured his father that it wasn't Fox and

politics coming between him and his other children. This, insisted
Lachlan, was just a stand-in for other stuff. Their issues weren't that different from other families, Lachlan mollified his father. And this might
have been true, except for the fact that Fox News was also pretty clearly
the pivot of American history in the last generation. For Grace and
Chloe, it was the harsh background of their entire lives, and of those of
their classmates at Yale and Stanford, those left-wing schools—dividing
the nation and electing Donald Trump. Well, what could he say to that,
mumble, mumble . . . He mostly blamed it on Trump. And Ailes, who
he had fired, hadn't he?

"They're woke," said Murdoch, glumly.

"Put James in charge," said Hall, taunting her husband.

Murdoch chose not to hear this or be reminded of his errant and
tenacious son outside the empire walls.

"James wants to completely blow Fox up." She made an exploding
noise.

Murdoch went back to the topic of DeSantis, though it took a
moment to follow where he had gone. But he seemed to mean that
whatever the problems were at Fox, and however that had infected his
family, DeSantis, a normal politician, would calm it all down, that anyone but Trump would calm it all down.

"He's a professional," said Murdoch, as though high praise.

"He's so conservative," said Hall with disgust.

"He's a professional," repeated Murdoch.

"Really, you should *just* put James in charge," Hall insisted, goading
him again. "You're megarich, why do you need more money?" pressing
the central point, as had his wife Wendi before, as did his (megarich)
children now. And he clearly did not—nor would he. There were some
friends he had asked about what they thought about him giving up Fox.
At least some of them had said that's exactly what he should do. He had
a great wife, fantastic places to spend his time, and how much better his

relationship with his children would be without the curse of Fox News. Not to mention, did he really want to be responsible for the reelection of Donald Trump? *Really?*

He continued on now about Ron DeSantis. It was going to be DeSantis. His insistence seemed to cancel out or disappear Donald Trump from his mind. That's what this year was going to be all about— Ron DeSantis. He had laid this out for Lachlan: they were going to keep Trump off the air and promote DeSantis.

"You see, what would he do if he didn't have Fox?" said Hall, understanding his helpless love for the game.

"I do own the *Wall Street Journal*," said Murdoch, affronted.

2

Tucker

FEBRUARY 24, 2022

This morning, Russia, in an air, sea, and ground assault, had invaded Ukraine, in a move that caught Tucker Carlson, as well as the world, off guard. For weeks, Carlson had been describing the US intelligence predictions of an imminent attack as fearmongering and propaganda aimed at *provoking* the very Russian response that had now occurred. *Irresponsibly provoking.* As though he saw it as a natural part of right-wing regenesis—ontogeny recapitulates phylogeny—Carlson had relocated himself firmly back in 1930s isolationism. America need not have anything to do with the obvious damnation of the rest of the world—why, for heaven's sake, would it want to? This view came with a searing disgust for anyone who might think otherwise, those same people complicit in a generation of fruitless and catastrophic wars—*they* were the real enemy, not Russia, not Vladimir Putin.

Carlson was a larger man than you might expect, loping down the main street of Boca Grande, an island off of Florida's Gulf coast, taller and fatter, and yet still with an arms-swinging boyish gait, looking from side to side, ready to see and be seen in a musical comedy way—hello world! But behind the open face—cheerful, winning, eager to please—there was a more conscious calculation. How was he being looked at and by whom? He was starting to see himself as a human Rorschach blot. What you thought about him was a gauge of . . . *everything*.

In the old days of television news, the great voices became nearly indistinguishable from the great events—Walter Cronkite, his breath catching, removing his glasses to compose himself and hold back his tears, when the announcement of John F. Kennedy's death came across the wire. But Fox had advanced that. Fox now *caused* the events. History turned on Fox. On Tucker. He was hated for what was happening—that is, what was happening to the liberals' world. And this, behind the hail-fellow country-club exterior, had for some time now started to fill him with both resolve and dread. He simply could do nothing about what other people thought: Even if *they* were after him. So what might happen? Disgrace? Prison?

Reversing the Rorschach blot, what he thought about everyone else had become the measure of his own anxieties and accelerating sense of good and evil.

He was, arguably, the second-most-famous person in the country after only Donald Trump himself, and, therefore, the second-most hated. But it seemed to him somehow unfair, or not classy, that this had spilled over to Boca Grande. Paradise had become darker for him. Whatever Boca Grande had once been—he and his family lived here in the home his wife's family had had for two generations, his high school sweetheart—it was, if not to the naked eye, different.

In fact, of all places in Florida, Boca Grande was among the places that had most stayed the same. A preserve of elite families, DuPonts and Bushes, the island had adopted extremely un-Florida-like zoning rules in 1980 just at the dawn of the most aggressive real estate years. "Nazi laws, which I am in favor of," said Carlson with signature hee-hawing laugh, stressing the irony of his real estate interests working against his otherwise self-styled libertarian views. This had produced in Boca

Grande something like a New England or Hamptons beach community except with palm trees—protected by a high toll for coming onto the island, and an exclusionary near cashless system of credit accounts at most commercial establishments. Still. Carlson could feel the change. Many residents thought *he* was the change. Boca Grande represented an older, genteel, tony Florida. Jeb Bush Florida. This was more and more at odds with present-day Florida, vying to be the new right-wing capital of America—with Tucker Carlson among its leading citizens.

Still. He was not so among the loonies as not to recognize that that his stance on Russia's invasion put him on a dangerous limb, out of sync with modern global behavior and logic. Behind a face of near untouched old-fashioned American optimism and innocence, a face from a 1950s television show, he was worried. He resented the idea that many people seemed to have of him as somehow cavalier and indifferent, when in fact he was consumed by worry—about the culture, his country, his family, the perpetual battle between good and evil.

And now, beyond his immediate worry that he might find himself in a shrinking minority, a minority of one even, about the war, he had another increasingly existential concern.

Fox News had been his home for thirteen years and for six years he had been its leading star. An astute player (he believed), he knew the Fox vibe, distinct from the tortured, quisling vibes at CNN and MSNBC where he had previously worked, and he didn't like what he was feeling. The Murdochs had their problems, God knows. Lachlan Murdoch was running the company from Australia, where he and his family lived. And Carlson had heard that the other Murdoch brother, who hated Fox, hated Carlson most of all. And Rupert was turning ninety-one. And Trump—he wasn't going away. How do you deal with that? And cable television! How much longer for cable? And the sheer crazed hatred in the country, directed at Fox and at him! He liked Rupert and Lachlan, he really did, but were they up to this?

A few days before, he had been visited by Lachlan Murdoch, his boss. The situation the eldest son outlined as they sat out in Carlson's lush garden was as potentially world-shattering (Carlson's world anyway) as the invasion he now, alas, appeared to have condoned (of course he did not *condone* the invasion, he just believed the invaders had been provoked to invade and wasn't *condemning* them for *that*).

The two men were nearly the same age—Tucker fifty-two, Lachlan fifty. And they were both attached by a lifeline to the continued success of Fox News, just passing its twenty-fifth anniversary of political and cable news dominance. Carlson and the Murdoch heir were its late-stage creatures. From a failing television career, Tucker, through a combination of chance circumstances, had gotten his prime-time spot at Fox in 2017, almost instantly transforming himself from country club respectability into the most compelling and protean right-winger in the country. The eldest Murdoch son, in 2018, after a meltdown and radical transmogrification of his aged father's empire, found himself leading America's most powerful news outlet. There were other similarities. Each man had had a precocious start in his career which had then crumbled into disappointment and resentment. Each was the product of a family experience so unusual that few could truly appreciate what motivated them. Each believed they had been both underestimated and unfairly maligned by . . . well, just about everyone. And each now depended on the other.

Despite having alienated half the nation, Tucker was an adroit politician. His varied circle included the casino billionaire Steve Wynn, the actress and Harvey Weinstein accuser Rose McGowan, the former *New Yorker* editor and chattering class doyenne Tina Brown, and the Nevada brothel owner Dennis Hof—at whose establishment he lost his virginity at the age of fourteen (taken there, along with his brother, by the family nanny at his father's direction) and at whose funeral he delivered the eulogy (along with porn star Ron Jeremy). It included, too, every journalist on the hunt for Trump gossip, which Carlson was almost always willing to supply with verve and finely calculated indiscretion. He was liked by almost everyone who had spent time with him. Carlson had devoted great effort to his relationship with the mogul son. Over the resentment of Fox managers, he had come to report directly to the largely absent CEO, meaning, in effect, he had no day-to-day boss and had achieved carte blanche to do with his show what he wanted.

On his part, the mogul's son was (not unlike his father) tongue-tied and inarticulate, socially uncomfortable except among his closest circle, prickly, resentful, and eager to be shown his due. He had been living in Los Angeles. It was a mogul's life: his home among the most expensive in Los Angeles. But with the sale in 2018 of most of his family's entertainment assets—especially the Twenty-First Century Fox movie studio and television production company—he'd found himself as just the Fox News boss, without entertainment industry clout, and grievously disdained in liberal Hollywood.

Rupert Murdoch and his children had been, for most of Fox's history, largely held at arm's length from the network by its chairman, Roger Ailes. Ailes maintained that he had extracted a promise from Murdoch never to interfere in the programming at the network. While Murdoch was famous for making and breaking such pledges at his many newspapers, in this instance he in fact left well enough alone. When Ailes's end came—by the sons' hands—the sons, eager to take over, were met at the network by suspicion and resentment. But among those willing to extend them the benefit of the doubt was Tucker Carlson, who Ailes had relegated to the dead zone of weekend shows, sending him on a grueling schedule every Friday from DC to New York.

Carlson is a whisperer, a trader of confidences, with a reliable archive of where the bodies are buried. Lachlan Murdoch has always depended on a series of mentors, or, perhaps more accurately, courtiers, in his father's employ, who might take him by the hand. Carlson and his boss fell happily into this role—Carlson supplying the insights into the Fox operation that the Murdoch heir was largely too remote to be able to learn for himself, and his boss's favor opening unlimited opportunities at the network for Carlson.

By the time of Lachlan's late February trip to Florida, the two colleagues had come to form an exclusive bond. They often spoke every day. There were few decisions that Lachlan did not run by his star. It was understood throughout the network that Carlson was not only the ratings leader but that he had the exclusive ear of the boss, even that he frequently spoke for him (Carlson encouraged this understanding). At that very moment, Lachlan Murdoch was planning his first significant address, a defense of Fox, and a statement of his own politics scheduled for the end of March in Australia, which Carlson was closely advising on if not writing himself.

But here now, in the Carlsons' tropical garden, was a different issue. Lachlan Murdoch was on his way back from the Persian Gulf. He had been in Riyadh in the Saudi kingdom and in Dubai in the UAE. He was there to meet with Saudi crown prince Mohammed bin Salman (MBS) and the Emirates leader Sheikh Mohamed bin Zayed (MBZ)—among, if not *the*, richest men in the world. The video game obsessed, cocaine-fueled Saudi crown prince had ordered the killing and dismemberment of Saudi dissident and journalist Jamal Khashoggi, becoming, however briefly, the target of the world's opprobrium. MBS had also hung up by his thumbs Rupert's most reliable investor and supporter, his cousin Prince Al Waleed bin Talal, forcing him to disgorge an impressive tithe of his wealth and pass it to him. Lachlan was trying to get some of this money back as an investment in his own Murdoch future. (He acknowledged the irony, but business was business.) Lachlan was similarly courting the fabulously wealthy Emirati MBZ, who often guided the even richer MBS in his investments. He needed the Gulf state money to defend Fox—against his brother.

It was a dirty and serious business, Lachlan confided in his star after Tucker's wife, Susie, left the garden, but it had to be done. The scion seemed exhausted and burdened—and noticeably carrying an extra twenty pounds—but summoning a new resolve. This was a positive sign. It was never certain how much Lachlan was committed to the job of running Fox. He was a distant owner, a global-maximum of time zones away in Sydney—his I'm-up-all-night protestation hardly even a pretense of active management. It often seemed that in a random game of musical chairs in the Murdoch family, Lachlan, unthinking, had snagged the last happenstance chair, and found it an uncomfortable one. To the degree that he had ever been at home in any parts of his father's business, it was in newspapers, especially the Australian newspapers. He had little television background. His politics were, at best, a nod to his father's politics, whatever they were—otherwise, amorphous. He had voted for Barack Obama and then for Hillary Clinton against Donald Trump. He had little appetite for controversy—certainly not Fox-style stuff. And inside the network, beyond Tucker, he had few relationships. His single reason for holding the Fox job seemed to be that his brother James actually wanted the job more than he did.

That now was precisely what seemed to be giving him this new determination.

He grimly outlined the current family dynamics for his friend (and employee). A showdown was inevitable. And it was seismic, for his family, for the network, for the nation—and it would be, too, for Carlson himself.

Brother James, having left the family in a huff (with his $2 billion cash cut), had reconstituted himself as a man of virtue, vowing to take control of Fox and to make it a "force for good." This sounded lame. But the family trust, which controlled the Murdoch companies, gave enormous powers to the four oldest Murdoch children—Prudence, Elisabeth, Lachlan, and James (and no power to the Murdoch daughters Grace and Chloe, who came after the formation of the trust). Although Lachlan was the CEO, in James's current alliance with his Fox-hating sisters (also with their comfortable $2 billion), it was perfectly possible, upon his father's death, that he could lead a vote against his brother and take control.

This was also a joke on itself. As whatever internecine struggle was unfolding in the Murdoch family, threatening to destabilize the country's politics (as Fox itself had, previously, destabilized the country's politics), such a drama was also playing out each season on HBO's *Succession*. Originally shopped as a drama specifically about the Murdoch family—at a time when the Murdoch family was still the most powerful family in show business and therefore not to be mocked by any other outlet in show business—it had been reimagined as a bitchy, vindictive, and knife-in-the-back soap opera of a Murdoch-*type* family. With reality imitating art that had imitated reality the show now seemed to have become an empowering agent for helping the otherwise uptight Murdochs to fully express, *en famille*, their full enmity and bitterness (with suspicions that one or more members of the family might be leaking family details to the show).

Tucker Carlson—always more or less playing a Tucker Carlson character on television—was now, in this internecine Murdoch war, stepping into a further television-driven reality. James Murdoch's conviction that Fox was a force for evil in this world and a personal moral albatross around his neck encompassed his belief that Tucker Carlson was, second only to Donald Trump, the most dangerous man in America, one to whom Fox was giving a platform and the very wherewithal to be president himself (as it had done for Trump). James was determined to stop both Fox and Carlson.

The reports of James Murdoch's wrath and righteousness served both to cement Lachlan's bond with Carlson and to make him dream that, both to spite his brother and to signify his own success, as his father sought to signify his own success as the power behind presidents and prime ministers, Tucker Carlson might in fact actually become president—the second Fox president. *His* president.

But for Carlson, sitting with boss and friend in the warm Boca

Grande night, the breeze coming off the Gulf, there was another equally obvious side to this. If James did succeed, Carlson's transformative, cometlike success, would abruptly, and ignominiously, end. That had always been part of the strange alchemy of Fox News. It made you— gave you a singular name: Tucker, Hannity, O'Reilly, Megyn—but somehow did not give you a star's independent life. Megyn Kelly, Bill O'Reilly, Glenn Beck, Greta Van Susteren, Paula Zahn, Fox superstars, had tried to go somewhere else and quickly faded away. It was a fate that weighed heavily on Carlson—that, in the blink of an eye, he might not be the second-most-famous and -hated person in the country.

His only alternative might be . . . to run for president. The White House. There it was, absent a note of irony: he could be unemployable but for the presidency.

Which was the other part of his alarm as he walked now to his lunch date, the invasion of Ukraine in progress for nine hours, earning him a nervous smile from all the people he believed were looking at him. He might be turning into Charles Lindbergh, that almost president.

A made-up war, a phony war, a not-going-to-happen war, had not only happened but what if Ukrainians were actually going to stand and fight the Russians? He had spent weeks now, nearly nonstop, excusing Vladimir Putin, if not praising him, if not outright siding with him, so a likely slaughter of thousands of Ukrainians was not going to be good for Carlson. And worse, perhaps, would be heroic resistance.

Curiously, of all the positions and views he nightly postulated and advocated and spun in his doom-and-apocalypse narratives, the one he definitely believed in (not that he *didn't* believe in the others, but this was, after all, television) was that the assumptions of American military and intelligence posturing and decision-making were always likely to be wrong and to lead to greater, not lesser, risk to the US. He put it on a personal basis. He had spent much of his life in the nation's capital, in the prestige circles of Washington, and he knew these people: They were self-serving, out-of-touch, heedless lemmings, and yes, quite often corrupt, too. Given their two decades (or this could be extended to the near seven decades since Vietnam) of failed performance and putting the US into harm's way for no advantage at all, there was some shit he, for one, was not going to eat. No Ukraine shit.

But, of course, that did not mean that this wasn't one of those times that the whole nation might line up against him.

Lindbergh, in the years before World War II, became the face of American isolationism, a profound impulse of practicality, family, exclusivity, and one's own place on earth—a racial consciousness without, at that point, a name (i.e., racism)—that Carlson believed yet existed in the American psyche. But for Lindbergh, it had turned to an enduring shame around the American hero (not least because of his bonhomie toward Hitler, not, many might argue, that different from the benefit of the doubt Tucker was extending to Putin).

Yes, yes, even given his weeks of Putin good cheer, he could of course walk it back now. This *was* television after all. And perhaps he should. Perhaps he might have to. While Lachlan Murdoch had opened up in Tucker's backyard about his own family problems, he had also— quite as an aside, but perhaps this was the real reason for his visit— indicated that he and his father might wish that Tucker modulate his feelings about Ukraine and Putin. But fuck it. Did America really care about Ukraine? Carlson found that hard to believe. And wasn't it likely that, this being war, soon enough it would go wrong, and he could say I told you so?

He woke up every day loved, apparently, by an ever-growing audience and hated by everyone who mattered—proof of the argument he tried to make every night: *they*—those nameless powers—don't care what you think, *they* are going to do only what's good for them. And if he was right—and he *was* right—*they* would inevitably come for him. "There is," he said darkly, "too much power and too much malice arrayed against me personally."

He had woken up and Russia had invaded Ukraine, and with Russia now airing clips from his Putin-praising segments on a constant loop, who didn't doubt that *they*, making him out to be some Tokyo Rose, were going to blame him—next only to Putin himself—for the war.

And one morning soon, as surely as the sun was going to rise, he was going to wake up, and the near ninety-one-year-old Murdoch (in three weeks ninety-one—Tucker Carlson was keeping close count) was going to be dead, the only person who, however unreliably, could maintain the status quo. For the time being anyway.

And then, a morning soon after, he might wake up and find James Murdoch—"full of arrogant anger"—coming for him.

And, in truth, however much he was the ratings star and the boss's favorite, he hadn't yet made enough money to walk away. Oh sure, everyone thought he was rich, of course they would—there was really no explaining otherwise. But he was still emerging from his lean years. And Murdoch was a begrudging cheapskate.

Carlson's countenance at the Pink Elephant, the clubby local restaurant on Bayou Avenue was as sunny as the day, his big and manic laugh booming across the room, his familiar good cheer and embracing banter thrilling to the waitress.

But his mind was focused. "How long," he wondered aloud, "before they get me?"

3

Lachlan

SPEARFISHING

Lachlan Murdoch's approach to dealing with his father's clear unhappiness about Tucker and Ukraine—and Tucker and everything—was to tell his father that Tucker really didn't mean much of what he said on the air, which seemed to somewhat mollify the older Murdoch. "Just get him to fuck over Putin a bit," Murdoch told his son, leaving it at that. And, indeed, shortly after the invasion Carlson did put some tepid blame on Putin. But perhaps more to the point what you had in father and son was a Frick and Frack demonstration of how conflict averse the two top executives of the most belligerent major media outlet in the country were, and of their mutual interest in looking for any excuse to avoid the problems at the network, even as Frick, the father, became more and more agitated about it, and Frack, the son, more agitated about his father's agitation.

His rich kid's life had always been a struggle. "Wounded," is how he described his life to a friend. This was because, he analyzed about himself, he "didn't fight back." In his view now, the enmity in the family—that is, with his brother—had only increased by not fighting back. It was not just that his break with his brother was complete—nothing now but an utter contempt between them—but that they faced each other over a battle line. The brothers would fight to the death—at least business death. Lachlan trying to hold on to Fox, James absolutely committed to taking it. Fox represented for Lachlan his patrimony and honest-work place in the world, for James it represented the world's evil. How do you deal with that? Lachlan could not even express how this made him feel. He was not evil.

Spearfishing had become his safe place. The two standout artifacts in his office were his large speargun propped in a corner, and a picture of his father hanging on the wall. His deeply engaged discussion of the nature of the sport and his experiences on the water and pursuit of kingfish and flathead got a lot more of his attention than his worries—or his father's worries—say, about his leading anchor's unpopular views on the Russian invasion of Ukraine. Just weeks before he had taken delivery of a new boat, not a gross super yacht but a finely restored forty-three-meter 1954 boat (only $30 million). Outdoor life and classic yachts were easy topics between the company CEO and his leading star (and the smart subject for everyone else who actually wanted to talk to the heir). At the same time, the star was more than a trifle concerned that his boss—and protector—was spending most of his time continents away, as well as underwater, instead of on the job.

It was not long into the pandemic, and quite in the dead of night, when Lachlan Murdoch and his wife, Sarah, with their three children abruptly disappearing from their Zoom classes, picked up and moved to Australia, surprising social acquaintances and their children's friends. Part of the background here was that Sarah, a former model and television personality in Australia, had, nearly incessantly, told everyone how much better their lives had been in Sydney and how much better their lives would be if they went back. Their Australian life, from 2005, when Lachlan left his father's company, until 2014, when, after years of his father's imploring, he returned, was quite a gifted existence. He was not just famous but something like a subject of national awe as the Murdoch scion; his wife, with her own television show, was famous in her own right. Plus, as an "investor" with no real job obligations, his hours were his own and his pace leisurely.

In many very large companies, there is a strategic practice carried out by a discrete inner circle to disguise the daily activities of the chief executive. This is because CEOs largely do what they want to, and, to both their boards and their employees, that often may not seem to have much relevance to the daily priorities of running a vast enterprise. But in the case of Lachlan Murdoch, maintaining the illusion that he was a CEO giving it his all was vastly complicated by the unavoidable admission that, with his great distance from anything that might be going on in his American company, he was necessarily only going to be a part-time presence.

The hope was that his absence would hardly be noticed in the pandemic; the tenuous or credulous cover story was that Lachlan would be keeping US hours and therefore be up all night tending to Fox business. When this failed to convince anyone, and with no sign of him returning as the pandemic abated, the new line was that he would be spending two weeks a month in the US, a week in LA, and a week in New York. But, after a year of this, it was hardly possible to find anyone who could actually account for those ten business days in one or another of Fox's US offices.

Who, then, was running the show?

It was, as numerous people who had known him for many years, including his family members, observed, exactly where Lachlan had always been: everything happening around him, he uncertain and vacillating and trying to escape the center of the action. It was not as though he hadn't made his ambivalence perfectly clear. His father had sent him after his graduation from Princeton back to Australia to learn the newspaper business. He had become a kind of happy mascot in the tough-guy Aussie newsrooms, mentored by the people wise enough to know the value of mentoring him. He reluctantly answered the call to return to New York in 2000 to an office near his father. Back in the US, he was most comfortable in the ever-retro newsroom of the *New York Post*, with its many Aussie imports, and its dedicated drinker's culture (possibly among the last true drinkers' outposts in New York)—here, too, treated rather as the mascot prince. But beyond the *Post* newsroom, a minor province of the empire, he found himself almost completely blocked off from any involvement in the larger company by COO Peter Chernin in LA and by Fox News chief Roger Ailes in New York.

In 2005, partly in a fit of pique over Ailes's constant insinuations about his social life, the thirty-three-year-old heir demanded that his father elevate him to an equal footing with Ailes and Chernin. When Murdoch demurred in favor of his executives, Lachlan retreated to Sydney. In a sense, this began the formal generational struggle. From here on, a significant amount of the older Murdoch's business time would be spent trying to both accommodate, and defend against, his children's interest, as well as to seek their approval, that is to leverage his assets to answer for all his deficiencies as a father (almost all of his top executives became involved in this generational undertaking).

With Lachlan barely speaking to his father—their engagement strictly on the level of shareholder and board member—Murdoch now elevated James, who in 2003 had taken over running Sky, the Murdoch controlled pay-television satellite system in the UK, to his likely successor. But at the same time, Murdoch began a ceaseless, decade-long campaign of emissaries, inducements, promises, and assurances, to persuade a largely immovable Lachlan to return to his side. Similarly, he continued to try to induce his daughter Elisabeth, who had also fled his employ, to return to working for him—although never quite as his possible successor. Wooing Lachlan as he continued to promote James closer to the top spot—moving him in 2007 from Sky chief to the chief of all the Murdoch international operations—naturally antagonized both brothers, as well as their sister.

It was finally in 2014 that the stakes seemed to be clarified and the competition leveled, at least between the brothers, with both of them given equal authority in the empire, with one of them eventually to take over. Lachlan may not have worked in ten years, putting him at a disadvantage, but James was yet in extremely bad odor over his responsibility for the UK hacking affair.

Lachlan, on his return to the US and his father's company, would be largely based in LA and James in New York.

With Lachlan's wife begrudging the move, and him years out of executive practice, his return was at best a diffident affair, even—to the extent possible when you command a lion's share of industry power in a company town—a low-key affair. They bought a $12 million house in Mandeville Canyon—befitting, that is, something less than a heavy hitter movie executive. Large but not too large. They greased the skids to get their three children into school, but not obnoxiously. They eschewed a security detail, that particular sign of LA status. Their social circle seemed purposefully or strangely limited to people *not* in the media business. They seemed, indeed, to surround themselves with service people—contractors, landscapers, car dealers. They were outside the industry power circles, without mover-and-shaker friends.

Lachlan was a frequent chaperone on school outings. The notable thing was that, while all other LA private school parents were, obsessively or obnoxiously or urgently, glued to their phones, Lachlan was not. He neither made nor took calls. He was either a perfect parent, or one without a job.

If his job was unclear, so was his point of view. When he had to engage on the subject of Fox or his father's long right-wing history—a red meat discussion in LA, and a sign of moxie to confront the bad man's son—he would shake this off as not involving him, not his bailiwick, not his interest. In the run-up to the 2016 election, the bathrooms at the Mandeville house featured toilet paper with Trump's face, reported visitors with relief and satisfaction. He told people that his wife and children cried when Trump was elected.

To community and coworkers, he was enigma or cipher. He seemed in waiting, but for what was not clear.

In contrast, his brother and coequal in the company was styling himself as the brother of big plans. Whether anyone was truly listening to James about these schemes might be beside the point. But he was a man with a mission. Despite the low odds, he was pushing for a complete takeover of Sky, which they controlled with only a 39 percent interest. With full ownership of Sky, this would then be the platform that Fox News would be integrated into and on its way to being cleansed as a new, international news brand. James, in New York, was the advocate for building a triumphal headquarters, a physical manifestation of the dominance of Murdoch media—a project Ailes was, with particular relish, dissing behind his back. And, in 2016, James worked to make Trump a line in the sand the company would not cross. Murdoch hardly, if ever, had given Ailes programming direction. But in May 2016, on James's prodding, Murdoch pushed Ailes to tilt Fox to Hillary Clinton, because she was going to win, and because Trump was a joke, and more importantly a loser.

When, in July, Gretchen Carlson launched her harassment suit against Ailes, James immediately hired a law firm—Paul, Weiss, the longtime Democratic powerhouse—to effectively carry out an internal prosecution of Ailes. In this lightning campaign, the brothers, led by James, enlisted Megyn Kelly for damning testimony that, in two weeks from start to finish of the scandal, brought Ailes down. Eight months later, when Bill O'Reilly, the network's ratings pillar, was confronted by sexual miscreant charges, James was at his father's side when now president Trump called Murdoch to try to save O'Reilly's job. "We'll pass," said Murdoch. James continued to propose himself as the man to take over and reform Fox—but here, once more, the father waffled.

Lachlan complained bitterly and often about James's management style—"a prick"—but at the same time, he was unable to define his own role as the cohead of the company. He seemed reluctant to involve himself in the closed-culture Hollywood studio world or to exert his authority over that world. James bumptiously insisted on his experience and acumen as a television executive in staking out a dominant position in the family's network, station, and cable business, and its hypothetical digital future. Lachlan, notably inarticulate, seemed uninterested in talking the talk and carving out a competitive position for himself as a CEO strategist and visionary. Plus, he had become well known for never making a decision. He seemed always in retreat. What was he doing? How did he fill his time? Who was he even talking to? What did he want to be when he grew up?

There was a disconnect, a laxness, and, in their Mandeville house, a sense not just of a lack of control, but of things being out of control.

Two of his children were beset by dramatic anxieties. Lachlan, to the horror of the rest of his siblings—all of them finding this to be a reversion to their father's long-standing and scowling views—rejected therapy. For a time both children had to be homeschooled. Lachlan told friends they were bullied because of Fox.

In the months after Trump's election, James began to build the case against his brother, to his father, his siblings, and to board members. Lachlan, James bluntly argued, was not now and never would be up to running a vast and diversified public company. He could hardly run his own life. It quite appeared he had neither the heart nor interest in running anything. Possibly he was depressed. At any rate, this wasn't working. Obviously. End of story. Nor was James willing to run the company yoked to his brother. A decision had to be made.

Nearly seventy years of public conflict, and yet Rupert Murdoch hated personal conflict. He retreated into a subverbal world in which he seemed to understand what was at issue but refused to clearly express himself. That is, he put his head in the sand and hoped it would all pass.

But James persisted, threatening to leave the company—this not long after his father's marriage to Jerry Hall, when, in one of the few times in his life, he seemed to want to work less. With his two sisters in tow, James brandished his ultimate political control: There was no future for Lachlan, so why should he be indulged in the present? If his father might not disagree about Lachlan, he was, at the same time, tired of the management effort that the impetuous and intractable James required. They both had had enough of each other. Hence, James's audacious gambit: sell it all to Disney. This was arguably—and a good argument, at that—the top of the market for television-heavy media companies that might not achieve ultimate scale (that is, buying everything). And now with British regulators—variously, under Murdoch's thumb, or, in this instance, determined to punish him—dashing the Sky deal, suddenly, they had no killer consolidation plan on the horizon. Largely through James's efforts and hobnobbing, Disney was soon making a top-of-the-market offer: $71 billion for the lion's share of the company's assets. With the prospect of only blood on the ground in a long-term succession fight, why not?

Murdoch, weary, lovestruck, and ever money-hungry, agreed.

Lachlan briefly, and not too credibly, petitioned his father to join with him and buy James out and let the family keep control. But his father, caught between one son's intractable enmity and the other's neediness, settled on an unbeatable price. Anyway, Lachlan soon got over it and took his consolation prize: $2 billion in his pocket and the leadership of Fox News.

Among his first moves was to bring in Viet Dinh as his chief lawyer and effective number two and COO.

For many years, the Murdoch sons, both when they were in the company or shunning it, had populated its ranks with various friends and proxies. It was their father's pattern to become impressed by this or that often random person and, with sudden enthusiasm, hire them to solve manifold problems. His sons followed, tapping both school friends and new finds and assembling their own ad hoc mafias within the greater company.

Viet Dinh had come to the US as a child refugee from Vietnam, soon piling credential upon credential in a legal and government career, from Supreme Court clerk, to Department of Justice high rank and influence, to major corporate law partnership. When Lachlan met him in 2003, at an Aspen Institute event, Dinh was a member of the Bush administration, the assistant attorney general for the Office of Legal Policy, a bureaucratic power base of significant and unaccountable influence; he was, too, an avid national security conservative (Dinh bragged often about his involvement with the design and passage of the Patriot Act). The chance meeting—exactly what events like the Aspen conference exist for—was gold for Dinh. He and Lachlan commenced a relationship which shortly resulted in him joining the board of the company as one of Lachlan's nominees and becoming a godfather to Lachlan's son.

The legal department in the Murdoch world has always had a paramount place, a crucial fulcrum helping to tip the company from its official status as a public company to its more characteristic identity as a private company—that is, the Murdochs were themselves the paramount clients of the company's lawyers. Your power as a lawyer within the company therefore came from your relationship with Rupert Murdoch and the members of his family. After James's departure from the company, Dinh left the board of News Corp and came over to the Fox side as board member and as the company's top lawyer. Lachlan seemed, practically speaking, to talk only to Dinh. In turn, Dinh began to act like the co-CEO. The seeming power grab was exacerbated by the fact that Dinh, secretive, uncommunicative, abrupt, generally charmless, and dogmatically conservative in the liberal entertainment industry, was widely disliked.

Lachlan, officially now the top Murdoch son, promptly bought a massive house in Aspen, Colorado, where his parents, when he was young, had once had an imposing home, though much more modest than their son's new estate. Why, friends wondered, would he buy a retreat in one of the most liberal communities in America where everyone was bound to hate him?

And then he traded his Mandeville home for one in Bel-Air, the most expensive house in the history of LA sales, a far larger home than his father's expansive Bel-Air house—indeed, ridiculously, the old *Beverly Hillbillies* mansion! So massive that nobody in his increasingly fraught family had to see each other.

There were several strands of statement here. For one, the Murdoch heirs had never actually had real money—their *own* real money—before. The Murdoch Family Trust, still controlled by their father, had kept the family fortune locked up in company shares. As some of the world's richest legatees, they were all yet on a short string. What's more, Lachlan had spent ten years palling around with and trying to punch in the same investment league as his friend James Packer, the son of another Australian media multibillionaire, Kerry Packer, whose vast fortune had already passed to his son (who was getting out of the media business and into the gambling business). So buying these megahouses was a sigh of *finally!* It was also an announcement of taking over. He wasn't yet fifty and his father was soon to be ninety. After nearly twenty years of open contention, the business, however diminished, was his. Hear me roar.

It was all a disappointment, of course.

Los Angeles is a town as binary in its appreciation of power as Washington. You had it or you didn't, with almost nothing in between. And, even if you had had it, if you didn't have it anymore, you were functionally useless. A cable news network was hardly worth noting in the movie business. There was more status and power in dissing this particular news network than owning it. What stature he might have had, and largely failed to take advantage of, as a TV and movie power—power that otherwise would have negated the hated Fox—was quite instantly gone.

Nor was he able to leverage his status as the CEO of the most significant political force in the nation—he just did not seem interested in trying. His father's pivotal allegiance to Fox, and to anyone who was running Fox, was wholly dependent on its profits, which any change might negatively effect—so best do nothing. Besides, Lachlan had no hands-on experience in the television news business, in managing television talent, or in the opaque particulars of cable distribution. Nor did he have any real politics, except trying to accommodate his father's more and more uncertain views. And, in fact, wholly putting aside the volatile future in both the television industry and politics, Fox, at least for the moment, managed itself.

So there was no reason not to leave LA for Australia. The more distance you gained from Fox, the easier life was.

Indeed, the one father–son decision, to allow an early call on election night 2020 giving Arizona to Biden, had immediately backfired, with Trump threatening a network boycott, the upstart conservative networks claiming new ratings highs, and internal tensions again rife with Fox talent (i.e., Hannity). No, do nothing. Anything you do upsets the ecosystem of profits. Just stay away.

Lachlan spoke to Tucker, and Lachlan spoke to Viet. And, even here, he spoke to them rather less than more. That was enough.

What he spent his time on was worrying about his brother. Everyone in the family observed his fantasy of a buyout with his trips to the Middle East with a certain amount of pathos. Lachlan was not a risk-taker. His occasional public bursts of right-wing-like enthusiasm also seemed more poignant to the rest of his family than macho—he was trying to be his father. He was desperate to secure that relationship, even as—especially as—his father became frailer.

Anyway, he described the incredible beauty of spearfishing to Carlson, and to anyone else who he could waylay, and his pride in his lovely, classic boat, the *Istros*. It was quite a life. And, just to be sure, he had a $147 million superyacht on order, too.

SPRING

4

Hannity

THE FUNERAL

Surely, to understand Fox News, to truly *get* the absolutely and for so long unique and unchallenged thing in American media and politics, you had to appreciate Roger Ailes. But perhaps stronger than any other effect they had had on the network, the Murdochs had wiped Ailes clean away. Here was a tour de force of corporate scrubbing: he was dropped from official accounts; nobody, except the tone-deaf, brought up how Ailes had done things in the past; and of course he was never to be mentioned on the air.

Sean Hannity often referred to Ailes, who had personally hired him out of Nowheresville in 1996 at the very dawn of Fox News, as "a king-maker," or, often, "the kingmaker." This seemed to mean both that Ailes had made Hannity a king, as well as generations of Republican politicians. Every Republican president since Nixon, Hannity ascribed, not entirely inaccurately, to Ailes's support and machinations. "The history of our time is due to Roger Ailes," declared Hannity in his own narration of American history. While the network at large had moved on from Ailes or pretended to, Hannity was one of the few who continued to quote him and to try to do what Roger would have done (not so incidentally slagging off the Murdochs in the process—also something that Ailes would have done). In the spring of 2022, this included trying to be a kingmaker himself. He was concentrating on the midterm race in Pennsylvania, successfully lobbying Trump, *that* would-be king and kingmaker, to support television personality Mehmet Oz for Senate and the right-winger Doug Mastriano for governor.

What had really gotten him going was that James Murdoch's wife, Kathryn Hufschmid, had in early 2022 donated $1 million to defeat them. This was straight-up Ailes stuff, that Fox News was in a battle, potentially a life and death battle, with the Murdoch kids (forget the liberals). This couldn't be better proof—*more* proof—of how right Ailes was.

For Hannity, there was one Fox News: Ailes's. He wasn't going to get twisted about this for anyone. Fuck them (that is, the Murdochs). There was right and wrong and they were obvious. If you had to think too hard about what was right and wrong then you were going to go wrong. He didn't think about it. If he had to define his politics, it was right there: don't ask yourself what's right; you know what's right. For so long, people had called him stupid. "I don't like brains, and you're not a brain," said Ailes, happily, to the $800-a-week talk radio host in Atlanta. But if his loyalty to Ailes was stupid, Hannity was fine with that. He was one of that very small circle from those first days in 1996. And he was the only one left on the air.

Hannity's allegiance was to *that* Fox. That *was* Fox. That's the world they were still living in—that's what made all the money. If that Fox disappeared, and eventually, without Ailes, Hannity guessed it would, then Fox disappeared.

Ailes had died twice. The first time had come without warning—those terrible and, Hannity stubbornly believed (mostly) unfair accusations, bringing Ailes down in just two weeks. The most important man in television, and in politics, gone. He had allowed his enemies (i.e., the Murdoch boys) to gather strength and let their enmity increase and when they struck they had killed the king—as they knew they must. (Outraged, Hannity had threatened to quit then. Well, privately threatened. And he probably should have gone through with it.)

And then, ten months later, Ailes had truly died, falling down in his $36 million house in his woebegone banishment among the tax exiles in Palm Beach—a week in a coma. Tragedy.

From $40,000 in Atlanta in 1996, Hannity had seen his net worth increase at the quantum leaps that Fox News itself increased—all because of Ailes. Hannity had invested in subprime real estate, going in heavily after the 2007 meltdown. So, he wasn't just rich. Likely, he wagered, he was the richest man on television. (Ailes, not a little sourly, was always guessing at Hannity's net worth—$200, $300, $400 million? "All the illegals live in Sean's houses," said Ailes.)

If Ailes was true Fox and if Hannity was the last man loyal to Ailes, then Hannity was now the true Fox. On that terrible day in 2017 (Hannity had been one of Beth Ailes's first calls: "He's gone, Sean") the powers that be—the *new* powers that be—had made it perfectly clear that it would not, if you had any sense at all, be a good idea to go to the funeral. Well, there was still honor in this world. Hannity might not be the smartest guy in the room, but he knew, as Ailes always knew, when to call the Murdochs' bluff. They weren't Fox News.

Who was? Who had the power within the nation's most politically powerful organization? Hmm? With Ailes there had been only one power center at Fox, quite unlike every other television news network, where so many knives were always out. At Fox, with Ailes, there was only ever one direction. That was Fox: no ambiguity. Everybody understood. And now, after Ailes?

Hannity's plane was on the tarmac at 7:00 a.m. at Republic Airport in East Farmingdale, Long Island. This was Sean Hannity's plane. So, Hannity was the immediate power.

Post-Ailes, everyone sensed Hannity's new swagger. Ailes's downfall *was* a tragedy. But it also meant a power vacuum. With Trump's victory, Trump became the most powerful voice at Fox—a lot more powerful than the Murdochs. And, with Hannity on the phone with the new president every day, really his closest confidant, his chief adviser, he was the single most important person, next only to Trump himself, in the revolution that was happening in this country, one that Trump was leading and that Fox was now following. "Revolution II," Hannity was calling it. "I'm like Thomas Jefferson, practically—wait, he had slaves, didn't he? Who's somebody like that who didn't have slaves?"

Bill Hemmer was there on the tarmac waiting for Hannity. Hemmer had moved over from CNN in 2005. Ailes had told him then, as Ailes told everyone, if you come here there's no going back. That is, you joined this side. The other side was the enemy, and you would be *its* enemy. This was brand consciousness as war. Hemmer certainly had things in common with the Fox identity. He was, generally, politically conservative, and he was a Roman Catholic—with an RC education, first at Our Lady of Victory in Cincinnati, then at Elder High School, the Cincinnati archdiocese's all-boys prep school. To be Roman Catholic, especially with a Catholic education, was an important Fox credential. But Hemmer was probably gay—at least Ailes thought he was gay. Don't ask–don't tell was acceptable to Ailes; suspicion would only preclude you from a prime-time anchor job (except if you were a woman: Ailes suspected most ambitious women of being lesbians). At Fox, the now fifty-two-year-old but boyish Hemmer had flourished as a roving reporter and daytime anchor. He was making $5 million a year—a considerable multiple from what he would be making at any other news network for similar on-air work. This too was part of the Ailes formula: with its extraordinary profits, reward the talent (at least the male talent—and not even the top-most male talent) for forsaking the non-Fox world (e.g., Brett Baier at $12 million, Neil Cavuto at $9 million, Hannity at $19 million—plus what he made from radio!).

Along with Hemmer, the small group on the early-morning tarmac now included Liz Trotta, who, at eighty, was one of the few veterans at Fox from the network news era—a hard-drinking, caustic broad (a term wildly out of favor with just about everyone anywhere, but which had still been a commonplace to Ailes), which, combined with her Catholicism and conservatism (held in moderate check at NBC and CBS where she had worked), made her, for Ailes, an ideal early Fox hire. Ailes had protected her from a running series of on-air gaffes and offenses (sometimes so off-note as to bewilder even Ailes).

Then there was Kimberly Guilfoyle. KG. There was a positive sense among many at Fox that one of the channel's virtues was its special tolerance, a kind of willing suspension of disbelief, for the peculiar outcasts who washed up there. Guilfoyle was certainly among them. A former prosecutor and an enthusiastic liberal groupie, Guilfoyle had been married to then San Francisco mayor Gavin Newsom, before breaking up with Newsom, moving to New York in 2004 for a television job at Court TV, and then, with an offer from Fox in 2006, making a dramatic conversion to the right wing. "Who knew?" said Ailes. She soon became an Ailes favorite. She was a Catholic, which for Ailes explained a certain right-wing inevitability; she was sexually forward, which for Ailes was the necessary attribute for any successful woman in television (the more forward the better); and she was a lawyer. There was something almost fetishistic about Ailes's penchant for women lawyers: a law degree played some tasty part in Ailes's dominance and submission fantasies. In Ailes's last days at Fox, Guilfoyle was an active Ailes agent, trying to cajole and threaten other talent into line behind him.

Guilfoyle, on the tarmac, was dressed in black widow's weeds, to sinister effect.

In addition to Guilfoyle, Hemmer, and Trotta on the tarmac, there were a few civilian friends for whom Beth Ailes had secured a lift, and one of the ever-paranoid Ailes's favorite security guards. The company had spent millions a year on Ailes's personal security (vastly more than it spent on the safety of Rupert Murdoch).

Thirty minutes late, Hannity swept in with the casual disregard of always having a plane waiting. Hannity prided himself on fame and riches not much changing him from a middle-class Long Island guy. Still, a plane was a plane. He had a jacket in a cleaner's bag and an untied tie around his neck. "What are we waiting for, the party's on—fuck, are we late? I don't think so." And he was climbing the steps with everyone following. "It's eleven, right, this fucking thing?" That is, the funeral. "So we have plenty of time."

Hannity plopped down on the back seat, one of those facing forward, put his feet up on the facing seat, and took out an electronic cigarette.

"They'll have stuff, breakfast stuff, as soon as we're in the air. KG you look like my prom date."

This was not exactly true: KG's mourning garb, a black body-con zipper dress, made her look more like a stripper or drag queen. What was also clear, if you wanted it to be, was that she was wearing no underwear.

Hannity, the everyman on air, was, actually, an everyman in person. Sure, his confidence had built over the years with his ratings and his wealth. And, unlike most actual everymen, he could speak in full sentences. But his body language was everyman. He was relaxed, uncaring, sloppy, a large body going where it pleased. So *loose*. Unprotected.

Airborne, the single flight attendant started to strip off the Saran Wrap from platters of fruit slices and bagels and muffins (refrigerated from the night before). "Come on, Hannity, where's the booze?" Liz Trotta called from the front of the plane. Hannity seemed to briefly wonder if he should be disapproving, but then shrugged and the early morning screwdrivers got underway. Trotta, barely sotto voce, muffled only by the small plane's hum, began dissing Hannity to Beth Ailes's guests ("an Irish bartender—we all know the type") and everyone else at Fox ("a nest of vipers") except Ailes ("what the sluts did to him . . . should be a public whipping").

Meanwhile, Hannity, in the back of the plane, working on his screwdriver, was contemplating his grievances. Not so much bitterly as basking in them. Owning them. Gearing up a running commentary, an on-air-like monologue: Yes, the Murdochs. It was Lachlan and James—particularly James—who seized the opportunity when their father was out of town, to oust Ailes. They wanted the network back and they had taken it.

Well, that remained to be seen.

Ailes's end (his first end), Hannity was expounding, had nothing to do with the accusations of years of systematic harassment. In the months since, it had become nothing but clearer: this was a political hit. Not politics in the left-right sense, but politics as a pure power play—old-fashioned television politics. The kids had organized the push against him, first the lawsuit by Gretchen Carlson, the former Miss America, with her bullshit allegations, then the others, and finally the mortal blow, paid for by the Murdoch brothers—Hannity knew for sure—struck by Megyn Kelly. Rupert Murdoch, an old man, had become weak and indecisive—plus he was fucking Jerry Hall, or *trying* to fuck Jerry Hall (*hee haw*). Hence, the sons thought *they* were in charge. The gay sons.

For Ailes, gay was a general characterization of good looks, the Ivy League, and liberal views, and included dark hints of what Ailes knew, and only he knew. Ailes's casual calumny had spread to almost everyone at the network, where a great number of people "knew a source," who had detailed information, names, places, practices. Ailes's scurrilous views had spread beyond Fox, been adopted in Trump circles, and become a favorite commonplace at *Breitbart News*. So now Fox, the bulwark of the right-wing movement, the mainstay of its thinking, more important than the Republican Party itself, was all but dependent on two liberal-leaning (one of them, in his own father's words, an out-and-out "tree hugger") poofters (an Aussie slur Ailes had picked up from Murdoch).

Hannity looked at the future grimly. "It's all fucking changing. If you think I'll be here in six months, you're crazy. There's only one reason I'm here now, and that's to protect Donald J. Trump."

Rupert was senile. And he was under the thumb of his sons. And of his new wife, Jerry Hall, and before that, his former wife Wendi, a Chinese spy (everyone now seemed to believe). Ailes had been the wall protecting his staff from Murdoch. "Rupert was fucking terrified of Roger," Hannity expounded, and beholden to his profits. It was in this anomalous relationship—in which, uniquely, the content side stood vastly stronger than the management and business side—that the modern right wing was forged. But now that was done. The Murdochs were back in charge—the thin layer of inept management that had replaced Ailes fooled no one. Everybody was reporting to . . . well, that was unclear . . . Rupert, Lachlan, or James, that is whomever was, at any moment, the stronger of the trio.

Now, everyone in television is always negotiating. Posturing. The next contract is always being negotiated. The better your ratings the more resentment, alienation, feelings of being unloved, and certain plans to quit, you had, or at least ought to express. To feel unappreciated was worth money (Ailes, for his part, paid you so much, you always felt loved—quite an anomalous feeling in the television business). "Hannity isn't happy," is the message Hannity wanted to send.

At the same time, the Murdochs *did* hate Hannity. Murdoch's own conservatism was business-class, market-based stuff, together with an appreciation of a certain style of one-upmanship argument (in this regard, he could appreciate Bill O'Reilly). But it wasn't populist. Murdoch was an elitist. He had no illusions about the people who read his tabloid papers—he'd take their money but they weren't part of his world ("Your readers are our shoplifters," a New York department store executive once told Murdoch, who was trying to get him to buy ads in the *New York Post*). The high point of his career was his purchase in 2007 of the *Wall Street Journal*. Hannity, the Irish bartender, was to that standard anathema. Hannity's on-air rants were not only often ignorant but incomprehensible ("a crackpot," was Murdoch's characterization of Hannity). For his Ivy League sons, it was worse: Hannity was an indefensible embarrassment.

"I'm their worst nightmare, an honest conservative," Hannity now bragged, "and fuck them." (It was axiomatic that if you were a true conservative, you were an honest conservative, that honesty defined why you were a conservative—except if you weren't conservative enough, then you weren't being honest.)

Against Hannity—and the Ailes legacy, and, make no mistake, against Trump, to boot—the Murdochs had made their first programming move, promoting Carlson, a conservative in a country club, college educated, Bush family mode—not in an Irish Catholic mode—to the 7:00 p.m. pre-prime-time slot. And then, after Megyn Kelly departed, into 9:00 p.m., and then, after O'Reilly was out, into the totally best slot, 8:00 p.m.!

Carlson, Hannity noted bitterly, wasn't going to show up at Ailes's funeral.

Nor, Hannity learned midflight, was Trump.

"What is wrong with him?" Hannity muttered.

But he understood that all was in flux, that a realignment was in progress. The one thing that was clear was that Donald Trump had the power—and, too, that Trump understood he was going to need Hannity's help in holding on to it.

"When I'm out of here, I'll go right to working for DJT. That's my only interest."

In the new nexus of employment at Fox and employment in the White House, it was Kimberly Guilfoyle's interest, too. She and her boyfriend of the moment, Anthony Scaramucci, a Wall Street promoter and frequent Fox contributor, were both desperately trying to find their way into the West Wing. Guilfoyle wanted to be press secretary. That was a job that Tucker Carlson had turned down, leading Hannity to doubt that Carlson had actually been offered the job ("You would take that job if you were Carlson, of course you would!") and also to crap on KG for wanting the job that Carlson might have turned down. Still, the larger point was that the Trump White House was a Fox White House. Or a Trump White House was a television White House—in so many ways a game changer, in ways nobody at Fox, or anywhere, had quite figured out. Ailes conceived of Fox programming as an overt message about an idea of American identity—American rectitude, virtue, patriotism, masculinity, which would once have been middle-class conventions but which, by the end of the twentieth century, had become an overtly political position. But he was careful that he was in control of the message. He was happy to have politicians fall in line behind it, but fierce about *not* falling in line behind them. He was the real kingmaker and not answerable to any theoretical king (except Murdoch, on occasion—but *rarely*), even ones he might have helped make (especially them).

Meanwhile, it was now beyond the point of keeping track of the number of pitchers of screwdrivers that had been consumed.

The more immediate issue was how the media would cover the funeral. The media was shorthand for Fox's two cable counterpoints, CNN and MSNBC (not exactly competitors, since the highly politized cable audiences were no longer transferable) and, perhaps even more to the point, the *Daily Mail*, that picture cavalcade of celebrities at their worst. Fox itself, the Murdochs' Fox, would not of course be covering the funeral of its founder and former leader.

Hannity wondered if anybody would pick up on Trump not attending—and not even giving the widow a condolence call (Beth Ailes had continued to call Hannity to report this slight). And how would that play? In Trump's favor for snubbing a sexual predator, which might please the *New York Times*, or against him for his utter lack of loyalty to a friend and key supporter? On this point, the passengers seemed confused about how to judge Trump's strategy.

Guilfoyle kept trying to reload her phone on the *Mail Online* page, furiously attacking the device when the connection failed.

"We're not there. Nobody's taken your picture yet," Hannity counseled, as the entourage loaded into waiting SUVs on the West Palm Beach tarmac.

If there was sarcasm here—there was—Guilfoyle paid no heed and passed around a slideshow of the *Mail*'s past scurrilous photos of her. She managed to mix here outrage and delight.

"Head high, Kim," said Hannity—unregistered sarcasm here, too.

It was Hemmer who seemed genuinely worried about the photographers, alarmed that Hannity's entourage might be arriving nearly an hour early, and suggesting everyone stay in the car until the church doors were open.

The church was Rose Kennedy's church when she was in Palm Beach—where she went to mass every day—Hannity noted. This seemed to be a positive Irish note, rather than a negative political note—but possibly there was irony here, too. Hannity further noted that Douglas Kennedy would be at the funeral. One of the peripatetic many children of Robert Kennedy, Ailes had befriended him and, certain irony here, recruited him as a Fox reporter (although never promoted him).

Sitting at the curb, watching through tinted windows, an estimation was made of media friends or foes among the onlookers gathering in front of the church. Then Hannity got restless and jumped out. The steps of the church were filling with the Ailes faithful. In the face of the cold shoulder by the greater Fox organization, Beth Ailes had declared the funeral to be by invitation only. The result was a gathering of the Aileses' true circle.

No casual well-wishers, no corporate obligations, no glad-handers, no hypocritical bullshit . . . not a funeral in which bygones were bygones, no Irish politicking, this was hard-core.

Well, there was some Irish politicking.

Laura Ingraham, the radio host, was working the crowd.

She was in intense buttonholing mode, irritating Hannity.

"Get her to cool it," Hannity told Guilfoyle. "And see if she's been drinking."

It was a martyr's mass. The theme was suffering. Ailes's enemies had tied him to the cross. Even among the faithful, it was possible to detect that this may have gone over the top. The professionally unsubtle Ailes nevertheless had his artfulness. Beth Ailes had none. Lacking a military guard, because Ailes had never served in the military, his widow had recruited a ragtag local police guard. The funeral was followed by a luncheon spread at the famously anti-Semitic Everglades Club. Yet unarticulated, Florida, and particularly Palm Beach, was on its way to becoming the redoubt of the new right wing, with its zero state tax and loophole bankruptcy protections. Sunny climes for shady people, that Somerset Maugham quip about the tax haven Monaco, applied now perhaps more aptly to Palm Beach. Trump's Palm Beach. Jeffrey Epstein's Palm Beach (a few months before his death, Ailes and Epstein had made a plan to get together, stopped only at the last moment by Ailes's aghast lawyers). If suffering had been the note at the funeral service, here now at the lunch it was defiance. This was defiance not even principally against the liberal monopoly (though of course that, too), but much closer to home. Defiance of the Murdochs, Fox women, and all those (and this was most) at Fox who had not in the last days stood up for Ailes. And this went on and on.

Hannity was expected back for one of his children's afternoon sporting events and was now having to make guilty excuses: "Do you like the life we have?" he was suddenly on the phone trying to push back against an aggrieved child. "Well, we owe it all to Mr. Ailes. So I'm going to stay as long as I have to."

And yet Hannity was impatient and seemed to traverse from doing the right thing to now needing to get on to so much more important business. Fox business, Trump business, whatever. Power exists. Even without Ailes. Fox was now up for grabs.

Hurrying out, his return passengers following behind him, the Kennedy-family contingent importuned him for a ride but Hannity apologized, feigning exigencies. Then, less than sotto voce: "Like I'm getting on a plane with people named Kennedy."

But worse, Laura Ingraham, staggering, reeling, her actual drunkenness a superb rendition of exaggerated drunkenness, latched onto Hannity's sleeve, imploring: "I needja help, Sean, needja help. Needja plane. You gotta plane, doncha? A plaannne."

Hannity hardly missed a beat, not hesitating, plowing forward, practically dragging her along until he pulled free, and continuing his commentary: "God, gross, her head in the john. Oh, man. These planes are too small for that!"

Five years later, Hannity was not only still at Fox—whatever the Murdochs wanted to do to Fox, they hadn't done—but he was still leading Revolution II, and not for a minute questioning the stolen election (well, not for much more than a minute), and preparing for what he also knew for a certainty (well, practically)—"I am absolutely certain!"— was the restoration of the forty-fifth president. On April 13, POTUS called in to his show. But then the bullshit from upstairs started: No more call-ins. Bad television. *Bad television?* Donald Trump bad television? This was great ratings-spiking stuff. Were they really trying to keep Donald J. Trump off the air? Really? Let's see how that works out.

5

Laura

RON DESANTIS

Suzanne Scott, the CEO of Fox News, was largely barred from instructing or even talking to the network's leading prime-time anchors and major moneymakers, Carlson and Hannity—what could she tell them, after all, that their ratings did not already say? It was Scott's management mantra: don't fix what isn't broken. Truly, what else could you say in the face of all that cash flow?

That left her Laura Ingraham, with her lagging ratings, as Scott's management project in prime time. Scott's message, not necessarily all that helpful, was that Ingraham had to distinguish herself. This was always a problem at a network that prided itself on the consistency of its message—how at the same time to be different from it. Ingraham's key difference was that she was a woman. That had helped Megyn Kelly because, in Ailes's analysis, if you weren't careful, the impatient and scolding Kelly might give you a spanking. Ingraham, from the Ailes perspective, had no sexual draw, and that was a waste (which is why he had never hired her!).

What she needed now in the 10:00 evening spot was a message

to brand her. It had to be, obviously, a right-wing message, but a *different* one.

Scott gave her the message. It was Murdoch's message, the message that everybody else had been running from: Ron DeSantis.

For Murdoch, the owner of the Trump Network, anybody-else-but-Trump was his paramount issue with no one evidently available *but* DeSantis. Trump's last call-in to Hannity had launched the beginning of an-all-but-policy embargo on the former president. It also marked the all-but-formal beginning of the Murdoch-designated campaign for DeSantis. Scott, after trying to shop this to both Carlson and Hannity, had given Ingraham the job of hosting the Fox town hall in Orlando meant to establish the-not-yet-proven-himself-ready-for-prime-time Florida governor as the clear breakout anybody-but-Trump Republican.

Rupert Murdoch had always dreamed of electing a US president. The joke on him was that the president was Donald Trump. Now he was going to rectify this.

In the Fox backstage chatter it was hard to tell if Ingraham was more discredited by DeSantis, and for so obviously carrying water for the Murdochs, or if DeSantis was tainted by Ingraham.

There were many strikes against Ingraham at Fox, including low ratings, Trump's own never-satisfied and widely shared barbed critiques of her, her long history as a laggard in the conservative media industry, and also, invariably, that she had been given such a prominent prime-time spot only because she was a woman, and then failed to pull the ratings to match it. But hardly just. There was really no bottom for how much you could be faulted at Fox for being a woman.

In the variegated ecosystem of Fox misogyny, Ingraham was derided as a hopeless drunk, a bad drunk, a puke-spewing drunk (Hannity's account of barring her from his plane had gone far and wide). And, too, that she had thrown herself, drunk or not, at every man in the conservative movement—this since her undergraduate years at Dartmouth, that particular hotbed of conservatism, in the 1980s, where she had first made her reputation. And yet never sealed the deal. (In a story that has long haunted her, she used a garden hose to flood the basement of a boyfriend who jilted her.) She had three adopted children now. She was, in the telling of many men at Fox and throughout a socially unreconstructed conservative movement, gross, pathetic, drunk, and a skank—cue the huge peal of laughter.

With Ailes's ouster, and the vivid exposure of Fox's casual and lurid workplace harassment, and, in short order, the expulsion of Bill O'Reilly amid more sensational revelations, followed then by the elevation of Scott as the first woman CEO and the Murdochs' much stated new commitment to a zero-tolerance workplace, it was dispiriting, if not shocking, to many at Fox that in fact not much had changed. But to others, possibly most, the terribly unfair thing was that the network had somehow earned this reputation as the absolute worst place for its treatment of women—when everybody knew that *every* television news division was a disgusting hotbed of mashing and misogyny. Ergo . . . Fox was just being pilloried for not being hypocritical about it. Indeed, Fox's reverse hypocrisy on this issue had always been something of a purposeful statement that it ought to be appreciated for.

Here, too, why mess with success?

Every on-air woman at Fox was selected for the feminine role she could fill. Ailes was very precise about who he was casting and for what role. Beyond that each woman needed to be not just white, but not ethnic—not to look Italian, Jewish, Hispanic, Greek, or too far from an Anglo-Saxon, Irish, Nordic standard—well-proportioned, long-legged, usually blond and in a hair style that said somewhere other than New York, and generally, to Ailes's specification, "a former beauty pageant type."

Each needed to have a more particular sexual-role function. The girl next door. The vixen. The disciplinarian. It was casting.

Perhaps most importantly, all had to rise to what Ailes called "the

American blow-job test." This was a homegrown Ailes theory, which he was pleased to frequently expand upon, about every man's evaluation of whether or not a woman would give head and with what verve and style (one of his favorite formulations: "To get ahead, you have to give some head").

Ailes saw himself as being the chief arbiter of all this—of both what men wanted and about which women would give a man what he wanted. This was part of his belief that his particular news specialty was picking the talent. "News is a variety show," he offered, harkening back to that favorite form of television programming from the 1960s. "It's sexy girls and outrageous men. It has to be clear what role everybody is playing—everybody needs to play broad, big, to character. Don't try to be subtle. This is America."

What's more, he saw this as part of his conservative principles—people wanted 1965—and, hence, when he was brought down, it was an attack on free expression (the right *not* to be a feminist).

His political, cultural, and programming sense converged into a single perception. It was a demographic appreciation of the radical disparities that had grown in American life—the wealth disparity, the education disparity, the generational disparity, the technological disparity, the gender disparity, the religion disparity, the white and others disparity, and the great rural-urban divide. There were two radically different countries, two dramatically different peoples. And this was not only a fundamental conservative belief in the traditional ways of life (idealized small-town, nuclear-family, churchgoing, know-your-neighbor—and agree with him—life), but a programming opportunity.

Rupert Murdoch's early intention in the television news business may have been little more coherent than a wish to compete with CNN—which he had tried and failed to buy. It was Ailes, who, given a budget far under CNN's global news gathering investment, focused on a cheaper-to-serve whiter, poorer, less educated, more rural, churchgoing, older audience. Having begun his career in daytime television, this had been his singular perception since the 1960s: the speeded-up culture was leaving a big and profitable audience behind. He had helped apply this to the 1968 Nixon presidential campaign: "the silent majority."

"The look of cable news," at the time when he launched Fox News in 1996, "was for somebody else. It was classroom stuff. I wanted Fox to look more like daytime television—or like daytime television used to look," he explained years later. Stubbornly unmindful of the new requirements for how to discuss gender in American culture, he went on, "So the women were important. Their job was to be familiar to other women in a nonthreatening way and yet still to have men want to fuck them—accomplishing both of those things was the vital part. Fox women are not yuppie women or aspirational women or professional women—they're television women. Game show girls. They come out of the American imagination. Television put them there."

Ailes's sexual penchants hid in plain sight. An overweight man and an ugly man, he apprised all women with something like greed and anger—a reflexive gaze that seemed to last far longer than he consciously realized. His conversation nearly always had a parallel tract of commentary about what acts a woman might be best at, invariably heading to what, with relish, he saw as forms of satisfying degradation. Ailes's defenders insisted, not inaccurately, that this behavior was hardly out of the ordinary for so many senior television executives, drawn to an industry that accommodated the baroque and perverse.

And then there was that other curious aspect of Ailes's obsessive and fetishistic view of women—Madonna–whore, submissive–ballbuster, beauty queen–yuppie. His thing for lawyers—"lady lawyers." That is, theoretically, smart, argumentative, stand-their-ground women, who he then liked to turn into babes.

By the late 1990s, with Fox, CNN, and the recently launched MSNBC, all in play against each other, none yet with a hard and fixed positioning, and with the Clinton scandals in the foreground, three women emerged as among the always-on-call right-wing figures: Ann

Coulter, Laura Ingraham, and Kellyanne Fitzpatrick. All blond, with long straight hair, all anorexically thin, in signature short skirts and, often, knee-high boots, and all lawyers. This became a significant subset of the quickly developing right-wing media movement. While it had been relegated to the voices of talk radio, and not-exactly-ready-for-prime-time politicians like Newt Gingrich—with his fleshy face and scrunched up features and inability to stop talking—now it had articulate and *attractive* public faces.

In fact, this most notable right-wing trio was created more by MSNBC than by Fox. MSNBC had been launched as a partnership of NBC and Microsoft in 1996—the same year as Fox. It had opened a newly built, self-consciously "techy," golly-factor studio—destined to become an immediate cliché—in a bunker-like structure in a moonscape setting in the Meadowland swamps in New Jersey, just across the Hudson River. (This was a strategy by NBC's parent, GE, to avoid the labor unions in New York City.) MSNBC's premise was to be new, and youthful, and high-tech hip (although, other than Microsoft as a passive partner, the network had no tech bona fides), rather than to uphold any ideological perspective. Its early programming concept was to recruit an assortment of "youthful" voices across the ideological and cultural spectrum and make them the floating talking heads of the 24/7 programming schedule. This included Ann Coulter, Laura Ingraham, and Kellyanne Fitzpatrick.

These were conservative voices, but not Ailes's voices. For one thing, he had not created them. And not slept with them—or been able to adequately position his growing power against their growing stardom. Ailes operated in a godfather sense of family hierarchy, of rank, debt, and due, and was at best suspicious of you if he couldn't place you in it. When liberal television tired of them and they had nowhere to go but Fox, he snubbed them.

But, in the two decades since, fortunes had changed. Ann Coulter had grown ever more anarchic, directing a pre-Twitter spew of startling and inventive invective in unpredictable directions. "I stay out of Ann's way and hope she'll stay out of mine," said Ailes, not without admiration. Kellyanne Fitzpatrick had married the conservative corporate lawyer George Conway—who, curiously, each of the women had dated—and largely retreated to a life of upper-upper-middle-class child rearing and would, as the proprietor of a small polling firm, reemerge in 2016 as a key face of the Trump administration. Laura Ingraham carved a talk radio niche that was never quite competitive with the higher rank of talk radio men—less riffy, less combative, less somehow aware of the larger joke (part of the broad joke was how seriously liberals took the lack of right-wing seriousness). For a right-wing media voice—a status marked as much by certainty, pugnacity, and machine-gun delivery as by ideology—Ingraham was oddly earnest and tentative, and her radio ratings steadily declined. With a growing family, and a fading radio career, she began to petition Ailes for a job.

Ailes, entertaining himself, strung her along for the better part of five years. But she somehow "keeps getting older," said Ailes jocularly and bitingly, adding that she got no better than a "C− on the blow-job test," also she drank, and, while Ailes had nothing against drinking per se, drunken women repelled him.

Not long after Ailes's departure, Greta Van Susteren, the legal analyst who had become a Fox fixture and one of its most identifiable women, was abruptly terminated (Murdoch didn't like her and thought she was paid too much). She was followed out the door by Megyn Kelly, the network's most prominent female figure and rising voice of a no-nonsense, practical, Trump-skeptical conservatism, a linchpin of the Murdochs' new ideas about how to remake the network, who took an offer from NBC. With the departure of both women, plans for programming changes were reduced in the spring of 2017 to the emergency of finding a woman for one of the three prime-time slots.

The contenders for the job, or at least those lobbying hardest for it, included Maria Bartiromo, Kimberly Guilfoyle, and Ainsley Earhardt.

Bartiromo, at forty-nine, had been for nearly twenty-five years a symbol of the last great boom period and moment of financial euphoria, a figure of deregulation and the dot-com era: the Money Honey, as she came to be known during her years as the headliner for CNBC, the financial news network. There she had befriended CEOs, emceed their dinners and awards ceremonies, married a scion of 1980s excess, Jonathan Steinberg, and, too, become a reliable voice of the new, arriviste, business establishment. She'd also become a Murdoch favorite (she had once hosted an awards ceremony where Murdoch presented an award to Italian billionaire and prime minister Silvio Berlusconi, and she also did a live interview with Murdoch at an investors' conference, where she largely failed to get him to rise above a mumble or deliver a comprehensible sentence). But in the years after the 2007 financial meltdown, Bartiromo became an addled-seeming figure and for many a broadside joke, unable to transition her previous unbridled enthusiasm to a new, tangled, and resentful world. With her star and CNBC's star fading, she accepted Ailes's offer to come to Fox Business News in 2013.

Ailes had launched the business channel at Murdoch's behest in the middle of the financial crisis. It was Murdoch's pet project and held little juice for Ailes. It was a back-of-his-hand effort, never achieving the mass ratings that Ailes lived for and failing to attract notable talent. This made even the faded Bartiromo quite a good catch. And for Bartiromo, it offered a possible route to the Fox News side. Her CEO-friendly politics pleased Murdoch. But Ailes found her to be exactly the kind of establishment cheerleader that he sought to distance Fox from. Bartiromo was nobody's populist. Her interest in finance seemed to be an interest in rich men; their interest in her, beyond her interest in them, seemed to do with her inability to articulate views other than those they fed her.

Or so it seemed to Ailes. However much this might be true, it also reflected Ailes's view of women: another female television personality as gold digger (he could, with rancor, enumerate the on-air women who had scored big-money husbands). He largely rebuffed Bartiromo's efforts to cross over from the business channel into greater prominence at the news channel.

But with Ailes gone, Murdoch was open to her taking the prime-time slot—former General Electric CEO Jack Welch, whose favorite Bartiromo had been at CNBC, was lobbying hard for her. Lachlan and James, vying to control the choice, wrote this off as another of their father's senior moments: both Bartiromo and Welch, figures from the long past.

Guilfoyle, who had arrived at the network in 2006, was confirmation for Ailes of several further hard beliefs he had about women in television: they would do anything, literally *anything*, to get ahead, and they were as sexually mercenary as any man in television. This transmuted into Ailes's belief that television was a level playing field for men and women, with Guilfoyle for him an almost comic book example of TV rapacity.

Guilfoyle was a former model who went to law school—a perfect marriage for Ailes. Better than just a lawyer, she had been a *prosecutor* in Los Angeles and San Francisco. Her 2001 marriage to Gavin Newsom, the future mayor of San Francisco and governor of California, united, many noted, two of the most avaricious people in the Bay Area, their brief marriage celebrated in many magazine spreads. Her transformation from ambitious liberal political wife to would-be conservative television star was, for Ailes, a sidesplitting example of human and particularly television-women do-anything-to-advance depravity. He saw this, too, as a competitive model: the liberals had Arianna Huffington—who had traveled from the power behind her conservative California politician husband to any-and-all lefty positions, no questions asked—and now the right-wing had gained Guilfoyle, with as much potential for spotlight hogging as Huffington.

During Ailes's last days—when it still seemed unlikely that he could truly be toppled—Guilfoyle became one of Ailes's hatchet women. She went down the list of Fox women, trying to hold support for Ailes and issuing not-too-veiled threats of potential punishment—or rewards— when all this passed and Ailes was, count on it, still standing. Her defense was not denial, but, with contempt, the hypocrisy of it all: everybody knew who Ailes was, everybody, in their own way, benefited from it, and, anyway, whatever he wanted was harmless, and, plus, who wouldn't fuck for more? This was television.

Meanwhile, as the campaign for the prime-time slot heated up— marked most by the indecision and squabbling among the Murdochs— Guilfoyle was tenaciously fighting her own battles with the "fucking hypocrites." She was about to become the most notable—and, arguably, the singular—woman taken down by #MeToo. As much as any man at Fox, or any man in television, she had long been conducting her- self with an unconcerned sexual recklessness: a constant and vivid and utterly indiscreet public airing of the details of her sex life, including her catalog of widely shared genitalia pictures, a variety of what-me- worry exhibitionism incidents, advocating to other women the merits of "fucking up" with detailed primers on her technique, and generally living what she called a "Samantha Jones" life after the *Sex in the City* character, well after this had passed out of cultural comfort. While all this was widely known and reported within Fox, making Guilfoyle one among many such company characters (Bill O'Reilly's long reign of sexual mashing and disregard had recently come to an end), the full and daily force of her polymorphous sexual self-dramatization became focused on a young assistant. In the post-Ailes climate of outside law- yers monitoring the HR situation at Fox, the assistant's complaints and threats of a lawsuit began Guilfoyle's end.

Nevertheless, at the same time she was lobbying to find allies within Fox to defend her—as she had sought allies for Ailes—she continued to lobby for the prime-time slot. Meanwhile, leveraging both Trump power within Fox and Fox power within Trumpworld, she was also lob- bying to replace Sean Spicer as Trump's press secretary. And she was dating Anthony Scaramucci (whose marriage would combust over the affair—and then heroically be repaired), who was pressing his own campaign to take over the Trump White House's flailing communication operation while promising to bring her along. He would succeed, but hold the job for only eleven days, brought down in a drunken rant caused by reports of Guilfoyle's new relationship—with the president's son Don Jr. Still, she persisted in her efforts to get the Fox job, recruiting one Fox colleague known to have a direct relationship with Rupert Murdoch to push for her. Just, however, as the colleague was about to bring this up with Murdoch, Murdoch himself, with the curious habit of abruptly unburdening himself, said he'd had a hard day with his lawyers and sons trying to figure out how to get rid of "this horrible woman we have."

That left in the immediate running for the job Ainsley Earhardt. The problem here was that she was Sean Hannity's candidate. He had made it nearly a second job lobbying for her. This, in itself, would have made her ascension difficult, because Carlson was hardly about to acquiesce to Hannity's handpicked prime-time choice. But beyond that, there was wide suspicion of the married Hannity's extra special interest in Earhardt—which Hannity stubbornly denied—and which, while in fact may not have actually been true at this moment, was shortly to be definitely true.

Although Laura Ingraham, at fifty-four, had spent the better part of the past twenty years trying to get a spot at Fox and not succeeding, now, post-Ailes, she was the useful—and in some sense, obvious—outsider. What's more, both Hannity and Carlson found her reasonably unobjectionable. She was, for both men—being an older woman—the contrast loser. A nonthreatening placeholder.

Although both Murdoch sons found her "retro," and "not inspiring," "a fucking dismal choice," in James Murdoch's description, she was hired.

Curiously, at the same time she was being considered for the Fox job,

Trump was pressing *her* to become his press secretary—the other job that Guilfoyle was after. Ingraham resisted Trump. Partly because the White House job paid a government salary versus a seven-figure Fox job (although a much smaller seven-figure number than she had hoped), but, if she needed other reasons, she understood the dysfunction in the Trump White House and was herself less-than-a-fully-signed-up Trumper. But Trump's interest in her had made him a party to the Fox discussions, with both Hannity and Carlson carrying his messages back to the network: Trump was annoyed that he might not get her as his press secretary (even though she did not want the job) and might hold this against Fox, and, as well, had a negative view about her television talents ("She's no fun, you can tell").

It was one of those television triangulations that got her the job but guaranteed a lack of success: getting her job as a foil to two more aggressive, swashbuckling, self-dramatizing men and in doing so incurring the displeasure of the central power at the network, Donald Trump, the president.

Pleasing to both Hannity and Carlson, and confirming their approval, Ingraham grabbed no issues of her own or assumed any distinct new right-wing identity, except an anxious one.

Now, however, to widespread how-could-she-be-so-stupid and general gender-based hilarity, she was making a play for Ron DeSantis and Rupert Murdoch's favor, and for a Fox future, placating an old man's whim to remake the known world, one without Donald Trump.

"And they say I'm the dumbass," said Hannity.

6

James

A FORCE FOR GOOD

Dismissive, angry, and rash, unable not to point out what was to him clearly right and clearly wrong with the views of everyone else, James Murdoch, as he contemplated his own Murdoch future, in the spring of 2022, nevertheless vowed to restrain himself. He was taking the advice of various CEOs of his acquaintance to hold his fire and demonstrate a new sense of gravitas (what was really meant was maturity) and let events play out in his favor, as they quite appeared to be doing. But at the least sign of interest from media, bankers, or heavyweight Democrats, James was delegating emissaries to make his case: his absolute intention to expel his brother, Lachlan, from the company's leadership, to take charge of Fox himself, and to turn this destructive machine into "a force for good" in the world. That was the official message and position: *a force for good*. He was forty-nine-years-old, had $2 billion in his pocket, and his time was coming.

"Does Lachlan actually think he can buy out Elisabeth and Prudence and James with Saudi money?" said the James emissary, a person of high political and business rank drawing a consultant's retainer, with the specific mission to lay out the scion's uncompromising position. "That is not going to happen. Lachlan has tried to buy out his siblings before—they will not be bought out. James is going to take control of Fox at some point in time and, yes, make it a force for good. This is not idle. This is meaningful. Both his intention and the mechanism to do it. He is a good person. A decent man. He is someone who has been raised in privilege and is extremely mindful of that and his responsibilities because of that. He and his wife are good people. Their desire is to do good. When Rupert passes his shares will be divided evenly among his four oldest children, that is irrevocable. The math is that three will aggregate around James, and Lachlan will be the odd man out. James will not take any amount of money to get out of Fox if that means leaving Fox as it is on the table. There simply is no amount of money that could ever cause him to leave Lachlan forever as the controller of Fox News. This is not a sustainable or defensible situation. It is a circumstance that has gotten out of control. You don't have to look beyond what is obvious: Fox has not been run rationally in many years. Why would you allow O'Reilly and Hannity to curtail the ability of the company to buy assets vastly more strategic than Fox itself—specifically Sky? The reason the greater part of the company was sold is because it couldn't grow. It couldn't grow because Fox News was being run in such a way that regulators would not approve the single most important deal ever before the company."

Many blamed the collapse of the Sky acquisition and hence the company's global expansion strategy—and the decision to sell off most of the company and with it the dreams of perpetual empire—on James's lax oversight of the phone-hacking practices of the Murdoch British newspapers. James now blamed it on Fox's politics. Both were probably true.

"James did everything he possibly could to correct this," the emissary continued. "But his father is very, very, very old. And you don't have to look beyond that. Really, really, really old. When he passes, if that is this year or next, yes, rationality can return."

In other words, a $15 billion public company, with its extraordinary political and cultural influence—among the greatest any American company has ever had—was in a state of play. At least if you chose to believe the determination and the certainties of one of its major shareholders and his conviction that, at the kill moment, he'd carry a majority with him.

James and his family resided in a double-wide town house in Manhattan on East Sixty-Ninth Street between Park Avenue and Lexington Avenue. There is a whole set of bragging rights among the owners of the limited stock of Manhattan town houses, whose costs start at $8 or $9 million and escalate to $50 or $60 million—frontage, depth, number of floors, garden size. But double-width trumps them all. Double-width, you're no longer really living in the often-taxing vertical experience of a twenty- or eighteen- (or sixteen-!) foot-wide town house—essentially middle-class dwellings, after all, in the nineteenth and early twentieth centuries—but in true mansion grandeur. James's $30 million double-wide, owned previously by the Muppets creator Jim Henson, and then by the Seagram's heir Edgar Bronfman Jr. and backing onto Woody Allen's single-wide on Seventieth Street, looks out, however, onto one of the Upper East Side's less becoming blocks, facing the institutional plant of Hunter College, part of New York's public university system. This has provoked a steady defensiveness on James's part. "I don't notice it." "I simply don't care." "I could care less about what Upper East Side bullshit block I live on." "What's the matter, are you against public education?" "I personally find Hunter inspiring." In this, he had made the double-wide house a beacon of his rebel nature.

Similarly, his point about his large property in Washington, Connecticut, a tony, bucolic second-home spot, was that he had chosen to buy here and not in the Hamptons, the more popular beachfront second-home choice for Manhattanites who, like James Murdoch, can afford the choice. His pride in Connecticut is frequently accompanied by a screed against the Hamptons and Hamptons people, and their riches, and tastelessness, and sheeplike behavior. And the kind of demanding social life he cannot stand.

The thread here is James's need to distinguish himself, even among options that don't really distinguish him, and to justify whatever choices he's made and actions he's taken as being of a higher order than everyone else's. He is aided in this by a natural hostility and overweening smugness and a punch-before-getting-punched spirit. This has resulted in the most frequent description applied to him by both family and friends. He's a prick.

Among the many novelistic facts of James's life is that only fifteen months separates him from his older brother and that, as Rupert Murdoch's two sons, throughout their lives one or the other was presumed to be their father's heir.

One effect of this for both boys was the insularity and peculiarity of their experiences. There was the private reality against the public reality: the tongue-tied father ever in the weeds of tactical business minutiae against the outside view of the all-powerful, world-beating colossus. Growing up in elite, cosmopolitan, progressive circles they saw their father's influence and fortune become anathema to all cosmopolitan and progressive values. And then there was the weighty or threatening assumption—on the part of father, mother, and all other family members—that one or another would receive the mantle of all this, would literally inherit an international power base. They had lived their entire adult lives in that fraught emotional bubble and chess-move tension. Who could appreciate this beyond maybe the Kennedys?

Their father's driving issue was a Murdoch dynasty. Theirs, Murdoch ambivalence. It was often less his children petitioning him, but rather him petitioning his children. These were entitled, American, New York, private school and Ivy League children, with no seeming limit on their worldly options. Despite his power and wealth, here was their father,

never American enough, spectrum-like in his lack of personal connections (his wife Wendi once accused him of having no friends; he
replied, "But I could have if I wanted to"), disconcertingly inarticulate,
seemingly stuck in a zeitgeist and emotional time warp, and barely able
to function outside of his closed circle of henchmen. Yes, he was Vito,
and each of the children saw themselves as some version of Michael.

All of his older children had tried to get away from him, with the
father having to woo them back. Elisabeth quit Sky in a huff; Lachlan
retreated to Australia in his huff; James only agreed, huffily, to work for
his father at three thousand miles' distance; and his oldest daughter,
Prudence, often his closest family confidante, had no interest in being
part of his businesses at all.

He devised strategy after strategy and ever more attractive inducements to try, unsuccessfully, to bring his sons back to New York. He put
both sons on the parent company board, where at board meetings they
openly bickered with each other—and with him. His increasing desperation gave them increasing leverage. And this preoccupation with
his media-business children, with his drive to get them to accept their
corporate patrimony and relocate near him, was a shadow that hung
over Murdoch's entire management team. It engaged the time and the
futures of every key executive: how to handle, accommodate, and survive Murdoch's detested children.

It is against this backdrop that Fox News first became a bitter issue
for the Murdoch children, with Ailes, backed by his ever-increasing
profits, leading the cold war against his boss's progeny—spreading
rumors about them and building alliances with other executives against
them. The family hatred of Ailes and Fox was personal before it became
political.

Ailes was the main culprit in forcing Lachlan out of the company in
2005, threatening to resign if Murdoch didn't check his son. The Murdoch siblings rallied in defense of their brother. It was the family's decision in 2008 to line up behind Barack Obama and to cajole their father

to largely do the same. This was met with overt hostility by Ailes, who used his profits to turn the father back again, and, with extra venom, turn Fox into the ultimate Obama enemy.

Here, too, emerged another theme: brand. Fox News, merely for the sake of shortsighted profits, was being allowed to damage the overall Twenty-First Century Fox entertainment *brand*, argued James. He got the future. Their future was as a *media-entertainment* enterprise not a *tabloid* enterprise. Brand was the passport into new markets and new technology.

It was in 2016 that the now co-CEO brothers, reporting to their more-and-more absent father, acted against Ailes. For Lachlan, struggling to navigate the interests of profits, his father, and the exigencies of a diversified multinational media company that he believed he was now leading (at least coleading), getting rid of Ailes was the first step in what he foresaw as a long process of dealing with the Fox problem. But James was thinking faster and bigger. So big. His plan to buy the half of Sky they did not own—and roll Fox in a new international strategy and "cleanse" it—had collapsed, thereby dooming the Fox entertainment empire. The company was hopelessly tainted by the news channel—and hobbled by his brother's small thinking and his father's old thinking. In what he would come to believe was nothing less than his own farsighted business acumen and pluck, quite measuring up to his father's, if he did say so himself, James opened talks to sell the lion's share of Twenty-First Century Fox's assets to Disney, recruited his sisters into the plan, and convinced his father, in spite of his brother's opposition—indeed, selling his patrimony out from under him—to go along, and thereby forge a new future for himself.

It was, though, an equivocal if not sour outcome for his big plans.

His fierce, even megalomaniacal ambition, was to trade his family out of the drawbacks of his father's brand—in its obeisance to, in James's characterization, "a hundred-year-old man"—and trade it up to control of the world's most powerful and best-positioned media-entertainment conglomerate, the Walt Disney Company. His gentle understanding with Disney's CEO, Bob Iger, in the final stages of his long run as the Disney chief (he would shortly retire from the company, but then, in short order, return), was that James would come into the company in a yet to be defined role but representing his family's holdings—next to only the mutual fund Vanguard as the company's biggest shareholder. He believed, too, that linking with Laurene Powell Jobs, the widow of Steve Jobs (to whose lefty save-the-earth politics he and his wife, Kathryn, were more and more active subscribers), and her large position from the sale of Pixar to Disney, could give him voting control of Disney. In other words, his plan was to astutely engineer a way around the inherent constraints of his father and fulfill the destiny promised not only by his name and his money but by his own acumen.

James's model for generational transcendence: John F. Kennedy, who, too, had been saddled with a rich and retro father.

Many deals have an unwritten upside. This is often the necessary suspension of disbelief that both sides accept to get the deal done. In this, Bob Iger appears to have indulged James Murdoch's aspirations to run Disney while trusting that there were enough moving pieces to stymie the plans of the heir, whose reputation for truculence and entitlement preceded him. Helpfully for Iger, neither James's father nor his brother were enthusiastic backers of James's plan for personal and generational triumph without them, dashing his Disney dreams.

Among the many points of family recrimination, this lack of support would be another James took with him as he exited all management responsibility for his family's remaining holdings in early 2018.

This did not, however, much alter the basic and increasingly existential question about fulfilling the destiny of his name, money, and talent.

A surprising number of people, who, having achieved inordinate success and then, by the random movement of moon, stars, and corporate politics, lost it, but who yet can call on vast financial resources, face this practical and philosophical question: What to do next? James's strategy was not much different from theirs. You rent office space, staff yourself with financial and deal-making professionals, and . . . wait.

As he waited for the deal of the century, or at least some clarity in an ever more iffy media business, still imagining an international play of visionary proportions, he brooded about Fox News—the ice pick in the heart of liberal democracy and his family. It threatened to drag his name and legacy into the annals of bad guy history. The Murdochs bore the responsibility for Trump's election; on their heads lay no small amount of blame for the near-lethal attack on the integrity of voting in America—an ongoing effort. And, too, with Fox's stoking of the anti-vax crusade, they would have to face judgment on the million American COVID deaths. They owned the divided country, mortally divided perhaps; what's more, Donald Trump's reelection, his return from exile, would only be possible with *their* acquiescence.

For many, this represented the power and vileness of the Murdoch family. James recognized that it in fact represented their weakness. The infuriating thing—the tragedy of it all—was that his father had only ever had the greatest contempt for Donald Trump. Murdoch's conservatism was merely of an old-man's kind. It was status-quo conservatism. Murdoch was certainly not looking for radical disruption, but now his own company was being used to undermine, upend, mock, and blow up those very views. Why? The money, of course. It was the brilliance of the tabloid ethos: figure out what the people want and give it to them—shamelessly pander.

Murdoch's special brilliance had always been his ability to use this tabloid power for his own ends. But now it was using him. Because, let's face it, he was too old. For twenty years—at least—his children had closely monitored their father's aging. Beyond his old-fool marriages, his chronically wandering attention, and, often, seeming near blackouts, James focused on the old man's inability, at virtually any level, to grasp the technological revolution which, James believed, he himself was quite a brilliant seer of. Their father's natural decline both represented the next generation's opportunity and impediment: no matter how much his executive function might diminish, his need for control remained his overriding instinct. But it was only the illusion of control. Sumner Redstone, one of Murdoch's historic adversaries in the media business, had sunk into senility abandoning all other desires but his sexual ones. With Murdoch, here, too, with everything else falling away, he kept showing up at the office—the office was his desire.

That's what pissed James off most about Lachlan. His pathetic and helpless need for their father's approval. To appease the old man, to suck up to him, to make it feel like it wasn't totally over for the old man, Lachlan made the ritual bows of the loyal lieutenant waiting for decisive orders. But the orders never came, and a checked-out Lachlan was incapable of stepping in himself. Hence, nobody was in control. Or, worse, Tucker Carlson was in control, or Sean Hannity—or Donald Trump!

So, yes, this had to end.

During the pandemic, James had retreated to his un-Hampton redoubt in Connecticut, as did much of his retinue of friends and associates tethered to once-and-future Murdoch possibilities. It was a near two-year bubble, a *Decameron* of media-business fantasies and heavy drinking, with James's righteousness and purported genius rigorously enforced. Of course, he had to take over Fox. What choice did he have? And of course he could. And, equally obvious, he *could* make it a "force for good." He said that—repeated it: "A force for good." His people insisted on that message: "A force for good." General scoffing and hilarity did not dissuade him. This was the future. James was the future. The old man was eighty-nine, then ninety, then ninety-one. But, having said that, James himself was forty-seven, forty-eight, forty-nine. Fifty was putting the pressure on.

7

Tucker

THE WASPS

On the weekend beginning April 29, 2022, Tucker Carlson was fishing at the Rolling Rock Club in Ligonier Valley, Pennsylvania. Rolling Rock, founded by members of the Mellon family, those nineteenth-century industrial and banking aristocrats, with streams stocked with trout and a set of riding stables with all manner of elegant hunting accoutrements, in addition to the usual golf-and-tennis country club amenities, is a stop on a particular twentieth-century White Anglo-Saxon Protestant establishment tour. How Tucker Carlson came to adopt and identify with this unreconstructed way of life and, with the passionate intensity unusual in places like the Rolling Rock Club, transform its once traditional conservative values into a down-market right-wing credo was part of what the *New York Times* was trying that weekend to understand.

The effort was deeply concerning to various members of the Murdoch family, who were easily wounded by their treatment in the liberal press, most of all the *New York Times*. And this was a three-parter.

Major historic and cultural developments in the world rated three-parters in the *Times*. This was that big. But why? Ostensibly, it was about

Carlson's journey to top-rated news personality and MAGA thought leader. But clearly the interest here was not so much to peel back the layers of this quite extraordinary phenomenon, a metamorphosis of class and values, a kind of moment-of-impact shot of old-fashioned conservatism and wing-nut cable. More, the *Times* story seemed designed to make clear the position that Carlson was the *Times*' enemy. Here was a subset of political commentary, media on media, the *Times* as upholder of progressive values taking on Fox, the upholder of reactionary values. It was a branding exercise.

This recalled another three-part series the *Times* began in 2007, when Rupert Murdoch bought the *Wall Street Journal*. That series similarly saw Murdoch—the first significant media disruptor since the left-wing provocateurs of the 1960s—as an offense against journalism and accepted modern values. (While the series promised three parts, it ended after two, with rumors that the *Times*' owners had become worried about editorial retribution from Murdoch.)

It had become a specialty of other journalism organizations to go after Fox and Murdoch, condemning them for their political and journalism offenses. It confirmed everyone else's journalism bona fides. CNN and MSNBC, Fox's direct cable competitors, used their open war with Fox as part of their fundamental legitimacy. Brian Stelter, a former *New York Times* reporter, who had replaced CNN's media correspondent Howard Kurtz (who, in more innocent times, went from CNN to Fox), was designated by CNN's then chief Jeff Zucker as the network's Fox besmircher. He regularly made Fox's broadcasts and personalities a subject of shocked outrage and then wrote a book, high in moral incredulity, about the network. (In 2022, CNN's new chief, Chris Licht, fired Stelter, at least in part because his sense of personal outrage seemed to trend into self-parody.) The *Times*' media reporter Jim Rutenberg, its designated Murdoch hitter, joined with CNN to produce a multipart series on Murdoch's journalistic perfidy.

The *Times*' treatment of Carlson, that spring weekend, was firmly in this oppositional and moral vein. Carlson had certainly become a liberal bête noire—his opposition to the US support for Ukraine, the ultimate topper. But the series now elevated Carlson to a particular and rarefied set of protofascist media precursors out of the all but forgotten past—Father Coughlin, Axis Sally, and Lord Haw-Haw, historic threats to liberal culture and democracy. Carlson was the threat of a new dark era. Like those figures, Carlson's paramount sin was nativism—valuing the past and its security and comfort, and, always, greater homogeneity over the present, and doing it in the harshest and most unforgiving terms. Carlson was Trump, but also somehow worse for not being Trump—being smarter, and cleverer, and therefore more dangerous. What's more, he might even be eviler than Trump because, it was the *Times'* implication, he did not necessarily believe what he was saying (as if Trump did). Rather, he was saying what he was saying merely for the ratings, which was some ultimate lapse of morality and propriety.

At Rolling Rock, Carlson declared to friends that he wasn't reading any of it—although he tweeted a smiling picture of himself holding the *Times* front page dominated by his picture. A man ever conscious if not overwhelmed by his sudden leap into the center of the most divisive moment in American history in more than half a century, he reiterated his blanket position of never reading anything about himself. But three parts in the *New York Times*, every barbed, surly, execrating, highminded word of it, would be for anyone, no less a media and Washington insider, hard to ignore.

Carlson's journey from flailing television humper on weekend duty to fame and infamy as, arguably, the second-most-celebrated and second-most-hated person in the nation was the *Times'* story. But that it might be as much a psychic journey as a political one was outside the *Times'* comfort zone. Here, though, was a view of keen interest among the people who knew Carlson well, one that might go to the heart of modern conservatism and Fox's future: Had this world of political Sturm und Drang driven Tucker crazy? Truly around the bend?

There was certainly an inherent fragility. His mother, variously described as a California 1960s type or as plainly disturbed, left her family when Tucker was six and his brother, Buckley, four, eventually moving to Europe (at her death leaving her sons a vineyard in disrepair in the south of France) and never seeing her sons again. They were raised by their father, Dick Carlson, who had himself been given up for adoption shortly after his birth—his birth father, at eighteen, committing suicide shortly thereafter—and, after further Dickensian chapters, adopted by a well-to-do New England family.

Dick Carlson became a peripatetic 1960s journalist in California, who seemed to slip, whether by intention or not, into politics and perhaps spying and to tread what his son would suggest was a fine line of international intrigue and profit. Several years after the end of his marriage to Tucker's mother, Dick Carlson married a Swanson frozen food heiress who adopted his sons. Valuing both adventure and a kind of class entitlement over career regularity, Dick Carlson had dropped out of college and was contemptuous of Tucker when he more diligently did his four years at Trinity College in Hartford, Connecticut. The Carlson world—the one in which the Carlson sons were sent off at first adolescence to the nearest brothel—took exception to all aspirational standardization, prescriptions, and behavioral demands, fitting in somewhere between the models of *The Big Lebowski* and of *The Royal Tenenbaums*, a solipsistic, entitled, not entirely sober world. Such was the family entrée into an unreconstructed, sorely attenuated, and self-conscious White Anglo-Saxon Protestant life, part rebellious, part among the last upholders of civilized standards. You could single out certain American families as part of this elevated archetype—the Sedgwicks and the Binghams, who would produce more or less tragic stories, or the Bushes, who would extend WASPism beyond its expiration date. It was an archetype that no longer fit into a clear demographic destiny, except eccentricity (or self-parody). It was through that lens that Tucker Carlson began to fashion a worldview of functional opposition to all authority. He was an outsider by dint of being among what he believed were a few true insiders.

He married his high school sweetheart, his prep-school headmaster's daughter, an act he would come to portray as one of social and sexual purity. He would take enormous pride in both his wife's lack of interest in anything outside the home—they had four children and generations of dogs—and her contempt, a snobbish contempt, for the political world in which, like Wallace Stevens going off to work in an insurance company, her husband was forced to make his living. He had a short stint as a political journalist, first at William Kristol's conservative magazine the *Weekly Standard* (funded by Rupert Murdoch), and then at Tina Brown's liberal magazine *Talk* (funded by Harvey Weinstein). At *Talk*, he immediately carved an identity not just as a conservative at a liberal publication, but one with a gimlet eye, even a scathing regard, for all authority, even Republican authority. In 1999, he tailed George W. Bush and produced one of the more insightful, funny, and trenchant profiles of the primary campaign. As a conservative liberals could like, he became in substantial demand, taking up a regular post at CNN, preferring talking to writing. In television fashion, he shaped his eccentric views—in bow tie, prep-school blazer, and floppy hair, he cut a standout figure—to the conventional repartee wanted from the house conservative. By his late thirties, his eight-year run on cable at both CNN and MSNBC, in which he had traversed from reasonable notoriety to increasing irrelevance as a good-natured conservative, seemed to have reached its expected end. As with most other used-up cable figures, the path to reinvention was hardly clear (wilderness radio, teaching gigs, as an ignominious pitchman?). He started a right-wing internet site, the *Daily Caller*, but Carlson was not a natural internet entrepreneur, and it never managed to compete with any verve against the towering Drudge Report or the increasingly aggressive *Breitbart News*. With four children and a big tax lien, here was his nadir. Ailes, offering some hope, toyed with buying the *Daily Caller* but was talked out of it by

Steve Bannon, then the Breitbart CEO. Taking pity, Ailes hired Carlson, but with the warning to Carlson that he should not expect a front-row future at Fox, and he didn't get it.

But, after Ailes's ouster, Murdoch curiously remembered Carlson from his time at CNN. Seeing him as the kind of conservative he could like (as opposed to Hannity and O'Reilly), Murdoch called him off the bench. It was a call opposed by almost everyone else at Fox, but Murdoch kept referencing Carlson's bow tie, which, in fact, he'd put away years before.

Carlson brought to his new assignment a set of pressing circumstances and views: an urgent need for more money, not least of all to pay the arrears on his taxes; long observation of the trends in the conservative media market; a nature that had only become more oppositional in his years in the wilderness; and, as well, a certainty born of experience that all cable news careers end inevitably and abruptly. Such were the exigent factors that helped turn his oddball and retro WASP cultural conservatism, snobbish and insular, into reactionary fury.

The *Times'* series saw Carlson's programming and ideological strategy as deftly positioning himself as MAGA forward but at the same time distancing himself from Trump. But much more strategically, and marking his programming breakthrough, he was distancing himself from Fox and its overwhelming Irish Catholic right-wing barstool identity. In this, he understood the more elemental point about right-wing media politics. You not only had to establish yourself within the hard-core conservative Fox audience but, as importantly, you had to distinguish yourself from your right-wing competitors. Bill O'Reilly succeeded as the most dogmatic barstool voice, meaning Sean Hannity, never as concise, scathing, and dismissive on his Irish barstool, was always the ratings laggard; Megyn Kelly succeeded in contrast to the right-wing guys as the voice of a woman ever irritated with those impractical, blowhard, perhaps drunken men. Tucker now succeeded with an even more glaring contrast.

"You know, I am not anti-Semitic, and I am not anti-Black, that's a complete misunderstanding of what I am," he would explain this side of the edge of irony. "I am anti-Catholic."

That was the retro message of the pale face, lanky hair, and prep-school uniform: WASP. In this, his atavism was a purer kind than that of Fox or Trump. His reached back further, recalling an even more absolute America. The tumble into a diverse, immigrant society began with the Catholics. Yes, take this fight back to the 1920s, when the sides were clear. The great mishmash in which anyone who even on occasion visited a church was broadly subsumed into being a "Christian," as though this was an uncomplicated designation, was very much, for Carlson, *ewww* thinking.

This was also taking the fight quite specifically and personally to Fox. While Ailes might have pity-hired Carlson, he was also straightforward in telling him that his future was limited at Fox—not just because he was a conservative who liberals could like instead of inspiring the reflexive hatred on which Fox thrived, but because, simply, he wasn't Irish Catholic. In this instance, neither man was fooled by catchall Christianity: Carlson, the Episcopalian, was not of our kind.

At the same time, the *Times'* story was Fox taking the fight to Carlson.

Irena Briganti was Ailes's feared and hated PR chief—"the fat beast" in Ailes's fond/contemptuous characterization. Briganti's powers within Fox were security police–like, a kind of enforcement arm that Ailes had believed he needed to counter the security operations he thought his enemies were running against him. In this, Briganti had a kind of counterintelligence and disinformation carte blanche seen only in the most secretive and paranoid corporations and usually not in public ones, at least not companies with strong compliance and human resource departments. After Ailes's exit, she had become useful to the Murdochs in their efforts to spin the departures of O'Reilly and Kelly, and then in Lachlan's war against his brother. But at the same time, she continued to maintain the power base that Ailes had given her and over which the absentee Murdochs had never quite established control. A year or so after Ailes's ouster, Carlson, with ever climbing ratings and in a new position of power, became incensed about leaks he believed were coordinated by Briganti regarding his friend the daytime host Brian Kilmeade, then in a contract negotiation. A righteous Carlson demanded that Lachlan Murdoch, his lieutenant Viet Dinh, and Fox News chief Suzanne Scott take action against Briganti. Carlson quickly came to understand he had overstepped even his rising stature and, at the same time, incurred in Briganti a fierce and permanent enemy, who now became a whispering source for the *Times*.

Carlson's snobbish Protestant conservatism, once the identity of the entire conservative establishment, had been upended by Ailes's protean right-wing Irish Catholic garrulousness. (Ailes had the furor of a convert—his own moral lapses had been balanced by acceding to his wife, Beth's, dedicated Catholicism, her uncle the priest often in residence in their guest room.) Fox and Ailes had helped unite Catholics and evangelicals in their crusade against abortion into a shorthand undifferentiated "Christianity." Carlson was sniffy toward both downmarket versions of Christian faith. The one other person at Fox who was not confused about Christianity's true schisms and class divisions, and who also harbored a historical contempt for Catholics, was the Calvinist Murdoch (even though his second wife, Anna, was a fervent Catholic who, annoying to Murdoch, had over many years tried to force the issue of his conversion). Murdoch, not unlike Carlson, saw the world in ethnicities far more nuanced than the modern brown-white divides. In their world, there was a whole range of white distinctions involving ever finer meaning and standing. Murdoch's view was firm, if not necessarily clear, when he described someone as "a Greek," "an Italian," "a Mick."

That, in sum, was the basic view that Carlson overlaid on the new Trump world: a pre–World War II sense of social hierarchy and norms, against which every incremental alteration was a step away from a more

desirable ideal—an ideal represented in the manly and salubrious pleasures of the Rolling Rock Club. Alas, there was little left of this world
after fifty years (at least) of avaricious aspirational social climbing, with
the institutions that once anchored this world, in Carlson's view, corrupt, vulgar, and mendacious. If he was worried that his position on
Ukraine might put him in Charles Lindbergh's pariah place, well, Lindbergh's life really *was* a pretty good estimation of the social milieu and
staunch principles (no matter how far out there—indeed, more worthy
for being far out) and time and place that Carlson admired.

So to the *New York Times*' question about whether Carlson believed
what he was saying or if it was all a cynical ratings affair, which the
Times clearly believed it to be, the more nuanced answer was that, while
he might not so much believe in lower-middle-class right-to-life, AR-15
worshipping, build-a-wall, trans-whipping blah blah, which on any given
evening he might defend, he did believe that somewhere around 1929
or so the nation had begun to go terribly wrong. And if that was racist,
well . . . Donald Trump had tapped into some down-market working-
class collective fuck you, heretofore without expression; Tucker Carlson
may similarly have tapped into a greater Protestant sense of rectitude
and moral exclusivity and lost innocence heretofore cowering in embarrassment. Both men were figures that self-consciousness or shame or
professional standards and sophistication might otherwise have kept
out of public life. Indeed, they are almost quaint characters in American culture. Trump, the River City con man Harold Hill, corrupt and
irresistible; Carlson, Jimmy Stewart as Mr. Smith (or, less auspiciously,
Alex P. Keaton). Narrow-cast modern media had allowed both men to
find their cartoon selves.

The *Times* was seeing this only in the lowest political terms, not the
higher dramatic terms in which Carlson saw it. Carlson saw himself on
the verge of tragedy and martyrdom. Like Mr. Smith, the personal toll on
Carlson was huge. Being the second-most-hated man in America—so
memorialized by the *New York Times*—had driven him to the edge of

something. He had sold the family home in Washington and he and his
wife had retreated to island refuges in Maine and Florida, where he
saw himself as a singular, lonely, and unbreakable voice, truth being
his cross, doubling down on his 1929-wrong-turn-by-America, Charles
Lindbergh great-man view, and making his proudly isolationist stand
on Ukraine.

And, of course, they were trying to break him. The biggest guns
in America—the *New York Times*!—were trained on him. So he would
double down again. What choice did he have?

As with most of the political discussion in this polarized time, the
Times story was only confirming the views of the people who read it
and was unread and of no consequence to the people who did not hold
those views—there was not even a tremor in Carlson's ratings after the
Times' takedown. There really was not a wavering audience. Except
for one.

Even though Rupert Murdoch had himself been attacked in the
starkest terms by the *Times* as outside of the bounds of *Times*-defined
political and journalistic acceptability, its attack on Carlson brought
Murdoch up short. For one thing, it had proved him wrong, no-fool-
like-an-old-fool wrong (the most pitiable kind of wrong): his view
of Carlson as a country club Republican, as a kind of well-mannered
Protestant reclamation of conservatism—which Murdoch was able to
maintain, even in the face of Carlson's Ukraine views, because Carlson
was, in fact, a well-mannered Protestant and an attentive and charming
dinner companion—was now seriously challenged if not dismantled by
the *New York Times*.

And worse, his children read the *New York Times*. So not only was
he wrong, but James, who had singled out Carlson as perhaps Fox's most
pernicious influence (he had been a helpful source for the *Times*' story),
was right. And even Jerry Hall, whose views Murdoch was always eager
to avoid, read the *New York Times* and was full of *How could you let him
on the air? . . . How could you support this? . . . And what are you going to*

do about it? And, pointing to another problem, Lachlan did not read the *New York Times*, part of his disengagement from the world in which his business functioned, not to mention from the business itself—and he was at a loss now to defend his star, except to say, as though this were a virtue, that he didn't really think, *underneath*, Tucker *actually* believed most of the things he said on the air. And now, the two youngest Murdoch children, Grace and Chloe—in college at Yale and Stanford, where people still read the *New York Times!*—were appalled.

So not for the first time Murdoch was brought to the point of what . . . ? Having to fire Carlson? He couldn't do that even if he wanted to, and not just because of the millions of dollars of prime-time revenue that depended on him, but because the *New York Times* wanted him to. But did he have to defend Carlson? That might make him seem like a Putin lover, which he most assuredly was not, and an anti-immigrant type, which was, for him, the worst kind of know-nothing conservative. Or did it mean he had to do something entirely different with Fox? But he could not imagine what that might be—as a television executive, which is what he had devolved to, he really had no good ideas. Or would he just have to keep sitting here being lambasted by his children, his wife, their friends, and by anybody he met in reasonably good company?

As for Carlson, at the Rolling Rock Club, the nature of being a martyr was also, at the same time, to be a threat. Carlson was starting to appreciate what he might be able to do with all his fame and influence, and now his anointment as the sum of all liberal fears by the *New York Times*. Trout fishing, he was in a contemplative mood: "As a philosophical matter I hate waste. If you have something valuable, you ought to use it, especially if it's fleeting, as this is. It'll be gone soon. What to do with it? I'm still not sure, apart from the obvious . . ."

The obvious being perhaps not so obvious—that modern presidential paradox: the more liberals attack you, the more the right-wingers might elect you.

8

Elisabeth

THE DAUGHTER

Against the locked-in-place enmity and static play of the sons, which seemed to hold the father with them in a frozen state, there was the wild card of his daughter and either her reasonableness or her ambition—which may or may not be one and the same.

"One night she got drunk," said Ailes, not long before his death, "and told me she was going to come back and kill her brothers."

In the spring of 2022, she was launching the hottest club in London. Camden Theater first opened in Camden Town in 1900, an Edwardian entertainment palace. From theater stage, to vaudeville, to cinema, to a BBC studio, to live music venue, to dance and new wave club, to rave factory, over the next hundred years or so it was a time capsule of the entertainment century. But in 2020 a fire largely gutted the place. Now under the name Koko, it was reopening with a near $100 million renovation and with Elisabeth Murdoch as its lead investor.

While the two brothers might, at his persistent behest, always be pushing to succeed him, it was Elisabeth who, their father speculated, might buy *them* out. He seemed oddly entertained by the prospect that the girl might upend the boys, even though, of course, he needed to favor them over a girl. Her father appeared not just tickled by her financial success (granted, largely backed by his funding), but to find it beyond his own capabilities. "She's great at *content*," he said, the au courant word sounding awkward in his old media vocabulary, "that's what you have to be these days, great at *content*." (At other times, he had extolled James's gift for *branding*, another, for him, newfangled media concept.) Curiously, what he was saying is that Liz had distinguished herself in the particular media world where he had not: elite media, cool media, *liberal* media.

By April 28, the day of the launch party for the House of Koko, the members-only part of the new multitiered entertainment complex, fifty-three-year-old Elisabeth Murdoch was among the most iconic and sought-after figures in social London, a particular inbred, intermarried, and inter-shagged set of political-, media-, and royal-connected celebrities and fixers. If there was any group that had most shunned her father after his arrival in London in the 1960s and who, in turn, he belligerently snubbed and quite defined his identity as being against, here it was, and it had become only more elitist—and left-leaning—in the intervening years. It was a trend-following, Zeitgeist-seeking, social-climbing, money-obsessed, competitively-of-the-moment set, as much as you might find even among the Hollywood elite in the US, the antithesis of Ailes's ever 1965 citizens and Murdoch's down-market papers. There was no better way to punch your ticket in this group than to be friends with Liz.

She was the pivotal voting member among her siblings, at different occasions aligned with each of her opposing brothers. Thrice married, and the mother of four, Liz had led perhaps the most unruly and defiant life among all the Murdoch offspring. Shy, nervous, skittish, and smart—blond and striking, rather a 1965-ish magazine model type, not unlike her mother—hers was an almost tabloid poor-little-rich-girl life of rebellion, wealth, status, excess, and possibly self-destructiveness.

Drugs, wild-side sex, domestic upheaval, social climbing in the show business demimonde, but at the same time with a successful, nearly self-made career (or what passed for one in this family). Hers was, among the Murdoch children, the most independent and accomplished business life.

To the extent that there was one, she had also become in recent years the family mediator, generally talking to everybody, and, against a strong family bias, with enough therapy to be willing to take on the family. She had also found herself, by proximity, temperament, or design, the adult daughter with the most responsibility for her aged father, a role that was hardly unique to the Murdoch family. Her father had spent a substantial part of the pandemic in London, at first because that's where Jerry Hall's family was, and then because that's where his daughter was.

Cooped up, he began to call her every day, and then multiple times a day. This was not only a rare show of vulnerability, but his conversation was often *not* exclusively about business—an odd development. The world's most renowned media mogul, famous for his coldness and impatience, was increasingly defaulting to a dependence on whoever of his children was willing to hear him out at growing length. Again, it was hardly happenstance in any family that it would be a daughter. His conversation, usually a litany of business minutiae, as though everyone else was as caught up in the details as him, was now filled with long recollections of time past (albeit mostly business time past), and more and more old man complaints, a list of personal ailments and dissatisfactions (in New York he had started to go to an "aging" specialist, who had many new theories and recommendations about how to fight nature and gain extra years). And, too, with uncharacteristic directness and emotion, he was on to facets of his life that earlier he would have brushed aside—his shrunken business, divided family, the sad fate of the newspaper business he loved, and his marriage to Jerry, perhaps not the wisest.

Liz's journey to finding herself now in proprietorship of her father in London had begun in the mid-1990s as, in part, a way to achieve distance from him.

Murdoch's relationship with both of his older daughters, Liz and Prue (nine years older than Liz, Prue was his child with his first wife, Patricia), was vastly more contentious than with his sons (and his relationship with his sons was hardly smooth). As the child of a strict-discipline, remote-parenting, socially restrictive Australian upper class, Murdoch seemed two or even more generations removed from his Upper East Side, fast-lane, liberal-elite Manhattan children.

He tried, without success, to cast Liz in the model in which he'd been cast, sending her to Geelong Grammar, the elite Australian prep school where he had gone (unhappily)—but she lasted less than a year. She attended the all-girls Brearley School in New York, which saw itself, even with an influx of banker children, as the true home of the children of people of distinction at the *New York Times*, the *New Yorker*, Columbia University, and in the New York theater, maintaining left-leaning academic and social airs (of the most establishment variety), conveyed with a most artful snobbishness and condescension, as though specifically to belittle Murdoch, "the Dirty Digger." (He would also send his younger daughters Grace and Chloe there—though by then money had perhaps trumped cultural airs.)

Liz went to Vassar, then at the forefront of becoming an unconstrained gay campus (years later Murdoch would still be grumbling about having to pay for a "poofter" school), and emerged in 1990 living with a Black man, Elkin Pianim, the son of a Ghanaian businessman and white Dutch mother, and intending to marry him. The ensuing family crisis—testing several generations of Australian views on race—was papered over by Murdoch's recent invasion of Hollywood, where, in 1985, he had bought Twentieth Century Fox. On the grounds of their new Hollywood mansion, the former home of golden-age movie mogul Jules Stein—bought with all its furnishings, including a complete library—the 1993 wedding, under a tent over the tennis court, was an out-of-time affair, featuring Bob Hope's orchestra, Les Brown and His Band of Renown, a guest list of New York bankers and dowager society figures, and the Reagans, with the former president needing to be led by the hand (the band striking up "Hail to the Chief"), as well as dozens of the groom's Ghanaian relatives in traditional attire (about which the former president seemed particularly perplexed). The couple's college friends were put up at the Hotel Bel-Air. Her brother James was charming in his toast; her brother Lachlan considerably less effervescent in his.

Launching his daughter's career, Murdoch financed for her and her husband the purchase of two television stations in California. Within a few years the couple emerged with a $12 million profit.

Elisabeth was accepted by Stanford's business school, which her father took as a hurtful slap ("What can they teach you that I can't?"). Instead, at his behest, the couple moved to London, where her father inserted her at Sky (then BSkyB), the still nascent and money-losing UK satellite television company that had come close to bankrupting him. Hers was an undefined eyes-and-ears role under the bullying and brilliant Australian executive Sam Chisolm, who redefined her undefined role as mere intern. In a pattern that would often repeat itself, Murdoch found himself unable to resolve the tension between his imperial desires for his children and his dependence on his executives. What's more, he was annoyed at his daughter for getting pregnant. Not once, but twice. She had to make a choice, her CEO father sourly told almost anyone who would listen, between business and motherhood.

And then, while pregnant with her and her husband's second child, she ran off with another man. Scandal, and fury from her father, ensued. In turn, Liz spurned her father, who had recently left her mother, Anna, his wife of thirty-one years, for Wendi Deng, thirty-eight years his junior. Elisabeth, the same age as his new wife, became the first of his children to turn her back on working for him. This seemed to come at the same time she appeared to jettison most of her American life, her closest school friends no longer hearing from her, and began to remake herself as a London social and media figure.

The other man was Matthew Freud, great-grandson of Sigmund Freud, proprietor of one of the best-connected PR firms in London (where PR is a quasi-political function), leading member of the demi-monde celebrity social set, and all around behind-the-scenes dark figure, with whom she would have two more children. Her father hated him. While both men were arguably very much alike in their calculation, ambition, and amorality, they were nevertheless poles apart in their politics, snobberies, social circles, and personal lifestyles, Freud's a louche road that Murdoch believed he was leading his daughter down.

Father-in-law and son-in-law (the couple married in 2001) would never find basic or even tolerable ground, with Murdoch somehow able to maintain the view that Freud, who had realized a considerable fortune from his business, was practically speaking a wastrel with doubtful career prospects.

Meanwhile, as Elisabeth was indeed taken down the louche road, with reports of her personal exploits regularly elided from the Murdoch press and by anyone else in the UK media who might end up at some point working for the Murdoch press (i.e., everyone), she had also identified, quite before it was evident, the coming insatiable worldwide demand for nearly unlimited television programming. From the early 2000s, until her father bought her out in 2011, she built Shine, a company in which she was the majority owner, into one of largest independent television production companies in Europe.

Her father used her success as a frequent reprimand for his sons, even as James, running Sky, became a leading media executive in Europe. Still, neither son had built anything successful himself, Murdoch reminded them. He continued, as he had since she had left her job at Sky, trying to lure Liz back into his company. But he would not or could not give up the assumption that it was inevitably or necessarily one of the sons who would take over, explaining this with a rationale that Elisabeth would not want to take over because she had many other things on her plate. This seemed to mean children, but also, more broadly, a life he yet regarded askance—that is, with Freud.

Murdoch believed Freud was organizing all his children against him. Further, Murdoch believed that Freud himself had designs on his company. Freud had certainly become influential among the Murdoch children. He was their in-house adviser on the future of the Murdoch legacy, including the various burdens of its association with Murdoch politics. Here were the beginnings of a conversation about mortality, succession, and a new Murdoch political identity that they all felt was critical but had yet to agree on. But here *was* one thing that they could all agreed on: Fox News was toxic, not just to American political life but to them personally, and that Roger Ailes was clearly some version of true evil and, more to the point, their personal enemy. In this, Freud willingly became the siblings' spear. In 2010, acting as the family spokesman, Freud told the *New York Times* for a front-page story that he was "ashamed and sickened by Roger Ailes' horrendous and sustained disregard of the journalistic standards that News Corporation, its founder and every other global media business aspires to," adding that he was "by no means alone within the family or the company" in his views.

Afterward, there was some dispute about what Murdoch actually knew about how far his children would go in crafting their public attack on Ailes and Fox. But the ire if not disgust toward Ailes had been brewing for some time in the family and had included Murdoch—"He's crazy, that's all," Murdoch kept saying about Ailes, although perhaps more as an excuse than condemnation. The cause of the increasingly open distaste was Ailes's ever more derogatory, and what the Murdoch children considered racist, views toward Barack Obama, who all of the Murdochs, including Rupert, had backed in 2008. It was at this point, with the persistent attacks on Obama—over his birthplace, his religion, and his allegiances—the family moved from seeing the news network as a profitable if obnoxious gadfly to regarding it as a destructive, ever more powerful family stain.

Murdoch had known something was coming from his children, and had let it happen, and yet, confronted by Ailes, Murdoch immediately backtracked. Indeed, he gave him a thumping bonus and raise. Here again, for neither the first nor the last time, the otherwise indomitable Murdoch shrank in the face of Fox's power. Whatever message Murdoch might have initially hoped to send, as in "remember who your ultimate bosses are," was inverted to mean Murdoch would always protect Ailes from his callow children, and, even, that there was profit in antagonizing them.

Not long after this, and again confirming the weakness of the next generation and Ailes's relative strength, the British arm of Murdoch's company was plunged into scandal over allegations of the phone hacking practices by Murdoch reporters. James was caught out in the investigations as either a feckless executive or a conspirator in an elaborate cover-up. Within the family, blame squarely fell on James—he had known, or should have known, what his British papers were up to. Elisabeth took her brother Lachlan's side in a willingness to sacrifice James to save their father (however much he, too, might have known about the phone hacking). Rupert, on his part, used all his power—in some sense exhausting all his influence and future business prospects in the UK—to save James from prosecution and to move him back to business respectability in the US.

Trying to paper over the family fissures the best way he knew how—with money—Murdoch bought Elisabeth's company (at what many complained was an inflated price), bringing her officially back into the corporate fold. True, it was hardly an ideal generational step forward. James, in disgrace, was back in the US operation without clear purpose or authority—persona non grata with nearly everyone in the company but his father. And Elisabeth, even with her nepotistic reward, was acting like her father's prisoner, and began almost immediately to waffle on her pledge to spend more time in the US. Still, Murdoch now had two children beside him.

This then became Rupert's primary focus, engaging them in running the family company while he continued to work on cajoling the third back in. The strategy for the prize he most wanted—a dynasty named Murdoch—was, at least with a little imagination and suspension of disbelief, starting to fall into place. But it was also increasingly becoming clear to his children that in order for any sort of dynastic plan to actually begin to take shape the major hurdle, and the key requirement for them, was getting rid of their father.

What Murdoch sought in his children was an alter ego, someone to walk lockstep with him and think what he was thinking. But what was he thinking? His executives had long learned to carve out spaces for themselves that he wasn't much interested in, and to otherwise patiently wait for him to make clear the course he wanted—theirs was a stealth management job. But from his children he wanted something more, though what this might be remained unclear. Murdoch lived in deep ambivalence. Hidden from view and almost entirely unexpressed—that is, he was unable to express it—he churned. He second-guessed. He doubted. He struggled. And then, often when you least expected it, as though spontaneously and often unrelated to any chain of logic, he decided—and you could not question that decision.

Meanwhile, he had also raised reasonably capable children, and given them experiences and put them in positions that might encourage them to believe they had high competence if not special capabilities. They not unreasonably believed they were independent thinkers, take-initiative managers, modern leaders, ready with spreadsheets and other analytics. But their job, well beyond modern business tools, was to guess what was in the black box otherwise known as their father.

Because this was a hopeless prospect, the children, one after another, had tried to distance themselves—geographically and philosophically—from the patriarch. But now Murdoch was on the verge of getting them all back again. He was luring them in with the promise—hardly the first time he had made it—of him gradually stepping back. The sons weighed the uncertainty of this against the certainty that, with their father now over eighty, a countdown had surely begun.

Liz, more realistic, once again pulled away. She was, if not jaded, clear-eyed. Her father was not going anywhere until carried out. Her brothers were more, and not less, hostile to each other. And Fox, as it became the vital profit engine of the company, was, she recognized, a time bomb for all of them. She had sold her company, earning her first taste of true fuck-you money, and her marriage was on the rocks. She was a respected media entrepreneur, a presence and quiet power in London, and, in her midforties, back in circulation.

While her alignment had been with Lachlan against James during the phone hacking scandal, she was now in an extended discussion with James about the media business—in which they both regarded their experience and acumen as far greater than their brother's, and, increasingly, their father's—and their company's future.

Twenty-First Century Fox—split from News Corp in 2013—was in the network and cable television business. At the very least, those businesses were going to require a reinvention that was probably beyond their octogenarian father, but that could not be done without him. What's more, in 2016, the Fox bomb seemed to go off with the election of Donald Trump—the family would be directly linked to one of the most bizarre and threatening developments in modern history.

Elisabeth sided with James: there was not going to be a viable succession plan; their future and fortunes could not be wed to Fox; they were at a market top; Fox had so poisoned the business air against them that the company was cut off from many future avenues of growth; and the premium Disney was now offering was big enough to move even their father. Do the deal. Get out.

With her initial windfall from the sale of her own company now augmented with her $2 billion dividend, she segued nicely into a new role as one of the most sought-after individual media investors in the world. What's more, in 2017 she got married again, this time to an artist, Keith Tyson, safely outside media and politics and the Murdoch world. She was turning fifty and it was time for a new future. By 2018, when Elisabeth Murdoch showed up at the British *GQ* Men of the Year Awards, that year honoring, among other discordant figures, Prince Charles and Rose McGowan, she was barely recognizable to people who had not recently seen her. Cosmetic surgery may no longer be a certain character note, but it can certainly be a vivid signpost in a life journey, an effort to stay the same and slow your path, or to break from the past and start again.

Alas. The past, held in intractable place by Fox News, still needed sorting out.

By the time of the pandemic, it was clear that Lachlan, even from Australia, was stubbornly determined to hold on to his role as chief executive and heir to the Murdoch companies when his father died, willfully seeing this as the future owed to him. Meanwhile, James had set his position: to take the company from his brother and transform the network, seeing this as his heroic destiny. Between these two poles was her father: uncertain what to do with his disengaged son, who yet seemed to desperately cling to his position and legacy, afraid of his righteous and wrathful son and the havoc he could bring.

In the fall of 2021, Liz hosted a ninetieth birthday party for her father at Tavern on the Green, that tourist restaurant in Central Park where her parents had hosted a party for her when she graduated from Vassar. The party was delayed by COVID from Rupert's true birthday date the March before (with some worry about whether he would make it or not). Liz sidelined her father's wife, Jerry Hall, in the planning. It was Liz's event, for which she produced a video of such hagiographic and interminable proportions that only part of it could be shown. James declined to attend.

The point was legacy.

It was no longer in her mind a business issue. There was no longer a business to grow or advance—the real business had been for all practical purposes sold to Disney. What was at issue for the future, for Liz and her siblings, and as much for their children, was the meaning of it all. That was the story, which, of course, she was making plans to tell. That was one thing she was spending her time on—it was in the works. Their father's extraordinary story—and it was *extraordinary*—of transforming the modern world. You could oppose him, you could dislike him, you could disagree with him, but what you could not take from him is that he was a historic individual, among a handful of singular individuals of his time, arguably *the* singular individual. *Succession*, which the family had tried to shrug off or laugh off, was such bullshit. Now was the time to get out in front of that and give the man his due. Now the real story was ready to be told.

Except for Fox, that fucking exasperating part of the tale.

SUMMER

9

Dominion

"FUCK HIM"

With the Dominion Voting Systems suit against Fox News now in its fourteenth month of litigation without a settlement, millions of pages of discovery material—email, texts, programming plans, video outtakes, the audio of off-camera exchanges—had been delivered to Dominion's lawyers.

"Do you want to tell me what this is about? Seriously? What could possibly be going on? What could they possibly be doing? Who could this possibly benefit? Who? Not us. Who is thinking this through? Could it be that he's had his fourth glass of wine at lunch?" Tucker Carlson fulminated to a friend. This was Viet Dinh's possible fourth glass he was pointing to.

"Is this fucked up or what? Seems pretty fucked up to me," Sean Hannity separately concurred.

The first rule of libel law for a media company—beyond the actual law—is never to go before a jury. Ordinary people don't like big media companies and are uneasy with the way the First Amendment seems to protect powerful organizations against littler guys.

The second rule is to avoid discovery—how the media sausage is made only compounds the problems. Therefore, media companies in libel actions have two courses: move to dismiss—that is, ask the judge to decide early in the process that the media is within its constitutional rights and to throw out the case. Or, failing that, settle, no matter how expensive.

In June 2022, the judge in Delaware's Superior Court hearing the Dominion case ruled that the suit could also include Fox Corporation and its top executives Rupert Murdoch and Lachlan Murdoch. The judge, Eric M. Davis, allowed that there was a reasonable inference that, after the 2020 election, both Murdochs had been directly involved in approving and creating the Fox News storyline that a conspiracy involving the manipulation of Dominion's voting machine was a cause of Trump's defeat, and that father and son specifically knew this storyline to be false—a necessary ingredient for a libel plaintiff to override US free speech protections for journalists. Judge Davis had previously ruled that there was sufficient evidence to believe Fox News had acted with knowing disregard for the truth in this instance, but his ruling now exponentially expanded the usual parameters of a libel suit. It wasn't just reporters, producers, and news executives responsible for the damaging statements, but the company's highest executives.

In media circles and among the libel bar there was a collective and unsuccessful effort to find any other instance where the highest officers of a major media company were personally implicated in a libel case, that is, where they themselves had participated in a coordinated effort to defame the plaintiff.

Just a few months earlier, on the beach in St. Barts, Murdoch had rued the $50 million the suit might possibly cost him. Now that amount had potentially doubled or tripled or much more.

Dominion had first filed its suit in early 2021. This had followed weeks of watching itself pilloried on Fox and other conservative news outlets in down-the-rabbit-hole fashion; the baroque storyline of international conspiracy, virtually none of it true, seemed to compound itself with each telling. According to Dominion, during this time it made more than three thousand complaints in writing to Fox. And Fox appeared to ignore all of them. This was, at the beginning, no doubt weird and then appalling to Dominion; then it was surely a cause for panic about the possible effects on its business. At some point, as this tiny company became the linchpin in the stolen election, it must have been an out-of-body experience. But then, for a company with relatively limited growth prospects, there was surely a recognition that a most extraordinary opportunity had been laid at its door.

This wasn't, as most libel cases are, a difficult circumstance of factual interpretation, hard-to-prove intent, and the need to overcome high-bar free speech protections. Here were grossly and willfully fabricated lies. In the weeks after the election, dozens of courts, election regulators, and most of the political establishment confirmed that the claims of election fraud were fantasy if not in themselves calculated acts of fraud. In the days after the election, when Trump's inner coterie of election deniers began to air the Dominion conspiracy, Trump campaign lawyers and operatives quickly commissioned a report whose conclusion was that neither Dominion nor any other voting machines were in any way involved with election fraud—a message clearly conveyed to Fox (Trump campaign staff and Fox producers and stars were in constant touch). Trump's own people—at least the "normies" in his circle—were appalled. Further still, *Dominion v. Fox News* joined a lineup—perhaps went to the head of the line—of proxy actions, with massive political and cultural support, against Trump himself. It may have been the surest libel suit ever filed since *New York Times v. Sullivan*, the 1964 case that vastly expanded the rights and wherewithal of journalism, turning all journalists into protected gadflies and would-be giant killers (and all libel plaintiffs into quixotic figures).

Fox, however, up until June, seemed unconcerned in its response. The company's chief legal officer, Viet Dinh, told people it wasn't on his

list of top twenty worries. With his own history as a Washington lawyer and Supreme Court clerk (often mentioned as a possible Supreme
Court nominee when Trump was president—or at least when Fox was
in good standing with Trump), the case seemed to have become part
of Dinh's own legal swagger. Oddly, he kept announcing that he was
willing to go to the Supreme Court, as though this was good news,
with Dinh himself somehow seeming to want to act as his own solici-
tor general.

Dinh even appeared to regard the case as a kind of Murdoch macho
proving moment. After all, for so long the Murdoch media had aggressively trodden fine lines in coverage of celebrities, politicians, royals,
ordinary folk in the headlights, businesses in the news, and of Murdoch's
own designated enemies. Just by sheer size alone, not to mention temperament, the Murdoch world was among the industry leaders in field-
ing libel complaints and suits—and largely undaunted by them. And
successful *in spite* of them. Or *successful* as a measure of them—an
intemperate voice paid the bills. Why should this libel suit be different
from any other?

The Murdoch companies had long had among the best libel lawyers
in the media industry. This does not mean, as other media companies
might construe it, that these lawyers were strict sentinels policing careless editors and reporters, nor that they were principled advocates of
the right to publish, helping to push free speech boundaries, as, say, the
New York Times might be proud of. Rather, the job of Murdoch lawyers,
evolved over decades and decades, was helping the company do what
it wanted to do: i.e., what other more cautious and deliberate media
companies would most often not do.

The practice of aggressive media lawyering, beyond standing behind
the first amendment, is a process of applying a close textual analysis,
really threading a linguist's needle, in an effort to observe all of the cave-
ats the courts have cited as well as to take advantage of all the protections
they have granted, so as to allow the journalist to safely make his or her

assertion. But few practice this very well, favoring caution over craft. For expert and bold libel lawyers, the practice also involves a constant risk assessment of whether the potential libel is against someone who will actually sue. Likewise, it's a power equation about whose resources and tenacity to fight a libel action are greater—media company or plaintiff. Libel, Murdoch's lawyers understood better than most, is a *real* world battle. And, too, it is a return-on-investment calculation: what does a casual if not reckless disregard for the literal truth get you, versus the cost of lawyers and settlements (as well as, though only marginally for most of Murdoch's outlets, public opprobrium). In this, the success of the Murdoch enterprise spoke for itself. He'd built an empire challenging people to sue him. Hence, Murdoch lawyers allowed the company to gamble, tenaciously fought the challenges that might arise, and then, if necessary, expediently settled (although Murdoch was in theory always ready to fight, his lawyers understood that as soon as they mentioned preparing him for a deposition he'd settle). In other words, Murdoch was willing to pay to publish—to be the publisher of what others might be too cautious or too principled to say. The trick was of course to pay as little as possible.

There was another subtler aspect here within Murdoch's newsrooms. Media lawyers, in the common corporate context, are a bulwark to protect the media company from the natural overzealousness of its reporters and editors. The executives, rather than the reporters and editors, are the client. But Murdoch had long ago achieved a fine symbiosis between his own interests and his newsrooms' overzealousness, leading to, arguably, journalism's most successful tabloid products, and the growth of his worldwide media empire (as well as to the phone hacking scandal that had nearly undone him). Murdoch believed, more than any other media executive, that he represented the true journalism impulse—that is, to say whatever you wanted to. In this, his lawyers had come to represent, with all the artful nuance that required, the symbiosis of Murdoch and his product. Their principal job was not to protect the company from libel claims, but to allow Murdoch's tabloid sensibility to flour-ish. Murdoch's direct disregard for his own expert in 1983 and personal authorization to have the London *Times* publish the Hitler Diaries, which his historical expert Hugh Trevor-Roper—Lord Dacre—judged to be fraudulent (and which indeed turned out to *be* brazenly fraud-ulent), had become something of Murdoch's legendary and ultimate standard: "Fuck Dacre! Publish," was Murdoch's now famous dictum. Don't let too much nitpicking get in the way of a good story.

In the Murdoch-Ailes symbiotic relationship, Ailes would single out Murdoch as, in his experience, the most fearless media execu-tive he had ever worked for. Murdoch's commitment, with a nuanced calculation of the risk/reward balance, was to again and again let Ailes push the limits of his freedom to say what he wanted. This rep-resented some political topsy-turvyness. Since the 1960s, the cry for journalists, writers, and media outlets to be able to express themselves freely had largely been the demand of the left. This impulse had fueled alternative media, moved sexual boundaries, and helped birth the internet. But with some of the same arguments and an added joie de guerre—and with cable television in the US out from under the juris-diction the FCC had over broadcast TV, and with the clout and legal resources of one of the world's largest media companies—Murdoch and Ailes essentially made Fox a zone of uninhibited expression, albeit right-wing expression.

Fox's favorite conspiracy theories, often drawn from single threads and then weaved into great new tapestries, became in essence a new conservative form, showcased if not invented by Fox. The truth could never actually be known because it was controlled and hidden by forces protecting their own power and interests. *Therefore*, you had to extrap-olate from the threads in order to make the greater and more "truthful" story, even though it might not actually be *true*.

Yes, this was taxing to lawyers. But many of Murdoch's lawyers had grown up with him and grown rich with him. Historically, he had

eschewed blue chip firms. For decades, he relied on a scrappy, politically attuned New York firm, first hired when he came to New York in
the 1970s, Squadron, Ellenoff, Plesent, and Lehrer. The firm expanded
as the Murdoch business expanded, with many of its lawyers moving
from the firm into his executive ranks. They thought as he thought; they
thought as he wanted them to think—a symbiosis here.

Anyway . . . they, along with the organization they protected, helped
define new boundaries to news. And life went on to the next disingenu-
ous, perfidious, and on occasion wholly made-up story.

The Dominion defamation was not exceptional at Fox, but to head
to trial with a jury that might hold you maximally accountable for it
certainly was.

Complicating matters, Murdoch's longtime lawyers—along with
the lawyers they trained and who, over generations, had taken their
places—were largely gone from the company, replaced by Lachlan's
choice of Dinh, and then Dinh's choices under him (curiously, as became
evident as the Dominion matter proceeded, Murdoch did not even
seem to know the name of the Fox News in-house counsel, Bernard
Gugar). Further complicating the company's practiced and efficient
response to libel complaints—bully-boy defense, coupled with best-
case confidential settlements—Murdoch's own personal actions were at
the root of what had occurred and were so confusingly at odds with the
company's interest that blame had become something of an existential
dilemma, best put off for another day.

Beginning the events that would result in the Dominion suit, shortly
before 11:20 p.m. Eastern Time, on the evening of November 3, Election
Day 2020, the election desk at Fox News, where in-house election data
specialists applied their own assessment to the voting data coming into
the network, decided they were satisfied that Joe Biden would win Arizona's 11 electoral votes. Grabbing for a journalistic coup, Fox proposed
to be the first on the air to make the announcement (television news
organizations had long become de facto election night authorities). This

would prove to be an accurate call, but it was also chancy enough that you might prudently want to hold it for a while (the election desk admitted as much in the days after). Other suppliers of election data were far from showing such convincing numbers—and at that moment, such a call might also have an undue influence on polls that were yet open. (In the view of *New York Times*' polling expert Nate Cohn: "Was the Fox call the result of the most sophisticated and accurate modeling, or more like being 'right' when calling heads in a coin flip? It appears to be the latter—a lucky and dangerous guess . . .") Anyway, while it turned out to be right, in the moment it was audacious enough that no one not named Murdoch was in a position to take responsibility for it—nor would have wanted to. The election desk's belief that it could legitimately make the call was passed to Suzanne Scott, then to Lachlan Murdoch, and then to Rupert Murdoch. The elder Murdoch, apprised of what the election desk was ready to do, said: "Fuck him." Fuck Trump, the preposterous president. The interpretation of this response, passed from Lachlan to Scott, was that there was no objection to the desk proceeding with its decision to have the on-air anchors announce that Biden was the winner in Arizona and Trump the loser.

The Trump camp saw this both as the first strong indication that its optimism from the early stages of the evening was misplaced and as a problematic influence on other calls to come in tight states. Indeed, it went batshit, contacting anyone of any standing in the Murdoch organization including Murdoch himself, who refused to reconsider. Trump saw it as the tipping point in his relationship with Fox: Murdoch, he understood, not without justification, was out to hurt him (certainly at least no longer to help him). Furthermore, it became in Trump's mind an indication that higher forces were doing whatever they do to put a thumb on the scale—which, in turn, became the suspicion and evidence (largely one and the same) of a certain conspiracy to deprive him of his victory.

Over the next several days—Biden's victory was not called until

Saturday, November 7—as the early positive numbers for Trump in key states inexorably eroded, there would be many culprits in Trump's sights. Fox was foremost among them.

Murdoch, with his "Fuck him," had allowed the network to seemingly take an overt position against its paramount franchise, the presidency of Donald Trump. (Subsequently, in his deposition in the Dominion case, Murdoch would demur on this point—Q: "Were you involved in the call of Arizona prior to it being called?" A: "No." Here, he arguably equated not intervening, or even directly affirming, with noninvolvement.) Fox had vastly expanded its audience as a by-product of its support for Trump (as other media expanded their audience due to its opposition) and nearly doubled its profits. In Trump's view this was a betrayal of him and of the audience that came to Fox because of the network's support of him. What he giveth he could take, in this view, and that became one of his clear post–Election Day messages—Fuck Fox. For the first time, this gave a meaningful market lift to the other fledgling conservative cable networks.

What had actually happened? Despite Murdoch's private detestation of Trump, the breach with him might in fact have been inadvertent: "Fuck him" more feeling than intention. For all his career, Murdoch had been uniquely engaged by election nights. It was the moment that most reflected his interests and his power. In another life, he would have been a political columnist or political operative, he often told people. Election nights were one of the things he worked for, a payoff. A moment of heightened reality. His true and only sport. He stayed up far into the night and often did not restrain his drinking. On election night 2004, when, as it happened, a key block of his voting stock was coming on the market in Australia because of a change in the company's listing, he sat up with Ailes, both of them reasonably shit-faced, toasting the Bush victory and neglected to buy back his own stock. Instead, John Malone swooped in and bought it, costing Murdoch and his shareholders billions to recover it. In 2020, his "Fuck him," likely as much impulse as policy, ended in a dramatic and wholly anomalous statement against the network's programming strategies.

Make no mistake, Murdoch was to blame. On the other hand, you *couldn't* blame Murdoch. He couldn't be blamed because there was no corporate or psychological mechanism for that. And also because it was never clear what he was actually saying. Everyone, most of the time, was merely inferring what Murdoch meant. But an unforced error had been committed. The call could easily, and more fairly, have waited—and still the network could have been first. Fox had made, if only by inference of Murdoch's desires, a personal attack on Trump.

Dominion was arguing that Fox's willingness to air the Trump camp's increasingly far-fetched if not deranged theories about Dominion was a strategic effort to win back the goodwill it might have lost with Trump voters, the Fox audience, and Trump himself due to its Arizona call. Airing the Dominion conspiracy was a premeditated plan to win a commercial advantage at unfair and egregious cost to Dominion. All this was true. But *truer* was not that it was a desperate new plan to compensate for the terrible mistake, but merely a continuation of the Trump storyline the network had been pursuing since Election Day 2016—essentially allowing Trump to write his own storyline. The network wasn't dealing with its impulsive, unaccountable Arizona call, it was—in a subtle interpretation that would not much help its chances in court—ignoring it.

For one thing, *not* to ignore it might mean having to confront Murdoch with it. *Is it the intention now—your intention—to disavow Trump? Do we, as a result of your election night call, remake the network? Change it all up? Is that what you want?*

That's an almost unimaginable conversation to have with a man incapable of discussing motivations or intentions or, really, being asked to explain himself beyond an utterance.

So, you ignore it, unless he utters it again. And, indeed, Murdoch immediately distanced himself as well as he might from the Arizona call and let the network storyline follow both its ratings barometers and its direct line to Trump sources. No matter the general cynicism of Murdoch and others at the network toward what Trump himself was saying—at best a secondary reality.

The Dominion story had not departed very far from the usual practices of the network. Or, if so, only by degree. The fantasy and reality-bending about Dominion was no greater than, say, Sean Hannity's bizarre trashing of Seth Rich, a young Democratic operative whose death Hannity put at the center of a vast and nutty conspiracy, or, for that matter, the allegedly dark mysteries of Barack Obama's birth certificate. A tenuous strand—in this case, that another voting machine company, Smartmatic (also suing Fox), was started by Venezuela nationals, and whose machines were used in a Hugo Chavez election, and who once owned a company that was sold to Dominion—is woven, through layers of internet interpretation, into an elaborate scheme gilded with possibilities and questions, which, because this is a conspiracy, implied, of course, that you could not know, really—*ever know*—the truth. Obviously. The most intriguing issue was not whether this was true or false (obviously false), or how the network could have been so brazen (brazen was its currency), but *how* had the lawsuit gotten this far, and not been short circuited in the courts, as most defamation suits are, or swept under the rug in a confidential settlement? How had it gotten to the point that a major media company's two top executives and controlling shareholders were themselves about to be hauled into court and found directly culpable? It was now looking like the most extreme instance of Murdoch corporate accountability since he and James were forced in 2011 to publicly account for illegal phone hacking practices in the British newsrooms. That had resulted in Murdoch's personal humiliation (and a literal pie hurled at his face), the shuttering of one of his newspapers, the forced division of his company, a block on his ability to increase his holdings in British television, and his son James's ignominious retreat from the UK.

Well, in fact, arguably, that's exactly what it went back to. From phone hacking there had begun a long arc of corporate reorganization and changing of the guard around Murdoch himself (from his top executives, to his closest lawyers, to his secretary of thirty years), including the elevation of his sons, to the sale of most of his assets. In the last decade almost everything in the Murdoch enterprises had changed—sixty years of corporate evolution handily disposed of—except Murdoch himself.

He remained the decision-maker. In some ways, at the age now of ninety-one, even more so. The company—this significantly smaller entity since its great sell-off to Disney—had been refitted with much weaker executives. The band of crafty lawyers and knowing executives, with their nuanced understanding of aggression and retreat, and of Murdoch himself, was no longer backing him up.

Lachlan Murdoch was now in charge and his basic management method was to always wait upon his father and then bend with him. This seemed born out of some true filial desire to keep the great man thinking that little had changed and that he was still great (in this, Lachlan was drawing a clear contrast with his brother, who was always telling his father his time was over). Likewise, he had recruited executives who would wait with him.

The Praetorian Guard that had grown up over more than half a century to protect Murdoch (often from himself), and which had created this remarkable machine whose expertise was to manage the politics and calculate the price of what he wanted to publish, was no longer in place.

Hence, at ninety-one, the great man was more in charge than ever, more the last word, more the necessary word, more the person on whom everyone waited. Except . . . he wasn't saying anything. Personally at fault for his election night "Fuck him," blaming Donald Trump as much as anyone, blaming his son too for being off in Australia, having little rapport with the people at Fox who were waiting on him for an answer, and as confused by the American political situation and where he stood in it as he had ever been, he seemed to be able to offer no direction, no view, or not one that could readily be interpreted.

"He's pissed off at everybody about this," his daughter Elisabeth was telling people—it was everyone else's fault but his.

"Absolutely nothing to worry about," Viet Dinh kept repeating, often after his multiple glasses of lunchtime wine, at exactly the same time that the lawyers were turning over the millions of emails that vividly illustrated the sausage-making technique of Murdoch tabloid reality.

10

Hannity

GIVE THEM A HEAD

Tucker Carlson was hoping that the fact he was back for the summer on his Maine island would help delay the subpoena server from knocking at his door. Sean Hannity was telling everyone to just bring it on, he had nothing to hide, which was, to everyone, the danger. There was an internal debate about Murdoch's possible testimony with some proposing to argue that Murdoch's memory had degraded too much for him to be reliable (this was not to be discussed with Murdoch).

Still, nobody doubted there *would* be a settlement. How could there not be?

After the Murdochs had been directly included in the action, the already onerous estimated figure of $50 million had risen to as high as $200 million, a fantastic sum in a defamation case. So settle now, *right now*, before it gets worse.

But Fox was having trouble even in engaging the other side at any level of settlement discussion. Beyond its financial interest, Dominion had become a historic player and a virtuous one. Inside Fox, among some, this suggested the possibility of an additional Dominion conspiracy: that it had recruited left-wing deep pockets—George Soros et al., or others such—to help fund its suit and to finance a floor so it didn't have to settle. This hypothetical left-wing billionaire consortium would guarantee Dominion several hundred million dollars no matter the outcome, letting them take this through discovery and, ideally, to a jury—no matter how much Fox might be willing to offer. Viet Dinh began to use this excuse to explain what otherwise seemed Fox's strange paralysis in squaring the suit.

But then Murdoch had an idea. This seemed to come out of his own heated response to the January 6 congressional hearings that had recently begun—with its day-by-day deft and sickening presentation of the video portrait of the Capitol under attack. His fury at Trump had been reignited. *Give them a head*, he proposed. *Hannity.* Hannity was the person he most equated with Trump, often coupled in his repeated and unanswered question: "What is it with Hannity and Trump?" As though this were a confounding mystery rather than a natural connection. A settlement of whatever millions would be sweetened with the understanding that within the short term Hannity would quietly leave the network. Done. Finally, Hannity gone.

What frustrations or incomprehension Murdoch had with Fox often seemed particularly summed up in Hannity and his bewildering balderdash. Murdoch often greeted questions about Hannity at social events with grimaces and scowls. In 2016, after Ailes's ouster, it quite looked like, and Hannity himself believed, that the Murdochs, open in their disgust for Hannity's pontificating and bizarro conspiracy theories, would get rid of him. (Murdoch, in random conversations, sometimes asked people if they "believed" Hannity, seeming to find it incredible that anyone could.) But then, with the exit of Megyn Kelly and Bill O'Reilly, the prime-time schedule was rejigged, elevating Hannity to the effective evening tentpole. From that perch, he had become part of the Trump-MAGA heart and soul, shifting, if as one, with the identity of the network. The way in which Murdoch would stew as he watched and then, in a steam of aggravation, switched off the network (in fact, he could never watch Fox for very long) seemed to confirm how part and parcel Hannity had become to the new MAGA-Fox.

But another side of this, complicating the blame circle, was how much Hannity was a natural character of Murdoch newsrooms. The idea that Murdoch would fire someone—even if he might want to fire them—because of outside pressure was literally the one thing that violated Murdoch's journalism principles. In this, he had enshrined himself as a free-speech absolutist—the right of his newsrooms to say anything, and to be as louche and incorrect (well before this became anybody's political measure) as they might naturally be. He may have thought Hannity had a screw loose, but for seventy years he had been a defender of people like Hannity. He took some higher moral virtue from defending his newsrooms' eccentricities, hijinks, cruelties, drunkenness, and crimes. Richard Johnson, his longtime gossip page editor in New York, was exposed running something of a protection racket on his page—pay him money, or grant him favors, and you were spared—but no matter. Johnson's Murdoch career continued for many happy years after his grift was exposed. Murdoch's defense of free speech—as absolute as anyone's—was not a defense of virtue, rather the opposite.

Murdoch's ideal newsrooms, while top down—from Murdoch at the top, or in Fox's case from Ailes at the top—were a survivalist culture of outré, semi-outlaw, class-bucking, unemployable-anywhere-else personalities able, precisely because of their lack of upwardly mobile socialization, to deliver a true tabloid product. This was Fleet Street, when it was still on Fleet Street—or the rat-infested warrens of the Murdoch papers headquarters just off Fleet Street on Bouverie Street—the true chemistry of popular news for Murdoch.

Here, in a direct line to Hannity and Dominion, the truth, such as it was, the prosaic truth, was goosed, inflated, sexed-up, dumbed-down, and sometimes turned on its head, to serve a higher truth, which was the satisfaction of an audience. That was unrestrained, unconstipated, unimpeded, take-the-pole-out-of-your-ass free expression.

Murdoch's best tabloid reporters believed, not just unquestioningly, not just absent moral compunction, but joyfully, that no life was as exciting and as satisfying as life in his sort of newsrooms, uninhibited by self-consciousness. *Do not overthink* might be the truest Murdoch news model. What you were allowed to do in a Murdoch newsroom became addiction, need, dependence. Others in the television business at other networks more self-conscious about the game might agonize about what was necessary to hold ratings, understanding that they were struggling against it, that a devil's pact had been made, but not Hannity. The high of saying what thrilled his audience was constant—no more so than since he and his audience had converged in never-ceasing-to-be-amazed admiration of Donald Trump.

Hannity's life, built with his office wife who had become his home wife too, in Oyster Bay, Long Island, was a life not foremost directed at fame, or money, or influence, but to working in television, living inside the process of being on the air, receiving the feedback from it, and going back on the air, 24/7, and subbing in radio to fill what time was left over—and accomplishing this in a say-anything quest for his audience's heart. In a tabloid newspaper reporter, this addiction, and the greater and greater lengths you might need to go to satisfy it, classically led to a life of personal disarray not least because the financial rewards of the job couldn't compensate for its demands. A prime-time slot did. An ever bigger house, ever more property, plus a personal plane, and all the placating that could be gotten from creature comforts—the best tickets to any sporting event—helps hold it all together. But even wealth can't satisfy the obsession for more air. Hannity wouldn't take five minutes off. He wouldn't miss a show.

During the Obama birth certificate mania, Murdoch sheepishly approached Ailes about Hannity's rants. Ailes spoke to Murdoch's high sense not by defending the story but by defending Hannity's willingness to say anything. "Hannity is not a good soldier; he is a great soldier. Give him another swig of the Kool-Aid and he'll head over any hill," explained a happy Ailes, apparently satisfying Murdoch.

"Most people on TV are morons who can talk the talk. Hannity is a moron who talks like one," Ailes said, expounding on his personal brilliance of picking Hannity out of the Nowheresville talk radio.

Twenty-six years and Hannity's personal mania for airtime continued. He wasn't bored, he didn't plateau, there was no introspective moment of *What more? Is there anything else?* In the Fox closed world, where his wife had as many friends as he did, it was common knowledge that their marriage, once a model—Sean, almost singularly at Fox, wasn't a jumper (as per Ailes: "Hannity looks but doesn't touch")—was breaking down. Sean wouldn't take a day off. He was addicted to airtime and the sound of his own voice. It was as if he had no consciousness beyond Fox News. It was a complete world. It was his wife who finally pulled the plug on her marriage to Hannity and to Fox.

Ainsley Earhardt, with the straight blond hair and Florida complexion of the archetype conservative woman broadcaster, arrived at Fox in 2007, recruited from her news reader job at a local station in San Antonio, Texas, a move resisted by her then husband who had been her college sweetheart, Kevin McKinney. Ailes had promised to make her the morning anchor and then reneged. Her marriage shortly broke down over her husband's argument that without the job she had wanted they should leave New York. Earhardt, however, at thirty-one a hopeful television lifer, countered she had made it to New York, into the top-rated cable news channel, and that her television career potential was limitless. In short order, she was appearing in her own segment on Hannity, "Ainsley Across America." Rumors that they were having an affair were not true; as per Ailes, in a variation on the theme: "Hannity is a dreamer, not a cheater." Earhardt's second husband, whom she married in 2012, was Will Proctor, a Clemson quarterback, with a penchant for women on television (his ex-girlfriends included the actress Mandy Moore). The quarterback was soon cheating on his wife, a circumstance he stoutly denied but which was widely shared at Fox News. There followed for the couple a religious retreat meant to help repair the marriage during which she got pregnant (a circumstance also shared among her Fox crew). By the time of the baby shower, the marriage was pretty well finished and the affair, widely shared and equally denied, with Hannity begun. By the pandemic, she was living in a house almost side by side with Hannity's large property on Centre Island in Oyster Bay, and they shortly stopped pretending and, indeed, quickly assumed the role of King and Queen of Fox.

It was a kind of ultimate Fox marriage (without in fact benefit of marriage), two people who had found absolute satisfaction at Fox, who were indistinguishable from Fox, who did not really exist without Fox, completely addicted to the sound of their voices on the air and the feedback from that, and entirely understanding that Fox's air is the most sublime kind, speaking to the rapt and converted. A desperate need to be on television is the thing that distinguishes almost everybody on television. But for most the eternal, and often painful, struggle is to fit yourself into whatever television demands, and these are often shifting demands—and knowing, or at least they should be knowing, that inevitably it will go sideways on you. If Murdoch could not personally comprehend Hannity, if Ailes had thought he was squarely among television's stupids, if nearly everybody else in the building would frequently roll their eyes about him, Hannity, almost everyone appreciated, had achieved some true synthesis with the form. His combination of casual conspiracy, everyman alienation, easy indignation, and daily hunt for liberal hypocrisies, all in a package of certainty, ebullience, and good cheer, was the soothing, reassuring, and inspiring Fox voice. Ainsley would tell people Sean had never been abroad. This was humble brag, and, curiously, not true. But it defined a higher truth: he certainly had no use for being abroad, away from the Fox set, and seeking anything that might suggest urbanity, polish, culture, savoir faire.

Throughout his career Murdoch had found and come to trust such voices. He didn't necessarily understand them, nor respect them, nor certainly think they represented any truth or level of reason—he often tended to see the people in his newsrooms as errant children—but he recognized that they got the form and spoke to the audience (something he would not have been able to do). They were poets, his tabloid stars, and he was their proud publisher. The literal world might not understand this—the more liberal, the more literal—but Murdoch himself understood that news was a creative form.

So, yes, Hannity might be stupid, but he was also a genius (like Trump too). And among the many reflexes Murdoch had developed over his seventy years of doing this was to absolutely defend this kind of genius. It was not a commodity; it was not replaceable. He had to defend it. When his competitors—and everyone outside his own company was a potential competitor—attacked his people it was just further proof of their singularity and their strength.

Nonetheless, he wished he didn't have to deal with Hannity who was, as he had found so many other of his tabloid stars to be, a personal annoyance. Hannity was a thorn in his side—"He's the stupidest we have," said Murdoch to an acquaintance, as though making a considered evaluation—as Fox was a thorn in his side. But that was the nature of the editorial freedom that he had always so profitably been able to tolerate.

Anyway, they could even pay a billion to settle Dominion (this was suddenly the worst-case number being whispered at Fox). They could, unhappily, *extremely unhappily*. But it would not break the bank. Murdoch had lost various billions many times before. Having said that, to save a buck, yes, he would certainly sacrifice Hannity—but quietly. His son was for it. If anyone had to go, Hannity for sure. Lachlan wondered if they could bump Tucker up to two hours and extend his bigger ratings into Hannity's hour, and at much lower cost. Indeed, there was Hannity's big pay package—losing that would be a sweetener for everyone.

But being forced into a public admission, Fox being publicly brought to its knees, that would cost a much greater part of Fox's value than any size cash settlement. And of the ninety-one-year-old man's effort over all these years to protect free speech, or his version of it. Everybody knew this was the old man's line in the sand. He simply was not going to be publicly forced to do anything, most of all to suggest that he had any doubts, discomfort, guilt, or embarrassment about what he had ever published or put on the air. To publicly sacrifice Hannity—or anyone in his newsrooms—would be to sacrifice himself. He would not be publicly humbled, would rather pay massively not to admit that there might be anything fundamentally wrong with his newsrooms. That was the precedent that in seventy years he had never permitted, the weakness he had never shown, the question he had never allowed anyone to suspect he might entertain (except for phone hacking, the grievous affair, still the most painful of his long life). In the face of how many years of people demanding that he reproach himself for what he did, he'd done everything possible to hold tough. And he had. Fuck them.

Still, this was business. And, in the end, Hannity's fate, if it were a silent fate, was *just* business. He was hardly wedded to Hannity, only the idea of Hannity. Murdoch used the Australian word "larrikin" here—a rogue, hooligan, thug, a fool with a heart of gold—seeing this as a perfect tabloid sensibility. Hannity was an idiot and if he could quietly get rid of him without sacrificing the principle of having to protect his idiots . . . why not? He would not trade the principle, but he was willing to secretly trade Hannity for a settlement. Jeff Zucker, the CNN chief, had been kicked out of his job for having a longtime affair with another CNN executive. Lachlan proposed that this could be the official excuse for bouncing Hannity, the Ainsley thing.

Of course, what the other side wanted was precisely the opposite, to publicly prevail against the principle that a Murdoch newsroom could say anything it wanted. They wanted heads and they wanted a public admission (as well as wanting the dough).

"We'll take it to the Supreme Court," Viet Dinh kept saying, with increasing stupidity, as subpoenas were landing on Fox doorsteps, including Murdoch's own, and as a trial date was set for the spring.

11

Tucker

UR-TEXT

Murdoch was increasingly agitated by reports about Carlson's possible presidential ambition—and the presumption of it. Whatever he might believe about politics, he thought politicians should be politicians.

"These are all fucking amateurs," he had taken to saying, dismissing most of the new generation of Trump politicians. He suspected—as did some of his other children—that Lachlan was encouraging Carlson in this preposterous thinking, that his son was fantasizing about electing a president. Lachlan had made a flippant remark to his father about what he might become in a Carlson administration. Was Carlson really thinking about running? His father sent him to find out if there was any truth to this at all.

Carlson laughed it off—and then shortly set out for Iowa.

The Hotel Fort, a redbrick building of substantial solemnity and little distinction, is a Des Moines institution, a hundred-year point of Midwest civic pride and usefulness, giving downtown a sense of early twentieth-century weight and authority. Every midsize city had its

leading hotel and department store. The Fort hosted local grandees, a
surprising number of visiting presidents, a century of traveling salesmen, and innumerable out-of-town journalists covering the quadren-
nial Iowa Republican and Democratic caucus race. Tucker Carlson
had been here in the run-up to the 2000 presidential election covering
the George W. Bush campaign and missing his three-year-old son's
birthday.

The hotel was then a musty, overstuffed, heavy-curtain affair in
need of an upgrade. The upgrade it eventually got, as part of Hilton's
Curio Collection, turned it into a medium-range boutique hotel with
little ornament, stain-resistant carpeting, central air-conditioning no
less noisy than the window units it replaced, and curtailed services. The
Fort is now connected to the rest of downtown Des Moines through a
series of labyrinthine pathways between buildings called the "Skywalk,"
as desultory as most airport passageways, designed to protect Iowans
from their bad weather, and where Carlson, in July, having flown in
(commercial) from his Maine island accompanied by his nephew and
college roommate, got lost coming back from dinner.

Quite a nostalgist, Carlson was back staying at the Fort to address
the Family Leadership Summit, a right-wing Christian group that had
come to assume great prominence in Christian Iowa because of its
record in hosting successful presidential aspirants (Donald Trump in
2015) and in turning out participants in the Iowa caucuses.

There are those who come here planning presidential runs, or to
shore up right-wing Christian support, or generally on the fundraising
hustings. And those who come to promote various versions of agitprop,
radio shows, political nonprofits, right-wing books and films. But there
are some, like Trump addressing the Family Summit—indeed, perhaps
Trump is the model—who come to see if they, being who they are, that
is, reluctant if not phobic churchgoers, effective atheists even, can yet
thread the needle with the Christian right.

It might be possible to argue, as some in the Trump camp did, that

it was precisely his lack of churchiness and ritual (and smarmy) sanctimony that made someone like Trump—and perhaps Carlson, the dis-
passionate Episcopalian—a contrast gainer alongside so many other
right-wing Jesus voices. Still, even if there was an increasingly less-
churchy conservative hard core, the religious right could certainly
not be discounted. The Family Leadership Summit was, for that,
a pretty good focus group for how much the religious right might
accept a conservative secularity if it yet delivered on their issues.
Could Carlson, for instance, come into this heartland and achieve a
level of Christian adulation without the ritual bromides and blah blah of
so many other less gifted rhetoricians? Of course, Carlson coming here,
to the Family Summit, was an indication that he full well understood
the power of the religious right, which, for religious groups, was almost
as good as smarmy sanctimony, and that it was a hedge against what
could, he suspected, become at any moment an uncertain future at Fox.

The morning of the event, Carlson was holding court before a gag-
gle of political ops and right-wing media types in the Fort's new coffee
shop, with its wide variety of sugar-coated brunch options.

The subtext was a presidential run, and semipublic agonizing about
whether he should do it. Implicit, there was simply no one else. Nobody
not corrupt, venal, stupid. But the sub-subtext was whether he could do
this without Fox. And not just being off Fox. The network's connection
to its biggest star might seem rapt—"crush" was the word often used
about Lachlan Murdoch's regard for Tucker. But, in the maelstrom of
the ever increasing passions around Carlson, he had become more and
more convinced that some nameless day of reckoning lay in his future.

"I can be totally fucking honest with myself here. Fox goes away like
that. Perfectly possible. Likely! I believe that. I think that's realistic. And
I could be taken out back and shot at any time."

He saw himself easily off Fox, and quite possibly *deplatformed* by it,
trying to imagine all that he had to say and having no place to say it—
again, what choice would he have but to run for president?

Carlson's opening page is always the sorry state of the nation. For an outwardly jovial person, his is an unrelenting bleak vision, even a dystopian one. There was no happiness in the American soul, neither liberal ones nor conservative ones, he said, beginning to work himself up in the coffee shop. There was psychic misery everywhere. There were no possibilities of fulfillment or contentment because the culture had delegitimized all those things that had once brought fulfillment and contentment. There was a collapse of morality. A topline point that might appeal to the Christian right. But what he specifically meant was honesty, and personal courage, and individual ethos (that is, not sexual or religious propriety)—not too dissimilar from the Ayn Rand-ish right-wing line. But on top of this was a catchall of moral compasses that included novels, poetry, art, Hunter Thompson—this is where you found truth (his wife, he noted, was a great reader). Along with truth, beauty was the issue here. Beauty had been lost—sacrificed. He had always refused to take his children to Disney World, not because, in the manner of Ron DeSantis, it had increasingly liberal values, but because it was . . . ugly. Disgusting. Disconnected from nature. Plastic. (Of course, Disney's LGBTQ-positive stand *was* another break from nature.) His villains were not so much atheists and liberals, but bureaucrats, apparatchiks, the cogs in the machine, and the collaborators with it. That is to say, the establishment: most politicians, corporate anything, the academy, the *New York Times*, the networks, and even, yes, the Murdochs. The problem with all the above was not their views or politics, but that they were inherently corrupt. Dishonest, unprincipled, bent, with an allegiance to no one and nothing except the expedient and themselves. They stood for nothing. Weak, lily-livered, gutless, craven, grotesque.

This was bleak, but he rendered his critique with incredulity, guffaws, head-smacking disbelief, laughter—that Tucker laugh—at the living, breathing absurdity of it all. The world might be in desperate condition but the critique of it was something to relish. No, he wasn't lecturing. He was riffing—and interrupting his riff to smile for a dozen selfies, as more and more coffee shop patrons gathered around. He was painting the picture of the hell in which we lived. It was Brueghel, a vivid, *compelling*, ugly chaos.

And this was just prelude. Because the real problem was ... the Republicans. The Democrats were so bad it wasn't necessary to mention them. And just because they were so bad you might think it gave a pass to the Republicans. But open your eyes, man! Could there be worse? Mitch McConnell, "that miserable old woman." He ticked the Republicans off with rank contempt. And Donald Trump? Nothing was required here more than a facial expression—and a suggestion, darkly, that Trump could portend a violent future. There was only one politician he spoke surprisingly well about: Barack Obama. In 2004, at the Democratic Convention in Boston, which Carlson was covering as a journalist (although by then, arguably, more of a television personality than a journalist), he had been walking along the street and a little-known local Chicago politician jumped out of an SUV—in the car with Jesse Jackson Jr., the troubled young scion, who Carlson would also express sympathy for—to shake his hand and to say how much he admired him if not agreed with him.

Anyway, this all set the scene and cleared the way, of course, for Tucker himself—the last honest man standing.

Attending the Tucker riff in the Fort coffee shop was Sam Nunberg— one of those curious, Zelig-like political figures whose inexplicable and marginal existence yet somehow greases the wheels of politics. Nunberg, who had recently lost thirty pounds, but still roly-poly in his T-shirt, was an acolyte of the political conniver, trickster, and Trump ally Roger Stone. Nunberg had become the first staff adviser to Donald Trump's incipient 2016 presidential campaign. He was generally credited with the idea to build the Wall across the Mexican border and thereby solve the immigration problem—and Trump's limited command of it. A drunk and cocaine addict who lived with his parents in Manhattan, Nunberg had been forced out of the growing Trump campaign—not necessarily because he was a drunk or a cocaine addict—by the next wave of more seasoned political operatives who came into the Trump campaign (who themselves would be forced out). While Nunberg's enmity toward Trump was without limits, he was credited with keen insight into him ("You don't get it, do you? He's an idiot!"), making him, in the Trump White House years, one of the go-to media sources to explain the inexplicable. His notorious on-air breakdown in 2018—multiple radio and television appearances after a night of prostitutes and cocaine—only increased his standing as an unfiltered and savant-like and useful-idiot source. It was Nunberg—nine months sober and having left Manhattan for a rented condo in West Palm Beach—who, at the behest of Family Leadership impresario Bob Vander Plaats, helped recruit Tucker. Now, he was here as a semiofficial hanger-on (in politics nearly a formal job) and an ad hoc Tucker Carlson press attaché, charged with dropping hints, lest it be missed, that Tucker might be a 2024 candidate.

Hence, Tucker's dissing of all other Republicans.

Of course, Nunberg dropping such hints did not at all mean Tucker was truly interested in being a candidate. While Nunberg was supplying the formal sourcing for reporters looking to report that Tucker was interested, he was at the same time telling reporters that, in his personal view, there was no chance that Tucker would actually run, which was part of how you teased out a run.

And that's what Carlson said too, he wasn't running—of course not! Who would want to do this? What reason could there be? He was not crazy. He liked to work alone. He never wanted to be told what to say. Never wanted to say what was supposed to be said. No way. But . . . if circumstances presented themselves, he said, if there was such a hopeless vacuum of Republicans, which [laugh] it certainly seemed like there was, well, then . . . you know . . . nobody could predict the political future in this day and age.

But, anyway, if there were to be future possibilities, he needed the Christians first not to reject him, and then to actively adore him.

The conservative cause, and its great half century of success, has been in strong part built around local and state organizations, becoming roughly akin to the great age of labor unions that built and supported the Democratic Party. The strength of the Democratic Party had stood on the backs of young men with young families engaged with a good-day's-work-for-a-good-day's-pay labor principles in the workplace. The conservative cause rested on the shoulders of older people, often retirees with ample time on their hands, connected to church and church-related organizations fundamentally opposed to the liberals' lack of church guidance and ever growing atheism, as well as defending guns, decrying abortion, and ferreting out new and appalling culture issues—the Fox audience.

Such was the Family Leadership Summit. Nearly two thousand people—attendance buoyed by the recent overturning of *Roe v. Wade* and by Carlson's fame—the overwhelming number over the age of sixty, had turned out for the 2022 summit. Almost all of them would be active participants and often dedicated organizers in the Republican presidential caucus in Iowa.

At most trade, association, and special interest conferences, participants tend to turn the gatherings into social and networking affairs, gravitating to hallways as speakers deliver pro forma remarks in half-empty auditoriums. The hallways in the vast meeting center in Des Moines were empty enough to suggest that the summit was a bust (in another corner there was a robust meeting of Iowa meat producers). But, in fact, the near two thousand elderly attendees (paying $75 per person) were attentively glued to their chairs (many had ambulatory problems) for the full day of speeches and presentations.

Speakers offered nothing they hadn't heard before. It was all straightforward in its Christian hortatory—the enemy: "Marxists, abortionists, and Hillary Clinton." Its prescription was an only lightly veiled radical dismantling of the political order. This included a lengthy and in-the-weeds presentation about a "convention of states," and a detailed explanation of how the Constitution offered a way around the pernicious and unholy weight of the federal government. States' rights was once the call of the segregationist South and it had returned with vigor as the blue/red schism deepened, and now as an overturned *Roe v. Wade* gave each state its own reproductive say-so. This proposed convention of states, however, was an effort not just to assert states' rights but to assert the *right* of states, through a constitutional overhaul, to impose, among other things, gun rights and abortion restrictions across all the other states. This had as much of a chance of success as overturning *Roe v. Wade* might once have seemed to have (not so much an ironical point as one about the random nature of perfect storms). But, nevertheless, a convention of states was a compelling vision of right-wing hope and a path to righteousness and vindication—a cool fix.

The catechism here was precise. There was no deviation. It was all call and response.

Standing outside the dogma, it was virulent, harsh, incomprehensible stuff. Inside it was just the common language of people who spoke no other—shared, direct, evocative, familiar, meaningful, reassuring. Nothing rankled. Easy listening.

Iowa governor Kim Reynolds was passionately opposed to transgender girls competing against other girls in sports events. Iowa senator Chuck Grassley, as well known for his conservatism as he was, at eighty-eight, for his political longevity, took personal credit as the ranking Republican on the Senate Judiciary Committee for the Supreme Court's conservative majority and, hence, the overturning of *Roe v. Wade* (the holiest of issues). But the politicians were wan figures beside the true rhetoricians, the conservative media performers.

Here was the stark contrast. Here were the amateurs Murdoch decried and who Fox cultivated. The conservative media—talk radio, cable news, religious programming, social media, and internet broadcasting—had nurtured a generation of inspirational speakers. They offered everything the dead language of politics did not. There was drama, there was story, there was a personal connection, there was a voice, there was a learned and professional understanding of the elements of narrative. The standard language of politics was policy prescription. This new political language was entirely theatrical, washed of all bureaucratic nuance. Conservative politics was relaunched in so many ways with Ronald Reagan, but perhaps no aspect was so important in his model as speaking technique and a crowd-pleasing performance. Indeed, while the conventional political career was electoral, lawyerly, administrative, and bureaucratic—Murdoch's kind of political people—conservative media had expanded politics out to lucrative performing careers. Fox itself may have established conservatism as a major media business, but more and more it occupied just a place in an industry that continued to expand around it.

Steve Deace, taking the Family Summit stage, was the son of a fourteen-year-old single mother, who was spared his own abortion by God's grace, and survived, by God's further grace, an abusive stepfather his mother married at seventeen. This was the personal basis on which he was confirmed into Christian politics and an inspirational career. Opposing same-sex marriage (as well as abortion) and a proponent of the birther conspiracy theories about Barack Obama, and, between stints on talk radio, a political operative for Ted Cruz, he had found a growing audience on former Fox host Glenn Beck's internet radio network, working his way into the top list of podcasts. His 2021 book *Faucian Bargain: The Most Powerful and Dangerous Bureaucrat in American History* had made it onto the *New York Times* bestseller list. He was now producing his 2016 novel *A Nefarious Plot*, a barn burner about a death row convict and his possession by the devil, a torrid philosophic inquiry into good and evil, as a feature film, financing it with righteous money and vowing that Hollywood studios would never be permitted to dilute its message about the demons threatening so many aspects of American life. And here was the movie trailer, screened for the first time—the wretched convict and the devil speaking through him. Anyway, it was all better than the standard dull dry bones of politics, bringing much of the crowd to its feet.

The question hanging portentously over the gathering was about the inclination and will to go beyond Donald Trump. With DeSantis quickly rising, with some polls closing in toward a contested center, and with various indictments threatening the former president, it was possible—well, it *might* be possible—that this was a hinge moment. The ritual nod to Trump by each speaker might not have seemed to produce the same ritual applause in return. There were MAGA hats, but not on everyone. So possibly—*possibly*—it was up for grabs. But who? Was DeSantis a true new inspiration or merely a hopeful default back to normal, and, after Trump, could normal—and that was DeSantis's likely secret, and perhaps fatal flaw, that he was normal and would soon enough be rattling those dull dry bones—ever be enough? What if Republicans were hooked on performance? On event? On voice? On talking some kind of visceral talk? On superior riffing? On what the Democrats, in their version of show business, used to call charisma. On all these years of listening to the confidences and hyperbole and insinuations and joyful in-your-faceness of right-wing performers.

Even at fifty-three, Tucker Carlson could still be a son to the great majority of people in the room. His youthfulness—chinos, sports jacket, and full head of hair (he was fond of explaining that he only ever used Dr. Bronner's; fond of explaining too the value of his daily saunas)— was quite a beacon in this crowd. It was the youthful look of a prep-school teacher—the hip teacher—from 1985 (indeed, when Tucker was in prep school), which might have been suspect in the cornfields, but perhaps Iowans, even on a slow-boat gentrification schedule, had now caught up to 1985.

Here was Carlson's aw-shucks, everyman, conversational warm-up,

following the political requirement to bow to all things Iowa and extol
the pleasures of being in a place where, all things being equal, no one
might otherwise come ("bad weather makes good people"; and the
food—"if you like steak and donuts—my two favorite foods"). He had
done, he said, the "full Grassley," that is, the Iowa senator's practice of
visiting every one of Iowa's ninety-nine counties on his election year
campaign swings—which, in Carlson's case, was probably literally not
true, but quite enough to embrace the sentiment, and, too, a forward-
looking nod for the benefit of press and faithful (he knew what it would
take to run for president).

But his true opening salvo was to define the vacuum of Republican
leadership. "It's easy to let your own side slide, when the other side is
unacceptable." Ergo, the Republicans, by their failure to seize the day,
were leaving the possibility open that the rough beast Democrats would
stay in power. Hence, the issue was not *really* abortion, guns, judges,
taxes, LGBTQ, and all the other heartfelt Republican issues for which
they might legitimately claim great progress if not outright success—
all issues that Carlson himself might be less a local yokel about—but
the greater, darker, ever coming, always corrupting threat of liberalism
itself. Like communism. Like cancer. And it wasn't even so much liberalism, but the *people* who are liberals, their certainty and condescension
and contempt and absolute determination to remake the world as they
wanted, and with a total absence of awareness that that's what they are
doing. Understand that the true moral fight is upon us—upon the good
Christian burghers of Iowa—and if they—*they*—do not find the right
person to lead it the moral void will keep closing in. Yes, who will lead?
Choose carefully now.

It was, just this side of explicitly, not Trump. It was certainly not
Nikki Haley—in his polite-boy way he yet managed to spit out her name.
Hardly a mention of the rising Florida governor. There was nobody.
And it was noon and the darkness was closing in—framed by his hyena
laugh at the absurdity of the choices at hand. A vacuum indeed.

You see, the issue wasn't merely abortion. It was so much beyond that—meaning he could skip over the prosaic debate and therefore, he, a relativist not to mention wan Episcopalian, avoid the absolutist demands of the argument. No, the true issue was . . . *corporations.* (He could easily snatch that liberal issue!) It was the insidious corporate state, with its shadowy means and motives and intentions, that wanted abortions, that advocated such ugliness, that could accept such soul-killing solutions—such final solutions. Corporations were trying to sell lives of anomie, loneliness, lack of meaning, torpor, conformity, Stepfordism—hence, abortion.

Abortion, a life without family, lives without the stability of true roles and true identities—to be precluded from calling a woman a woman!—was all a terrible break with . . . *nature.* And, indeed—of course!—it was the liberals, the bureaucrats, the corporate interests, modernity itself that had broken us from our vital connection to all things nurturing and good. The Democrats, and their corporate allies, were making a case against having children (not, mind you, a case about when life begins, or women's rights, or bodily autonomy), "making a case for devoting your life to some soulless multinational corporation," making a case against fulfillment and human destiny. "When I hear people say abortion is the most important right we have, I ask myself what are they really saying?" (He swallows here, "I am a pro-lifer just to be completely clear," because it is not necessarily clear, and rushes on.) "We can debate the issue, and what limits should be put on it"—as though acknowledging at the very least a middle ground, otherwise anathema to most of the people here—"but that's not really the issue." He pivots: "We need to take three steps back and ask what they are really saying. The corporations—Citibank, Nike, Dick's Sporting Goods—these huge companies that are affirmatively promoting abortions—are really saying, 'it is more important to serve us than to have a family. You'll be happier as you rise within our company than you would be by having your own children.'"

And nobody among the two thousand Family Leadership Summit attendees seemed to be scratching their heads. Nobody seemed to be aware that this was a bit of bait and switch on their most fundamental issue. That Carlson was expressly not arguing about murdering babies but, rather, was confirming that there was a choice that you could make—family or career—and arguing that he thought family was a better choice. Such was the power of the rhetorician. Everybody was rapt. His story was simply more interesting, more embracing, more modern—and, yes, smarter—than the street soldiers of the pro-life movement and their political yes-men. (Of course, everybody here might leave this hall and ten minutes later say, hey, whatever happened to the bloody cut-up fetus.)

And Ukraine. But the issue was *not* Ukraine, no way, that was just pure sideshow—the *issue* was . . . social media and its manipulation of what was important, urgent, and *true*. ("Twitter isn't real. It's the domain of super unhappy people with empty personal lives and creepy political agendas.") He absolved himself of any allegiance to Vladimir Putin ("despite what you may have heard") and instead made his position a resistance to the false flags of social media and its pernicious and creepy hold over the political system and indeed daily life. Ukraine, he declared, in his personal estimation, was on the top of no American's list of the most important issues facing them. Hence . . . to resist the rush to support and arm Ukraine was to resist the evils of social media that had put Ukraine on the top of that list. (No head-scratching evident.)

Here was the rhetorical strategy. You might think the issue is this, but in that you have been misled—by politicians, by social media, by corporations, by special interests—and the true story is really *this*, so much more important, and dramatic, and meaningful, and threatening, and represented by Carlson. And he veered: "The rising price of fossil fuel is not an inconvenience, it is the whole story . . . Cheap energy, cheap fossil fuel, make the difference between living in the Central African Republic and Des Moines. . . . If you were to isolate the single largest factor contributing to prosperity, life expectancy, politically placid systems, it would be cheap fossil fuels . . . Gasoline is autonomy. I get my truck and drive anywhere I want. It's freedom." So much for global warming.

Indeed, the abortion debate and the Ukraine debate and global warming added up to the same issue, which all Republican candidates should be focused on: "Can your children grow up in a country pretty much like the one you grew up in?" Main Street, Rotary Club, chicken-in-every-pot, local department stores, real food not fast food (he was here in Ailes's perpetual 1965, but also back to Murdoch's country club Republican before all this became a racial clarion call).

He veered again: "And beauty. I don't think I've ever heard a politician mention beauty. And I think about it constantly. In the beginning was the word. It starts with the word, always. It's how we know if an ideology is a good one. Noble ideologies produce beautiful results. Poisonous ideologies produce ugliness. Super simple. There's a reason the architecture in Bulgaria in 1975 was hideous. Because Sofia in 1975 was controlled by the Soviet Union. Soviet architecture was horrifying. . . . Beauty reminds you that the more important things in life are eternal, unchanging. Beauty has balance, symmetry, and grace. Why? Because it's derived from nature. It's derived from God's creation."

Here, in this somewhat bewildering loop, he had seemingly—you could feel the audience's relief—returned to an acceptable Christian point.

"Virtually everything built after 1945 is less attractive, less pleasing, less human-centered than everything built before. The closer you get to our current moment everything looks like a dollar store. And the Republican party has somehow found itself in the position of having to defend the aesthetics of the dollar store. Some libertarian think tank was paid to tell us that the dollar store is attractive? . . . The Republican party should be for nature."

Again, some worry. Was nature . . . "the environment"? No, he confirmed, nature was God, and he took a stab at ugly wind turbines. Plus, boys and girls. One or the other. Nature. Beauty. So, yes, this worked for conservative Iowa Christians.

Every issue was elevated to metaphor. If the usual politician's strategy—indeed, a middle of the road politician—was to avoid commitment, and to preserve wiggle room, with a cotton-mouthed, policy-oriented, as opaque as possible response, Carlson had found a much defter, more enticing way. You made the human condition your true issue and then threw everything into a unified field theory of happiness and unhappiness, of righteousness and corruption.

It seemed startlingly likely that his source material, his ur-text, was from Norman Mailer, of whom Carlson was an avid fan, and who in the 1950s and 1960s, at his most soaring moments of drug and alcohol inspiration, bundled technology, bureaucracy, corporations, the break from nature, the threat to masculinity, and rotten architecture ("bad men make bad buildings, and bad buildings make bad men") into the prime cause of cancer and left-wing worldview. Indeed, there were many counter-intuitive connections between Carlson and the literature of the 1960s—Mailer, Richard Brautigan, Kurt Vonnegut, Joseph Heller, Ken Kesey, and of course J. D. Salinger. Carlson might very well, in his prep-school dorm room in the 1980s, found himself in a heady weekend transformed by these writers.

The fact that he was now serving this 1960s lefty, drug and psychiatric culture point of view to the Iowa Christians was both topsy-turvy and for Carlson part of the logic of how far liberal America had spun away from the good. These were all writers whose dubious status, if not formal cancellation, among liberals now, only supported—at least in Carlson's own mind—his detestation of the modern left and its snobberies, hypocrisies, and certainties. It was, too, it was possible to suspect, on Carlson's part his own private joke.

Or truly messianic.

12

Elisabeth

THE THIRD OPTION

Not long after Murdoch's ninetieth birthday party in October 2021, he closed on his $200 million purchase of a 340,000-acre ranch near Yellowstone National Park in Montana. This was supposed to be safe space. Jerry Hall was less fond of New York City, which Murdoch preferred; their alternative life in London, Hall's social epicenter, was exhausting him. Her children, that is, Mick Jagger's children, with their rock 'n' roll heirs' social life, often kept her out after Murdoch's bedtime. But Montana was also to be at a distance from his children. His youngest children, Grace and Chloe, were, Hall felt, spying on her and supplying their mother with gossip that echoed through overlapping social circles. They hate me, she told friends, and on one occasion, had sneaked shellfish into a pasta dish, despite being aware of her intense shellfish allergy.

Hall had felt particularly excluded by Elisabeth Murdoch from the ninetieth-birthday preparations and worn out by the Murdoch family's seething state of political play leading up to the event. The level of rancor among the Murdochs was at a consuming pitch, with each child mapping out competing territorial claims on their father, his aftermath, and his legacy. Equally, the Murdoch children saw Hall as trying to use COVID as the cause to become their father's gatekeeper, keeping them at bay.

Elisabeth told friends she "did not like what she was seeing." She felt Hall's social demands were humiliating her father. He was literally falling asleep in his soup, with Hall's friends and family chortling around him. Murdoch seemed always drawn to women who took over, who supplied the conversation and the social face that he could not—in Hall's case this included frequently lecturing her husband on all manner of his lack of social justice concerns as well as the horror of Fox News.

It is a converging line, the wherewithal and desires of one of the world's richest and most powerful men to live his life with impunity, and the frailty and dependence of his age. How the line proceeds is often about who has best positioned themselves at the point of convergence. Hall failed to secure that spot.

Prompted by his daughter Elisabeth, Hall's walking papers were delivered (as they were delivered to Wendi Murdoch, prompted by what his children believed were her casual humiliations of their father, including less than discreet infidelities). Hall released a statement saying she was "truly devastated," but at the same time friends were delegated to say she was "vastly relieved" to be out of the Murdoch drama.

Among the social events of the summer—which Hall had been planning to attend with her husband—was the marriage of Elisabeth's daughter Charlotte. The background here was, as in all things in the Murdoch family, both scripted by the prerogatives of a billionaire clan—the entire family arriving in England on their separate private planes for the nuptials—and so glaringly off script that no one in the family seemed to bear, beyond the money, any relationship to the other. Murdoch, having tried to draw a tight and exclusive circle, had instead produced not just enemy camps but nearly foreign entities.

Charlotte, twenty-one—her age not the foremost issue of her marital suitability—was the daughter of Elisabeth and Matthew Freud. There were many in-law issues in the Murdoch family, with each sibling's spouse invariably finding him- or herself in an oppositional role to the larger family dysfunction and dependence, and each the subject at some level of disapproval from the patriarch, suspicious around all outsiders. But none so much as Freud, who he treated as a predatory intruder (James's wife, Kathryn Hufschmid, would come to take this place).

Murdoch's relationship with his daughter had dramatically improved since her divorce in 2014 from Freud—or "Fraud" as he was frequently known in Murdoch circles.

The heavily tattooed Charlotte, in addition to being very young to get married, had already a long history of drug abuse. She'd met her husband-to-be in rehab. They were now both trying to forge rock careers. Charlotte was just the most obvious cautionary tale about the now rather sprawling fourth generation of the Murdoch dynasty (dating from Murdoch's father, Keith), and how, everyone acknowledged, it would inevitably diverge farther and be so much less, if at all, in the Murdoch mold (no one from the fourth generation had yet to enter the family business). The Murdochs liked to come back to the Kennedy family model of generational torch passing (notably, they never used what might be the more apt royal family model) as a way to characterize both the uniqueness of their experience and their determination to achieve on their own terms—with each of Murdoch's three media-executive children believing their careers were profiles in exceptional accomplishment. But the Kennedy model, with drug problems, botched or nonexistent careers, and strands of strange politics, also suggested how far, alas, from the tree the apple can fall. For the Murdochs, you could measure the distance the family had traveled from Elisabeth's own 1993 Beverly Hills society wedding with the Reagans to this rehab rock-hopefuls union in the Cotswolds.

The glaring sore thumb in the middle of the wedding party, besides the two brothers blanking each other, and the rehab couple, was the ninety-one-year-old patriarch, still, at least in every sentient aspect, the 1950s son of Victorian-age Scottish Presbyterian parents, with his unreconstructed buttoned-down never acknowledge weakness or sentiment conservatism. Here he was amidst his great family dysfunction, every aspect of which you could read as a personal repudiation of him—indeed, with the event itself in its way quite a celebration of a new live-and-let-live, suck-it-up-this-is-life, we're-all-a-mess ethos among the Murdochs.

The bride's mother, along with the bride, was dressed entirely in white. Holding on to Elisabeth's arm was her father, dressed also entirely in a white ensemble, but for a pair of red velvet shoes—possibly the most unlikely red velvet shoes ever worn. You might chart Murdoch's sartorial style by the women who were dressing him at any given time, from British pinstripes in his early London years and, later, bland New York business dress when Anna was dressing him, and sleeker designer stuff when Wendi ran the wardrobe, and then wealthy retiree-casual, even jeans, when Jerry made her contribution. But now the white and red were at a level so uncharacteristic, so curated, so ridiculous as to suggest a whole new level of influence and control. He was dressed like Elisabeth's doll—so here was the obvious and grim question after the guffaws: who was running the show?

The nonagenarian's health and basic sentience had long been the most significant question at the heart of his Après-moi-le-déluge empire. It was answered by extremes of wishfulness and denial. Everything might change after he fell or fell apart but, the assumption went, until then everything would safely stay pretty much the same. During his sixties, when the subject of succession began to lurk in the background (there was his promise to his then wife that he would retire), through his seventies, and then through his eighties, when it was the glaring backdrop right up until the sale of so much of the company when he was eighty-seven, when succession might seem to have come to a resolution, with Lachlan running what was left of the company, he was yet still on the job, reliably, relentlessly, doggedly showing up. And, yet, he was eighty-eight, eighty-nine, ninety, and now ninety-one . . .

His mother had lived to a hundred and three, but his father to only sixty-seven.

Beginning at some unclear point, but probably most pointedly around 2014, after his fail-safe executives had been ousted or sidelined and his sons installed, the question, in low tones, became more or less a constant: *How does he seem?*

The answer always, nearly without equivocation, was . . . "good," "fine," "great," "sharp as a tack." This was part of the required affect, but it also skirted the parallel issue, that it was, and always had been, hard to tell. Murdoch, by character, often seemed out of it. For at least ten years, he had been, much more than was comfortable for the people most frequently around him, dropping off in midsentence. He went into some fugue state. The first time you witnessed this it was possible to think he had stopped breathing, even that he had just died. Gary Ginsberg, one of his longtime and most sentry-like PR aides, would rush to explain that this was him concentrating—*really*. And then there was his natural low mumble, in which he might go on, or wander off, at some length, with almost no one, except the most practiced, comprehending what he was saying or even the subject he was on—he certainly appeared to be in a different, remote world. Once, when the Murdochs were living in a Trump-named-and-managed building on Park Avenue while a renovation of their Fifth Avenue triplex was underway, Trump himself boarded the elevator along with Murdoch and a guest. Murdoch offered a neighborly greeting to Trump in his fitful, mumbling, and distracted manner. "Let me ask you," Trump said, turning to Murdoch's guest. "Do you ever understand a word he's saying?"

True, at the same time, he could seem determined, decisive, focused, but this was side by side with the out-of-it stuff. And yes, this had come to seem natural, or the natural Murdoch state. He might not be an introspective person, assuredly he was not, and yet he clearly lived a lot of the time alone in his head. This partly had to do with the fact that he really did have a pared-down range of interests. And if you were not as eager as he was to talk about one of those interests, then, in short order, he would be less present, or as though gone. He was hopeless in groups where the conversation and the topics at hand were likely to be random (at gatherings he always surrounded himself, or handlers knew to surround him, with practiced insiders). And he wasn't hearing that well. There too his was spectrum nature—"he's actually very, very shy," was the explanation here—a lack of ability to appreciate social cues and, as the years went on, with power and money insulating him, less and less interest in trying. This was Murdoch.

One problem this presented is that you might not necessarily know if this was *just* Murdoch, the way he always was, or a sign of an approaching senility, or his characteristic mental wandering merging with senility.

His age, through his seventies and much of his eighties, was almost never spoken of by his retainers—and a subject he himself steered carefully clear of. But at ninety-one, his age elasticity was now sorely limited.

So what did this mean for *right now*?

There was, surely, a resolution destined to happen post Murdoch, possibly a fiery one. But there was also, potentially no less significant, a gentler curve toward a resolution that might already be in progress, one that could be just as profound.

He was a black box and there was only limited access to it. Still . . .

Elisabeth was the daughter most notably on-site for him, a situation not meaningfully different for a world-beating billionaire than in any other family of older children and old parents where the daughter with the closest proximity invariably gets the job. In addition to the Kennedys, as their historical model, the Murdochs had often looked to other media families for more practical concerns—the Sulzbergers at the *New York Times* and the way they had structured the family's long-term control of their paper; the Bancrofts, who had owned the *Wall Street Journal* until Murdoch had snatched it away from them; the Bingham family in Kentucky, with the *Courier-Journal* and their statewide media empire, dissolving into acrimony; and more recently and vividly the Redstones, owners of Viacom and CBS, with the patriarch sinking into his humiliating final years. Murdoch had often ridiculed Sumner Redstone, seven years Murdoch's senior, for having "lost his marbles" in his last years. In fact, that billionaire's decline, while more operatic than most, was also similar, in its helplessness, to many ordinary folk. Redstone's daughter, Shari, overlooking their fraught relationship, became his support and protector in the end. The difference from ordinary-folk families is that this enabled her to take over his multibillion-dollar enterprise, a cautionary note not lost on the Murdoch brothers.

Elisabeth was not only distinguished as the most demonstrably successful businessperson among her siblings, but also distinguished among her brothers as the sibling speaking to them both. And, too, by removing herself from leadership contention—or, as a woman, being sidelined from it—she had no direct stake in the longtime head-to-head management deadlock. Still, friends always counseled that it was unwise to underestimate her ambition, that it was stronger for being thwarted.

Unlike her brother James, she was eager to protect and venerate her father; unlike her brother Lachlan, she was not directly dependent on her father's favor for her future. She had accrued, as the family voice of reason and moderation, and as the child offering her father the most drama-free care and attention, a special influence with him.

She also knew the key to his heart: return everything to a discussion of the fundamentals and variables of the media business. It was Murdoch's inexhaustible subject—his spectrum retreat. He could out-consider almost anyone on both the micro-elements and the grander trends (and on the currents of gossip underlying so much movement in the business). For years and years, he had been talking his executives into the ground on the industry's day-to-day chessboard developments.

Elisabeth was using her great fortune to invest across the gamut of new media opportunities, from her hundred-million-dollar club, to streaming projects, to podcasts, to social media content. Transfixed, her father could sit for hours, for long periods almost motionless, absorbing the details.

Whether by strategy or for further diversion, Elisabeth began to go deep with him into the transforming drama of the television industry. And here she was able to connect two divergent topics: her family's dysfunction and the industry's dysfunction.

In her family's dysfunction, her father, after siding with her brother James to sell the greater part of the company to Disney, had as consolation prize settled the remainder—most notably Fox News—on her brother Lachlan. But the continuing hostility between the brothers had left their father annoyed with and confounded by them both—Lachlan for his passivity (and unaccountable retreat to Australia) and James for his refusal to leave well enough alone.

And while that dysfunction appeared to be intractable there was, Elisabeth advanced, a yet even bigger dysfunctional picture.

Beyond their other problems, where they were as a family was in the cable television business, with its declining and aging audiences, falling ad revenues, massive new sources of competition, radically changing technologies. If within recent memory being in the cable business meant you had hit the jackpot, now it was infused with pathos. Forget Tucker, and Hannity, and Trump. Cable television, no matter how successful, was just never going to become more valuable than it was today.

Was there a business case for owning a single cable station? To ask the question was the answer.

Her brothers—both looking at this largely through the noneconomic logic of their personal $2 billion—had staked out diametrically opposite answers to this question, not only from each other but from her. Lachlan wanted Fox because it had been given to him and he was going to rise to the occasion of running it as his father had more than risen to the occasion of running what had been given him. James wanted to take Fox from his brother to cleanse the family legacy and demonstrate his own next-gen Murdoch or anti-Murdoch leadership.

Elisabeth, in her intimate moments with her aging father, letting it percolate with him, now staked out a third opposing position, a business solution to the family's existential ailment: sell it. Sell Fox.

There may not be a lot of obvious buyers, no conservative media owners big enough for such a deal, and no private equity players eager for the controversy that might come with even this cash flow windfall. But there didn't have to be. The Murdochs could just pile on a lot of debt to the company, take their cash, roll Fox out as an independent public company, and wash their hands of it. Fuck it. The money they might fairly get for their stake would be greater now than it ever will be again. Take it.

Here was an argument that her father, doddering on her arm in his red shoes, no matter how much he was or wasn't with it, and after a lifetime of bitterness toward every penny he had ever left on the table, might likely appreciate.

13

Hannity

POTUS

There was an internal number said to be floating around at Fox that broke down exactly how much money could be credited to Donald Trump, that is, the *additional* money, the pure profit, Fox had made since Trump became the main draw, and what kind of rating boost each time slot had gotten because of him. Trump had heard about this too. Or perhaps he started the rumor. Whatever, there was no one who wouldn't agree that the golden goose that was Fox was so much fatter since Trump.

Since the 2020 election the specter of no more Trump had haunted American media everywhere, no more so than at Fox. But, in a media miracle, he hadn't gone away. Now, though, they were trying to chase him away.

"Fucking no Trump? Are they fucking out of their minds? You want to tell me what Fox is without Trump? Trump is running and we're what? For Ron DeSantis? And when he loses? Tell me? Biden? Is that it?" Hannity was flabbergasted.

And maybe that was it. Murdoch just seemed crazed on the subject.

How far would they let the channel fall? Would they destroy their network because they hated the guy Fox had made president?

It was impossible to imagine Fox without Trump. For Hannity, and he'd bet for at least a 30 audience share, there was no Fox without Trump. Hannity, seeing everything at stake, was not going to let that happen.

But here he was between the Murdochs, who wanted to fuck Trump, and Trump, who wouldn't get in gear: "I'd rather be playing golf."

"That's Trump," said Hannity, not so much frustrated, or resigned, but just riding the Trump train, which had so far been a magical trip.

Hannity was confident that when Trump *really* started to run everything would change, and it would be the Murdochs who'd understand they'd be fucked without him.

Still, it was Hannity's job to be the voice of political reason, quite a fantastic development in and of itself.

By the late summer of 2022, a few months before the midterm elections, Trump had over a hundred million dollars in the bank, raised mostly on the basis of his ceaseless railing against his stolen election, of which, so far, he had hardly spent a dime. The dire calls over the summer to Hannity from Trump's circle were all about enlisting Hannity to get Trump to open the spigots for Republican candidates.

"This is the moment. You've got to support your guys," Hannity pushed POTUS.

"They've got my endorsement. There's nothing more valuable than that."

"Spending reinforces that."

"It doesn't need reinforcing. They'll be fine. This is my money. People gave it for *my* election. They don't want me spending it on other people."

"Mr. President, I really think they want you to do what is best."

"That's what I'm doing!"

The Dominion stuff was getting intense and freaking out everybody—everybody had gotten subpoenas; everybody's emails were going to be ripped open. And, even more than usual, the Murdochs were being such assholes. Rupert had launched the *Post* and *Journal* against Trump—basically stuff that could have been written by the liberal press. (Trump, for one, did not see a meaningful difference between Fox and Murdoch's papers—it was all Rupert!) Suzanne Scott was afraid for her job and desperately trying to read the Murdoch tea leaves—DJT came to DC, his first time since leaving office, and Fox didn't run a single second of his return speech (though it did go live to a competing speech by Mike Pence—*Mike Pence!*). And the truth was that a lot of the women and the whole libertarian bunch at Fox—a surprising number of less-than-orthodox right-wingers—weren't comfortable with the *Roe v. Wade* stuff. So blame *that* on Trump. What's more, OAN, the smallest conservative news network, but unwavering in its abject support for Trump, was practically dead, dropped by key cable carriers. And the Dominion suit could bankrupt Newsmax. Trump and his Dominion bullshit, for which Hannity had carried so much water, were, ironically, going to destroy the competition leaving Fox free to become less-Trump television.

Plus, Tucker wanted Trump out of the picture. An open Republican primary with Carlson as potential kingmaker—with Carlson as potential *king*—was what he wanted.

That's what it came down to. The Carlson-dominated right-wing future or the Trump-Hannity-dominated right-wing future. Fuck the Murdochs and DeSantis.

This was a ratings game, and, to Hannity, in a ratings game it was surely ludicrous not to bet on Donald Trump. Betting on Donald Trump and his ratings had made Sean Hannity—this is what he sometimes said after a few drinks—the most powerful man in television, even the second-most-powerful man in America.

But where did he go with that?

He could walk away from Fox and suffer no strains whatsoever on his or even his children's future lifestyle. Unlike Carlson, Ingraham, or really anyone else at Fox, Hannity had true fuck-you money. The others at Fox, with no other place to go, would all be financially stranded, as well as just plain washed up.

And yet Hannity, however rich, *because* he was so rich—and counting on becoming richer—was right where he wanted to be. In him, Trump and Fox had merged.

A reliable character in television news portrayals is the dumb-ox anchor, a person so dense that his lack of self-consciousness, total absence of concern about television's inherent stupidities, and eagerness to hold on to what in a world outside of television he might never have reasonably achieved give him startling advantages and, as well, an annoying swagger. At Fox, Hannity was that character. Ailes's twenty years of joking about Hannity's what-me-worry intelligence level and happy lack of self-awareness had made dumb Sean a given, a happy one (Sean's general good cheer was real) of Fox culture.

His devotion to Donald Trump was seen as a natural alignment, and somehow confirmation of Trump's own natural place at the network. There might in fact be great skepticism at Fox about Trump, even personal incredulity and embarrassment, but then again there was that about Hannity too—everybody was accustomed to suspending disbelief, the by-product of ratings success.

Hannity could merrily pursue inane and convoluted conspiracy theories, theories often shared by Trump (or vice versa), laughable to most everyone else at Fox, because Fox had provided a thriving audience for them. Both Hannity and Trump were garrulous to such an extreme that they occupied a force field shielding themselves from any exterior conditions or even information; this constant exercising of their own voice made them not just their own best entertainment but supremely talented broadcasters (most people on television had long ago lost the ability to listen). What might otherwise have been a babbling force field separating them (Trump did not like listening to anybody to an extreme that distinguished him even among television people) became their connection. A direct line to the president gave Hannity both the kind of ratings and the centrality he had never managed to achieve in his long career; and, for Trump, with a kind of primitive respect for anyone with command of a television audience, Hannity's eagerness to channel him turned them into beloved and dependent brothers. Each was quite likely the only person the other *actually* did pause and listen to.

Murdoch had dwelled on this, prodding Lachlan to find out exactly how much his anchor was talking to the president. With his conventional understanding of power, it confused Murdoch that anyone, particularly someone who worked for him, would have better access to power than he had. There was also his irritation that his employee might be encouraging Trump in his Trumpness. Here was the feeling that he could never directly acknowledge, but that seeped out in the low growl sounds he made: he ran the great Trump enabling machine.

Within the Trump White House, Hannity was seen as the effective real chief of staff, with each of the various actual chiefs of staff having to forge a relationship with Hannity as the person who could reliably and, in his manner, sagaciously offer advice and counsel to the president. Within Fox, Hannity was the curia cardinal who most reliably had the ear of the pope, not just one who could carry messages from him, but who could put words in his mouth. The fact that it was the dumb-ox anchor who had achieved this place further magnified the internal Trump irreality at the network and reinforced the obvious: it was absurd and certainly pointless to question it—so just give in.

From Hannity's point of view, he never had it so good. Trump was his buffer against Fox personalities smarter than him and with better ratings (for years he had put up with O'Reilly mocking him), and against Fox management, thin as it may have been, and, perhaps, most of all, against the Murdochs, baffled and cowed by Trump, who they disdained but who had become their inadvertent profit center. In addition, Trump gave Hannity new, undreamed of, possibilities. He could be anything he basically wanted to be—an ambassador, secretary of state, whatever. Trump, in fact, was always offering him this or that high-ranking job (with Trump himself often forgetting that the place he most wanted Hannity to be was prime time on Fox). Everybody in the White House sucked up to him. As Trump transformed America, and Fox, he had transformed Hannity's world.

Of course, Trump was also an act of great fortitude. Trump, Hannity recognized, was quite the dumber ox. Hannity, in Trump's presence, was the clear contrast gainer, the considered, methodical, thoughtful one. Hannity had developed a wide tolerance for Trump's wild swings, his shoot-from-the-hip fantasies, his constant and random character assassinations. He waited him out (storing up all the shit Trump said as gossip to be retailed later). He consulted the people around Trump for their estimation of the boss's general equilibrium and the seriousness of his passing obsessions (as they in turn consulted him).

Trump was Trump and he, Hannity, for the sake of Fox, and for his own sake, as well as the country's, had learned how to handle him. Once, he and Carlson had raced across Europe against each other on the promise of a Trump interview. That was Trump shit. In the end, he had given back-to-back interviews to both Hannity *and* Carlson. Trump had played them for two hours of airtime. He was a genius. But it was genius shit like that that upset the Murdochs. The man was incapable of staying within the lines.

Hannity accepted a sense of personal responsibility for the unruly child. Given Trump's value to him, and the network, and the country, Hannity had a strong interest in protecting the president, not least in protecting him from himself. In this, in his own mind, Hannity had become something like a statesman.

People outside Fox, but also many people inside, really were incapable of understanding the history he was making. Hannity did not *need* anybody's respect, but he deserved it.

No one ever in the history of television news had ever achieved such direct political power as Sean Hannity.

"Donald J. Trump is my business," he declared without journalistic equivocation.

Hannity's efforts during the 2020 election, as he viewed with growing alarm the consistent wrongheadedness if not incompetence of the campaign—daily calls with the president; then, in Trump's name, calling campaign officials to give instructions and strategy—began to reflect most of all his own desperation that he, Hannity, might lose his place at the top of the world.

But after the initial incomprehension of the 2020 election news, Hannity, like Trump, understood that nothing had ended here, that the business went on—precisely because the ratings went on! It was about Trump refusing to go away, of continuing to make the news.

If Trump continued to exist on television (on Fox), then he continued to exist in the hearts and minds of the American people (the MAGA people), which was just democracy.

"That's why the Dominion thing is so fucked up. People believe what they believe and they have the absolute right to believe it. There are tons of people saying it's not true and yet tons of people still believe it. So fuck everybody. A lot of good people have made up their minds," defended Hannity, with a logic that to him seemed perfectly transparent.

When Murdoch was brought reports of Hannity's on- and off-air defense of Fox's postelection coverage, he perhaps seemed to justify his anchor: "He's retarded, like most Americans."

On January 6, and in the aftermath, Hannity's immediate panic and consternation was not principally about the events themselves but that, as he said widely that day, Trump was "ruining everything." But any doubts Hannity might have had, expressed in his frantic messages to Trump and Mark Meadows, Trump's actual chief of staff, as the January 6 calamity unfolded, were quickly swallowed by the theme, in all its ratings, fundraising, and organizational and imaginative possibilities, of the restoration of the Trump White House. The exhilaration of the new Trump fight for vindication was already feeling like they were back on top. It was, as he was seeing it in the weeks after Election Day, "eight more years of Donald Trump" (the POTUS of Mar-a-Lago and then back in the White House).

While liberal media tried to wish Trump away and saw a commensurate drop in ratings, Fox remained (mostly) defender and torch bearer sustaining its great Trump ratings run. Hannity continued as Trump's point person at Fox, Trump's most influential media and political adviser, and as one of the people who might benefit most from Trump's return to the White House. Trump, even more than Hannity's own serious fortune, had become the anchorman's true fuck-you money.

But then that had started to seriously change. The message from the second floor was not clear but it *was* clear. The last time Hannity had gotten Trump on the air was his phoner in April. Then, after that, there was the bullshit new policy about phoners. And DeSantis, the new Murdoch boy. It was as though they were in some other universe that people could think DeSantis, that stiff, had any future against Donald Trump. If you thought the Dominion story was crazy ("It got a little out of control," Hannity admitted), the DeSantis story, making him out to be the fucking front-runner, wiping up Donald J. Trump, was crazier. How messed up was this? Ailes had always said that the Murdochs had to be kept away from Fox because the real truth was that they were snobs. They thought they knew better. And what's more, they weren't *real* Americans—to state the obvious. And what you had to remember, *always* had to remember, was that Fox had an audience of real Americans, and if you had to ask who they were then you were never going to know. That's how fucked up this was; Fox was out of touch with itself.

Ron DeSantis. It wasn't thinking straight. How could you even think of giving up on Donald Trump? This was *Donald Trump*! Hannity might be dumb, but he knew that never before had a television news network been so identified with the news itself—nobody had ever been as skilled at getting attention as Donald Trump and it was to Fox News that people came to give him attention.

"I don't get this, do you get this?" Hannity went around asking everybody. "In what universe does this make sense?"

And Trump was starting to get pissed. In what universe would you piss off Donald Trump? In what universe would you ever sell Donald Trump short?

Whenever he had been with Murdoch—"a weird dude"—he'd thought that Murdoch had condescended to him, had barely tried to be pleasant. If that was smart, Hannity was grateful to be stupid. Ron DeSantis, it boggled the mind.

So the fact is that Sean Hannity was going to have to save Fox for Trump—and save Trump for Fox. He got it that a lot of people at Fox did not like Trump. ("What can you say? He's Trump.") But everybody was being too smart for their own good. Trump was not going away. He was going to run for president again and it would all happen once more (and more like 2016 than 2020!). He wondered, with some anticipation, what the Murdochs would do when they realized that Trump was not going away—in fact, was here to stay.

And Tucker. He was too smart for his own good too. Tucker wanted to compete with Trump. Again, if that was smart, Hannity was just fine with being stupid.

Hannity wanted to be the power behind the throne—and he wanted to be on television. He could not understand the problem. Fox was as profitable as it had ever been. His own ratings were as high as they had ever been—and so were basically everybody else's. Fox had no real competition in conservative media. In fact, while every other kind of media was coming undone, Fox was basically unchanging. Plus, Donald Trump was going to run for president again. What more could they want? You would trade that in for Ron DeSantis? Why? Because you felt guilty over Donald Trump? Come on. Shame had no place in television.

Anyway, Trump just had to get in gear, and it would all fall into place. No matter how much anyone might want to change it, Fox would do what it did best.

14

Suzanne Scott

THE SECOND FLOOR

There was no question that Suzanne Scott was going to lose her job. Everybody knew this. Lachlan Murdoch was saying as much. Plus, Rupert was down on her. The shadow of the Dominion lawsuit hovered over her head. Murdoch's—and the Murdoch family's—confidante in London Rebekah Brooks, who ran Murdoch's international operation, had put her finger on Scott as a clear issue in this obstinate Dominion problem, which desperately needed someone upon whom the blame might fall. (Brooks worked for Murdoch's other company News Corp., but her influence was wide.) There really seemed to be no question: a shake-up was coming.

Fox was making more money than it ever had and yet it all felt so precarious. Dominion, Trump, ninety-one-year-old Rupert, Lachlan off spearfishing, Viet Dinh drunk (this was a report in fact spread by Scott), Tucker off the reservation; who was in charge? That question echoed throughout Murdochland.

Joel Klein, the former New York City schools chancellor, who Murdoch had crushed on and given wide portfolio in the empire before

Dinh had eased him out, ran into a journalist who closely covered Fox
one day when he was out walking with his wife Nicole Seligman, the
former CEO of Sony, on Madison Avenue, and right away plunged into
the head-slapping question: "Who is in charge over there?"

It was a situation of no one taking anything in hand that surely
needed to be taken in hand.

Scott was the obvious place to begin. "It's happening," Viet Dinh told
a colleague who was wondering why it was taking so long. (Dinh and
Scott were a yin and yang on many issues of Fox blame—if Dinh wasn't
being blamed that meant Scott must be.) Fox people were telling outside reporters it was certain to happen, and, at the same time, fishing
for news about when. *By the summer* was the timetable. But then July
was finished. So the question began to reverse itself. Not as to when she
would lose her job, but why did she still have it?

The answers seemed to confirm both why she *should* be fired and
why perhaps she *couldn't* be. She *should* be because she had not, in the
four years she'd been the Fox chief, taken a forward leadership spot
at the network. Her lack of vision, her lack of ownership, her lack of
command had more and more moved the Fox shadow over the Murdochs' head (if she was the weak executive, then the Murdochs were,
by default, the strong executives). The complex process of navigating
Fox out from under the Trump years toward some new model—one,
of course, as profitable—was Scott's job, but instead she was ducking
it, letting Fox continue on making its gigantic sums as though on auto-
pilot. But that was then the difficulty in getting rid of her, because she
had so successfully not put her name on anything, not stood out to any
degree at all. She was perhaps too small to take the blame. There was no
message in firing her.

Lachlan Murdoch proposed they put out some stories on Scott to
increase her profile, precisely so she could be fired—and, in fact, the
New York Times would duly oblige and positioned her as the fulcrum
Fox leader.

There was another reason why firing Scott made sense. She really was a representative of everything that Fox had been but which now the Murdochs wanted to undo—well, not undo the money it made but the aggro it was causing them. But this augured against that outcome too. In some sense it is much easier to fire big-name, hired-gun executives (of the kind James Murdoch had wanted to bring in when they jettisoned Ailes) than it is to fire executives whose careers are intricately tied into the very DNA of the organization's bureaucratic bloodstream. To say the least, Scott knew where the bodies were buried. She had been here literally from day one, a 1996 Ailes hire—one of the feisty, TV-savvy blondes he preferred ("TV is a blonde world, fire anybody who thinks they can change that"). But in Scott, they had gotten the exact opposite of Ailes—a woman for one, an executive who eschewed attention instead of seeking it, who had no instinct or appetite for a cult of personality, who had few if any personal politics, and who did not seek to run her own independent show, which is what they wanted. At the same time, in Scott, they got someone who didn't want to tamper with what Ailes had built. With something like modesty—or fear of the unknown—she understood that the Ailes formula was what made the money (and it continued to make astounding dough), so don't mess with it. The Murdochs wanted this too, without necessarily admitting it.

This was a good news/bad news situation. The money continued to roll in—and Fox continued to poison every aspect of the Murdoch family's presence in the world. That contradiction, seemingly unresolvable, so far continued to bind Scott to her job.

Post-Ailes, the Murdochs, in their initial period of paralysis—as surprised as anybody that they had succeeded in killing the king—had kept Ailes's management team, largely a team of yes-men, in place. Bill Shine, Ailes's loyal lieutenant and key apparatchik, stayed in place in the short term and was even given the impression that for the long term he might be cool. But to the extent that Ailes had created his hermetic North Korea, cut off from outside influences and basic social norms, everybody on the second floor—who had even visited the second floor—was pretty clearly complicit in his exclusive and often pervy world.

In the family politics, after Ailes's ouster, James Murdoch argued for a clean sweep, specifically wanting to bring in David Rhodes, the head of CBS News, who had begun his career working for Ailes at Fox, but now had mainstream cred too, and, in addition, was the brother of Ben Rhodes, ensconced as a senior foreign policy adviser in the Obama White House. "Heterodox" is how James billed him to lead the orthodox Fox world. Rupert and Lachlan resisted this professionalization of the network perhaps less because it so obviously seemed to presage a major change in the nature of Fox News than because James was so adamantly for it.

Instead, Rupert and Lachlan chose to look a management level down, though staying very much on Ailes's second floor—the floor where so many of his abuses occurred—and chose Scott, a woman, in official contrast to her misogynist predecessor.

Overnight, Scott became one of those people who had had absolutely no idea at all about what Ailes, with whom she had spent most of her career, had been up to or who he really was. She spoke in deeply wounded terms about the mark Ailes had left on everyone—the world wondering if *she* had traded sex to get hired, or if she knew, or if she had helped cover it up. This was sexism in itself, outrageous if you knew anything about her at all! Why, even to imply it . . . The unfairness!

Anyway, for the Murdochs, this was declared another country and Scott was officially deemed de-Ailesified. Scott knew how the place worked and seemed ready to do what they wanted her to do—even if they did not know what that was.

Among her management virtues was that she was a woman, but, that said, she was a woman. And this was very much a man's network world, one led by a chairman who was uncomfortable with women

and fronted by on-air right-wing men professionally (as well as personally) unreconstructed in their gender views, so she was paired in
the management suite with Jay Wallace, another Fox lifer. The married
Wallace, however, it turned out, was having a not very well-hidden
affair—open snogging in the Fox parking garage—with his young assistant. In bureaucratic terms, this elevated Scott and made Wallace her
human shield. She was protected by his glaring vulnerability.

This became her management signature, to rise higher and retreat
farther, and push others into the line of fire. Fox, which had always been
the least bureaucratic news operation in television, with Ailes's voice
and priorities leading and dominating, became as layered, encumbered,
and abstruse as any other (television news operations build bureaucra-
cies not least of all to keep managers far from the controversies and the
ensuing blame that news invariably creates).

Here was a puzzling metamorphosis for so many people at Fox
with whom Scott had grown up, confided in, and seemingly been a
happy office cohort. Especially for the tight circle of women at Fox,
joined together by the network's parallel gender cultures—like nuns and
priests, in its fashion—who regarded Scott's rise as hopeful evidence of
cultural transformation. For them, Scott's there-but-not-there elevation was a fact of significant meaning although no one could decipher
what that meaning necessarily was—except it certainly didn't seem to
be transformation.

Ainsley Earhardt, who often seemed notable for saying out loud
what you were supposed to recognize but keep to yourself, kept widely
asking if anyone knew why Suzanne wouldn't speak to her anymore.

Dinh and the Murdochs talked only to Scott (except for Lachlan,
who talked also to Carlson), and Scott talked only to her three lieutenants, the VPs of morning, daytime, and prime time, who carried the
"second floor" word. The days of Ailes on the phone, or Ailes directly
through your IFB earpiece—prompting, cajoling, joking—the man in

whose name everything occurred, now became simply an amorphous second floor. "Here's what the second floor is thinking today . . ." It was Mafia stuff with no fingerprints or way to track anything back to any person on the second floor. Except it wasn't even a hidden capo giving untraceable orders, rather it was someone who herself had no real standing or authority to give orders, and who certainly did not want to be held accountable for those directions she might be forced to offer. This is partly what happens when you inherit the most profitable business that an industry has ever known—any change is likely to get you blamed for screwing it up.

The three principals—the two Murdochs, father and son, and Dinh—had little experience in television, almost no background at all in programming, and an aversion to talent management. What's more, Murdoch, when he was uncertain and frustrated, and faced with circumstances that he did not understand, tended to retreat into his place of inexpressible mutterings. Lachlan Murdoch seemed to choose more and more not to interpret his father, and instead to temporize, equivocate, and avoid standing in on his behalf. For Dinh, structural paralysis accommodated his long afternoon lunches. Nobody was eager for anyone to do anything.

Murdoch's lightbulb ideas of how to reinvent Fox, when they intruded, seemed to revolve around many of the conservative figures he had worked with in the past—Bill Kristol, who had started the conservative magazine the *Weekly Standard*, which Murdoch had backed; John Podhoretz, a longtime columnist at the *New York Post*; various gray figures from the *Wall Street Journal*. On his own say-so, he gave a show, in the low-rated Sunday evening slot, to Steve Hilton, a Brit with libertarian views, unknown in the US market, who had been an adviser to former conservative prime minister David Cameron, quite a liberal in the Fox context. Murdoch's impulses were all toward conservatives not just mostly of a different generation, but ones who had rejected Trump, the MAGA movement, and all the things that Fox had most successfully embraced and become. Lachlan, Dinh, and Scott, understanding that this path was going to benefit no one, let most of Murdoch's brainstorms drift off.

Indeed, the general drifting off and indecision and putting things on the table to give some further thought to, ably facilitated by a CEO gone to ground in the maximum number of earthly time zones away, became the fundamental management methodology.

"If it's not broken don't fix it," said Lachlan Murdoch, describing for a friend his guiding view of running Fox.

The friend expressed surprise, recalling that Lachlan had said that Fox was a train wreck heading for a crash.

"Isn't everything?" the scion replied.

One of the things that frequently drifted off were the meetings with Scott. They just didn't happen, leaving Scott to take no action, and to leave well enough (that is, the fundamental profit engine) alone.

The principle that all power vacuums are inevitably filled was curiously contradicted here—nobody stepped up, nobody wanted to. The less you did, the more Fox appeared to do what it did best, to become what its audience wanted. In this it was one of the most successful media paradigms ever created, no more so than after Donald Trump's election.

"I create monsters and they bring in monster ratings, but then I have to control them," Ailes often expounded.

In fact, it appeared that not controlling them brought in even greater monster ratings.

In Ailes's view you needed "persona—on-air persona." Persona, as Ailes described, was not a made-up or invented role, it was exposing your truer self. "They have to go with what they feel their authentic persona is, that's the only way they can go out and be compelling." It was the Strasberg Method. "They don't take off until they take that risk." And, indeed, that produced voices of a type that had never been heard on American television—not just voices of certain politics but voices at a new pitch, fever, and mania. A new reality.

But in seeing his people as actors, as extraordinary talent that he had created—or unleashed—he saw himself as the director. This was his ensemble, his orchestration, his show. This was his voice in your IFB.

As it happened, when that voice went away—not to be replaced by anything other than a vague "here's what the second floor is thinking . . ."—the personae became more vivid, the risks that were taken greater, the monsters off the leash altogether—and all this tied to the greatest persona, monster, risk taker in the land, *in American history,* who was living in the White House!—and the ratings soared.

The Murdochs, curiously, took this as confirmation of their management acumen. They had gotten rid of Ailes and things got even better! They weren't dependent on him. Just look at the results. Even if, at the same time, Fox was . . . well Fox. And becoming even more . . . *Fox.*

One thing the new Murdoch management did aggressively was control costs. Ailes, spending Murdoch's money, had an expansive view of what to do with it. Murdoch, spending his own money, set out to take back, new sheriff–like, what Ailes had spent.

Ailes had used Fox's great success as his own management tool. He paid his people (well, at least the men) at extraordinary levels. He bought loyalty and devotion—that's how much he was paying people (men). In the end, the great sums he heaped upon the men in his favor helped create the disparity that would contribute to pitting many of the women at Fox against him—what did they have to lose, really?

Melissa Francis, an on-air anchor and correspondent for Fox Business and Fox News, making $1 million a year, confronted the network with the wide disparity she had meticulously documented between the salaries of men and women at Fox. She sued; they fired her; then they thought better of it. Her settlement: $15 million.

But meanwhile, for the men on this incredible gravy train, the cash confirmed Ailes's genius and wisdom.

It pissed off Murdoch—one of his fundamental business beliefs being cheapness—to have to pay so much. He carried around salary lists, focused deeply, and with incredulity, on pay packages. Ever skeptical, if not averse, to women in the workplace, he now seemed to be delighted with the women at Fox because, compared to the men, they made so little.

The effect here, beyond annoyance and resentment on the part of the new post-Ailes personalities and stars—Carlson making a third of what Hannity made, even as his ratings climbed higher; Ingraham making much less—was to recast the hierarchy from top down to a satellite system. There was no central management. Everybody worked for themselves. Each an individual entrepreneur in the new far-right marketplace.

The satellite structure became even more clearly part of the basic relationship between talent and management with COVID protocols: everybody working in remote studios, no one even coming into the building, 1211 Sixth Avenue—ever.

The relationship to management consisted of nothing more than ratings. If you delivered ratings, you had delivered what was wanted. Like salesmen in the field phoning in orders. Scott had neither the authority, nor the interest, nor the reason—if the ratings were good—to alter this management relationship.

Indeed, for Fox talent, the relationship to Trump, and how his mercurial desires were managed, was vastly more important to success than the relationship with the second floor.

The full-scale panic that ensued after Election Day 2020, now encapsulated in the Dominion lawsuit, represented an end point in that long slide from Ailes's North Korea regime. At the moment of crisis, of internal contradictions so great that the system rebelled against itself—both undermining Trump and then rushing to do anything at all to save him—there was no message, no strategy, no controls, no communication, no agreement. No one in charge.

Anyway, the Murdochs weren't going to fire themselves. And probably not Dinh, their main guy and lieutenant, almost a family member (almost). So Scott, obviously. Right? The network CEO.

It had to be her. Everyone agreed.

15

Laura

THE BRAND

Laura Ingraham was willing to be what a Fox anchor needed to be. Every evening she seemed to push herself as far right as she must, an act, it often appeared, of supreme will. The one person who seemed to sympathize with her discomfort was Murdoch. "She's got a brain," was one of his excuses for her lower ratings. "She's not a crazy," he said in her defense. That she seemed desperately trying to be a crazy was beside the point. She was caught up in the same hard position that he was in: there was Fox and its burn-everything-down views on the one hand, and, well, a conservatism much more choosey about what had to go (mostly taxes) on the other. It was a disorienting delta for them both.

The conservative movement that had emerged with the Reagan years—a notable instance: the *Dartmouth Review*, and its small group that included Ingraham—was marked by its intellectual conceits and a Jesuitical debate style (with William F. Buckley Jr. still its highest exemplar). Out of this grew a circle of conservative media personalities, a protean new column of political activism, and the rise of the neocon front rank—with Murdoch's avid support. In 1995 he funded the launch of the *Weekly Standard*, a kind of in-house journal and promotional vehicle of the awakened (and ambitious) conservatives.

Murdoch's own views were generally anti-left, pro-business, suit-and-tie stuff, mostly unread and knee-jerk. The more pro-business the better: Reagan, Thatcher, good; a new conservative establishment versus a liberal establishment, sign him up; not much interested in social stuff. Arguably, his greater politics was the politics of expediency, and in the UK he threw over the Conservative party to support Tony Blair and New Labour. His conservatism aligned with the 9/11 terrorism state advocated by the neocons, often in the *Weekly Standard*, and the Bush administration. He was delighted to buy the *Wall Street Journal* whose pro-business, neocon editorial page was saying what he might have said (if he could articulate anything). But there, mostly, his views stopped advancing.

The increasing conservative hostility to immigration, its evangelical tilt and abortion politics, and the racial animosity toward Barack Obama, was outré and low-class stuff to Murdoch—however much all these empowered and profited Fox. Indeed, in 2008, perhaps because he could not control Fox and Ailes himself, he invited Ailes to accompany him to a sit-down with Obama, then the Democratic candidate, and sat passively by as Obama tongue-lashed Ailes about his racism—a moment Ailes would hold against both men.

Laura Ingraham had come of ideological age during the eighties and nineties, emerging among the new generation of conservative media personalities. Murdoch, who tended to form unwavering impressions, in this instance of Ingraham as a thinking man's Republican woman, saw her addition to the Fox lineup as a voice that he would appreciate and as part of his new, purposeful, I'm-in-charge post-Ailes engagement with the network.

Murdoch might have, mostly, succeeded in turning a blind eye from his own network's domination of the new right wing, but Ingraham, making her living as a conservative radio host, needed to keep up.

Except she kept falling behind. The gap between eighties and nineties conservatism and what had blossomed after the Iraq War, the financial meltdown, and with the presidency of Donald Trump was only by a factor smaller than the basic liberal-conservative divide—anti-worlds to each other. Indeed, many of the major players of the former tide had become anti-Trump figures, if not Democratic voters. Staying in the right-wing game required a level of reinvention and theatrical ability and, even, a balancing act on the mental health line (displayed in one example by Dinesh D'Souza, Ingraham's former boyfriend also out of Dartmouth, whose political extremes and provocations would result in a felony conviction and pardon from Donald Trump). Even before her unexpected move to Fox prime time, Ingraham's radio career had been dwindling off, her conservativism sounding more crabbed and unhappy than provocative and protean. At Fox, she had been given the opportunity to become a lightning rod but, as much as she tried, she often seemed exhausted by the effort.

Like Murdoch himself, Ingraham's long journey through the radical transformation of conservative politics, from Ronald Reagan and a new class of clever, often Ivy League, talking heads, through the rise of right-wing performers and entrepreneurs, to the new populist-nativist-racist-separatist heartland, had left her awkwardly off brand (and Fox could monitor such things—tracking minute-by-minute ratings had kept Fox, through two decades of tumult, remarkably on brand).

Brand was the point. Fox's was as vivid and powerful as any television network had ever been. You either capitulated to it, like Lachlan Murdoch, recognizing that it could not be altered or amended or redirected, so why try; or your alternative was just to destroy it, as James Murdoch seemed to understand; or like Tucker Carlson to wholly embrace it—if you did its power was yours. While all this would seem so obvious, the astonishing thing is that there were still some people yet obtuse in the face of it.

Murdoch himself certainly seemed this way, giving the impression that he regarded Fox as a place of lively, conservative-leaning repartee, or, at least, that he had decided this is what it could reasonably be. Why, he continued to wonder, weren't there "more voices" on the air? More (at least *some*) "serious" shows? Why, he wondered, wasn't Mitt Romney on more?

The Murdoch family itself, its cultural character, was so comically at odds with the Fox brand that you merely had to discount this as having no relationship to reality whatsoever—even though it was quite the pivotal factor. More aspirational than he could ever acknowledge (he might descend into mutterings about "tree huggers" and "champagne sippers"), Murdoch had watched his children become rich, internationally oriented socialites and corporate managers. That is, the diametrically opposite sensibility from Fox and its hoped-for sacking of the elites and their liberal social order.

Now, from London, from atop the media and celebrity social set, Elisabeth Murdoch was having a brainstorm. It was an audacious idea. And for anyone who had ever actually watched Fox News a baffling one.

For a talent programmer like Elisabeth Murdoch, Laura Ingraham's weakness in her time slot seemed like a fresh opportunity. The boss's daughter saw this through a normie lens: in television, better ratings were always on the horizon. Try something new and see if it works—it just might; what did you have to lose? Liz was good at this. In 2002 she brought the British show *Pop Idol* to her father. It was recast for the Fox Broadcasting Network (necessarily to be distinguished from the Fox News Channel in decades of brand confusion) as *American Idol*, and, over its fifteen seasons at Fox, it had become one of the most successful television shows of all time.

Now, Liz saw possibilities here at Fox that could boost ratings *and* solve other problems for her father and for the greater Murdoch interests. "We can make Fox work for us instead of just us working for it," she said, aptly diagnosing the problem, if overconfident about the solution.

In England during many of the COVID months, Murdoch had taken to showing up at his London operation—his once *mighty*, now shrunken London operation. The *News of the World*, the prime hacking offender, was closed, his son James run out of town, his newspapers separated from his larger empire, and his own political influence reduced to a shadow of its former self, the London operation—principally the *Sun*, the London *Times*, and the *Sunday Times*—had become quite a backwater. The *Sun*, once the cash flow engine of the empire, was now, like the *Times* and the *Sunday Times*, a money loser. Sky was his no more (sold to Comcast in 2018). The British operation was staffed by older Murdoch retainers, saddled with an aging tech infrastructure, and was generally resigned to a declining corporate existence. It was unclear how much Murdoch appreciated this and how much he truly yet saw himself as able to will the British media world to his vision. Anyway, stuck in London, he was grateful to have an office to go to.

The UK company was run by Rebekah Brooks, the former *Sun* editor who had been subjected to months and months in the dock at an Old Bailey trial for the phone hacking scandal. Brooks was a personal Murdoch favorite, indeed a family favorite, one of his few relationships that appeared to transcend business—"like a third daughter," was how it was reliably expressed, putting aside that he had an actual third and a fourth daughter. She had befriended Elisabeth upon her arrival in London in the 1990s and introduced her to Freud. She had been one of James's key lieutenants when he had the job of running the company's international side. After she was acquitted in the phone hacking scandal, she was rehired by Murdoch and shortly given the top job in London. She remained both deeply embedded in the Murdoch family and highly attuned to her opportunities in it. She had shifted her allegiance from James, in exile from the company, to Lachlan, whose leadership abilities, almost everyone agreed, needed support.

And, too, Rupert needed support, or at least distraction.

Brooks's great notion, as the newspapers she was running sank into

economic if not quite yet social irrelevance (although this was accelerating too), was, naturally, television. Except, of course, the company, once a dominant UK television presence, was a presence no
longer. What's more, the UK television market was neither fluid nor
thriving. But pay no attention, it was now a streaming world. Brooks's
save-the-store notion that Murdoch enthusiastically bought in to was
a streaming news channel that would be more Fox-like than other UK
video news, but not *that* Fox-like; in other words, quite the proposition
that Murdoch and his family might like for Fox News in the US (i.e., for
it not to be Fox).

Based on many promises of resources and staying power, David
Rhodes—the former Ailes lieutenant who had leapt into mainstream
media to run CBS News, and who James had tried to lure back to Fox
to make the network less like Fox—moved his family, wife and two
school-age children, to London to run the operation. Alas. Murdoch's
long history of digital initiatives—from Delphi, one of the first internet
ISPs, to a pre-Google web directory, to the Daily, an early tablet app,
to MySpace (at the time the largest social network shortly to be wiped
out by Facebook)—was one almost exclusively of failure. Here was no
different. Months after it began, Murdoch's British streaming network
was abandoned.

The failure was directly on Murdoch. He had eagerly made the project his own and then seemed unable to make decisions about it, or follow
through on plans. In fact, he never seemed to fully comprehend how the
streaming world might differ from cable news. His embarrassment now
seemed different, at ninety-one, from embarrassments past—beyond
screwup, pathos—and there was something of an all-hands effort on the
part of his closest circle to salvage the mess and help him save face.

Liz Murdoch and Rebekah Brooks together conceived a way to
reboot: call in their mutual friend Piers Morgan.

Tabloid news, Murdoch tabloid news, in the British and Australian
sense is populist, drama-and-conflict based, scandal (sex), crime and

blood, sports, and showbiz—with Morgan among its leading practitioners.

Morgan, fifty-five, had one of the most high-flying and dramatic careers in British tabloid journalism with a history of scoops, fistfights, lawsuits, and controversial personal financial dealings. A favored Murdoch protégé first at the *Sun* and then as the editor of the *News of the World*, who jumped, in a brief Murdoch betrayal, to the *Daily Mirror* where he was felled by a scandal of his own, publishing, unaware, faked photographs of British atrocities during the Iraq War. There followed bestselling books, a stint as Matthew Freud's partner in various media projects, a perch as an attention-getting columnist, a scabrous and inevitably news-breaking celebrity interview column in British *GQ*, his reinvention as a television presenter, and a contestant on Donald Trump's *Celebrity Apprentice*. In 2011, he replaced Larry King as CNN's prime-time anchor. His British accent and tabloid sensibility combined with a British sense of Americans as often psychotic (advocating gun control became one of Morgan's primary issues) made him quite a puzzle to the US audience and low ratings took him off the air in 2014. But within short order he returned to British television prominence as a host of ITV's morning show *Good Morning Britain*, where he generated daily contretemps and ratings-winning battles. In 2021, conceiving a passionate contempt for Meghan Markle and her besmirching of the royal family, he stormed off the set during a live broadcast when he was accused of racism toward Markle.

Not long afterward, his friends Elisabeth Murdoch and Rebekah Brooks saw their moment. The plan was that Morgan would become the headliner for Murdoch's revivified streaming service TalkTV, not an enviable job (in fact, nobody wanted it; a long negotiation with Andrew Neil, a conservative-leaning and news-making interviewer at the BBC had previously fallen apart). But it was made much more attractive in a package that would include carrying the show on Fox Nation, the digital Fox network, which had so far not fared well. But the true sweetener, in addition to a bundle of cash, was the quiet promise that Morgan could replace Laura Ingraham in the Fox prime-time schedule. In addition to solving the immediate problem of the lame streaming effort without a headliner, by slipping him into the Fox world he might be the Trojan horse for returning Fox to the true tabloid sensibility that it had in fact never had. And, in doing so, Liz the peacemaker went so far as to hope, might help find the point of accommodation between the two brothers. In other words, Ingraham who could not quite keep up with the demands of the Fox brand would now be replaced by someone, a gun-control, pro-choice advocate, anathema to it.

Here was also a curious effort to pay apparently no attention at all to Fox as it actually existed—as though Murdoch and *his* journalistic history were the bigger brand. Elisabeth Murdoch, who had lived in the UK for almost thirty years, and Brooks, who had hardly ever been out of the UK, seemed unconcerned with the fact that Morgan's conservatism—a British kind of conservatism—was a foreign language, an utterly dumbfounding one, in the Fox lexicon.

To boot, when his show debuted on the new streaming service—certainly demonstrating Elisabeth Murdoch's ability to make things happen in her father's empire—he landed an interview with Donald Trump and confronted him with the ludicrousness of his election fraud claims, whereupon Trump walked off the set. Delighting Rupert Murdoch, if no one else at Fox News.

As part of his forced introduction to the Fox world, he was promoted through a series of interviews on Fox shows, including with Hannity and Carlson (not Ingraham). In every instance he was greeted with on-air befuddlement. "Where, God, is Rupert going with this?" read the thought bubbles over everyone's heads. It was not even so much anger that management might be pointing in a new direction, or that some suit (or owner's daughter in a suit) might be tone deaf, but something so much more uncomprehending than that. There was just no point of commonality or intersection or mutual space or possibility, even if all the powers in the world commanded it, of Fox living in the same world as Piers Morgan. So much so that, really, it was not even worth anyone at Fox worrying about, no matter how much he was sponsored by those far above. Piers Morgan was just someone's (the sister's) asshole tragic folly, not worth another thought.

Except there, not to be missed—and the *Daily Mail*, delighted by Murdoch vulnerabilities, made sure no one would miss it—there was the patriarch in his white suit and red velvet shoes being paraded around by his daughter on the church grass.

Indeed, where was this going? And who was taking it there?

AUTUMN

16

Lachlan

IN PLAY

On September 15, 2022, Anne Kantor, eighty-six, one of Australia's leading philanthropists and a frequent supporter of left-wing causes in Australia, died after several months of illness. Her brother, Rupert, the long-suffering but loving and loyal brother to all his "socialist sisters," failed to show up for the funeral. For nearly forty years, Murdoch had been dependent on the votes of his three sisters and mother as he expanded his father's company. It was only in 1991 that he finally bought them out, forcing their hand—his mother sobbing at the conference table—and causing him a permanent sense of guilt that somehow bound Australia's most famous family even closer. That the only brother was absent from his sister's funeral (he and his sister Janet Calvert-Jones were the remaining siblings; their sister Helen Handbury had died at seventy-five in 2004) was immediately noted by the permanent rank of Murdoch sentinels in Australia. There could be only one reasonable explanation for why he wasn't there.

It was the earth-shattering one, the one that upended everything, the black and white reality—and the reminder to put in place what you need to have in place, to secure yourself for the coming storm, before it is too late.

Murdoch's impending death is always foreshadowed not just because it is an obvious, if not foremost, concern to a far-flung network of newsrooms around the world, anxious about their own fates, as well as always hungry for advance word. And he has almost died on many occasions, at least according to the informal death-watch wire. There was his prostate cancer; the time he was hit by the boom on one of the family boats; there was an incident, riding with Elisabeth, when he fell off his horse and could not seem to be revived; there was his bout with COVID, which hospitalized him early in the summer. The death watch is on a hair-trigger alarm given both his age and that these are mostly *his* newsrooms, and that this is what reporters do, keep watch over the lives of the very powerful, none so powerful as their owner.

He had planned to go to his sister's funeral. He had tried to go. The plane was on the tarmac ready to take him. But he just couldn't get on it. And with that—picture the clickety-clack of a telegraph—there was a collective updating of the Murdoch obit files already in the can around the world.

Most public companies—or truly public companies—are obsessed with succession and maintain standing board committees whose function is to deal with any events that might impede the chief executive's ability to do his or her job. But not Murdoch's kind of public company. He is treated more like the pope, or a Supreme Court justice, or any other position—not many such—in which a person might continue, at his own discretion, at any level of health and sentience. And, unlike the Vatican or the Court, where at least the internal gossip is trying to keep up with the reality, such gossip, at least among those in Murdoch world who *truly* know something—an extremely small group—is, at best, highly circumspect. Death yes, that would be news. Decline, don't speak openly about it.

To say that there would be corporate disarray after him would hardly be to grasp the true deluge of fundamental business issues: divided leadership; long-unresolved management conflicts; the inevitability of major asset sales (who, really, wanted all those money-losing newspapers?); and a strained structure of holdings sustained only by Murdoch's personal legacy and stature. And all this would need to be dealt with by the four siblings beset with their personal and ideological rivalries, two not speaking to each other—a divide now so deep there likely could never be a bridge—and all so vastly rich that even an obvious economic rationale would not necessarily unite them (and, that slight problem, of two lining up against two, with no tie-breaking mechanism). Death would certainly be the deluge, but what about now, this . . . drift, uncertainty, vacuum . . . ?

In the middle of October, News Corp and Fox Corp, those two separate public companies that are the pillars of the Murdoch family holdings, announced that they were considering a proposal to reunite nine years after being split apart, which would thereby give Lachlan Murdoch theoretical control over the entire Murdoch portfolio, consolidating his position now, under his father's name, while that was still possible.

The painful split of his holdings—painful for Murdoch himself, if for no one else—had occurred after the great phone hacking scandal of 2011. His own management team, with the push of his major shareholders, and the support of his children, had used the opportunity of the disgrace perpetuated by the Murdoch newspapers to protect the far larger and more lucrative entertainment assets from the newspapers' sour odor and, more importantly, from their low growth and dwindling markets.

In the new plan, all his worldwide print endeavors—the 70 percent of the Australian newspaper market he controlled; the *Sun*, the largest circulation paper in the UK, and the *Times* and *Sunday Times*, two of

Britain's "quality" papers; the *Wall Street Journal* and its Dow Jones data operation and the *New York Post* in the US; and the American and British book publishing giant HarperCollins—were to be siloed together into a separate public company under the legacy name News Corp. His entertainment holdings—movies, network TV, cable channels, sports programing licenses, and its interest in Hulu, the streaming service—were sequestered in another public company under the Twenty-First Century Fox name. Split apart, the only thing these two companies really had in common was that the Murdoch family continued to control both of them.

One model here, for both having taken the companies apart and now contemplating putting them back together, was the Redstone family holdings, which, in 2006, had been split into Viacom, largely a cable and movie company, and CBS, a television network. At the time of division, network television seemed to hopelessly lag behind the growth of cable. But when they were rejoined in 2019, the media industry judged those businesses hardly different at all. Together, they represented the industry "scale" so desperately and aggressively sought after—synergy, added clout, cost reductions.

But this was a hard argument to make about the Murdoch family's holdings. Newspapers and entertainment were now regarded as different enough from each other as to offer in combination neither scale nor efficiency. Indeed, newspapers had only become even more unwanted by and antithetical to the greater media business since the Murdoch companies had split. The proposition now to the Fox Corporation was, in effect, "Hey, great idea, let's buy a newspaper company!" In fact, each entity might penalize the other: the money-losing papers a drag on Fox's profits; the open-ended Dominion lawsuit (and the Smartmatic and further election suits to soon follow) together with the taint of Fox News serious negatives for News Corp.

The announcement that both companies were mutually exploring the combination suggested high-level contacts between management principals on both sides. That was true only in the theoretical sense. More exactly, it was an exploration between father and son, and possibly even more one-sided than that, this being Lachlan's strategic vision with his father's less than attentive approval.

Murdoch's interest here, to the extent that he had a clear interest, seemed wholly sentimental. Bringing the companies together again would cure an old wound; plus, his newspapers would regain the support of his far healthier media businesses; what's more, it would make it somewhat more difficult for his children to shed their newspaper legacy after his death (fuck them). Despite his public shareholders, here was a matter of the heart.

And there was another one, too: Murdoch's sentimental loyalty to the ever loyal Rebekah Brooks. With the radical changes in his companies over the last decade, few of his faithful retainers remained in place. But Murdoch's historic style was to manage through the people he was most comfortable with—he needed people who could interpret what he wanted. Brooks had remained in place for more than three decades and was among the closest corporate relationships he had.

Fifty-four in the fall of 2022, she had grown up in provincial England, and without much education joined *News of the World* in her teens. By thirty-two she was its editor. From the editorship of *News of the World*, she then took the editorship of the *Sun*, Murdoch's flagship in the UK. She married British television star Ross Kemp, a relationship that shortly became a tabloid staple itself, including headlines from a night in jail in 2005 from his charges that she assaulted him. Murdoch himself immediately appeared on the scene to offer his editor public support after her arrest. (She married racehorse trainer Charlie Brooks in 2009.) Murdoch often applied his favorite tabloid accolade to her: "larrikin," the kind of reprobate he liked.

From the *Sun*, she was promoted to CEO of all the Murdoch British papers, reporting to James Murdoch, then the London-based chairman of all the Murdoch European holdings, and became his key lieutenant and effective business partner. In 2011, taking some heat off James, she became the face of the company's phone hacking scandal, forced to resign from the company (receiving a $15 million payout), and enduring a six-month trial (during which it came out that she'd had a longtime affair with codefendant Andy Coulson, editor of *News of the World* and later press secretary to Prime Minister David Cameron). When she was acquitted, Murdoch immediately restored her to her position as CEO of his London papers.

A curious point is that, beyond her role as a family courtier, Brooks had a resounding lack of corporate success. Whether or not criminal behavior could be pinned on her, phone hacking occurred under her leadership and cost the company a newspaper and, ultimately, its ownership of Sky. What's more, on her watch, the *Sun*, once one of the profit drivers of the Murdoch empire, and the *Sunday Times*, the profitable sister of the always money-losing *Times*, both descended into the red (newspapers are, of course, a bad business, but the *Sun*'s most direct competitor, the *Daily Mail*, remains solidly profitable). But Brooks, now aligned with Lachlan Murdoch, became a strong advocate for the recombination. In this scenario, she would dislodge her current boss, Robert Thomson, the CEO of News Corp, and be positioned as Lachlan Murdoch's chief operating officer in the new combined company.

As so much in the company has so often and so inexplicably been designed with her benefit in mind, so too was this recombination. It was not a small consideration that Brooks's longtime friendship (despite some ups and downs) with Elisabeth Murdoch might soon enough be very valuable to Lachlan Murdoch. Nor was it to be missed that the clear drift of the company was to a kind of sentimental management—the nearest and dearest finally reaping their rewards.

On his part, Lachlan too had personal rather than business interests in the recombination. His larger plan seemed to be to merge the two entities and then to delist the combined company in the US and relist it—as it once had been—in Australia. This certainly made sense for

Lachlan because he and his family *lived* in Australia. What did not make sense is that he was currently running a largely US-based company from a home base many time zones away (or, conversely, spending too much time away from his family, and in a state of befuddled jet lag). But a company with an Australian headquarters at least made it easier to explain what its CEO was doing living there. Lachlan too believed that Australian corporate rules would give him greater leverage in a control fight with his siblings than would the state of Delaware where Fox was now corporately domiciled.

Lachlan's good friend (many would say his only friend) was Jamie Packer. For two generations, the Packer family with its substantial newspaper and television holdings had been the key rival to the Murdoch family. Rupert Murdoch and Kerry Packer—Jamie Packer's father—were the contrasting Australian tycoons, each inheriting his father's media holdings. Rupert was, by temperament, restrained, focused, bottom-line, and internationally oriented; Kerry Packer was an exuberant brawler and gambler (regularly staking millions of dollars in casinos around the world) with his business and identity committed to Australia. Both men and companies fought business battles— and street battles too. Murdoch thugs and Packer thugs squared off in a fight over the sale of a printing plant (Murdoch naturally had photographers there to record the fight and score a front-page scoop). It was less than a pleasant turn of events for Murdoch when his son Lachlan, in exile from his father's company, joined with Jamie Packer in various not too successful business deals. In recent years, and since the death of his father in 2005, Jamie Packer had sold much of his family's media holdings and profitably redirected his fortune into the gaming business—specifically Crown Resorts Limited, one of Australia's largest casino groups. Lachlan was now confiding his interest in doing something similar. In a roundabout rationale for the recombination, News Corp had certain gaming assets in Australia, which might give this plan a jump start—but in order for Lachlan to make use of those assets he had to control News Corp. And too, in Lachlan's plan, this could be the way to deal with Fox, use its great profits to buy gaming assets, which would in turn produce profits great enough for Fox not really to be vital to the company anymore. Voilà!

The failure to settle the Dominion suit and the announcement of the intention to put the Murdoch companies back together seemed almost of a piece: not just head-scratching but lacking any sense of business forethought or even adult supervision. The large institutional shareholders in both companies were alarmed by a scheme so heavily weighted to the Murdochs' personal interests.

Then, on second look, they began to sense opportunity.

Murdoch had a long and impressive history of doing things that, in many instances, the theoretical adults in the room would probably not have done. This included the move to London, and then the move to America, and the launching of a fourth television network. All were, in their way, quixotic. But Murdoch could make those moves, even with skeptical shareholders, because he had always made sure he held control of the voting shares. That was the fundamental nature of being Murdoch: it was always his call, no matter how incomprehensible, or, for that matter, economically unwise (he had kept the *New York Post*, the *Australian*, and the London *Times* alive for decades absorbing their grievous losses).

But this, putting the companies back together, would uniquely require approval of the plan by a majority of *all* their shareholders, not just the ones with voting rights. For the first time, the Murdochs' disenfranchised shareholders—understanding, though not always happily, that to be a Murdoch shareholder meant going along with what Murdoch wanted—would get a vote. What quite appeared to be a wholly noneconomic deal designed around the Murdochs' personal interests would now be subjected to a vote by people who had *only* an economic interest.

The overriding question was not which way such a vote would go,

but why would anyone have concocted such an obviously losing proposition in the first place.

And yet they had. This required each company to hire bankers
and impanel a committee of independent directors to analyze the proposal and to make a recommendation as to the economic benefits of
the combination. All of those involved in this time-consuming and
costly process could only have understood that because there was no
economic advantage—few cost savings in the combination of the two
businesses; no clear new opportunities in the relationships of publishing and video—the chances of them being able to recommend this deal
were near nil. And if there were any doubt—and there wasn't—outside
analysts began to weigh in on the foolishness of the plan. Likewise, funds
that controlled large blocks of heretofore nonvoting common shares
made it clear that they would vote against the deal.

In other words, it was all absurd.

The ninety-one-year-old man still officially in charge was either
incapable of appreciating any reality outside the one he had always
controlled, and now proceeded into the face of failure (and humiliation) based on a reflex that no advice (and there certainly was such
advice, if only asked for) was apparently able to dissuade him from. Or
he was just not paying attention. Or he had found some philosophical
peace and was letting his son and heir hang himself and thereby learn a
valuable lesson (even one that could result in his corporate death). Or
the heir had gone off half-cocked, rushing to squeeze the last drops of
authority out of his father's stature in a desperate attempt to secure as
much of his own future as possible.

Where were the advisers to say: *You'll instantly be shot down if you try
this.* Here you might be able to see the last days of a Murdoch presence:
an institutional incapacity among company executives, lawyers, board
members, even understanding the inevitable outcome, to challenge the
illusion that Murdoch was fully calling the shots.

Meanwhile, James was publicly opposing the deal. This provided an opportunity for James to privately offer investors and analysts—that is, the Street—his views on what the hell was going on inside a company entirely premised on trusting Murdoch's instincts if not sagacity. Flash: he couldn't be trusted any longer. Because the instincts at work here either were failing or were the instincts *not* of one of the most vaunted business minds of the era, however dulled by age, but of the callow son who had demonstrated no business acumen anywhere ever.

The precedent suddenly being established was that the Murdoch shareholders, who had never behaved like shareholders before, now had to pass judgment on the fate of their companies. I.e., Lachlan Murdoch should not get a free ride, or even the benefit of the doubt.

And shareholder disapproval of Lachlan's first major corporate move wasn't the least of it. The proposal to join the companies clearly suggested that greater shareholder value should be unlocked. If this merger was not the way, then what else might be? What else had been set in motion. If holding assets wasn't the best strategy, then that very obviously prompted the opposite approach: sell.

The question then became: what should be sold? Might the parts be worth more than the whole? What was the independent value of the *Wall Street Journal*, of HarperCollins, and, if the family's assets were now being valued, inevitably of Fox.

In some surprising, serendipitous (for some), and assbackwards sense, Lachlan Murdoch may have put his company into play.

17

Rupert

IN LOVE

A lonely Murdoch, his split from Jerry Hall announced in June and finalized in August, kept flying into his new Montana ranch and out, trying to get people to join him, anyone who would. In October, Boris Johnson, out of office, flew in to discuss what business he might do with the Murdoch papers—with Murdoch footing his travel bill. Coming and going, it was unsettled, distracted, sometimes frenzied-seeming activity. Certainly it was not focused on what might otherwise have seemed to be the heart-stopping issue facing his company: what to do about Dominion.

To say the least, Murdoch's romantic life, shuffling wives in his eighties, now at ninety-one looking for love again, was confusing to many. Even with two much-younger wives, one an intern in his company, the other a famous fashion model—and two wives before that—almost no one saw Murdoch as a man who regarded women as a central concern of his life. He could easily seem without physical or emotional need. He certainly did not chase women—he was not *that* kind of media executive. In fact, he barely talked to them. Finding Murdoch caught in an elevator with a woman—worse, a young woman—was a scene of paralytic awkwardness.

And yet the bottom fell out when he was without a woman.

During the last year of his marriage to Wendi Deng, when she was largely absent, and the year after, before he met Jerry Hall, his sons believed that a cognitive decline had become evident. That was part of the reason they agreed to their comanagement role in 2014. But his marriage to Hall revived him. Indeed, the marriage ended in part because Hall was no longer adequately attending to him in a way that, at least his daughter Elisabeth felt, helped him keep going.

The basic chemistry of his romantic life was the hovering proximity of his partner and his remoteness. His female companions largely attended to his physical self—his schedule, his dress, his diet, his vitamins, his medications, his house details, his social life. Jerry Hall judged her central purpose to make him his scrambled eggs in the morning. And while this might seem to be a superficial, even transactional relationship, with the thinnest connection to his emotional life, without that day-to-day real-world anchor he seemed like a lost soul, almost frighteningly so, fading, depressed, disassociated.

The consequential summer of 2022, at the age of ninety-one, after his break from Hall, and coming down, not long after, with a difficult COVID case (Hall had been vigilant about protecting her high-risk husband), found him in a state that caused a renewed and anxious discussion of his "status," as Lachlan dubbed it. "Fine," "great," "sharp as a tack" became "Is he up to it?"

That was a broad question, but also a specific one. Was he up to Dominion?

Where months before, the Dominion suit might have been handled as one more overhead expense, it now had become a ticktock of corporate destiny—the fate of so many at Fox possibly riding on it. The opposing sides had gone before a mediator but Dominion, every day gaining more and more confidence about its position, refused to put a new offer on the table, and now added an ultimatum about "reform." This seemed to be suggesting a kind of consent decree, almost of the type that the Justice Department might force on a company to settle criminal charges. Fox could even have to agree to have outsiders monitor how it did business—an outside truth squad. The parties walked away. Without a settlement, discovery and depositions proceeded. Each of the key figures on air and in the company's management hierarchy either had already testified or were now scheduled to sit before Dominion's lawyers. Murdoch was headed for his turn.

This was its own crisis. How, in his present state, could he possibly sit for hours and hours of detailed and hostile questions?

And yet somehow there was no stopping it. Perhaps because only he could stop it at this point.

Internally, as the deposition process went on, incredulity mixed with fury. Every one of the key on-air faces of the network had been exposed in email conversations expressing obvious skepticism about the Trump camp's claims that Dominion was part of a conspiracy to steal the election, and more generally that there was any doubt about the election at all. The Trump claims were laughable, the people making them on his behalf demented, everyone understood. And yet, on air, key Fox voices furthered suspicion about Dominion and the legitimacy of the election. They were caught. They were all guilty of defaming Dominion. Testifying was only going to make the guilty seem even guiltier. Everyone was being hung out to dry. It was now a scramble to find the worst offender to blame.

"Everybody's on their own. So why is Fox not defending us? Because they are stupid or because they are venal?" an aggrieved Carlson said to a friend.

One visitor to Murdoch's Montana ranch found Murdoch absolutely unwilling to consider any view in which Fox could be considered at fault, even though, glaringly, it was. Murdoch, the visitor found, was stuck in a place far from the real world. The Dominion suit had somehow become an attack on him and on his long career. He seemed angrily trapped in the company's desperate and preposterous logic, that it was just airing the newsworthy opinions of important political figures.

"Why don't you just settle?" asked the visitor.

This provoked a Murdoch rant, lots of it hard to follow, but with the sense that Murdoch had found himself alone, up against everyone else who wanted him to settle, but he, if no one else, was going to stand up for free speech. And at any rate it wasn't Fox's fault. It was Donald Trump's fault. He wasn't going to pay for what Donald Trump did. Sue Donald Trump. The visitor came away wondering how this famously cold and analytic business mind had become such a hot mess.

His loneliness had seemed to fuse with his contempt for Trump. Trump had guided the Fox audience, hence forcing Fox to follow. Hence, this was all Trump's fault. He had lost the election. But by refusing to concede and then mounting a campaign to convince his base—Fox's base, and a base that would largely believe anything he said—that he had won, Trump had pushed the network into its untenable position. You see, Trump's fault! As much as Trump could not leave the subject of his stolen presidency, Murdoch dwelled, his anger only increasing, on how Trump and his claims had damaged him and his business. A close Murdoch confidant—speaking to him every other week at the very least, which was near the maximum contact outside of his family and a select few executives—described Murdoch's loop of Trump obsession as possibly "early dementia-like." Murdoch could not get off the subject; he returned to it from conversation to conversation, as though the prior conversation hadn't ended, his pitch constant, infused with unrelieved anger.

The Murdoch court, more virtual at this point than present, was worried.

Concern for him on a personal basis has often seemed to fall to the wives of his friends, the billionaire and men-of-high-standing social circle in which he moved. Henry Kissinger's wife, Nancy, for instance, kept a well-known (and closely followed) eye on Murdoch's personal life. In the weeks after his split from Jerry Hall, his informal, though dedicated, network of wives started to go into action around the unmoored Murdoch.

For his children and executives, it has been both a marvel and an inevitability that, on the market, he finds someone. Over the summer, a series of gatherings was organized by Murdoch friends to help occupy him and introduce him to new people (that is, women). One of the world's wealthiest bachelors (no matter that he is such an old one—no doubt among the oldest) is apparently always a draw.

Murdoch is resistant in social situations, with no game for small talk. He often seems particularly frozen around women—his scowling doesn't help. But he is unexpectedly amenable to any woman with the zeal to take control, even compliant when a woman energetically seeks him out and leads him into conversation.

Ann Lesley Smith, a wealthy sixty-six-year-old Californian widow, came to a small "wine tasting" at Murdoch's Bel-Air vineyard over the summer. She was a former vineyard owner herself, and, too, a media proprietor, with radio and television stations, all inherited from her second husband, former country music star Chester Smith, who she married when she was forty-seven and he was seventy-four, and who died four years later.

Wine, media, her experience with older rich men, her eagerness to engage Murdoch, and the fact that she had no children—with Murdoch exhausted by his own and by Jerry Hall's—made them immediately compatible.

Like both Deng and Hall, there is something headlong and unconcerned about Smith. She has a raucous laugh like the two former wives. And like both other women, she treated Murdoch with a flirtatious amusement. All three women regarded him in a way, in the disapproving eyes of his friends and family, that was at odds with his stature and seriousness.

The people who had worked to set him up almost always felt he chose wrong. Indeed, through his whole life the people closest to him believed he had chosen the wrong women. His mother and his sisters believed that about his first two wives; his children about Wendi, his third wife; the matchmakers in his circle about Hall and now Smith.

No matter. Hall reported that he married every woman he had ever slept with and proposed marriage on the second date. His romance with Smith took off.

If he was depressed without a wife and unable to focus on business, he was elated in the first flush of new romance. This happiness was now widely blamed for his continuing lack of focus and for the fact that Dominion was still not addressed.

His personal life had become the acceptable excuse for his drift.

The truth was that for several years now, marked by some as following the sale of so much of the empire to Disney, it had become increasingly difficult to get clear decisions out of Murdoch, or to get him to engage or follow through.

Most centrally, this included an unwillingness or inability to clarify a management structure that appeared, with a largely absent Lachlan, not to give anyone clear authority. Viet Dinh, who held the title chief legal and policy officer for Fox Corporation, was generally thought to be Lachlan's designated day-to-day operator, but if so he hid in plain sight (one longtime Fox correspondent, in a discussion in the fall of 2022 about internal Fox politics, had never even heard of Dinh). Dinh's official role might otherwise have put him in charge of the Dominion suit, but he blithely seemed to wave off that responsibility. In a particularly peculiar development, it turned out that Dinh had failed to properly establish his law license in California where most of his legal activity took place, hence the privilege of many of his communications related to the suit as the company's chief lawyer might be compromised. At the network itself, its CEO, Suzanne Scott—with her more clearly administrative than leadership role—continued to be regarded by almost everyone as in daily danger of losing her job (that she had not lost it so far, after months of everyone thinking she would, did not seem to change the assumption—just confirming the sense that no one was in charge enough to even fire her). In other words, there seemed to be no ultimate decision-maker or strategic planner, except, by default, Murdoch himself, who, depressed without a wife and then excitedly pursuing a potential new one, was even less present than his son.

The Murdoch organization had for so long and so often succeeded because Murdoch himself was the point-person decision-maker, over-ruling bureaucracy and ordinary caution and putting risk upon himself. That structure yet remained in place, but more and more without Murdoch's attention. Hence, Dominion took on a greater life of its own, with, at every advancing day, the decision to settle and shut the case down a more and more momentous one that no one other than Murdoch could make.

An alarmed Carlson confronted an unconcerned Dinh who told him not to worry, repeating what seemed to have become his fail-safe security, that they would take the case all the way to the Supreme Court if they had to, even though by then pretty much all the damage of the lawsuit—devastating discovery, humbling testimony, mountains of bad press, internal blame, a humiliating, inevitable multibillion-dollar award—would have been done.

After Election Day, November 8, 2022, when, as though miraculously, the Republican wave failed to materialize and Donald Trump seemed cast into at best an uncertain limbo—many of Trump's chosen candidates were humiliated, and a prime opponent and the current Murdoch hope, Ron DeSantis, elevated with a landslide result—Lachlan Murdoch began to tell people that they were going to focus on Dominion and get it resolved. But, after the midterms, Murdoch seemed to further focus a new manic energy on punishing Trump rather than resolving Dominion. Dominion wasn't the problem, Trump was.

As the weather turned cold, Murdoch headed to St. Barts, this year with Smith instead of Hall, with friends observing that Smith's certainties and querulousness merely replaced Hall's—though where Hall had been significantly to the left of Murdoch, now Smith was far to the right.

18

The One-and-Only Channel

BEN SHAPIRO'S $110 MILLION

S ean Hannity and Ainsley Earhardt, if they were not at Hannity's compound on Centre Island in Oyster Bay, were in Palm Beach at their quite unlovely, cookie-cutter condo, just down the road from Mar-a-Lago. Trump had offered them Mar-a-Lago membership, but Hannity found himself annoyed at being sucked (or suckered) into being just another among the many far-flung Republican politicians and snowbird billionaires that formed the former president's daily court. Still, if he had to locate himself, and his prime-time show, and additional radio hours, ground zero was closer to Mar-a-Lago than it was to 1211 Sixth Avenue, the Fox News headquarters. As Trump became more indignant and choleric toward Fox, Hannity seemed to join him—like, what the fuck was going on there, who was in charge? At the same time that Dominion might trade for his head, and the Murdochs might possibly be considering giving it, Hannity, with his great fortune (he had seriously beefed up his security in Oyster Bay) and his near and dear relationship with the once and maybe future president, seemed to live in another world. Fox, in whose office he had sat for twenty-six years, seemed more and more like someone else's problem.

The tight Fox family, anomalous in television news, a product of right-wing exclusiveness and of Ailes's patriarchal (and predatory) control, was increasingly a set of separate business centers. Fox was merely an umbrella brand for the like-minded—and they weren't that like-minded anymore. More and more they seemed held together merely by the assumption that Fox couldn't come apart.

In Palm Beach, shortly before Christmas, someone, expressing concern, had asked Ainsley about the Dominion suit.

"Is that still going on?" she replied. What was represented here was both Earhardt as ditzball but also that the first couple of Fox was no longer merely part of the Fox apparatus, but true celebrities untethered to their community's concerns. Too big to care.

The liberal critique of Fox as a force for evilness, possibly surpassing even Trump himself, made the network out to be a top-down system as efficient in promulgating its views and protecting its own interests as any political organization had ever been. And it was true, during Ailes's twenty years, he had, with obsessive focus, unique belligerence, and open checkbook, herded cats. But in the six years since his demise, Fox had reverted much more to the standard television news model: virulent interpersonal enmity, parallel and unbridgeable worlds of stars and non-stars, fearful executives, remote owners, and warring fiefdoms. It was, like all television news operations, among the most unhappy places of business on earth. With COVID, and the creation of home studios and separate satellite worlds for each Fox star, and the practical disappearance of any center of common overlap and consideration, the idea of brand coherence and shared interest, even ideology, was growing more fragile.

Carlson and his family had arrived in Florida, back for the winter in Boca Grande after finishing out the grouse season in Maine where Carlson, the preppy sportsman (an attribute in common with the Trump sons), had two exceptional spaniels, the best, he marveled to friends, he had ever shot over. He and his wife were only now assessing the damage of Hurricane Ian, which had hit the west coast of Florida that fall with historic ferocity. The Carlsons' house, just off the beach, had no insurance—"Insurance is for pussies," Carlson told his incredulous wife—and yet, living in their closed Maine-island world, they had paid little attention to their closed Florida-island world. In fact, while there had been a path of serious damage through Boca Grande only Carlson's sauna had really taken a hit ("Don't tell people that. . . ." his wife sagaciously advised). Like Earhardt, Carlson had little idea of what was going on at 1211 Sixth, except the obvious inference that nobody was in the driver's seat. Should he care? Unlike Hannity, Carlson didn't have hundreds of millions, laughably far from it. In the new economics of television . . . he was still a salaryman, even if it was a large salary. So he applied a straightforward way to deal with his need and his insecurity.

This was a test. He went out to LA, making a point to be there when he knew he could get both Lachlan and Viet in a room together in their office on the Fox lot, now owned by Disney. (Why you had to go to LA to meet the two top executives of a company whose business activity mostly took place in New York was another unresolved piece from when Fox was an entertainment company, and, too, for Lachlan's convenience, Australia being closer to LA.) Carlson made them an offer they ought not, reasonably, refuse. The network's ratings leader—the ratings leader in cable news—had two years left on his existing four-year contract. It would hardly be out of the ordinary to begin talking about renewal at a sizable jump—a 50 percent jump over four years would not be exceptional for someone as advantageous, even necessary, to the network as Carlson. But he made the network what should have been a much more attractive offer: if they extended his contract by eight years, instead of the standard four, he'd renew on his present terms. In the new world of cable television, in the uncertain if not ever odder world of Fox News, he'd trade off a huge premium for security.

Lachlan and Viet said they weren't interested.

As a test, this yielded some important information.

The network was unwilling to lock into its present course for the future. Not unlikely, this was because there wasn't anything like agreement about what that future was, because—again this persistent point—the patriarch wasn't making his intentions clear (at ninety-one, planning for the future might not seem so pressing).

Carlson was the ratings leader, generating approximately $80 million a year (at a cost to Fox of under $20 million a year), but every day they found him more and more nettlesome, and, yes, even possibly racist—though, at the same time, to Murdoch, "the smartest we have"—in his views. But would they get rid of him for that?

And, possibly, they were still holding their Dominion cards, and yet unsure how to play them. At what price might they need to sacrifice somebody? *But Carlson?*

Or, simply, there was no reason to worry about extending Carlson's deal because management believed, with the kind of arrogance that seemed to enable them to disregard Dominion, Trump, the state of cable, and the roiled conservative moment, that Fox owned the market, and that Carlson and everybody else had nowhere else to go. The upstart conservative cable networks Newsmax and OAN had only a small fraction of Fox's audience. And they, too, were being sued by Dominion for their election coverage. While this was bedeviling for Fox, Dominion threatened the competitors more. Newsmax and OAN could well be bankrupted by Dominion's suits. Major cable operators, seeing the downside of Newsmax and OAN's bad PR and little upside from their limited audiences, were dropping them—whereas Fox was too big to drop. So Fox had no reason to haggle with its talent—they were stuck.

Or, perhaps, there was something even more sinister reflected in Fox's strange behavior toward its right-wing celebrity cash cows.

It was a smooth segue from the conspiratorial plot lines that wove through the Fox daily programming narrative—that opera of liberal and establishment hypocrisy, hidden agendas, and false flags—that such a mindset would become a way to decipher the growing weirdness of Fox itself. (Murdoch may have regarded Carlson as weird, but Carlson, likewise, was putting out daily calls to friends and supporters in growing consternation: "What's happening here is getting weirder by the day.")

The reason this might be happening—Dominion ongoing, nobody clearly in charge, conflicting and muddled messaging, stalled contracts—shifted quite naturally to the suspicion that someone was *letting* this happen. But who?

In 2019, Murdoch had hand-selected Paul Ryan, the former Speaker of the House of Representatives and vice presidential nominee on the ill-fated 2012 Romney ticket—who had fled Washington in the Trump years—for a seat on the Fox Corporation board. Perhaps more than even any liberal, Ryan was a number one enemy of the Trump MAGA base. His villain-ish standing was diminished only by the fact that his sort—professional political class, fiscally focused, legislatively oriented Republicans—were so out of fashion. But indeed, despite his stewardship of Fox, Murdoch's own political temperament seemed well reflected in Ryan. The former Speaker was now, in the conspiratorial interpretation, the spear of a new corporate fifth column within the network. Republican politics, after the midterms, were approaching an existential inflexion point and, in the conspiratorial imagination, the powers that be at Fox—Ryan, the spear—had aligned in a vow not to let Trump win again.

Of course, as in all conspiracy theories, this one rested on the assumption that there are in fact powers that be. People who are actually working with diligent attention and in concert to operate the levers of control.

Details of the conspiracy theory had Murdoch increasingly frustrated with Lachlan, and making a rapprochement, at the urging of his daughter Elisabeth, with James. Working hand-in-hand with Paul Ryan, representing the establishment politics that James so much wanted to be part of, James was adamantly spelling out for his father that it was now or never, this was the moment to act, that the reelection of Donald Trump and the end of America would be on his head if Fox were not remade. *Don't be an old fool—your legacy is at stake!* And, if management could not turn it around, if the Trump-MAGA-weirdo-right-wing voodoo was too strong (and those peculiar new players Marjorie Taylor Greene and Lauren Boebert had recently seemed to surpass even Trump in Murdoch's assessment of the craziness of the political crisis), let Dominion blow the whole thing up!

Who was the author of this neat plot line (to the extent that conspiracy plots have a single author)? Steve Bannon, that reliable Trump advance guard, who retailed so much of the right's most useful and all-purpose unified field theories, and who had never seen a dark political shadow that Paul Ryan was not part of.

Beyond the dubious cogency or zaniness of Bannon's many intricate and rousing conspiracies—this one or any other—his personal antipathy to Murdoch was real. It was not just the natural bad blood between essential elitist and poster-boy populist, or between process conservative and anarchic right-winger, but between successful conservative media mogul and would-be conservative media mogul. Breitbart, Bannon's news platform before 2016, had led the Trump charge in part as a way to challenge Fox. And Bannon had plotted with Ailes, after his ousting from Fox, to launch a competing conservative media organization.

Of the many areas of friction that had developed between Bannon and Trump, one was Trump's continuing awe of Murdoch in the early months of the Trump White House. "A pathetic need for the approval of an old man who clearly regards Trump as a despicable, low-class specimen," said a disgusted Bannon. Murdoch, in Bannon's view, might have been forced to tolerate Trump, but would surely lay in wait for an opportunity to screw him. (And here Bannon was right.) For many Fox personalities, most notably Hannity, Bannon became the serpent's voice about Murdoch and his sons' true intentions. No matter Fox's importance to Trump, Bannon correctly identified Murdoch as a stalwart of the group that the Trumpers hated most, the old guard, RINO Republicans.

But there was something else that helped make his whispers about the dark shadow of the conservative establishment within Fox even more compelling—he was making money on his conspiracy theories! Bannon had found a podcast/livestream/over-the-top audience for his podcast/livestream/over-the-top *War Room* that, more and more, directly refuted the Fox singularity. Bannon was proof of opportunities outside of the network.

Internally, this was one of Fox's most potent myths. Right-wing fame, influence, big contracts, book sales, speaking gigs, brand extensions all flowed exclusively from the Fox platform. (Curiously, this was a similar myth to that maintained by the left-leaning *New York Times*, that its institutional weight distinguished its people and their influence and without it they were nothing.) And indeed that its audience—an older, more rural demographic—was glued to old-fashioned television, and reachable in few other ways.

Bannon's *War Room*, loosely organized, light on production, dismissive of otherwise costly professional concerns (a "top misinformation spreader," according to the *Times*), had launched early in the pandemic, as part of Bannon's wide portfolio of trying to keep himself at the center of conservative news. (This included his build-the-wall project, which got him indicted; his refusal to testify about January 6, which got him a contempt indictment and conviction; and his effort to start a conservative social media network with the Chinese billionaire dissident Miles Kwok, aka Wengui Guo / Ho Wan Kwok / Miles Guo, who would himself be indicted.) Bannon, who regarded Trump with as much skepticism, if not contempt, as most others who knew him well, focused the *War Room* after the 2020 defeat on a gadfly advocacy of virtually every cockamamy stolen-election theory (even embracing Rudy Giuliani who, for years, Bannon had accused of senility and constant blackout drunkenness), and then as a defender of the most virulent January 6 cadres. This had attracted a dedicated audience that put Bannon in the top handful of podcasts, generating more influence (and attention) for himself than he had had since his short stint in the White House, and garnering a substantial steady income nearly for the first time in his checkered career. In other words, the certain secret of conservative broadcast success was not just the Fox platform. It was also, as everyone at Fox certainly understood, the Trump platform—and maybe the Trump platform most of all.

And then, as further indication that the Fox center—and the entire cable center—might not be holding, there was Ben Shapiro, the prickly young conservative media performer and impresario out on his own. His multiplatform success was both a noteworthy and an irritating phenomenon. A Bannon acolyte at Breitbart (who he would later fall out with), a Harvard-educated lawyer, an Orthodox Jew, the thirty-nine-year-old had found an audience that, unique in conservative media—he was arguing to possible investors and sponsors—was young and affluent.

In late 2022, the greater Ben Shapiro enterprise, piggybacking advantageously off of Facebook, and consisting of podcast, streaming, syndication, newsletters, speaking, and seemingly primed for whatever media was yet unknown—and recruiting other people to his "platform"—began to circulate materials that included his financials in order to seek new investment and executive managers for the quickly growing company. Ben Shapiro's number, $110 million a year, was news that ripped through the conservative media world.

Here was evidence—wasn't it?—that there could be big-money conservative life outside of Fox. If so, what did that mean to Fox's captive voices?

The Fox world, the Fox power, the Fox effect, the Fox heavy foot on twenty-first-century America had come because of its conservative mind-share monopoly. It owned its audience. Its audience had nowhere else to go. What's more, Fox had held its audience in part because— and this was not said too loudly—its viewership had a preponderance of lagging tech adapters. They were old. They were behind the media times—their attention was focused and not scattered. True, this had made Fox's voice quite as astoundingly powerful to its audience as mainstream media had been in the heyday of its audience's undivided attention. But . . . they were old. And there was a younger, techy, right-wing world, cutting the cord, too.

Was conservative media about to break up? Or, forget that, could you possibly make more money, much more, outside of Fox than inside?

19

James

THE SISTERS

Dominion's lawyers wanted James Murdoch's deposition, too (they also wanted Liz's). James had argued that he had no role whatsoever in the company during the period that was the subject of the suit. That was technically true. Not that he didn't want to *help* Dominion; its victory would aid the chances of *his* ultimate victory. It would have been quite in character for James, full of righteousness and vengeance, to have publicly excoriated his father and brother. But he was pursuing a new tactic now—a *tactful* one, uncharacteristically.

In the upstairs-downstairs split at the network, the downstairs staff saw James Murdoch, to the extent that they saw him at all, as having washed his hands of the company and taken his marbles home. Hadn't he? The person most trying to upend their lives—with his two billion dollars, his righteousness, and his eye on a majority of the voting stock—was, among the downstairs people, given almost no thought at all.

"He's totally out of the company," said Hannity to a colleague on the subject of James's liberal views, "what is *he* going to do?"

James Murdoch saw his political future within his family (and, because he was nothing if not self-important, he saw the country's political future this way, too) as having a constituency of two: his older sisters Prue and Liz. James's ability to turn Fox from a political force of reaction and deception to a "force for good" depended on his sisters. When their father died—and the countdown to his ninety-second in March was on—their two votes would decide which of the brothers might be left with control of the Murdoch business. Or, in fact, whether there would be any businesses left at all. Of course, the sisters would also be central to Lachlan's constituency if *he* hoped to hold on to control.

Family members, close Murdoch retainers (lawyers, bankers, trustees), and the highest-placed company executives presumed that the internal dynamic would pit the brothers against each other with the sisters choosing between them. The choice the sisters faced—if the choice remained between the male siblings—was put in acerbic family terms that might or might not contain an amount of affection: between "chucklehead" or "hothead."

There were no illusions about Lachlan's general business muddle, indecisiveness, and dependence on his father's views; nor was there any rosy way to mask James's temper, in-your-face certainties, and inability to play nicely with others.

Murdoch, even in his reflexive business preference for his sons, did on occasion acknowledge the possibility of Liz's leadership role. Early on, he'd had high hopes for her business potential and still harbored annoyance that she had left his employ. At other times, he had speculated that Liz, the only one of his children who had made real money independent of him (although nothing in the media world was truly independent of him), might buy out her brothers and take over. But then Murdoch would slide back to the simpler variable of one son or the other. He, after all, had been the business heir among his three sisters. Anyway, that had been the overriding assumption for most of the past twenty-five years: one of the boys.

The wrinkle was that the father could not unilaterally choose a son, or for that matter anyone, to be his successor. He had no power here. That decision—the course of the future—would be up to a vote of four.

Curiously, or wickedly, the trust agreement negotiated in his divorce from Anna did not offer a tie-breaking mechanism. But the assumption was that there would not be a tie because a conflict-averse Prue (or detached Prue, or a caring-much-less Prue, or an actually good person Prue) would reliably make a plurality of two a majority of three. The sixty-five-year-old resident of Australia and mother of three—with, like her other siblings, $2 billion in her pocket—had only ever skirted her father's businesses, with apparently little temperament or temptation to compete with her siblings, or with her father. Perhaps, as a result, she has had the easiest relationship with him, although that followed, during her childhood, the most difficult. When she was nine, her father left her mother for his second wife, Anna, starting a new family, and largely moving to London and then New York and leaving Prue behind. There followed years of her own mother's struggles, and Prue's fraught relationship with her stepmother (she moved in with her father, stepmother, and new siblings for an unhappy period). But now with her own family, maturity, distance, money, and years of therapy, she might be her family's most fair-minded and tolerant member, above the fray. She was hardly a business naïf. In addition to having her own fortune with its attendant lawyers and managers, her first marriage was to Crispin Odey, one of the most famous, and at times richest, British hedge fund investors (and frequent subject of sexual harassment charges). She seemed to have made a considered personal evaluation that there was little upside in actively engaging in her family's internecine business disputes. Against her wishes, her father had recruited her second husband, Alasdair MacLeod, into the company for a time, but that ended in more or less normal corporate attrition (Murdoch in-laws receiving no special protections) and MacLeod is now in the cattle business; and none of her children, all of them of working age, have joined the company (there is still no fourth generation of Murdoch players). Burdened with her vote, Prue would cast it, the family logic went—an untested logic—always with whatever coalition of two had formed.

If that proved to be true, then James's foremost constituency was one: Liz.

The American political future, the democratic model, the US Constitution, the last best hope for man, was in her hands (well, it would be in *his* hands, but first he needed Liz to place it there). But in his campaign for his sisters' votes, he was trying to keep his natural grandiosity, penchant for absolutes, and fury when anyone contradicted him under control. It all, he believed, was going in his direction. But it was too important for democracy (and for his own career) to let his righteous certainty get away from him now. Even if he believed he had his sisters' votes, he knew he had to show that the young hothead could now be a fifty-year-old level head.

This was not so easy. The family history and emotional patterns had been carved in stone: their father's inaccessibility, their mother's censoriousness, Prue's absence and separateness, Liz's rebellion, Lachlan's sulkiness, and James's splenetic, unyielding certitude.

In his diaries, Alastair Campbell, Tony Blair's press secretary and close adviser, describes, with quite some shock, a twenty-nine-year-old James upbraiding his father in public during Blair's courtship of the mogul in the 1990s, publicly dismissing his father as "talking fucking nonsense."

Board meetings often featured James's diatribes against his father and brother. At Sky, when he was the CEO, with little patience for consensus and collegiality, James surrounded himself with a coterie of yes-men, all of whom seemed to look like him and dress like him (thin, fit, white, in dark suits and open-necked white shirts—the Kendall Roy look before Kendall Roy). His sister Prue described him as an OCD automaton, unfeeling in his judgments and perfectionism. It should not—and did not—pass notice that one of the businessmen James seemed to admire most was Elon Musk, the model for unforgiving corporate superiority and intolerance (Rupert Murdoch, too, was a Musk fan). In 2017, shortly after James exited his own family's company, Musk put him on the Tesla board.

As part of his effort to craft a new persona, James followed Musk's playbook, hiring Musk's own strategic makeover adviser, the Washington-based media consultant Juleanna Glover. Knowing everyone there was to know in government and media, Glover was among the most accomplished establishment whisperers. She was whispering now about James's astuteness and liberal and corporate gravitas. Here was a make-over directly for his sisters' benefit—to show he had officially forsworn spouting off, and that he could keep his emotions in check. But it was also meant to position himself for when he stepped back into a public role as a serious, politically moderate, corporate citizen. The corporate club of like-minded billionaires was where James most comfortably saw himself. The process of making himself more clubbable was to stay out of the press, restrain his visceral responses, not engage in public succession drama, and to wait for his moment.

His public pose was to wave off Fox. He wasn't involved. He had no part in it. He was a serious investor pursuing his own interests—socially and environmentally sound investments. He was a Murdoch in name only. At the same time, a great deal of his private emotional energy seemed to be invested in confidential gadfly activities meant to undermine the public Murdoch course. Possibly this was a sign of maturity. He wasn't mouthing off; he was a behind-the-scenes player; this was an insider's game. His father and brother, with some critical interpretation, were the outliers with their weird attachment to the Murdoch legacy and to Fox. He was the technocrat Murdoch who understood the cold business realities and the establishment interests.

The fallacy here, or chink in the new James model, was that he seemed to actually want to run Fox. But why would he? Why would anyone who did not want Fox to be Fox want to run Fox? Could there be any greater nonrational and emotional response than to want to run Fox News as a liberal?

James's logic was Sky News in the UK. That's what, in always some exasperated fashion, he pointed to when people wondered about how he might remake the network. Sky News, over which he'd had direct control for four years, and whose success he put on his list of accomplishments, worked under the British government's impartiality media rules but yet managed to be fast-paced, declarative, visually compelling, and personality driven, a contrast to the BBC's more traditional, if not dour, approach. So why was he even being asked about what he would do with Fox? He had done this before, hadn't he? It was obvious how to make popular news programming without political provocation, not to mention outright lies. His fundamental answer to how he would dramatically distinguish his dreamed-of Fox from CNN or basic network news, all doing a fraction of Fox's business, was again annoyance that it was not clear to everyone that he obviously knew what to do.

A similar ideal of television news had been the generally plaintive and none-too-successful dream of almost all non-Fox programmers for the past generation. And every year the dream had receded further. Just the facts, or "straight news," was simply not—at least there was no successful model for it—the medium's message. CNN, in its latest corporate incarnation combining its parent WarnerMedia with Discovery, had declared, with new fight, that it was going back to straight, or straighter, news, and had promptly plunged in the ratings and lost 25 percent of its earnings. (Discovery was run by David Zaslav. Ailes had been sidelined at NBC, leading to his job at Fox, over an anti-Semitic remark he had made about Zaslav, also at NBC at the time.)

James resisted saying the obvious: that Fox, in order to be a better citizen, would need to be willing to shed a billion dollars or more in earnings. It was a modest estimate of the cost of his planned makeover, but he insisted instead (hotly) that he could make Fox a "force for good," while keeping it a money machine. You wouldn't catch him hobbled by his brother's ambivalence even if the force-for-good Fox continuing to make big money was plainly ridiculous.

This is why Elisabeth's steady argument, divorced from the network's politics and focused strictly on business reality and how to realize value, was, in the view of some Murdoch advisers, both eroding Murdoch's support for his son Lachlan, who clearly did not have a plan, and undermining even the remote chance that James might ever win his father over.

In her role of hands-on daughter to and protector of her legendary father (in his metamorphosis from testy, crotchety, querulous, and dismissive to legendary), the British social doyen with $2 billion and then some, a mother of grown children, remade from resistant, noncompliant family member into peacemaker and sagacious business adviser, Elisabeth continued to be seen as aligned with James. But she was not yet excluding Lachlan, either.

Almost as background noise, she continued to voice the view that, in slow motion—but one day soon it would seem to happen overnight—the industry was witnessing the death of cable, or at least cable value. Forget politics, this was about the transformation of media and the future of technology. Fox's long dominance was on the edge of a pin. There was no reasonable scenario in which this dominance was not chipped at and then hacked at. Even if it could maintain *cable* dominance, that would be an awfully diminished kind of dominance. She argued, too, that the idea—somehow yet clung to by so many media operators—that transformation was possible was laughable, particularly in Fox's case. Fox Nation, its digital offering and streaming strategy—a subscription video-on-demand service—was a bust. Since its launch in 2018, there had been a mad scramble at the network not to have anything to do with it. So . . . again, what was stopping them from selling? The fact that Murdoch had—out of support for his son Lachlan, and his own need to stay in the game—waved off this argument (literally waving in the air to indicate he didn't want to hear was different for Murdoch from disagreeing with it or dismissing it) did not mean that he would not cut his losses and at a moment's notice decide to get out. Elisabeth compared this to how his marriages ended—largely overnight. The possibility that one day Murdoch would wake up and decide to sell Fox was, anyone with inside Murdoch knowledge understood, always a certain existential variable.

The argument to sell also potentially put Elisabeth at odds with James.

For Fox, its fate might not be one brother or the other. Instead, the likelihood that the liberal sister would side with the liberal brother—the expected outcome—might have another twist. Liz, carrying Prue along, might side with the illiberal brother, or be joined by him, in an agreement to dump the network (that is, make it someone else's problem). This might be a better option for Lachlan than the humiliation of being ousted by his siblings from his job; and it could well give him the consolation prize of running the newspaper company with all its Australian papers (certainly a job that no one else in the family would want).

But for James, selling Fox was a solution that did nothing to solve the larger problem—Fox as the out-of-control monster, as threatening a force as any in the world against reason and institutional probity. It would do nothing to spin it off, spin it free. The likely method for doing that, loading on debt so that the company could buy out the Murdoch interest and control, would only force the network to pander further to its most dedicated and most reactionary audience. For the Murdochs to get rid of the problem would only make the problem so much worse for everyone else—and, too, of course, leave them with the historic blame.

James had become the avenging Murdoch—avenging what his family had wrought. It was not enough to save himself and his family and the Murdoch brand from Fox. He had to save the nation. His was a study in the character development of an heir, possibly even more dramatic than his heretofore defiant sister's transformation into matri-arch, caregiver, and voice of reason. He had gone through a series of distinct phases. The hip, cutting-edge, culturally gifted (in his mind) entrepreneur, putting his early marker down in a music company and dot-com investments (both activities coming to naught, but put that aside); then the disciplined, MBA-forward (though without an MBA) martinet, an unsentimental media manager, running Sky and the Mur-doch international operation (put aside that this, with the hacking scan-dal, came a cropper); then, as co-CEO of Fox, a mogul manqué, with visionary bona fides (he was convinced), happiest when he was con-sorting with other moguls (believing that with the sale of so much of Fox to Disney, he would officially join its ranks as Disney's CEO); and, finally, now . . . out from under his family's enterprise, at arm's length from its interests, with his own vast fortune secured, and with nothing very much to do, he saw himself, by right of his name and $2 billion, as a person of pissed-off and righteous destiny.

Lest it appear that he had reversed all stripes and become a move-ment left-winger—of the Hollywood or Bernie Sanders type, as his father seemed to believe—in October 2022 he hosted a fundraiser at his double-wide on East Sixty-Ninth Street for Joe Biden. He had become a prominent establishment player in the Democratic Party. In some sense, his transformation here was even more dramatic than it would have been into dedicated ideologue. His father's entire career had been an expression of suspicion, resentment, contempt, insecurity no doubt, and competition toward insider liberals. His apostate son had now officially joined—been welcomed into—their ranks.

One of the leading enemies of his new set, the wealthy and connected who commuted between financial institutions in New York and Dem-ocratic political and policy circles in Washington, was, of course, Fox. You could not restore the once liberal-ish nation until you solved the Fox problem. And no one knew how to do that because Fox was so good at what it did, raked in so much money doing it, and was so unresponsive and immune to normal social and commercial opprobrium. Hence, only its owners could fix it by will and decree. Rupert Murdoch, despite his liberal wives and the chastisements of his corporate peers and establishment conservative allies, had so far been unable or unwilling, and his other son was God knows where . . . that left his son James.

What do we do about Fox? The answer, the liberal establishment great and good were concluding, was James Murdoch, philanthropist, donor, billionaire next door.

He was being called.

In 1907, J. P. Morgan stepped up and put his own funds at risk in order to calm the panic sweeping the financial markets. James Murdoch could see himself in that role. He was a media titan (although one currently without portfolio) ready to put himself (and Fox's shareholders) on the line for the good of the country.

Would his sister(s) give him the chance? He was confident.

If only his father would die. He did not want his father to die, of course. On the other hand, his really, really, really old father *was* going to die. And every day his father did not die, and an unreconstructed Fox remained on the air, was another day toward democratic Armageddon (all right, attrition, but steady, certain, eating-away-at-everything attrition).

He could not say this to his sisters, about the death foretold. Liz particularly, as part of her reimagining of her father as a historic personage, seemed now to cherish every additional day of his life (no matter the forbearance required).

James's whole goal now was not to say the wrong thing. This was frustrating, infuriating, that the fate of the nation depended on his good behavior. That his own destiny was being held in check—as it really had been for the whole of his career—by his father's continued heavy presence.

WINTER
2023

20

Rupert

DIE, TRUMP, DIE

Rupert and Lachlan were, most mornings, on a call with Suzanne Scott. On the one hand, this might have been a sign that she was part of the inner circle, their confidant, and their instrument. On the other hand, this might have been a sign of their impatience with her—she was just not delivering what they wanted, hence their insistence, their hectoring. It could be much worse, given this critical moment—Dominion; Trump; vast, internal confusion. She could be their fall guy, as almost everyone expected her to be. But frankly, it was hard to tell where the bosses were going.

Truly, everything hinged on what Murdoch wanted and didn't want. The fact that, at ninety-one, this had become less clear and less orderly, did not matter. His was still the word that everybody waited for—without it, or without its accurate interpretation, it meant . . . well, that was the point, no one knew what it meant. Nor could you acknowledge that you didn't know what it meant.

Murdoch's seventy-year-rolling inner circle had largely been made

up of successful interpreters, men—except for a few favorite women—
who observed him closely enough to believe they got him, and who,
having convinced themselves of his unique and farsighted business intelligence (well, *mostly* convinced themselves), were confident enough to
express it—"he wants," "he thinks," "he feels"—but never to make the
mistake or give the impression that it was them talking and not him (as
soon as you began to think of yourself as "Rupert's guy," you would not be
for much longer). Although it might have been them. Even that was often
unclear. That was his accomplishment, to convince people that he knew
what he wanted and that their job, their highest order, was to figure out
what this was. That was your accomplishment: what he wanted; interpret-
ing this mandate, however unclear—with a preternatural urgency in its
lack of clarity—became the sixth sense of anybody who wanted a future
in the company. (Ailes's gift was, for so long, to almost unfailingly be able
to convince Murdoch that what he wanted was what Murdoch wanted.)

What he adamantly didn't want by early 2023—this was clear—was
Trump. Of all Trump's implacable enemies, Murdoch had become a
frothing-at-the-mouth one. His relatively calm demeanor from the early
Trump presidency where, with a sigh, he could dismiss him merely as a
"fucking idiot" had now become a churning stew of rage and recrimination. Trump's death became a Murdoch theme: "We would all be better
off . . ." "This would all be solved if . . ." "How could he still be alive, how
could he?" "Have you seen him? Have you seen what he looks like? What
he eats?"

Like much of the Republican establishment—and this seemed
to include anyone in Republican politics not part of the Trump
establishment—Murdoch had convinced himself that Trump was,
finally, vulnerable. That his hold on the base and on Republican politicians had weakened enough that now was the time to kill him off, finally.
This had been Murdoch's operative view through his long life of political
influence—arguably longer than anyone else's. In every major election
in Australia, Britain, and the US from the 1970s on (only in recent years

had his attention sometimes drifted), he had tried to put his finger on the scale. There was no significant political figure in each country over these decades who Murdoch did not have a detailed opinion about, who he did not have dirt on—or at least believed he had dirt on (it was a way to curry favor with him, the implication that there was secret reporting in the files—Ailes, especially, was always hinting at a bottomless trove of dirt; and Murdoch's London papers were actively in the dirt business). Throughout his long career he had kept careful tabs on all potential candidates, and the Republican candidates with an especially proprietary sense. It was his real calling, to have been a party boss (of the smoke-filled-room type), or political columnist. (Jann Wenner, the *Rolling Stone* founder and editor, had once complimented Murdoch on an unusually astute political column that, incongruously, appeared in the then Murdoch-owned supermarket tabloid the *Star*. Murdoch admitted he was the secret author.) In 2015, he and Ailes judged the then New Jersey governor Chris Christie to be a serious threat to Jeb Bush, the safe and reasonable favorite, and, together decided—with boyish pleasure—they would lean in hard against Christie. (Per a jolly Ailes: "Rupert and I are killing the fat man off.") And yet Trump, from his rise in early 2016 through his presidency, had been untouched by Murdoch's barbs, grunts, scowls, and wide variety of other subverbal imprecations—Murdoch seemed to be able to make nothing happen against him. An empire schooled in his signals wasn't picking any of them up. It was as though Murdoch did not exist.

Now was going to be different.

Liberal journalism bishops and congregants have always been bitterly appalled by the interference of corporate owners in a newsroom's product. This is classic church and state, a moral separation. In Fox's case however, the liberals had been appalled that Murdoch did not interfere. The sins that Fox committed were Murdoch's sins. The fact that he seemed helpless to interfere, that perhaps he did not even know how to interfere through most of the Trump presidency, that the militant approval of

Fox's audience kept him from interfering was a weird journalism paradox. Fox's journalism and its audience's enthusiasm for it was far stronger than its corporate owner's personal agenda. Of course, the owner
was making gobs of money out of it, which perhaps had something to
do with his evident passivity. But now, with Murdoch committed to the
no-more-Trump cause, it seemed here was a real test about who was
stronger: owner or newsroom.

Or, really, owner or audience.

Here was the stumper: in one of those unexpectedly anomalous
developments in journalism, the audience had truly become the decider.
Respectable journalism always put the moral weight on the audience:
the first loyalty is to readers. In reality, this has always meant a mix of
what readers want, usually inchoate, and what they will tolerate, with
a certain faith that the audience can ably (or gullibly) be guided. At
Fox, at least through the Trump presidency, it seemed crystal clear what
the audience wanted: as much Trump as possible. From the beginning,
Fox's conceit had been to give media voice to the media voiceless. It
succeeded to the point where the heretofore voiceless were dictating
the network's words. Fox, with its twenty-five years of propaganda, had
inculcated an audience that was now militantly loyal to the message—
and now the message could not be so easily challenged. Most of the
Dominion discovery evidence—judged appalling by the mass of liberal
journalists—was that the Fox newsroom was tuned into what its audience wanted to hear, and would give them nothing less.

You could argue that all media was going this way. Here was the
natural result of audience sorting and targeting: every audience was
now efficiently defined by what it wanted. Was that bad? The newsroom
reported to its audience. The audience held so much power that even a
bigfoot owner—the biggest bigfoot owner who had ever lived—could
not interfere.

Well, he would try.

To review: for most of Fox's twenty-five years, Murdoch had been remote from what might be fairly judged as his most influential and profitable creation—his cable news station. He was a newspaper guy, not a television guy; had never produced a television show, hardly ever even sat in the control room; he had wholly empowered one man to control every aspect of the network and its product, and then eliminated him without replacing him. Lacking clear leadership, the network ran by pure audience response, with the audience under the extraordinary influence of a single newsmaker—a charismatic, intemperate, would-be showman, a ratings-producing one, who also happened to be the president. But now, a few months shy of his ninety-second birthday, the absentee owner wanted to change all that, wanted to take back control.

Suzanne Scott was the hapless middleman between the owner's wishes and the network's independence, its *incredibly profitable* independence.

Yes, it was clear how much antipathy Murdoch had personally built up toward Trump. But at the same time there was no change in his expectations as the owner of the country's ratings-leading news channel, dropping $2 billion to the bottom line. Like his son James, in his magical thinking of how to transform the colossus into "a force for good," Murdoch was also not ready to admit that his strongest impulse, a determination that had become possibly as close to a moral imperative as this otherwise amoral businessman had ever gotten, could cost him billions. He seemed emotionally incapable of squaring this contradiction. He had the guts not to make money, to invest in quixotic, ego-fueled enterprises—none more so than the *New York Post*. But losing money that was so successfully being made was not something he could temperamentally accept *even* as he unmistakably wanted, with wild-eyed moral fervor, the other thing.

It was left to Scott to parse these two contradictory ideas.

Murdoch delivered his desires less as directions or decisions and more as utterances which then needed to be turned into prescription.

In terms of Trump, it seemed clear: in addition to being an "asshole," an "idiot," a "fool," "plainly nuts," who "couldn't give a shit," who had "no plan," who "just wants the money," "a fucking crazy man," he was a "loser," which was among Murdoch's worst imprecations. Trump couldn't win. Here were Murdoch's true politics: there's nothing to be gained from a loser. Against an incumbent president, a Democratic Party united against him, and with a marginalized message and his vast organizational disarray, not to mention certain looming indictments, the end was obvious: "Loser." Without other alternatives, Murdoch, dismissing or denying practical doubts, had subbed in Ron DeSantis. He was, in one of Murdoch's good words, a "professional," exactly the sobriquet DeSantis was trying to avoid and that Fox viewers might reasonably flee from. Indeed, everything Trump-like about DeSantis, everything he had so carefully worked at in order to seem Trump-like, Murdoch waved away. He wasn't like that, that was all just because he had to, strategy stuff, he was a Florida Jeb Bush Republican.

At the same time, despite how his attention might wander, Murdoch's acuity for numbers remained both keen and compartmentalized. Whatever else was happening and for whatever reason, he seemed always to be up to date on the internal reports and focused on the faintest trends downward. And to do so with impatience, sourness, displeasure, and a profound lack of understanding about how you could have allowed this to happen. Bad numbers were *your* fault. You only had one real job to do, that was to bring good numbers. The message was clear: He might despise Trump, but Fox must remain the dominant cable news channel, holding and increasing its market share.

There was another feature here to Murdoch's thinking, which might have to do with Trump, or with Murdoch's appreciation—subconscious or otherwise—of the potential conflict between high numbers and deep-sixing Trump. Or with having to be on calls about Fox when he didn't want to be. He was in an incredibly bad mood when he had to focus on Fox business—very possibly because he had an attentive woman waiting for him. For an uncommunicative man, being able to read the nuances of his moods was important. For many years, his executives charted his moods against the jet lag of a man logging more air miles per year than few others (often commuting back to Australia from Europe or the US—flying commercial until the late 1980s). In his bad moods, he seemed to bridle against all suggestions and opinions; he might have no clear vision himself but did not want to listen to anyone else's. It was his default business state of mind: testy, snappy, agitated, unquiet. Almost everything he saw on Fox—and it was unclear what he was seeing, or with what regularity he was looking—seemed to irritate him. But perhaps most of all as a tell, he was openly frustrated with his son. He interrupted him; he shot him down; he seemed to wholly disregard whatever Lachlan might say.

Could it be that the father had had it with the son?

Whereas he had had it with James, because he was a know-it-all, because he talked over everyone and talked down to everyone, because his own politics had become as important as his father's politics, because Murdoch simply did not trust most of James's business certainty—now he seemed to have had it with Lachlan, too. Because of his disengagement, because of his lack of point of view, because of everyone else's influence over him, because he was just going through the motions, a diligent son, but nobody's idea of a CEO. At any rate, of all the problems facing the business, Lachlan was offering no solutions at all (not necessarily that his father would have wanted to listen to them).

Six years ago, when he was eighty-six, with an appreciation, however unspoken, of his own mortality and a deep dissatisfaction with his sons as the would-be leaders of his colossal enterprise, he had sold off the lion's share of it. But here he was now, within weeks of turning ninety-two, and it was still just him alone, with his remaining and yet still vast holdings, having to figure it out.

So maybe Liz was right.

The most familiar place for him to retreat was the great media chessboard in his head. This put immediate problems into perspective—they

really did not matter against the realities of industry dominance, technology development, and capital trends. It was a comfortable place
because he had been here, on the chessboard, so long, knowing not just
the rhythms and moves of the game surely as well as anyone else, but
the players, too. If he was excited about anything—excitement at near
ninety-two being a relative condition—it was a sense that the game
might be, once again, afoot. A sense that his competitors were trying to
work out their own intractable problems. A sense that another round of
musical chairs had begun—with a need to secure your position before
the music stopped.

At the critical center was the existential question of what to do about
television with technology altering, nearly beyond recognition, television behavior and business models. That reliable Murdoch competitor
John Malone had amassed a television power with the combination of
WarnerMedia and Discovery. But, in quick order, he seemed ready to
sell to a greater power—likely Comcast. The television business might
become a Disney–Comcast duopoly. John Malone and Brian Roberts,
the Comcast chairman, were certainly thinking such things, which
meant that Murdoch, even with his last breath, would be thinking such
things, too—he would not want to be the last man owning a single cable
station!

In the end, and this being close to the end, Fox was his last historic
move, in a lifetime of shape-shifting moves.

But meanwhile, beginning in 2023, he was looking at another presidential season—with the overwhelming likelihood that it would be his
final one.

He really didn't speak to anyone else at the network beside his son,
Dinh, and Scott. And he would prefer to speak to just his son—he didn't
like Scott very much. But he didn't have confidence his son was deliv-
ering the message to Scott—in fact his son didn't like to speak to Scott.
Lachlan more often was leaving that to Dinh, who was, as the *New
York Times* put it, "up for a drink at lunch." So, Murdoch, even with his

deathly long fades and pauses, his mumbling locution and unfinished sentences, and cryptic, unanchored utterances was, more or less oracularly, setting the agenda.

The top line—and that was largely all that Scott got from Murdoch's abstruse muttering—was *Trump bad, Trump loser.* From that, she had to make the programming day. But Scott herself did not talk to many people. Rather, of the three or four people to whom she communicated *Trump bad, Trump loser,* she might hope that, if ratings fell it was their interpretation that could be blamed. Likewise, those three or four were communicating with producers in such a way that if ratings were to fall it would be the fault of individual shows and stars.

Trump bad, Trump loser, and the patriarch's deep, abiding revulsion, was the hot potato.

The immediate result was a hope-against-hope credulous sort of DeSantis fever, quite in keeping with the strained efforts to like the not-very-likeable Florida governor going on throughout the Trump-fretting or Trump-scorched circles of the Republican party. And then there was a Jesuitical effort to find pretexts to keep a live Trump off the air, and to somehow keep from its Trump-loving audience that the former president had all but been banned at Fox News.

In June 2016, Murdoch had come down to the second floor to tell Ailes, with disgust, that Trump was a loser and that they should obviously be tilting to Hillary. In a way, here they were again. The larger point was that Murdoch could no longer move events, no less his own network. Or, certainly, between the two men, Murdoch and Trump, and the true heart and future of Fox News, you would not necessarily want to bet on Murdoch.

21

Tucker

MIGHT HE? SHOULD HE?

"**I**'m fifty-three," Tucker Carlson addressed a friend, almost a year to the day after the invasion of Ukraine—a year during which the hard-core or MAGA (by whatever name, it was an ever stauncher and implacable presence) Republican base had more and more adopted his position that Ukraine was an elitist folly, power play, and cultural flash-point. ("Has Putin ever called me a racist?" asked Carlson, in a weird inverse of Muhammad Ali's "No Viet Cong ever called me nigger.") In the face of his boss's urgent feelings otherwise—to Carlson, quite an accurate barometer of establishment views—his own feelings had become even stronger, and resentments larger. "Where do I devote my energies for the next fifteen years. . . . I'm feeling very open-minded."

That is, he had an increasingly narrow outlook on Fox—and a slightly paranoid one, too. Was he of Fox, after fourteen years, or shocking to it?

In weeks, he would air his biggest scoop—and nobody named Murdoch, and nobody talking to people named Murdoch, seemed happy about it. The leadership of the new Republican congressional majority, acknowledging Carlson's canonical role in the new MAGA party, had turned over to him the congressional video surveillance tapes taken on January 6, during the mayhem outside and inside the Capitol. Whereas the Democratic majority had impaneled an investigative committee to build a narrative about what happened that day, the Republicans were letting Carlson do it.

Whatever Carlson actually thought about January 6—and that included a revulsion toward the heavily tattooed riff-raff mob—the tapes fed his constant urge toward reverse agitprop (that is, the diametrically opposed narrative to liberal agitprop) and to a meta revision of liberal media. Since so much of the Democrats' case against January 6 had been based on—or at least dramatized by—the miles of footage, Carlson would use more miles of that footage to show the opposite story. In fact, both cases would be correct—that is, correct about what story you could tell from the footage. This was, with a little critical interpretation, not a political point, but a television point. Television news always edited footage to complement or reinforce or hype or fabricate the story it wanted to tell. How often did the pictures turn reality on its head? Not all the time, but often. Carlson, in his own mind, wasn't making a prosecutorial point, like the Democrats; he believed he was making a larger point about truth, justice, and media.

And he was getting frequent cautions from the proverbial "upstairs" and "second floor" at Fox (a more and more attenuated relationship and metaphor since Carlson dwelled so far from the actual and corporate Fox—plus "upstairs" was also in Hollywood with Viet Dinh or Australia with Lachlan or with Rupert himself from God knows where) about what he was doing with all this and where he was going. Murdoch was still holding to the shocked, appalled, horrified position seemingly everyone held in the immediate aftermath of January 6, but which, for the right wing, had now morphed into—Fox's general position morphing with it—the view of misunderstood protesters and left provocateurs and liberal propagandists. Would anyone at the network seek to curtail, flatten, or interfere with Carlson's show? This might be a true test of Murdoch's anti-Trump dictates. Carlson, counting on a major audience share, was betting not. But he was also trying to think one step ahead of the sheriff.

The sheriff could be Murdoch—Carlson imagined a flailing, destroy-everything, Shakespearean king in his final days. Or it could be James. Carlson had given up on Lachlan's staying power—he was, Carlson clocked, spending greater and greater parts of what should have been his business time on his various boats (a reference to "spearfishing" in the Dominion discovery document had turned this into the meme for Lachlan's out-to-lunchness). James, the would-be usurper, seemed poised to succeed. Or—and Carlson was currently leaning this way—they'd sell. That was a development that might be good for Carlson, to be judged in purely economic terms, but he really didn't want to find himself depending on the world of private equity. He was prepared.

But in a way he was worried about none of this happening soon enough.

He had two years left on his contract—two years during which the next election would occur, during which his voice would likely be at its most powerful and valuable. The guidance he was getting was absolute: no way they'd let him out. They weren't willing to extend his contract for the long term, but they certainly weren't willing to let him compete with them in the short term.

There was a way, however. . . .

His desire to keep doing what he was doing, talking for a living about all of the assholes who he held in visceral contempt (and who held him in visceral contempt)—a job he could yet hardly believe his good fortune to have gotten—was now oddly converging with something else that he was so far too self-conscious and fainthearted to openly admit he wanted, but a job that, for the past few years, he had been running for at least in the privacy of his own mind.

If he did really, truly, run for president, even if he took steps to explore, they'd have to let him out of his contract (no network, not even Fox, could have an avowed, or even likely, candidate on its payroll—this involved not just perception, but campaign finance implications). Getting sprung from Fox might be reason enough to run.

But if you looked at the field as it was shaping up, there was pretty clearly an opening for him—or someone like him.

A few weeks before, the DeSantises had come to lunch at the Carlsons'. There had been quiet urgings at Fox for Carlson to be open-minded about Murdoch's favored candidate. And certainly, for DeSantis this was a significant moment, to reach out, to break bread, to make nice, to suck up to a plausible kingmaker. The DeSantis strategy, to the degree that he had one, other than the media dream of any alternative to Trump, was to make quick proof-of-product inroads into the MAGA base, for which he was heavily dependent on Fox. Winning Carlson over would be an important part of using Fox.

Carlson put DeSantis's fate to a focus group of one: Susie Carlson. Carlson's contempt for politicians might be boundless, but Susie Carlson's contempt was pure. When they lived in Washington, she wouldn't even see politicians. Carlson himself may have known everyone, dirtied himself for a paycheck, but not his wife. She was the kind of true conservative, like that last Japanese soldier yet up in the hills. In her heart, it was 1985 and still a WASP world, absent people, in Carlson's description and worldview, who were "impolite, hyper-ambitious, fraudulent." She had no idea what was happening in the news and no interest in it. Her world was her children, her dogs, and the books she was reading. So, the DeSantises were put to the Susie Carlson test.

They failed it miserably. Theirs was a total inability to read the room—one with a genteel, stay-at-home woman, here in her own house. For two hours Ron DeSantis sat at her table talking in an outdoor voice indoors, failing to observe any basics of conversation ritual or propriety, reeling off an unselfconscious list of his programs and initiatives and political accomplishments. Impersonal, cold, uninterested in anything outside of himself. The Carlsons are dog people, with four spaniels, the progeny of other spaniels they have had before, who sleep in their bed. DeSantis pushed the dog under the table. Had he kicked the dog? Susie Carlson's judgment was clear: she did not ever want to be anywhere near anybody like that ever again. Her husband agreed. DeSantis, in Carlson's view, was a "fascist." The pot calling the kettle even blacker. Forget Ron DeSantis.

Of course, presidentially, Trump was the much greater issue. Carlson regarded himself as in a small circle of clear-eyed people who knew Trump well and who knew exactly who and what he was. This circle might be as small as Jared Kushner (who Carlson detested), Steve Bannon (who he mostly detested), and a handful of others who had come, through long experience, to see Trump as a simple (and, as well, effective) machine. This understanding had removed the mystery and fear and the still prevalent sense of his magical properties. The reach of his gold-plated, say-anything-to-get-a-rise, stark contrast with the empty-suit, pole-up-the-ass professional political class was well defined, with Trump being permanently limited by his inability to do anything different than he had always done. If the field was Trump, DeSantis, and various hopeful brand builders and gadflies, then Carlson, the second-most-famous person in this race—with that new political x factor, a television persona—might realistically become a true MAGA Trump alternative.

Carlson's considerations here were hardly just practical and strategic. They were existential and went to the heart of the roiled country. In his seven years of partisan fame—or infamy—he felt that he, perhaps more than anyone (Trump being unfeeling), had absorbed the true, otherworldly levels of insanity, rage, and viciousness that it was useless to even couch as "under the surface." He had told the story of the unraveling, much of it through the crazies that populated his show (he wasn't without realistic judgment about their sanity), but speaking some sort of truth—these were perceptual guerillas, as well as opportunists (he had become an early supporter of Democratic Party apostate Bobby Kennedy Jr., acknowledging that he might be crazy, and liking him for it). At the same time, he weighed the power of the cold-blooded establishment and its organized will to do anything at all—*anything*—to crush the challenge to its intellectual hegemony. And, in his own immediate world, there were the Murdochs, and what they might, at any moment, do to him.

He had risen on the Fox–Trump juggernaut, but that, he was concluding, was a spent force—and broken partnership. He had spent nine hours in his Dominion deposition. The Murdochs and their executives had dumped their problem on him. You don't want to work for people who you think might hurt you, he offered darkly. He had become what Fox demanded, and now he could be, he feared, left out here on his own. How bad could this get?

He had recently focused a show on the mystery of billionaire sex offender Jeffrey Epstein and his convenient suicide—with the clear point that Epstein, in prison, had been done in by individual or collective uber forces of self-interest. Well, he could end up there himself, he felt. Sometimes he even expected to.

Sometimes it seemed that he regarded running for president as a further part of his belief in an inevitable martyrdom (as well as to get out of his contract). But if he *did* run, he knew what he would run on— he had been thinking about that. Duly noting what was to him the tragedy of Charles Lindbergh—that giant of a WASP Republican—he would run on foreign policy. A year into the bog of Ukraine, his views had only hardened: the foreign policy establishment, followed mindlessly by the entire political establishment, was risking everything—a functional world order, economic stability, as well as Armageddon—in a conflict that would only result, without the active involvement of NATO troops, in Ukraine's capitulation. *Be realistic!* Here is what gripped him, not just that Zelensky was a fake and Putin, you better believe, real, but that liberals, and he would include here the Republican center as effective liberals, weren't even really talking about Ukraine—supporting Ukraine was just some accepted aspect of good manners and public virtue. Well, fuck that—here was a reason to run. He had a message. *He* was the anti-war candidate.

Frankly, it was hard to imagine, not just because it all sounded odd or fanciful or far from a winning approach, but because Carlson, as he had become more and more public, had retreated further and further from public life. His career thrived on massive, unrelenting, nearly universal liberal vilification, but not, well, his soul. In some sense, his hour on Fox every weekday night was a hologram of a Tucker character, with the real-life version otherwise occupied somewhere else. Since selling his home in Washington, so frequently and rudely under siege by left-wing rabble, he and Susie, and whichever of their four children were present, spent six months on their island in a glacial lake in Maine, their own kingdom, with plenty of acreage and houses and a separate hunting lodge (with the same paint that had been applied in the 1920s when it was built still on the wall), which he almost never left. That is, until the end of hunting season, when they packed up and moved to Boca Grande, their Florida island. In each place, he had his Fox-provided studio setup. The Carlsons had no television and imported a social life of heterodox or dissenting celebrities, recently, Mike Tyson (who cleared it first with his hosts that he'd be smoking pot the whole time he was their guest—"Guess who's getting high tonight in your bedroom?" Carlson texted his daughter), Russell Brand, and Tony Robbins. It was a happy life, this most public man insisted, cut off from the world. So why would he want to be president?

Because everybody does. That is, every deeply ambitious man (yes, man), still of a certain general mode and vanity and generation, drawn to the promises and interactions of power, impatient with everyone else's claims that they might know the answers and be better at being president.

Still. Carlson also thought you needed to be "called." And he was still waiting for the voice to be absolutely clear.

At the same time, he acknowledged that Trump's 2016 calling—idle gesture, business opportunity, branding exercise, just the obvious contrast to everyone else—changed the spiritual nature of this. Politics and media were the same job, the same life. Running for president was no different than being on television—votes, with only a slight critical adjustment, were the same as ratings. If the Democrats yet maintained some treacly pretense about political process and civil society, the Republicans—part of their new character trait—had wholly thrown pretense away. It was all performance; it was all media—it was all attention.

Carlson had saved his career and reinvented himself as often as anyone in television. If Murdoch, with his last breath, was trying to make Fox his own political weapon (distinct from the political weapon it had become and for which he was blamed), waging an irritating battle for yesterday's Republican politics; if he was going to die anyway, leaving the network torn between his children; if cable television was itself a dying animal; then the fifty-three-year-old Carlson needed his next move.

Ben Shapiro's $100 million–plus enterprise was a model; so was Steve Bannon's *War Room*; and Megyn Kelly, Carlson had heard, was pulling down impressive sums from her deal with Sirius Radio. But, of course, there was nothing here remotely on the level of what Fox prime time got you.

So, the question was not if you wanted to be president, but what could be gained by running for president? You became a star because you had the platform and the canny or shameless wherewithal to focus attention on yourself. If you were a star who ran for president, cannily and shamelessly using the world's largest public platform, might you not make yourself into the largest star ever?

It was a platform world.

During the 2016 campaign, Donald Trump was asked that question designed to reliably trip up a candidate: Why exactly do you want to be president? But Trump had responded without a second's hesitation or moment of doubt: to "be the most famous man in the world."

Still, Carlson was suffering about this. Were he to run, he believed Fox might spitefully wipe him off its platform. Could you be a successful Republican candidate without the overt or implicit backing of Fox? Among the subplots of 2024, Trump was testing Fox's power. Putting aside Carlson's own plans—and whatever exasperation and incredulity he felt about Trump—he was full of respect for Trump's willingness to confront the network. It was another existential line: What would happen to Fox if Trump, a vindictive Trump, actually won?

If Carlson were asked why he wanted to be president, his answer, at least the honest one, would be similar to but qualitatively different from Trump's. It would be: to be able to keep talking. (In this, he might not be dissimilar to anyone else who had been on television and faced the prospect of not being.) He saw running for the presidency and the presidency itself as part of the greatest opportunity ever to keep talking and to have people listen to you. There was something pure here: you would rise or fall on the singular power of what you said. From a conservative point of view this made exemplary sense: politics should not be, foremost, about policy—that was for small minds and for the self-interested (a clique that included the people Carlson hated most)—it should be about ideas (even harebrained ones).

Six years ago, he was on weekend Fox duty, working the lowest-rated part of the Fox schedule, and having to commute to New York to do it. But then, disregarding Murdoch's misimpression of the new moderation he might bring to the air, he had understood as well as anyone the new media dynamics of Trump's America. This had elevated him into some stratosphere of performative and psychic polarization, now far out beyond where the network that made him wanted to be.

Murdoch, presented with rumors about Carlson's possible interest in the presidency, blamed this on Lachlan, making him responsible for not controlling the ratings winner at the network—who, of course, precisely because of his ratings, could not be controlled. Murdoch told friends, with disbelief, that Lachlan *wanted* Carlson to become president. "My son wants his own president." It seemed intolerable to Murdoch that he might be responsible for another president representing conspiracies and populist emotion—that is, representing Fox. And so he dismissed it (indeed with almost the same words he had once dismissed Trump's prospective candidacy): "Won't happen."

Carlson, meanwhile, as he considered the presidency, also considered, as a reflection both of the divided country and perhaps his own divided psychological state, a different kind of end, the most extreme result of what he saw as the politics of zero sum and retribution—a jail cell. Martyrdom. He could not believe that Steve Bannon—whom he mostly disliked, but occasionally admired, and who, overall, he'd concluded was some sort of mad genius—was not, in the face of the various prosecutions lined up against him, fleeing the country. Carlson dwelled on the issue as though with clear personal stakes. "Why wouldn't he just get the fuck out?" Only because he's "just so wrapped up in his own shit." In this, there was a cautionary tale, both not to get so wrapped up in your own shit, but also—rather starkly contradicting that advice—to understand that, when you became anathema to those who had the weight of the system on their side, prison was a real possibility, which Carlson, as the second-most-hated person in the country, was keeping clearly in mind (mindful that the most-hated person in the country might well end up there, too).

What were your options then, Carlson wondered, but to flee, or "go Eric Rudolph," *or* to run for president?

"Nobody gets out of cable news alive—but imagine being the one guy who made it. Escape from Stalag 13."

22

Hannity

INDICTMENT

Since his election in 2016, Trump had always found reasons not to blame Rupert Murdoch for the reports that might be brought to him about the mogul's belittling remarks, or for Fox's deviations. He had even resisted putting the blame on Murdoch for the 2020 election night call for Arizona. Murdoch had remained firmly in the category of billionaires who he didn't challenge. It might be unrequited love, but still love. Even as Fox had soured on him, pushing harder and harder for DeSantis, Trump apportioned the blame out: it was the once loyal *Fox and Friends* morning show that he hated; it was the disloyal Laura Ingraham who was screwing him; it was Fox Business's Neil Cavuto who couldn't be trusted; it was his former press secretary Kayleigh McEnany, who needed to be smacked; it was Jesse Waters who was in the tank for DeSantis. It was Lachlan, the "gay" son, and a list of "nasty" executives. But now he had crossed the Rubicon. It was Murdoch, in Trump's private-but-not-too-private parlance, who was a "piece of shit."

It was only Hannity who stood between Fox and Trump and all-out war. And it was Hannity who was carrying the message to POTUS: the Murdochs were no better than CNN.

Hannity always scoffed at the liberals saying Fox was all about a planned and calculated political message, instead of just the obvious counterargument to the other side's planned and calculated message. But this was *really* now a planned and calculated message! Scott's instructions, to everyone who would take her instructions, were clear: fuck over Trump. Where was this coming from? Above.

They were consciously trying to destroy the one true golden goose of the network (in fact, of cable television). Even more ridiculous, *they* were trying to replace him with . . . *Ron DeSantis*. How was that going?

DeSantis was now virtually exclusive to the network, his coming candidacy constantly prepped on the Fox air. In more than two months of this since the beginning of the year—definitely marking the unofficial launch of the Republican race—the numbers were showing that DeSantis was flatlining or even causing a ratings dip in every Fox spot he was on. And his national polls went down the more he was seen on Fox. Hannity was in I-told-you-so mode and drawing a clear line between his operation, the greater Hannity broadcast enterprise, and the other fools at Fox. This wasn't complicated stuff. DeSantis was a stiff. A suit. A politician. Everybody was getting this so crazily wrong, that Republicans wanted Trumpism (in the form of DeSantis) without Trump. Insane. What they wanted was Trump! Anyway, with DeSantis's increasing exposure he was self-destructing—and with him Fox News.

Laura was being pushed out in front on DeSantis and it was killing her. She was like a sacrificial lamb. (Every time a Fox person went critical on Trump, they got massive liberal praise, which was its own sort of punishment.) She would pay for this. Say good-bye to prime time, Hannity thought.

Hannity and Trump saw the Murdoch conspiracy. It was Murdoch's *Wall Street Journal* and *New York Post*, too, after POTUS.

But Hannity was just waiting this out and telling POTUS to do the same.

He knew how this was going to go. Whatever they were trying to do, whatever Murdoch thought he could do, the story would play out as Hannity knew it would, with the Trump line on the ratings graph rising, rising, rising—"Wait for the hockey stick," Hannity kept saying. As much as Hannity genuinely felt the indictment of the president was police-state stuff, he could hardly wait for it to happen. That was going to super-charge everything. And as much as they were trying to keep Trump off the air, he would be back, 24/7. This was the thing the liberals never, never, never understood (thank God). The more attention Trump got, the more conflict he caused, the more his poll numbers went up—"Go figure," Trump would always say, cat-that-swallowed-the-canary—and the more Fox would want him front and center. And someone would have to be blamed for being the numbskull who thought otherwise. That was Scott. Dead lady walking.

Hannity was Hannity because, from day one, he had been Trump's go-to guy at Fox. Virtually at every moment of crisis (these really weren't ever *crises*, at least not like other politicians experienced; for Trump these were opportunities), Trump would come on the Hannity show to savor the moment and his victory. Whatever crazy stuff was going on, Trump would just lay it out as he saw it, which was always Trump on top of the world, gently rocking back and forth, his hands between his legs. This had made Hannity the second-most-important person in the country—this was a joke he kept making, but, of course, it was also true (he was annoyed when people referred to Carlson as, behind Trump, the second most!). And, he continued to joke, with Trump out of the White House, it had probably reduced him now no lower than the third-most-important person in the country. And it was the kind of *importance* that made him give very little thought to this Dominion bullshit. That was all just a liberal fucking sideshow.

The second floor was now trying to screw with him—Suzanne Scott carrying messages from the Murdochs. Scott could not tell him what to do with his show, who to have on or who not to have on, what to say or what not to. She neither had the power nor the temerity. But she could be a pain in the ass. It was obstruction and delay. It was mostly obstruction by delay. Scott was not going to call him and he was not going to call Scott—so that meant she was able to create a lot of misdirection and obfuscation in between. The second floor might not be able to say no to him, but they could drag their feet on saying yes. Well, Hannity was a lot more worried about losing his job with Donald Trump than he was losing his job with Fox.

Several times now he had to find his way around a reach out from Trumpworld on potential on-air calls and even sit-downs. Now it was a legal consideration, the second floor was saying, with the lawyers raising issues: Did they really want Trump live on the air saying something that could mess with the Dominion lawsuit? That was of course bullshit. They didn't want Trump on the air because he was Trump (although, true enough, you couldn't predict what he would say!).

Anyway, the point was he was going to have POTUS on the air when he wanted him. No question.

An indictment was coming. It was a countdown. A federal indictment, a New York indictment, a Georgia indictment. Nobody was sure which would be first. But the first would be the biggest. The Trump people thought it would probably be New York. That would be fantastic—on the steps of the New York courthouse, thousands of people, helicopters overhead. This was O.J. This was television!

On Saturday morning, March 18, from the golf course, Trump announced that his indictment in New York was coming on Tuesday—more Trump total brilliance, raved Hannity, to make the indictment his story, and not let a dipshit prosecutor have it. This was one of those moments, like the ride down the escalator in Trump Tower in 2015, Hannity announced, that would go down in Trump history.

The reach out came from Mar-a-Lago.

Obviously, Hannity would do a sit-down—run of show, of course—as the indictment came down.

The second floor—Scott—wanted to make sure when the indictment was. Let's not let him spin it before we know what it is. By Tuesday and Wednesday an indictment still hadn't come down, and Hannity was a little irritated himself. But more so, he didn't want to be put on the schedule the second floor wanted him to be on. He was on Trump's schedule.

Anyway, Mar-a-Lago was certain it was coming (even as Trump was telling everyone the case had fallen apart—of course!). But what Trump had in mind now was something a little different than just waiting for the indictment to fall. He was stage-managing the indictment rollout. The first mega rally of the Trump 2024 campaign would be held in Waco, Texas (that eerie right-wing symbol), on Saturday, a tens-of-thousands-strong rally. So why not do the interview, the run-of-show interview, on that Monday, and build anticipation for the coming indictment?

The second floor was furious. This was Trump using Fox to control the indictment narrative. They were exactly where they didn't want to be: part of the Trump spin machine. Hannity felt a bit played, too. On the other hand, he had to admire it. Trump had already seen a fifteen-point climb in his polling numbers. This was a Trump-at-his-best media play. Plus, Trump, in practically open war with Fox (though not with Hannity), had put one over on them. The second floor went into their own crisis mode to dissuade Hannity from giving Trump the airtime—and, if he had to, why not one segment, instead of the full hour?

Hannity and Trump were in this together. They were openly plotting together against the network. Trump was in fine form, mocking and attacking Murdoch, "the old man" who had just announced his fifth marriage!

"Why's he getting married at ninety-two, what the fuck? Only one reason why: prove you can still fucking do it even though everyone knows you can't. It's a fake news marriage," Trump hee-hawed.

What could Scott do? They had tried to keep him off the air, but here he was, about to be indicted, *making news*. Monster news! And Hannity had the interview.

They were insisting he tape it. They didn't want to risk Trump live. What if he said something about Dominion? What if he said something about the Murdochs?

"Fuck it, I don't care," Trump said, quite understanding Fox was getting back, one way or the other, in the Trump business. "Let's do it."

Hannity set out from his condo in Palm Beach to Mar-a-Lago for the taping.

Hannity had seen Trump at all kinds of moments. Sometimes it had been so bad, Trump's thinking (*thinking!*) so hopelessly jumbled up that they had to give him the questions beforehand so he could prep his answers, and still he rambled on. But he now was as sharp as Hannity had seen him. He was back—and on Hannity. It was starting all over. Hannity could hardly believe it, that it could all be beginning once more. Here was Trump again: *Indictments? Just another way of stealing an election—that was all it was, more of the same. Ron DeSantis, well, he'd be working in a "pizza parlor place" if it wasn't for Trump helping him get the Florida governor's job.*

Trump was back.

Murdoch watched the interview early, believing that Trump came off like a buffoon, and urged Scott to follow the interview with "tough" coverage.

What unfolded the next day after Hannity's interview had aired, with Fox News covering its own newsmaking event, was perhaps the kind of conservative-leaning news channel that Murdoch, or at least his better self, had always wanted. Indeed, it was close—or closer—to what news more purely is, more remote, more disengaged, skeptical. Old-fashioned news. "We should act like journalists," Scott had actually said, perplexing for all.

Murdoch told people how much he thought Fox had put Trump "in his place," and how this was an example of how they weren't going to let Trump "use" Fox anymore. Over the next several days, he repeated to a handful of people, "Fox is a news channel."

Three days after Hannity's interview aired on March 27, Trump was indicted in New York by Alvin Bragg, the Manhattan District Attorney, for various business frauds. And instantaneously at Fox, any doubt that Trump was anything other than the main and all-consuming event, or that there was any taint of moral conundrum, evaporated in the wonder and excitement of the moment. The protagonist, the *hero*, was under attack. And it was all bigger than anyone—anyone at Fox—could dream.

Trump giddily called Hannity and asked if he thought being indicted was bigger than being impeached.

Fox was back. Its message, full of ratings magic, was back: the powerful, pernicious, conspiratorial, fake, Democrat machine was doing anything it could possibly do, bending reality itself, not to mention the entire justice system, to humble Donald Trump.

What were they going to do on the second floor? What could they do? There was only one drama. There was no Republican primary race; there was no existential battle at the heart of the party; there was no Ron DeSantis; there was no Rupert Murdoch and his quislings' politics. For seven years the witch hunt had wanted to indict him and now they had. And likely they would do it again! And even again!

What could the Murdochs do about that? They—and their network— were in the same position as every person who might hope for any standing or legitimacy in the Republican party. Even a judicious, wait-and-see view (forget the outright condemnation of Trump that Murdoch himself favored) would mark you as a hopeless outlier; there was only support for Trump and denunciation of his corrupt enemies.

Murdoch told Scott he had spoken to Mitch McConnell, the Republican Senate leader, who, perhaps even more than Murdoch himself, was the Republican who most reviled Trump (putting aside that he was also the Republican who had helped pass the Trumpism agenda, such as it was). Murdoch did not tell Scott what McConnell had said (he often left thoughts unfinished and crucial points unexpressed), which, in this instance, seemed likely to mean he did not have to: for both men there was nothing to say; they were, hardly for the first time, captives of Trump events, and without practical options.

Scott's months of triangulation, to accommodate Murdoch's anger, to help push a new Republican chapter, to move but not confront the audience, involved depriving Trump of the one thing that he most needed to survive (at least Fox knew this if not the liberal media): airtime. It was, if not an outright ban, an unofficial embargo. That was the message to her lieutenants: keep him at arm's length, at least until the race heats up. No front-loading. No letting him spin.

Hannity had broken through, and Scott was still kicking herself for having not short-circuited that. But she had told the Murdochs, father and son on the call, that there would be no further issues until at least the summer. They could certainly be Trump-free until then.

But on indictment day, with Bret Baier, Fox's official political correspondent and one of Scott's reliable factotums, bowing to the new reality, it came to this: "I'd like to put in the call right now," Baier said on the air. "If the former president would like to phone in, we'd love to have his reaction to this news tonight."

There followed, for the next six hours on Fox News, nonstop Trump news, nothing but Trump.

23

Trial

THE DEAL

A baby-faced white guy with a fluffy beard wearing a green windbreaker was excused, and then immediately thereafter, an older white man, a blue-collar type, was excused, both replaced by Black jurors. A nondescript middle-aged white man was replaced by a middle-aged white woman with a pageboy haircut. Then a heavy-set Black guy in a polo shirt was excused, replaced by a white woman in a sweatshirt and backpack, who was herself immediately excused, to be replaced by a heavy-set white woman.

It was a modern, low-ceiling, unbecomingly lit court room with sports-bar-like screens and marble-effect panels—instead of actual marble—and office furniture and poor airflow. All as though designed to remove any sense of drama here in Superior Court in Wilmington, Delaware, with its favorable laws for corporate organization. And yet there was a powerful demographic tension, a countdown.

Another white woman was excused and replaced by a man of indeterminate racial background in a fluorescent roadwork safety windbreaker who was then immediately replaced by a Black man in a fluorescent but sporty windbreaker. A young Black woman was excused and replaced by a young Hispanic woman. Another white woman was excused and replaced by a white man in a polo shirt, in his forties, seemingly recently off the golf course. Then another middle-aged Black woman was replaced by a young Black woman, who was then promptly replaced by a middle-aged white woman. And then, finally, the white woman with the pageboy was excused and replaced by a young Black man.

In the end, the jury that was seated for *Dominion v. Fox News* was composed of eight African American men and women, one Hispanic woman, two white women, and one white man, all drawn from a jury pool in this overwhelmingly Democratic city, to pass judgment on what might not unreasonably be described as the "white-man news network."

Opening statements, beginning with the plaintiff, Dominion Voting Systems, and already delayed by a day, were scheduled to start at 1:30 p.m., immediately after the lunch break, and would play to a packed courtroom.

But the journalists and curiosity seekers (overwhelmingly more journalists than the passingly curious) who came to Wilmington, Delaware, for the media trial of the century, many planning to stay for the full scheduled six weeks, had been brought there under false pretenses. There was never going to be a trial.

Rupert Murdoch, a month and ten days after his ninety-second birthday, was scheduled to be called as the trial's second witness. Fox's lawyers had failed in every effort to exclude him from testifying. Murdoch had already had to sit for an extended deposition, a performance on his part described as, with a good face, "painful," or, less generously, a "fucking mess."

Days before the trial, there was a practice session for Murdoch's testimony. But this was not really practice, as in an expectation that Murdoch's performance was going to improve enough for anyone to be able to believe they could limit the damage of his testimony. Likewise, there was no circumstance in which Murdoch, finding himself here on the eve of trial, was going to be happy with the people who had not found a way out of this for him.

The catastrophe looms. This is the moment of all options closing; it's dread and panic; it's helplessness. Who is to blame? The two versions of Murdoch's practice session reported by participants are Rashomon versions of the long history of this lawsuit and of the utter lack of wherewithal to go forward, an admission of not just defeat but of hopelessness. While each interpretation of the run-through session was diametrically opposed to the other, it might yet be that both were true in their clear understanding that it would be impossible to proceed.

In one version, Murdoch during and after the session found himself utterly disgusted with his lawyers. They weren't prepared; they failed to understand any of the political nuances; they couldn't grasp the nature of what Fox did, nor of the kind of journalism his company was so successfully built upon. This was Viet's fault. It had been his idea to switch legal teams last July after the ruling that brought Murdoch personally into this suit. They had moved from Fox's original litigator, Chip Babcock, from a big Houston-based firm, to Dan Webb, a Chicago lawyer who handled the pink-slime-beef defamation case against ABC (an ABC reporter described a beef product as looking like pink slime—ABC settled the case). Webb, at seventy-seven and hunched over, seemed old, decrepit—"that old man," said Murdoch. They couldn't possibly go to trial with this crew. Hence, Murdoch finally made up his mind that this had to be settled.

In the other: his run-through was tragic, dire, fatal. Even worse than his deposition. He seemed haplessly befuddled, out of it, stumbling into all kinds of fatal and unnecessary admissions. It was not just that his testimony would be devastating to the case, it would be the ultimate, career-ending humiliation for the ninety-two-year-old man. They could either settle now or they would be forced into a settlement for vastly more money as soon as Murdoch got off the stand.

Of course, it really didn't matter which was true: both were to the same effect, a trial wasn't possible. It had *never* been possible.

This, of course, had *always* been known, because media company defendants don't go before juries, and plaintiffs positioned for record-breaking settlements don't risk it in court—and Dominion had been looking to break the defamation record for the better part of the last year. (Excluding the $1.4 billion award against Infowars and Alex Jones, which would likely never be paid to the Sandy Hook parent plaintiffs, the next highest defamation amount was the pink-slime settlement at $177 million.)

Both sides worked throughout the weekend before the trial was to begin; the judge agreed to delay the start of the trial by a day—that Monday—but insisted on moving forward on Tuesday with the seating of the jury. But it did not begin at 1:30. Nor 2:30. By 3:00—now too late to begin opening statements—the formally icy defense and plaintiff's counsel were showing an obvious new affability toward each other, unmindful of the restless court. The judge returned to his courtroom just before 4:00.

Announcing the settlement—a foregone conclusion and yet somehow still a breathless surprise in the courtroom ("What did he say? What did he say? Was that it?")—Judge Davis, a headmaster type with iron-gray hair, rimless glasses, and a long face, sheepishly rationalized for the jury that while their presence was for naught, actually, just having them show up and sit there had had a bracing effect.

He did not, and did not have to, single out the lone white man in the jury box.

The jury simply held up a mirror to the glaring flaws of Fox's defense: Fox's world, its logic, its behavior, its conspiracies, with its 1 percent African American audience, its billionaire owners, and its Trump-loving hosts, hardly had a hope of translating—even without its long incriminating paper trail—to an urban jury in an overwhelmingly Democratic city.

Plaintiffs in libel cases painstakingly pick through the evidence looking for that one instance—all it takes is one—where a responsible figure in a journalism organization might admit that what was said was known to be false. A plaintiff and his lawyers rarely find such indubitable clarity. Here, though, in *Dominion v. Fox*, there were hundreds of such instances—all of them head-smacking. Reduced to a bare-bones literal interpretation—and that's what a trial was—what you had was a mountain of evidence showing that the defendant, despite knowing otherwise, had broadcast lies for its own profit. And larger than that, here was a news operation whose very business model was to feed its audience a false vision of the world.

But perhaps worst of all for the network, by setting up its stars for public humiliation, exposing the wide gap between what they said and what they believed, putting them on a witness stand where they could be compelled to admit their fraud might do serious damage to the network's ability to keep doing this profitable work.

Not to mention, there was a former president responsible for vast profits at the network, whose perfidy and mental balance would surely become an issue at trial, who might well be president again, and if so, would hold this shit show against them.

And a brother trying to protect his patrimony from his siblings, about to face a trial that could only embolden their case against him.

But the even greater point was that none of this had to be made clear to anyone. These circumstances were the same at the beginning of the lawsuit as at the end. The most devastating and fateful legal rulings were themselves almost a year old. So, the fact that they were here, minutes away from a trial without a settlement, was in its way a much greater indictment of the company than the lawsuit itself. No one could stop the runaway train. The company's true monetary and reputational exposure kept increasing inexorably after the judge ruled that the Murdochs themselves were culpable—before that they might have extricated themselves at 10 percent of what this would ultimately cost.

In front of a jury, there was no cap on the punitive damages. How much would a Wilmington jury make Fox pay for destroying American democracy? That is how the issue would invariably be framed.

"Trillions," offered Carlson, not too facetiously, who was scheduled to be among the earliest witnesses, planning to fly into Wilmington on a moment's notice, and told to expect he'd be on the stand for two days.

Coming into the weekend before the trial, Dominion's settlement position was $1 billion. Fox was at $500 million.

A majority stake in Dominion was owned by Staple Street Capital, a relatively small private equity firm which had invested $38 million with Dominion in 2018. For a good part of the last year, there had been a degree of tension between the investors and Dominion's CEO John Poulos, who had come to see the lawsuit as both profitable and righteous. And indeed, his pushing forward with the lawsuit, which had yielded more and more favorable rulings, as well as the motherlode of discovery filings, had confirmed both the likelihood of great profit as well as his righteous mission. But now, Staple Street argued—insisted—it was time to take the money, the highest amount that could be extracted, rather than looking years out through the appeal process, trillions aside.

By the weekend, it had come down to Murdoch making a prideful last stand not to go to ten figures, and Dominion looking for its best case over $500 million.

Still, at this point, Murdoch remained a wild card. His age, as well as meaning he should *not* go forward, might also mean he was unrealistic enough to do precisely that (why else had it gotten this far?). And, even as much as any of the sums on the table would be transformative for Staple Street and Dominion, could Fox truly dismiss the righteousness factor, the willingness of Dominion and its investors to put off their payday for heroic stature?

Murdoch kept citing the Infowars–Alex Jones number, not wanting to be associated with that kind of craziness. "We are not Infowars," he kept repeating, insisting on what he apparently saw as a big-business difference between Fox and this other right-wing, conspiracy-mongering upstart. Murdoch now focused the blame on Dinh for switching lawyers. Dinh, in turn, was trying to hold firm at $500 million, hoping to claim this heretofore unimaginable sum as his victory.

Dominion, while it held out for more money, also continued to press for righteousness in some form: an apology, an admission, a head on a stick. Particularly if there was anything *less* than a billion dollars.

They had more of a chance, the Fox side believed, of extracting a billion from Murdoch than contrition.

Dinh, who had now stepped in to personally oversee the negotiations, bringing in settlement consultants to make the case for what he had so blithely ignored (that the need to settle was absolute), also had his own future to protect. A billion would be personally fatal for him, he thought; anything shy of that survivable.

The trial lawyers, ready to get underway in Wilmington, were largely shut out. The real negotiation, taking place in New York, was between Dinh, keeping Murdoch father and son in the background, and Staple Street Capital.

With Dinh trying to hold at $500 million—here was his heroic stand—Hannity's head, which had long been floated, got put back on the table. But not as a public admission, not even as part of the deal. Five hundred million and assurances you'll see certain steps taken that will satisfy you—Rupert had been thinking about this anyway.

Yeah . . . no. There only might be something to talk about if this were public. So still a billion.

Any suggestion that this can be called a billion-dollar settlement just won't fly with Rupert. It's Rupert, you know.

As that man in the shed goes—that intransigent behind-the-scenes figure in a negotiation, implacable, and not necessarily rational, and yet the ultimate decision-maker—Rupert Murdoch, after seventy years of legendary deals, was quite a good one, perhaps even better now for being ninety-two, and possibly less rational.

We're just not going to get to a billion. But really we are not kidding about change and . . . Hannity. It just can't be a quid pro quo, obviously. It's Rupert.

Public settlements often have confidential side deals. But it seemed improbable that anything in writing in this case could stay confidential. Nor did it seem likely that Murdoch would accept anything that might ever look like he had made a quid pro quo deal. But neither would he accept a billion. For Dinh, the pressure to make this happen for under a billion was getting to make-or-break.

On Monday, Murdoch called Carlson. The call should have been to say that a settlement was in the offing, hold tight—those were the messages Carlson had been getting since late the week before—but an aggravated Murdoch instead said Dominion was still off by a zero.

The positions were: Fox's—or Murdoch's—continued determination not to go to a billion, but with anything under it seeming to be fair game; Dominion's expectation that it had considerable room to go above $500 million with the hope that it could yet break through Fox's billion-dollar resolve.

Dinh kept putting Hannity back on the table, but without a side letter. This was a sweetener of the most tepid goodwill type. But Dinh could make this happen. Rupert had always wanted to get rid of Hannity. In this, the things they might have done without this suit, and might do in the future anyway, became convenient, psychologically, and tactically, to the deal at hand.

But no agreement, no real acknowledgment even, that they were doing this in any other way but coincident with the deal, and hence, obviously, no enforcement mechanism. A gentlemen's agreement. *Really*? Practically speaking, after a settlement is reached the parties have a period of time, often up to a week, to file the details with the court. Technically a settlement could come apart in that time if anticipated conditions or actions were not met. So Fox would make its gesture, this coincident event, happen that week. *Really.*

But Dinh's offer of reform—to *trust* him with reform—at $500 million was soft enough to still keep the number moving upward. At some point on Monday, the logical midpoint between $500 million and a billion started to come into view. Dominion understood that it would be able to better its position by a few hundred million—almost $300 million by the end; likewise they were far enough away from Murdoch's billion-dollar line in the sand to approach common ground. How to nail it?

Murdoch's annoyance with Carlson, especially over Ukraine, was balanced by how much Murdoch enjoyed his company, looked forward to speaking to him on the phone, and appreciated the fact that Carlson had built a good relationship with Lachlan. Murdoch even liked Carlson on the air, except for when he was spouting his obvious bullshit. But even that he did well. He didn't think Tucker was actually a racist, although he thought he could really be an asshole. More and more, though, he was bothered by the reports that Carlson might run for president. It seemed ludicrous—like Trump running for president. It just lacked respect for politics itself—the thing Murdoch most respected. He was pissed at Lachlan for not reigning him in. Still, he really did like Tucker. He liked him much better than he liked Hannity, who he didn't like at all. But there was, too, a sense that the issues he raised were greater than his value, though his value was great. Among his children, the Fox backlash could often seem to be the Tucker backlash. Without him, you might take down the Fox temperature by what? Twenty percent? Thirty percent? Maybe more? This was a Murdoch calculation: How much could you cool things and still have Fox be Fox?

Hannity had been offered as a sweetener. Carlson, the ratings leader, more and more the real hard-core face of the new demagogic right wing, was sweeter.

He won't go to a billion. He just won't. Not going to happen. It's Rupert. You know, Rupert and money, when he digs in. So that's it. We're here.

Seven hundred and eighty-five million dollars. *There it is.* Far and away the largest defamation award ever made, outside of Alex Jones and Infowars—*and Jones isn't good for it and we are.*

And while we're not making this a part of anything—he can't live with that—we do understand what you want and things will happen. And you don't have to trust us. It will happen by the end of the week. It will be done.

Can you live with that? Can you live with $785 million and Carlson?

24

Tucker

THE LAST SUPPER

In 1998, when Rupert Murdoch announced the end of his second marriage, unsettling the entire Murdoch world, he did it through Liz Smith, a columnist at the *New York Post*. Ever after he used the *Post* to curate, and underplay, the increasingly dramatic signposts of his personal life. On March 20, 2022, less than a month before the Dominion trial, and little more than six months after first meeting Ann Lesley Smith, he used the aged *Post* columnist Cindy Adams (Liz Smith had died in 2017) to announce his engagement at ninety-two to Smith, unnerving his close circle and especially his children for whom the announcement came as a bolt from the blue. The announcement felt awfully like he was hurrying to try to publicly prove something, or, even more disconcerting, that Smith—the thumbnail that attached to her: "a 66-year-old former dental hygienist turned conservative radio host"— was trying to prove something and make it binding.

It's a modest assessment to say that almost everybody near him— his children, executives, the circle of former executives who still checked in with him, and the small group of billionaires and notables, the Kissingers among them, with whom he kept up—was concerned. And for some there was a lot more alarm.

Decline is not binary, but it is inevitable. Here was a vastly wealthy individual and the controlling shareholder and paramount executive of two listed companies. His public face did not acknowledge any difference between ninety-two or eighty-two or seventy-two. Even within his companies—and he did not directly interact with all that many people; to a great extent he was hidden from view—he had become something of a construct that emphasized where his acuity remained consistent and minimized everything else. His memory failures, physical fragility, attention lapses, and hearing deficit, and general decline of executive function, were yet somehow rationalized in terms of his stature—he was Rupert Murdoch after all. And, yes, he had good days and bad days, and often the good really did outweigh the bad. But no one was going to give him that benefit of the doubt in his personal life. Here he was *also* Rupert Murdoch, and his romantic relationship record was hardly good—two marriages had ended in eight years. And it was not likely that it would be better, here at ninety-two.

Why actually did he *need* to get married was a most basic question for a man who regularly proposed on the second date.

For his children, his prospective fifth marriage was a potential disruption to the new and hard-earned status quo: his final years, however limited, were to be theirs. No matter how fractious they were among themselves, at least there would not be a wife with a voice and interests of her own. Against the background of already maximal family drama, the literal last thing that anybody wanted was an additional wild card. Not unfairly, a sixty-six-year-old widow of a much older man, with an apparent history of intra-family contretemps and litigation (a court fight with her husband's children over the estate), who had managed to catch the eye and fancy of the world's most famous mogul, was judged to probably have some serious moves.

She was a striking woman, forthright and sure of herself. She seized a conversation and was emphatic in her views. Often these were black-and-white Fox-ified views. The government was doing this, don't you know? A mysterious "they" peppered her analysis of the modern world. For instance, beyond the North Pole, she told a Murdoch friend over lunch in St. Barts, there is a tropical oasis, a lush paradise created by genetic engineering and protected by secret security forces—she knew a couple whose private plane got too near, and, well, they were shot down (in her telling, the couple's children were in a separate private plane that got away—that's how she knew!).

Elisabeth Murdoch, who had helped talk him through and out of his marriage to Jerry Hall, proceeded patiently, pragmatically, and strategically in her conversations with her happy father, concluding that he knew practically nothing at all about his future wife.

What emerged, to her surprise, was her father's apparent disregard of Smith's evangelicalism. "She's a bit of a Jesus freak, maybe," he acknowledged, but as an afterthought.

The modern conservative movement and a great part of the Fox audience are built on the charismatic fervor and retro social values of the religious right. But Murdoch as an unemoting Presbyterian and, together with his children, long lapsed from their mother's Catholicism, had not only an ideological antipathy but a class contempt for this down-market world. The family, Murdoch included, were in this regard wholly internationalists, taking the upwardly mobile worldview that America, with its fundamentalist deinstitutionalized Christianity, had a screw loose. Murdoch's sudden ability to overlook what would previously have horrified him was just another sign of lost key faculties.

But, anyway, here was a useful wedge and Elisabeth had kept coming back to the subject, probing for more details, and trying not to let her father gloss over it.

The other thing Murdoch told his children and others without apparent concern and, indeed, as though it were one of his fortuitous calling cards—but raising a further red flag with all—was that his fiancée was a huge Tucker Carlson fan.

And, hence, on March 31, at his fiancée's request, Carlson's boss, hearing that he would be in Los Angeles, invited him to dinner at his vineyard in Bel-Air.

For Carlson it was an unexpected invitation but a reassuring one. The Dominion trial would start in little more than two weeks with Carlson scheduled as an early witness. Carlson was aware that his emails, included in the discovery evidence, had caused concern among Fox executives (this was relative—there was a firehose of emails from all parts of the company causing concern). He knew Murdoch had been unhappy with his recent January 6 congressional videotape package and continued to object to his Ukraine views. Still, they had always seemed to get along, with Murdoch hungry for and enjoying Carlson's vast store of political gossip. Carlson liked Murdoch, or, at least, found him to be a character of great fascination. He might be a savage animal, but he also had great manners: you were well received in his company, and he seemed to like to hear what you had to say (not many billionaires actually listened to you). Anyway, whatever other issues there might be, Carlson had enormous respect for Murdoch's vast accomplishments, and, as well, generally thought Murdoch respected him in return. Carlson's opener was one of the few things Murdoch reliably watched on Fox, complimenting Carlson's "style" when others watched with him.

At the vineyard, it was just the three of them, and Murdoch's dog. A social and convivial evening. Drinks first in the living room. But from the get-go there was a discordant note.

"I feel like I'm going to faint," said Smith upon meeting Carlson, grasping her hands together.

Her rapt focus didn't let up. Carlson was a television star and used to undue reactions, but this went over the top. Given that this was the boss's future wife seemed to make it significantly more awkward, with Carlson unable to deflect what was quickly going beyond basic star-struckness.

The general political talk was continually interrupted by Smith's slavish praise of Carlson at random moments.

Murdoch, pro-vax in all regards, chided Carlson, wondering if he was still crazy on the subject, with Smith jumping in to support Carlson and to express incredulity that anyone—in this instance, Murdoch—could defend "the kill shot."

As dinner was served, Smith put her hand on Carlson's and said, "I believe you're a prophet from God."

"Obviously a wise woman," said Carlson, trying to joke.

"No, it's true," she insisted. She would prove it, she said, and got up from the table and returned with a bible.

She then read passages she had previously noted presaging Carlson's arrival in this world, his Christian purpose, and the message he would bring mankind.

This might be nuts, thought Carlson, but on the other hand, the couple seemed very much in love, and it was a happy evening.

Carlson stayed in LA until Sunday to interview Elon Musk and then flew back to Florida that evening.

On Monday morning, Murdoch called to say how pleased he was that Carlson had come to dinner and how much his fiancée had liked Carlson and enjoyed the evening, repeating, with a note of amusement, that she thought Tucker was a prophet from God. Murdoch wanted to make particularly sure that Carlson would be available to come to their wedding in the summer. There was also another reason for Murdoch's call. *Wall Street Journal* reporter Evan Gershkovich had been detained in Russia by state security officials days before with the Russians seemingly ready to charge him with spying. Murdoch wanted Carlson's help in getting him out, with an implication that Carlson found somewhat disconcerting.

"I'm not actually a friend of Putin, you know that, right?" Carlson said to Murdoch.

Nevertheless, Murdoch asked him if he would use *whatever* influence he had. Carlson promised to run a segment on his show about Gershkovich's arrest as soon as possible.

An hour or so after his call with Murdoch, journalist Gabriel Sherman, who sometimes wrote for *Vanity Fair*, texted Carlson.

Sherman was the author of the 2014 book *The Loudest Voice in the Room*, a particularly critical biography of Roger Ailes, for which some of the Murdoch children had been background sources.

In the text, Sherman said he had it on good information that the engagement was off.

"I can tell you that is totally not true," responded Carlson, to whom Murdoch himself had just, effectively minutes ago, confirmed the wedding plans.

Sherman then accurately described details of Carlson's Friday night dinner with Murdoch and Smith, most pointedly the religious exchange.

Carlson, who had yet to share any of the details of the dinner with anyone else, not even his family, immediately called Sherman on the phone, concluding that the description of the dinner had come from inside the Murdoch family—probably through Elisabeth, he believed—and that it had surely come to her from her father. Carlson figured that perhaps there was some article in the works about Smith, and now Sherman was fishing for some critical comment from Carlson. It surely was no more than just a journalist's gambit, all this about the engagement coming apart. Carlson repeated that it was nonsense.

But later that afternoon *Vanity Fair* posted Sherman's entirely accurate report that the two-week engagement had ended—somewhere between the happy dinner on Friday evening and Monday morning, and, it might even seem, somewhere in the short time between Murdoch's call to Carlson and the journalist's text to him.

Of all the reasons that this might seem concerning, Carlson could not help thinking of the Dominion trial, now two weeks away. For months and months, the focus on the trial, that is, the lack of focus, had seemed peculiarly out of line with the stakes. Now, on its eve, a broken engagement, broken in peculiar and unnerving fashion, on the part of the key decision-maker in the suit, seemed like it might be an especially fraught distraction, and, too, an indication that the decision-maker might not be making all his own decisions.

In days following, Murdoch spoke to Carlson several times about the trial (the dinner and broken engagement did not come up). Carlson had been hearing that there was an intense effort to settle, but Murdoch seemed resigned to going forward, his stubborn refusal to pay a billion dollars very much at the forefront of his thinking.

Four days before the trial, Carlson spoke to Dinh, trying to get a greater sense of strategy and confidence levels. Dinh, who Carlson thought had perhaps been drinking, told Carlson he was reconciled to being the fall guy. "That's okay with me," he said, stoically, but eyeing, Carlson understood, a rich payout from the company, if worse came to worst.

On Monday, April 17, the day the jury was supposed to be seated and opening statements begun—before a day's delay was declared—Murdoch told Carlson Dominion was still holding to its b-word demand.

On Tuesday, Fox had a plane on the tarmac at the private-use airport not far from Boca Grande waiting to take Carlson to Delaware for his testimony that might begin as early as Wednesday morning. Slightly before 4:00 p.m., he was notified that a settlement had been reached. He would not have to get on the plane. It was over.

The general with-us-or-against-us protocols at Fox News have reliably meant that a notable defenestration—and there had been ample dramatic ones—is proceeded by a series of leaks and reports so that when the firing comes it isn't entirely a head-spinning surprise for the audience. This also sets up a case for arguing "cause," a legal reason not to pay out the remainder of a contract. Anyway, to be fired at Fox was never wholly a surprise. Fox's PR arm, led by Irena Briganti, Ailes's "fat beast," had a practiced playbook for besmirching anyone soon to leave the network (by choice or otherwise).

But in this instance, there was no prelude. Briganti and her people did not learn what was about to happen until 5:00 that morning, Monday, April 24, six days after the settlement.

At 11:00 a.m., just as Carlson had begun his work on that evening's show, Suzanne Scott called. After some idle chat, Scott said, "Listen, I think we have to go our separate ways."

"Go where?" said a baffled Carlson.

"No, we're taking you off the air."

"Why?" asked Carlson, so perplexed that he remained unruffled. "For how long?"

"No, we're taking you off the air permanently."

"Are you firing me?"

"No, but we're taking you off the air."

Now concerned, Carlson said, "Have there been accusations against me?" There was a recently filed suit by a former Fox booker accusing Fox and the Carlson show of sexism and harassment—but the booker acknowledged that she had never personally met Carlson. "Are you saying that I violated my contract?"

"We're not going to get into specifics at this point. But we would like the statement to acknowledge that our parting is by mutual agreement."

"You would first have to tell me what I'm agreeing to."

"We're just agreeing that you won't be on the air. Can you agree to that?"

"Suzanne, why don't we step back a moment and actually see what we can reasonably agree to. We obviously don't want a war."

"We definitely don't want a war. But we're announcing this right away."

"When?"

"Immediately. So, if we can't agree, then we should end the call."

"All right."

The announcement followed less than a minute later, with no suggestion at all as to why the network's top-rated star would be abruptly
taken off the air—not to the public at large, nor to Carlson, his lawyers,
or to anyone inside Fox. Carlson's company email was cut off, and the
security guard provided by the network was told to pack up. As a measure of how much Carlson had become a political phenomenon in the
nation—and with no reasonable explanation forthcoming—for nearly
two weeks his abrupt removal consistently ranked among the top stories, as large or larger than any other political, social, business, or international news in US media.

A few days later, while the Carlson household was getting ready
for its summer move to Maine, Murdoch called to thank Carlson for
his fourteen years at the network and his contribution to all the success
they had had together. "I just hope you know I'd like to stay friends,"
said Murdoch. "I hope we can."

25

The Talent

CARLSON AND TRUMP

Four hours after Carlson was sacked, Elon called.

Almost simultaneously, Trump, who had run his political campaigns as well as his White House largely through Fox News, was finalizing his move to CNN.

How to maintain a monopoly is the central job of any monopoly.

Fox News began as a play to take market share from CNN, then the singular cable news giant. It not only succeeded in its ratings war with CNN but broke the cable news market—and, practically speaking, the culture at large—into a hegemonic conservative audience and everyone else. Its ownership of this suddenly self-identifying counterculture reached a level of generational media dominance and cultural power achieved only in the rarest instances—in the 1960s perhaps with *TV Guide*, harnessing the lion's share of the television audience (a bigger audience than each network itself), and, more recent, Facebook, owning social media (but only for a few years). Here is channel control and influence that not only produces unprecedented profits, but changes (or dictates) behavior and culture. It's a one-voice phenomenon (Facebook had a multitude of voices, of course, but curated and data-selected them into a remarkably consistent effect).

Ailes's singular goal was to protect what he had built, dominating every time slot, controlling the Fox message, targeting Fox's enemies, using the power of brand and of the Murdoch company's horizontal media reach to achieve maximum industry leverage, and uniquely making one of the two major political parties his mouthpiece (not least of all by making Fox News a high-paying career alternative for Republican politicians), that is, truly, his bitch.

His significance has now almost disappeared under the cloud of his sexual sadism and fetishism, and because of the Murdochs' determined efforts at Fox to cleanse Ailes from its history. Hence, it might be missed that his exit from the scene, and with it his autocratic hold on Fox, is nearly as important as his appearance on it.

"Fucking Donald," ruminated Ailes, two weeks before his death, about his friend, the unexpected president, foreseeing Fox's new predicament, "he's been on television for fourteen years. The president of the United States is a television star, do you have any idea what that means? Reagan was a former star who wanted to be a politician. Believe me, Donald doesn't want to be a politician, he's all star. He won't have any idea how to run the government, nor care, but he knows how to pull every fucking string in television. He knows his audience. Really, he knows good television, no other politician does. Rupert is so fucked if he thinks he can control that."

He did not even try. Or, without basic television skills, and, for twenty years keeping a careful distance from the Fox News corner of his empire, and then having to stand between his squabbling sons vying for the Fox job, he was really not in any place where that was possible. By the time of Ailes's death, the Trump White House was in daily if not hour-by-hour contact with the producers and on-air talent that were largely controlling daytime and prime time at Fox, with Trump himself devoting hours a day to coordinating his own coverage. There was an effective open line to Bill Shine, Ailes's number two who had stepped up to number one. A year later, Shine joined the White House as communications director, maintaining his open line to the Fox control room. That key precept of the Ailes monopoly—Fox leads, the politicians follow—fell with Trump in the White House and Trump in effective control of cable news ratings.

Trump's unbreakable hold on the network during his White House years, the near billion dollars that his colossal nonsense of election fraud and Fox's codependent abetting of it had now cost Murdoch (with the prospect of another billion or more in further lawsuits), and with the grim prospect of his new campaign and horrifying restoration had—a dollar short and a day late—made Rupert Murdoch among his leading enemies. In a final effort of his seventy years of media dominance, an agitated Murdoch had spent as much energy as he could muster over the past year trying to break Trump, and, as much as might be possible, to patch up his own legacy. At the same time, he refused to acknowledge that it needed to be patched up, and, too, in a contradiction he could likewise not acknowledge, expected everyone to maintain Fox's dominance and ratings.

More than the uncharted legal perils Trump faced, Murdoch's efforts to keep the former president off the air seemed to be the actual real crisis of Trump's incipient campaign—to be deplatformed from the primary channel to his core supporters. But this then prompted the existential question for both Fox and Trump. Who was bigger? The Fox monopoly backed by the will (and money) of the most powerful man in the history of media, or the former president and television personality who had become the most famous man on the planet?

Trump placed his call to CNN.

Trump, the simple machine, almost always makes the obvious and characteristic countermove. Fox controlled its world and the conservative politics needed to work within it—that was Ailes's ecosystem and the power of monopoly. But Trump, with his abiding reference that true fame is bigger than anything, was untroubled by that. So, yes, he understood that of course CNN would be willing to put aside its own years of casting him as democracy's Golgotha and a common criminal, as well as Trump's own constant efforts to mock and demean CNN, to improve its own fortunes. (CNN would justify this as strictly a news choice—but what's newsworthy and what's profitable are, ideally, the same.)

The Trump town hall on May 11, less than three weeks after Carlson's firing—with a Fox audience in essence bused into CNN—had originally been set for 9 p.m. to avoid competing with Carlson's high ratings. Trump would go against Fox, but, in a subtle but important point about the growing individual powers at Fox, not against Carlson, who was still in his place at the network when the CNN arrangements were first made; he'd challenge Hannity. This provoked great agitation in the Hannity camp and remonstrating with Scott: *This is what's going to happen, you see, you see! We're up against Trump.* Then, after Carlson's defenestration, CNN was told by the Trump camp that it had to move the town hall to 8:00, which it had little choice but to oblige. Without the higher-rated Carlson to cater to, Trump could now extend a courtesy to Hannity, reminding him whose favor he most depended on. (Then Hannity begged Trump not to let the CNN town hall run over into his hour when, in fact, he had an interview scheduled with Mike Pence!)

"You see," said a Trump inner circle staffer with happy sarcasm, "you can't say all those years of fellating POTUS on air didn't pay off for Sean."

In a single move, Trump had turned CNN into his instrument and given it the wherewithal to compete against Fox. He showed that he owned Fox's remaining star. And gave Fox a demonstration of what eighteen months of the Trump campaign's guerilla attacks on its programming schedule might look like. Fox would simply become another Republican outlier for Trump to run against. (Not incidentally, the Trump weight broke CNN just as it was threatening to break

Fox: the town hall was the direct cause of the firing of CNN chief Chris Licht a few weeks later.)

In the days after the CNN Trump town hall, Murdoch told friends, in a new ironic tumble of virtue, that he would never have allowed Trump—whose performance at the CNN town hall was quite a singular encapsulation of his many years of Fox-enabled gaslighting and shamelessness—to do that on his watch. Meanwhile, the Trump campaign was in discussions with every other network for prime-time appearances (including Fox as well).

Within the space of a few weeks, Fox lost both an exclusive Tucker Carlson and a virtually exclusive Donald Trump, its two ratings pillars. In a taped interview with Bret Baier in early summer, Trump jauntily attacked Murdoch, with remarks later cut from the show.

The official line from Fox, internally, to advertisers, media, and the industry, was that it had lost big stars before and, beyond the short term, had suffered very little.

It was protected by its monopoly.

That monopoly system—Ailes's system—with its blunt-force strength and unforgiving enforcement arm, went to work in the days after Carlson's defenstration. Irena Briganti set up a war room tasked with retailing the multilayered case for why he was fired: in sum, general perfidy, moral turpitude, and bizarre views. This was his formal exile from the only game in town.

Not having had any warning of the move against Carlson or the time to build a slow-burn case that might make his end seem inevitable, nor have an actual reason for why he was fired, Briganti piled it on in particular shocked-shocked fashion. (It was also personal for Briganti. Fox—that is, Briganti—released to its corporate sister publication, the *Wall Street Journal*, snippets of Carlson's damaging emails, including the fact that he had called a senior woman executive at Fox a "cunt," implying that this was Scott, the network's senior-most and nearly singular female executive, when in fact it was Briganti herself, which fact Briganti conveniently elided.) Background briefings from the network cited a shadow world about Carlson that would soon be revealed.

Not long after he was fired, Carlson wrote his former bosses:

> Dear Rupert, Lachlan, Viet and Suzanne: I just heard from two reporters that Fox is shopping a story that I behaved in sexually inappropriate ways with staff, including with Fox contributor Jessica Tarlov, with whom I supposedly had an affair. Reporters are further being told by media relations at Fox that I committed "improprieties," exhibited "problematic behavior," and that "extensive" details of "further accusations" will soon emerge. All of this is a lie, as you well know. As the happily married father of four children, I feel deeply threatened by it. I haven't said a word publicly about Fox News since you pulled my show, and I hope I never have to. But this is too much. It's also unnecessary. I've always been grateful to Fox, and to you four. It shouldn't be hard to end this amicably. Let's. I'd ask that you put a stop to this immediately before it escalates in a way that hurts everyone very badly. Thank you.

Murdoch assured Carlson that no such efforts were underway or would be tolerated.

One ironic aspect of Briganti's campaigns against Fox's own people— not limited to Carlson—is that they so often take place through the *New York Times*. That is, the *Times'* animosity toward Fox made it the oddly perfect vehicle through which Fox might damage its own people. Briganti's voice had been trackable through the *Times'* three-part critique on Carlson a year before his removal; it would be evident in the *Times'* account of Fox's poor handling of the Dominion legal strategy, with the blame placed here on Viet Dinh (quite an indication either that the

Murdochs were imminently planning to get rid of him, or Briganti herself was taking him on—or both).

Fox's case against Carlson, retailed through the liberal media in the weeks after he was taken off the air—while Fox ritually denied there was a leaker or even that there was a case against him—was a case against itself. Fox might be white, chauvinist, nativist, and conspiratorial in its views, pushing those views further than almost anyone dreamed they might be pushed, but Carlson was this, in a dialectic that could translate only if you ignored the slapstick of it, *and more*. Carlson, in his six years in prime time, had become more Fox than Fox—that was Fox's effective case against him.

Unable to admit that Carlson was a casualty of the Dominion settlement—and this had become such an unwritten secret at the highest echelons of Fox that the secret seemed no longer to exist, with Murdoch waving off the settlement as Dinh's—Fox itself now had to find its own rationale that, as it happened, with unintended symmetry, effectively accepted the liberal case against itself. He had to go because . . . he offended the *New York Times*!

This was going to be hard to explain to its own audience. On the other hand, it was not really trying. In some sense, this was a case being made almost entirely for people who did not watch Fox. When the *Times* had gone after Carlson in its three-part series, it had had no effect on his ratings—his audience stayed in place, unaffected and perhaps largely unaware of the *Times*' furious critique. Now, as the ratings came in, more than half of Carlson's audience failed to show up, uninterested apparently in what Fox might offer in his stead.

After a week of disastrous ratings in the 8:00 hour and spreading across the evening, Murdoch began to actively panic, blaming Scott and his son for not having better programming suggestions, and reviving the idea of Piers Morgan in the slot. Murdoch also proposed putting in Carlson's place a round table of *Wall Street Journal* editorial writers, "wise men," in Murdoch's programming concept. A month later, MSNBC, the historic last-place news channel, was beating Fox in key time slots.

The case Briganti was making against Carlson was indeed a case for "cause"—that is, the rationale by which Fox could cancel its contract with Carlson and walk away from its obligations. But, contradicting the public case it was making, it wasn't doing that, it wasn't firing him. In fact, it was adamantly refusing to sever his formal employment. As Carlson's lawyer, in the weeks afterward, pressed more and more for a resolution that would allow Carlson to return to broadcasting in time for the election season—even offering to forgo the payout on the two years left on his contract—Murdoch himself, as the time-slot numbers plummeted, became more and more insistent on keeping Carlson from competing with the network.

"We might not get the audience, but no one else will," Murdoch said, seeming to arrive at some point of satisfaction, and casting two million or so right-wingers into a political and media void.

Still, by the summer, as Carlson seemed intent on baiting Fox into suing him with a regular schedule of Twitter broadcasts, Fox seemed reluctant to press beyond threatening letters. Will Carlson's shtick work in a different medium—Twitter monologues? That is likely not the right question. Rather, how many new shticks will Fox be facing? How many new voices will Trump, that ultimate shtickmeister, profitably inspire to the far-wacko right of Fox?

Nearly two months after Carlson was taken off the air, Fox finally rejigged its schedule, demoting Ingraham to the 7:00 hour, leaving Hannity in place, and filling out prime time with Jesse Waters and Greg Gutfeld, both more insult conservatives than ideological ones. ("Do you think they're funny?" an unconvinced Murdoch was asking people.)

Carlson and Trump were talking together about how they might team up in a series of counterprogramming events and go head-to-head against Fox. Trump began to casually discuss Carlson as a possible vice president, a wicked maneuver against Fox and Murdoch. Trump's political wars were always as much against Republicans as Democrats. It was natural to now take the fight to Fox.

Like all monopolies (and religions and single-party states), Fox was built on a great, uncompromising, stubborn, black-and-white, simple-machine literal-mindedness: us against them. Appropriately it is felled not just by its own overreaching and sense of impunity but by something like a conflicted conscience: the Murdochs feel bad, about Tucker, about Trump, about themselves.

Too late, they try to reject the monsters they have created.

But the monsters, Trump and Carlson, the first- and second-most-famous and most-hated figures in the land, are by this time bigger than the network that made them. In that age-old media tension, the best talent becomes larger than the platform by which it has been nurtured—and walks out the front door. Elvis leaves the building.

In the bittersweet department, accompanied by the wild laughter of his enemies, you have the lonely figure of Rupert Murdoch, ninety-two-year-old Rupert Murdoch, now shaded by doubt, ambivalence, regret, and bafflement, and the harsh and clanging voices of his children. Not the best mindset with which to hold a kingdom.

Epilogue

Rupert

APRÈS MOI

He dies.

His voting shares in the Murdoch Family Trust are equally distributed among the four remaining voting members, Prudence, Elisabeth, Lachlan, and James Murdoch. All decisions impacting the management of these assets become, upon his death, at the discretion of the four votes. Without a tie-breaking mechanism, a unanimous vote of four or a majority of three is needed to take any action. His two youngest children, Grace and Chloe, have a financial participation in the trust, but not a voting right—that is, no voice at all in what happens, except that they, like their four siblings, each have a net worth of approximately $2 billion, so they have lawyers, too (probably separate sets of lawyers), and a right to have their financial interest equitably dealt with and fairly protected.

The four voting members are unlikely to get in a room together, not even on a Zoom call. Lachlan and his brother James have not had direct contact, except through legal representatives, in more than five years; contact now would reasonably be deemed not productive, even ugly.

Anyway, there are professionals for this, the legal and banking advisers of each trust member, all with their own teams (and billable hours). With their father's death, there is obvious new urgency, but conversations have been going on for some time, anticipating both the "event" and the uncertainty, conflict, and potential fallout to follow. The family members who are talking to each other will also have conferred, along with their teams, and may or may not have arrived at mutual positions. The trust charter has a mechanism under which a meeting and vote can be called at the earliest moment—and James, for one, has been insisting there is no time to lose. Still, there may be reasons in the short term for that meeting to be delayed, not least because there are a lot of advisers to assemble and because it's impossible to predict how the impact of the "event" itself, no matter for how long it has been anticipated, might suddenly change the field of play. What's the media reaction? How will the obits read? What will the stock market say? When the formal meeting is called it will most likely be attended by proxies and nominees and perhaps none of the principals.

The trust holds control of the assets of the Fox Corporation and of News Corporation, approximately $25 billion in market value—potentially much more in a sale of individual assets—plus a variety of privately owned interests, including extensive property holdings. Without resolution and a unified expression of the view of the controlling shareholders, it is hard to imagine how management of these two companies would proceed, except in a state of stasis, with present management acting as passive caretakers trying to avoid future shareholder suits.

Currently, one of the four voting members, Lachlan Murdoch, fifty-one, a resident of Australia, has day-to-day executive control of the $15 billion US-based Fox Corporation. The other three, Prudence, sixty-five, living in Sydney, Elisabeth, fifty-four, living in London, and James Murdoch, fifty, living in New York, currently have no formal involvement in the corporate decision-making, but two, Elisabeth and

James, regard themselves as sophisticated media business managers and dealmakers. Prudence has had no professional interest in media or in her father's businesses. News Corporation has a separate CEO unrelated to the family, Robert Thomson. Rupert Murdoch occupied the position of Executive Chairman at News Corporation and Lachlan Murdoch, who now holds the position of cochairman of the board, might move to immediately have the News Corporation board appoint him to the top executive position—no doubt antagonizing family members, and possibly provoking what might be the first of many related lawsuits.

Lachlan Murdoch's stated intention is to maintain his job as the chief executive of Fox Corporation, and to that end has been raising money to buy out one or more of his siblings to give him effective voting control of the company. In 2022, he tried to combine both of the trust-controlled public companies to help him in his effort. That tactic failed.

James Murdoch's stated intention is to take control from his brother with a plan to grow the Fox News brand beyond the US cable market and to move it far away from partisan political news.

A curious aspect of this is that while the trust controls a little over 40 percent of the voting shares of Fox, its ownership stake when the nonvoting shares are considered is much less. For each of the six beneficiaries the monetary value of Fox might be substantially less than a billion dollars. For the two warring brothers, the calculation is surely that control of a powerful and influential media platform comes at a discount price. For each brother, Fox, at less than a billion, is a deal worth fighting for.

The sisters, not directly benefiting from this power, and, currently, feeling Fox's negative impact, might seem logically to feel otherwise.

Elisabeth Murdoch, maintaining her relationship with both brothers, albeit from a separate country, has advocated selling all or parts of Fox Corporation, including Fox News. Prudence Murdoch has expressed a knowing skepticism toward both of her half brothers, but otherwise does not appear to have a strategic corporate view but might logically see the value in cashing out.

In addition to each trust member's legal and financial teams, Lachlan Murdoch, as the Fox Corporation CEO, along with his own personal advisers, would be gearing up his company to defend against what might be understood as his brother's efforts to lead a hostile takeover. Similarly, the Fox board, accountable to all the Fox shareholders and not just the Murdoch trust, will have retained its own legal counsel and financial advisers in the event that the interests of the other shareholders in the company diverge from both the company CEO and the controlling shareholders. News Corporation, too, will have its advisers in place anticipating the uncertain actions of its major shareholders. The trust itself, because it has two beneficiaries, Grace Murdoch and Chloe Murdoch, with only a financial interest, may need its own counsel to safeguard their positions.

Lachlan Murdoch's plans for a buyout, of course, depend upon his efforts to raise money from outside sources—his sources in the Persian Gulf, for instance. The cost of a buyout is further complicated and increased because the trust controls two companies—investors may be interested in one and not the other. (Combining both companies would have made this easier, but that effort came to naught.) He would presumably need to buy out his two sisters to be able to break the tie—and, indeed, the trust itself may have to be dissolved by a vote of three before any individual buyout is possible. Given the vast wealth of each of the parties, the economic incentive is limited, yet at the same time, given the lack of a direct economic incentive, there is no reason *not* to hold out for the maximum return. So, playing into his sister Elisabeth's view, if Lachlan is making an offer to effectively control the company they might just as well open the field to other bidders and seek the full value of each individual piece of the corporate holdings. You can, after all, never be too rich.

Of course, the two sisters could choose to neither press for a sale nor to support their brother James's more drastic plan for corporate overhaul, and leave their brother Lachlan in place, at least for the time being. Perhaps there would be concessions—Elisabeth joining the board, for instance, even as board chairman. But the more or less liberal and socially well-placed sisters would in that case presumably want changes to Fox's editorial position—but then, why leave the status-quo brother in control?

Depending on how effectively in the last few years their brother James might have impressed them with his views and plans, they could well support him in his plan for radical overhaul, as he believes they will. This might be seen as the legacy move. They make a statement and show their mettle by dismantling Fox—likely sacrificing billions of their shareholders' money to do it.

Each company is currently controlled by a board of directors. Assuming Lachlan remains recalcitrant and yet in control of his board, in order to oust him the three votes would need, first, to use their controlling position in the trust and as the controlling shareholders in the company to replace the board members in Lachlan's camp—and then have the new board fire him. That was the procedure by which Sumner Redstone's daughter, Shari, ousted her father's former allies.

But Lachlan could fight his siblings. Viet Dinh might likely be urging as much, both because this is exciting corporate stuff, the kind of occasion that lawyers rise to, and because, at the very least, the fight increases Dinh's own personal bargaining position. Certainly, Dinh has a doubtful Fox corporate life otherwise—he would be fired under James's management. This might go, too, for Robert Thomson at News Corporation who could well be incentivized to join this battle. Both men might count on maximizing their exit packages in an effort to settle what would be a prolonged and costly corporate fight. Still, it would be a stiff, and probably impossible, proxy battle. The trust controls over 40 percent of the voting shares; a certain number of shareholders don't vote, and a rock-bottom minimum of 10 percent would certainly default to voting with the family trust, easily giving the trust a majority.

It would be a long, debilitating battle. Taking this through a series of suits and countersuits easily puts a resolution a year away, perhaps two, during which various future plans for trust members would be put on hold, the businesses themselves paralyzed, outside advisers enriched to an infuriating degree, and media coverage unsparing. Would the siblings truly have the stomach for this?

So is there a more rational, less absolute way to parse these rather vast assets to arrive at a tolerable solution?

In the days after their father's death, the sensible, grounded question would probably revolve around what Lachlan might accept to give up his control of Fox News. If he can't buy out his siblings, can his siblings buy him out? What would it take for him to go away? Well . . .

It's probably unlikely that Lachlan would just take the leadership of News Corporation and let James run Fox Corporation and turn the news channel into his "force for good." But what if James and perhaps his siblings were willing to trade their interest in News Corporation for Lachlan's interest in Fox, thereby giving Lachlan full control of a company with substantial Australian assets? He could stay home in Sydney and be the most powerful person in the land.

But this would likely bring James, and his sisters, if they came along, face to face with a harsh reality: Would they be willing to pay the current value of Fox knowing that James's plans might destroy a substantial part of its worth? Even the very, very wealthy might, at this point, have second thoughts about the cost of making the world safe for democracy (of course, the lion's share of the loss value would be absorbed by the Fox shareholders).

Beyond implacable family rivalries, and the meaning of their father's historic legacy, and with the stakes involving the most powerful political voice in the country, it's still business. Alas. The dominant activity of the

Murdoch family business in Australia is newspaper publishing, with almost all the papers there—70 percent of the Australian newspaper market—losing money; the biggest cash generator is the family's joint ownership of Foxtel, a subscription TV service on a steady decline. Would Lachlan really want that? The *Wall Street Journal* and Harper-Collins yet make money, but they are a newspaper and a book publisher, with no one in the family showing keen interest in print media. What's more, their full value would likely only be realized in a sale where ego and synergies might unlock a premium price. As for the cable television business, and a single channel in a heavily consolidated industry at that, what might you say? Except that with a consistent nosedive in advertising, endemic cord cutting, and the shift to direct-to-consumer subscription models, the foreseeable future only holds decreased revenues and audiences—the death of cable, in other words, slow at first, then off the cliff.

In the end, what is the important value to the rich?

Grudges, sentimentality, ego, and liberal politics aside, there is high personal advantage in a clean exit, free of ongoing legal entanglements, negative press, and always the relentless anxiety of the next shoe to drop. Indeed, the sorting of personal issues, and the irregular demands of family members in a public company with heavy family control, invariably lead, in a fraught environment, to lawsuits from the other shareholders, whose issues remain wholly economic. You're not only fighting each other; you're fighting everyone else.

Plus, the voting members of the trust have a fiduciary duty to the nonvoting beneficiaries of the trust—Grace and Chloe—who, with their own lawyers to guard against the trust's assets being wasted, represent another extended negotiation or potential battleground.

All this might be put aside, as families with contentious assets often do, and a clean exit accomplished by turning the holdings into cash and equitably dividing the proceeds. That would certainly increase the fortunes each of the Murdoch children already possesses, if that matters, and, curiously, it always seems to.

Rupert Murdoch was a shy and inexpressive man. But power and money, and the drama that created around him, and the identity that created for him, kept him, compulsively, at the center of the action. Money alone, as central as that was to him, was not enough. He needed passions to be swirling around him. But without that need, his children—who have consistently fled the eye of his storm—have created different lives for themselves.

In the aftermath of the storm, what do they do? When the day clears, they start the cleanup and begin to appreciate the nice weather.

Acknowledgments

This is the fifth book that I have published with Henry Holt since 2017. In each instance, Holt has sprung into action with an all-hands enthusiasm and can-do efficiency. Instead of the typical book schedule of many months, publication has happened in weeks. Amy Einhorn, Sarah Crichton, Chris Sergio, Caitlin Mulrooney-Lyski, Caitlin O'Shaughnessy, Marian Brown, Anita Sheih, Janel Brown, Chris O'Connell, Meryl Levavi, Emily Walters, Peter Richardson, Carolyn Telesca, Natalia Ruiz, and Conor Mintzer have not only offered enthusiasm, insight, and good ideas, but their evenings and weekends.

In the UK, at Little, Brown—my fifth book there, too—I have been lucky to have the support of Charlie King, Sameer Rahim, Jane Phillips, and Maddie Mogford.

The Wylie Agency has been an invaluable partner on this book and the many before it. As always, I have depended on the counsel and support of Andrew Wylie, Jeffrey Posternak, and James Pullen.

The mistakes here are all my own. But there are far fewer of them because of Amy Morris, who has fact-checked the book with patience and care.

Once more, I cannot offer enough thanks to Eric Rayman for his wise, understanding, and perspicacious legal review. This is our sixth book together.

I am grateful for the time and advice of my early readers: Edward Jay Epstein, Janice Min, Dylan Jones, James Toback, James Truman, Leela de Kretser, Chris de Kretser, Michael Jackson, Renata Adler, David Rhodes, Joanna Coles, Stevan Keane, and David Margolick.

The many sources who have helped me with insights, background, personal recollections, and knowledge of all the personalities at play in this story are probably best thanked by not being thanked here. But you know who you are and I am in your debt.

My wife, Victoria, my children Elizabeth, Susanna, Steven, Louise, and Jack, are either in noisy distance as I have written this or otherwise always in my thoughts. I do this with them.

About the Author

Michael Wolff is the author of the bestselling, authoritative trilogy about the Trump White House: *Fire and Fury*, *Siege*, and *Landslide*. His other books include the seminal biography of Rupert Murdoch, *The Man Who Owns the News*. A two-time winner of the National Magazine Awards, he has been a columnist for *New York* magazine, *Vanity Fair*, British *GQ*, the *Hollywood Reporter*, and the *Guardian*. He lives in New York City with his family.

The Teaberry Strangler

A TEA SHOP MYSTERY

THE TEABERRY STRANGLER

LAURA CHILDS

WHEELER
CHIVERS

31.99 *LARGE TYPE*
Childs, L.

This Large Print edition is published by Wheeler Publishing, Waterville, Maine, USA and by BBC Audiobooks Ltd, Bath, England.
Wheeler Publishing, a part of Gale, Cengage Learning.
Copyright © 2010 by Gerry Schmitt & Associates, Inc.
The moral right of the author has been asserted.

LIBRARY OF CONGRESS CATALOGING-IN-PUBLICATION DATA

Childs, Laura.
   The teaberry strangler / by Laura Childs.
     p. cm. — (Tea shop mystery ; no. 11)
   ISBN-13: 978-1-4104-2500-3
   ISBN-10: 1-4104-2500-2
   1. Browning, Theodosia (Fictitious character)—Fiction. 2. Map dealers—Crimes against—Fiction. 3. Murder—Investigation—Fiction. 4. City and town life—South Carolina—Charleston—Fiction. 5. Tearooms—Fiction. 6. Charleston (S.C.)—Fiction. 7. Large type books. I. Title.
   PS3603.H56T43 2010b
   813'.6—dc22   2010009545

BRITISH LIBRARY CATALOGUING-IN-PUBLICATION DATA AVAILABLE

Published in 2010 in the U.S. by arrangement with The Berkley Publishing Group, a member of Penguin Group (USA) Inc.
Published in 2010 in the U.K. by arrangement with The Berkley Publishing Group, a division of Penguin Group (USA) Inc.

U.K. Hardcover: 978 1 408 49178 2 (Chivers Large Print)
U.K. Softcover: 978 1 408 49179 9 (Camden Large Print)

Printed in the United States of America
1 2 3 4 5 6 7 14 13 12 11 10

For my old Mission Critical Marketing gang

ACKNOWLEDGMENTS

My thanks to Sam, Tom, Niti, Bob, Jennie, Dan, Moosh, Asia, Elmo, and the fine people at Berkley who handle design, publicity, and sales. A special thank-you to all tea lovers, tea shop owners, bookstore owners, librarians, reviewers, magazine writers, websites, and radio stations who have enjoyed the ongoing adventures of Theodosia, Drayton, Haley, and the rest of the Indigo Tea Shop regulars.

The poem "My Fragrant Cup of Tea," from which Drayton so freely quotes, is from the book *Tea Poetry,* compiled by Pearl Dexter, editor of *Tea: A Magazine.*

1

A back-alley crawl had certainly *sounded* like a tantalizing idea to Theodosia when she'd first conceived it.

A blue-black Charleston evening in early March. Candles flickering up and down the narrow cobblestone alleys that snaked behind Church Street's charming shops. And shopkeepers in historic costumes throwing open their back doors to invite visitors in for tea, Charleston cookies, steaming mugs of crab chowder, and special prices on antiques, oil paintings, giftware, sweetgrass baskets, and leather-bound books.

And, as far as Theodosia Browning was concerned, entrepreneur and historic district booster that she was, the event had been a rousing success.

Hordes of folks, locals as well as tourists, had thronged the back alley, dashing from shop to charming shop. And a whole lot of

11

them had dropped into her tea shop, too. She'd doled out more fresh-brewed cups of Darjeeling, tea sandwiches, and miniature quiches than she could remember serving in a long time.

But now, as the back door of the Indigo Tea Shop snicked shut, Theodosia peered down the length of the alley and suddenly had second thoughts about venturing out alone.

For one thing, the hour was late. Almost ten o'clock. And where visitors had swarmed up and down her alley some forty-five minutes ago, now there didn't seem to be any foot traffic at all.

Spooky, Theodosia thought to herself, as palm trees thrashed in the cool wind and dim, yellow gaslights glowed faintly in the mist. She wondered, just for an instant, if she shouldn't run upstairs and snap a leash on Earl Grey. Let her frisky guard dog Dalbrador prance along beside her. Or perhaps she should pop her head back into the warm, fragrant tea shop and ask Drayton, her master brewer and right-hand man, to accompany her.

"Silly," Theodosia murmured. "I'm only going a few doors down."

Pulling an old-fashioned cloak around her shoulders, the cloak that had served as her costume this evening, Theodosia gathered up her basket of tea and scones and set off down the alley. She was headed for the Antiquarian Map Shop, just down Church Street. The owner, Daria Shand, was a dear friend and probably in need of a little sustenance by now.

Theodosia felt the first drops of rain hit her shoulders and immediately thought, *Frizzies.* With masses of curly auburn hair to contend with, Theodosia sometimes projected the aura of a Renaissance woman captured in portrait by Raphael or even Botticelli. Smooth peaches-and-cream complexion, intense blue eyes, and the calm, often slightly bemused look of a self-sufficient woman in her mid-thirties. A woman who possessed a fair amount of life experience, but still looked forward to a wide-open future.

Flipping her hood up, resigning herself to the steady rain, Theodosia picked her way carefully along wet cobblestones. The squall that had been threatening for days had finally blown in from the Atlantic. Thank goodness it had held off this long.

She was passing the Cabbage Patch gift shop when a gust of wind flipped her cape up and threatened to send her airborne like the Flying Nun.

Theodosia fought the elements for a few moments, feeling like an umbrella turned inside out, then finally got her cape and basket righted. Glancing up as rain spat harder, she suddenly stared down the dim alley and beheld a bizarre scenario.

Theodosia's first, fleeting impression was of two people locked in a lover's embrace. Three seconds later she realized a nasty struggle was taking place.

A struggle? Really? Or were her eyes playing tricks on her?

With rain streaming in her eyes, the two figures appeared more like ethereal blue-black shadows, dancing and twisting in some grotesque embrace. But as their dance turned even more macabre, one figure grasped the other by the neck, forcing the other to drop to its knees.

Oh no!

A sharp burst of lightning lent bizarre special effects, leaching color from the landscape and giving the floundering figures the appearance of a slow-moving film negative.

"Stop!" Theodosia yelled. "Don't . . ."

Her plaintive cry was drowned out by a sharp crack of thunder that rattled nearby windows then continued to grumble ominously.

One of the figures was completely down on the ground now, unmoving, while the other bent over it, flailing like mad. Then, as if suddenly cognizant of a witness, the figure straightened up and gazed down the alley at Theodosia.

Theodosia's heart played a timpani beat in her chest as she sensed anger and rage, and she feared this person might turn on her. Instead, the figure spun and darted off into the pounding rain.

Dropping her basket, Theodosia sprinted for the downed figure.

Panic triggered by recognition shot through her like another bolt of lightning. It was her friend Daria Shand! But not the tall, reddish-blond beauty she knew and loved. This Daria's face was a grotesque mask of purple, her eyes half open and pupils staring into nowhere. And seemingly not breathing!

What to do? Call 911 or chase after the assailant?

Calling 911 won out, of course. And as Theodosia knelt in the alley, pummeled by wind and rain, clutching her cell phone, pounding frantically on Daria's chest, trying to recall her long-ago CPR training, a wave of helplessness washed over her.

Was there nothing she could do? But

15

Daria still hadn't drawn a single, strangled gasp, and the words *crime scene* were swirling sickly in Theodosia's brain.

Minutes later, two shrieking squad cars, red-and-blue light bars pulsing, rocked to a stop in the alley. They were followed by a boxy orange-and-white ambulance.

"Help her!" Theodosia screamed, though she feared Daria was beyond help. Probably, she was in her Creator's hands now.

Theodosia was caught in a swirl of activity then. EMTs working over Daria, more police officers arriving to cordon off the area, an officer firing questions at her, taking notes, trying to get a firsthand account.

At hearing all the commotion, Drayton and Haley came running down the alley from the Indigo Tea Shop, fear and concern etched on their faces.

And a familiar burgundy Crown Victoria slid to a stop in the alley.

"Tidwell," Theodosia murmured when she caught sight of the car.

Detective Burt Tidwell, overweight, articulate, and perpetually suspicious, headed the Robbery-Homicide Division of the Charleston PD. He was prickly rather than gracious and routinely brusque with everyone who got in his way. Though his suit coats rarely buttoned over a stomach that sometimes

16

resembled an errant weather balloon and he could sometimes look the buffoon, Tidwell was as predatory as they came. Smart, canny, a dogged investigator.

Pulling himself from his car, Tidwell donned an enormous black rain slicker and lumbered toward the victim, who still lay in the exact spot she'd fallen. At that same moment, the back door of the Antiquarian Map Shop burst open, and a bearded man in a blue-and-white-checkered shirt suddenly cried, "Daria! Is that Daria? What happened?"

"Who are you?" Tidwell asked in his big cat growl.

"Her boyfriend, Joe Don. Let me through. Let me see her!"

Tidwell raised a hand, and two uniformed officers immediately barred the way.

"Later," Tidwell told him. "Questions first."

"That's not right," Theodosia said, speaking up. "He's her boyfriend. He has a right . . ." She stared at Tidwell, anger and grief on her face, thinking he looked for all the world like a bloated vampire in his dark, shiny rain slicker.

"And you are here, why?" Tidwell asked her in a clipped voice.

"She discovered the victim," one of the

17

officers told Tidwell.

"And only doors down from your little tea shop," said Tidwell, turning his unblinking gaze upon Theodosia. "How very convenient."

"Be serious!" snapped Theodosia. "She was my friend. A good friend!"

"My sincere apology," said Tidwell, though he didn't sound one bit sincere. Or apologetic.

Theodosia shook off Tidwell's insensitivity and took a step closer to where Daria still lay. "It just doesn't make sense," she mourned. "Why would someone want to kill Daria?"

Tidwell leaned in and peered at the lifeless body that lay sprawled like a rag doll cast aside. And in a flat, almost impersonal tone, murmured, "Maybe they thought it was you."

2

"I simply loathe Tidwell's suggestion of mistaken identity," sputtered an outraged Drayton. "Why on earth would someone want to kill Theodosia? The notion's utterly preposterous!"

"Calm down," cautioned Haley, as she rubbed a silver teaspoon against her white chef's smock, polishing it to a lustrous patina. "That was just Tidwell running his yap again. Trying to be the hotshot homicide detective."

"Which he is," said Theodosia. She was putting the finishing touches on an arrangement of tulips, lilies, and orchids in a tall, straight-sided glass vase that had been wrapped with a piece of white birch bark and then a snippet of raffia. The effect was artful and pretty, but did nothing to alleviate the sadness she was feeling.

It was just before nine on Tuesday morning at the Indigo Tea Shop, and Theodosia,

Drayton, and Haley were setting up for the day. Although they were all doing their darndest to pretend it was another normal day, they all knew in their hearts it was not. One of their own, a fellow shopkeeper and friend, had been brutally murdered. So that nasty reality hung heavy over their heads like a dark shroud.

"I can't fathom what the killer's motive might have been," said Drayton. Setting a pink Royal Doulton teacup onto its saucer with a gentle clink, he pinched the tiny handle between his fingers and arranged it just so.

"Passion," said Haley, pulling a pack of matches from the pocket of her chef's jacket and lighting one of the tea lights. "It was probably a crime of passion. That's what they said in the newspaper article."

"But passion can also translate as rage, obsession, or even lunacy," said Drayton. He straightened up and gazed solemnly about with hooded gray eyes. A stickler for perfection, Drayton always dressed with great care. Today he sported a classic Harris tweed jacket with trademark bow tie, which made him look aristocratic in bearing and every inch the southern gentleman he was.

"Maybe there's a serial killer loose in Charleston," speculated Haley. She pushed a hank of long blond hair behind her ear and stared at Drayton with guileless blue eyes.

"Don't even *think* such a terrible thing," Drayton admonished her. He turned toward Theodosia, who was now seated at the small table by the fireplace, checking her reservation book. "Our dear Haley has quite the runaway imagination. Chalk it up to youth, I suppose."

"Maybe so," said Theodosia, glancing up. "But Haley's probably just being realistic."

Drayton pursed his lips and let his tortoiseshell half-glasses slide down his aquiline nose. "Excuse me, you're implying you and I are idealistic?"

Theodosia managed a weak smile. "Most of the time we are." She gazed around, studying the cozy interior of the tea shop. "We work in an environment where people flock to us for good conversation, excellent food, and a refined atmosphere."

"And that's exactly what we deliver," said Drayton, a touch of pride in his voice. "There isn't a lovelier, cozier tea shop in the entire city."

"In the state," added Haley.

"And we serve jasmine, Darjeeling, and Earl Grey tea, just to name a few," said Theodosia. "And Haley's prodigious baking skills turn out the most marvelous sweet potato scones, cranberry muffins, and banana bread you'd ever want to eat." She smiled. "And between our tea and baked goods, the atmosphere is so deliciously fragrant it's like a dose of aromatherapy for your soul."

"Hmm," said Drayton, frowning slightly. "I *suppose* I see where you're going with this. We do exist in a slightly rarefied atmosphere. You might even say the entire historic district's that way. Antiques, gorgeous mansions, cobblestone streets bountifully lined with live oak trees."

"You wouldn't want the Indigo Tea Shop to change, would you?" asked Haley. "Dump our old-fashioned ways and switch our name to Tea Biddy's or something equally silly so we can hustle customers in and out with to-go type food?"

"Goodness, no," said Theodosia. "I don't ever want to change a thing. All I'm saying is we should probably be a little more cognizant of what's going on. Realize that even our own little slice of Charleston can be a dangerous place."

Drayton's brows beetled together. "Is the back door locked?"

Haley shrugged. "Dunno."

"You see?" said Theodosia. "That's what

22

I'm talking about. Vigilance should be our new watchword."

"Right," said Haley, peering at Theodosia. "But you're the one who's always on top of things. You're our watchdog, so to speak."

"She's right," said Drayton. He hesitated slightly. "Case in point, you were able to give the police a fairly good account of last night."

"But not as much as was reported in today's *Post and Courier*," said Haley. "They made it sound like you could *identify* the killer."

"Which I can't," said Theodosia.

"That might present an awkward problem," suggested Drayton. "If some maniac out there thinks you can."

Haley wrinkled her nose and fixed Theodosia with a serious gaze. "Have you . . . um . . . been able to remember anything more? I know you told the officers and Detective Tidwell about everything you saw. But have you come up with anything else?"

"Like a clue?" asked Drayton, edging closer to Theodosia. "You've got a pretty solid record when it comes to crime solving." He ducked his head, having just uttered the words Theodosia probably didn't want to hear.

"I saw the struggle," said Theodosia, nod-

23

ding. "Although at first I thought it was Daria with her boyfriend. Being . . . I don't know . . . romantic, I suppose."

"But it was someone else," said Haley, in an ominous tone. "So . . . what else can you recall?"

Theodosia closed her eyes and tilted her head to one side. Tried to think back to last night. Conjure up the memory of darkness and rain-spattered cobblestones and two shadowy blue-and-black figures locked in a life-and-death struggle. An image that bordered on film noir. *And what else?* she wondered. *What else did I see or hear or think? Maybe* . . . She wracked her brain, trying to dredge up something, anything. *Maybe a faint minty fragrance?*

"Mint?" came Theodosia's whispered reply.

"Mint?" said Drayton, sounding dubious. "Seriously?"

Theodosia slowly opened her eyes, as if returning from a hypnotic trance. "I had the strangest feeling that's what I smelled last night. The closer I got to Daria."

"Pretty strange," admitted Haley.

"Maybe," proposed Drayton, "there's a simple explanation."

"Like what?" asked Haley.

"A mint plant growing nearby," said Dray-

24

ton. "After all, this entire area's overrun with flora and fauna. There's a reason Charleston's backyard gardens are so famously intriguing."

"Probably that's it," agreed Theodosia, exhaling slowly.

"Should we be doing something for Daria?" asked Haley. She seemed quiet and thoughtful now.

"Maybe send flowers to Daria's mother," said Theodosia.

"Don't you think we should wait until we know funeral details?" asked Drayton, always a stickler for proper etiquette.

"No, let's go ahead and do it right away," said Theodosia. "Daria's mother is a dear friend of Aunt Libby, so . . ." Her voice trailed off. Aunt Libby was Theodosia's only remaining living relative. A tiny, dynamic woman who lived at Cane Ridge Plantation out by Horlbeck Creek. The plantation where Theodosia's father had grown up, where her parents had been married. Now Aunt Libby watched over the low, flat fields that stretched to meet piney forests and cared for her myriad flocks of birds.

One of Theodosia's fondest memories was watching Aunt Libby tote heaping buckets of thistle, black oil seed, and cracklings down to the lake for all the migratory waterfowl that showed up. Of course, once they discovered what a fat deal they'd lucked into, they stayed on like a pack of mooching, shirttail relatives. But Aunt Libby adored them all. Her dear creatures, as she called them.

"I'll order the flowers from Floradora," said Haley. "Theo, you just stay put and compose your thoughts. I assume Detective Tidwell will be dropping by soon. He *said* he would, anyway."

"He'll be here," said Theodosia, though she wasn't sure what more she could offer Tidwell by way of details or faint impressions. She'd racked her brain all night for another nugget of information to feed him but had come up dry.

"Changing the subject," said Drayton, pulling a tin of Assam golden tips tea off the display shelves of an antique highboy fashioned from native cypress. "How are your move-in plans shaping up? You're charging ahead, I assume?"

A few months ago, Theodosia had been fortunate enough to come into a windfall of money. And had decided to move from her apartment above the Indigo Tea Shop to an adorable little English cottage a few blocks away, a former carriage house that bore the name Hazelhurst. A down payment had been made, agreements spelled out in writing, but she *still* didn't have a specified closing date or move-in date from the churlish owner.

"There are a few problems." Theodosia sighed.

"Always are," said Drayton. "No real estate transaction ever goes smoothly."

"Apparently," said Theodosia, "the wiring's not up to code. Which is why the lights keep flickering and the housing inspector has requested the sellers to replace a buried cable. I suppose I'll have to call Maggie and have her run interference." Maggie Twining was Theodosia's Realtor.

"Maybe your cottage is haunted," said Haley as she crossed the tea room floor, a pot of Darjeeling tea in one hand, a plate of fresh-baked cinnamon scones in the other. "That would sure explain the flickering lights. And let's face it, your place wouldn't be the first home in Charleston to have ghosts and supernatural beings wandering around."

"Charleston is supposedly one of the most haunted cities in America," agreed Drayton. "Although I can't say I'm a true believer in that particular spirit world."

Knock, knock, knock!

"Oh!" said Haley, suddenly startled.

"It's the *door*," said Drayton.

"Tidwell," said Theodosia, dreading his visit.

Burt Tidwell, looking bearish and slightly smug, sailed across the floor, dodging tables like a chubby matador, and plopped himself down at the table alongside Theodosia. Then his head swiveled toward Haley, his nose twitched eagerly, and his beady eyes fairly gleamed. "Miss Haley," he asked, "are those items, perchance, fresh-baked?"

So, of course, Drayton laid out a plate, teacup, and silverware for Detective Tidwell. While Haley ran back and grabbed tiny silver dishes filled with Devonshire cream and strawberry preserves.

"A feast," declared Tidwell, tucking into the scones and preserves while Theodosia poured him a steaming cup of Darjeeling.

"I'm glad you have an appetite," Theodosia remarked in a droll voice. She herself did not. Fresh in her mind's eye was the heartbreaking image of Daria's crumpled, lifeless body. *Tragic,* she thought. *Simply tragic.*

"I count on your lovely tea and baked goods to fortify my body as well as my spirit," responded Tidwell. "Preparation for all the difficult work ahead."

"And what is the work ahead, if I might ask?" said Theodosia.

"First course of action," said Tidwell, poised with a tiny butter knife in his big paw, "is the homicide last night. Determine motive."

"How's that coming so far?" asked Theodosia.

"A number of interesting ideas are spinning in my head," said Tidwell. "You don't know this . . . of course, you wouldn't . . . but quite a nasty struggle had gone on *inside* the Antiquarian Map Shop."

"Really?" said Theodosia, grimacing. She hated to think of poor Daria, bravely fighting off her attacker, while maps were flung everywhere and files and bookshelves overturned in the process.

"Place is a huge mess," said Tidwell, munching away. "Maps strewn all over the place. Old family records, too."

Theodosia nodded. Besides selling antique maps, Daria had amassed a fine collection of historic documents, old letters, photographs, and family records.

"Some of the documents had been ripped to shreds," said Tidwell. "Like someone had gone utterly berserk!"

"A maniac," Theodosia said in a low, hoarse voice. Of course, it had been a

29

maniac. He'd strangled Daria, hadn't he?

Tidwell reached for a second cinnamon scone.

"Why would someone want to rip up maps?" Theodosia asked.

"No idea," said Tidwell, popping a bite into his mouth and chewing appreciatively.

"But you will get a handle on this, right?" Theodosia sounded more than a little hopeful. After all, Daria had been a good friend. And her murder had occurred dangerously close to Indigo Tea Shop turf. What Theodosia considered *her* turf.

"Solving last night's homicide is a foregone conclusion, Miss Browning," Tidwell assured her. "My detectives are working numerous angles even as we speak." In Tidwell's former life, he'd been an SPIC, a special agent in charge, with the FBI. Old habits died hard with Tidwell, and he still subscribed to the get-your-man-or-else dictum.

"When do you think you'll have something?" asked Theodosia. She was itching to hear about suspects and suppositions.

"Soon as I get a few questions answered," replied Tidwell. His bright eyes bored into her.

"I don't know what else to tell you," said Theodosia. "I pretty much told you every-

and we'll be catering a book signing at the Heritage Society on Saturday night, although I haven't quite got the menu planned for that one."

Peering through eyes that were narrow slits, Tidwell looked colossally bored. "That's not quite what I had in mind. I was talking about your *personal* involvement."

"You mean something I might have, uh, meddled in?" Theodosia gazed about the tea room, saw that it was rapidly filling. Friends from the neighborhood come for their morning cuppa and scone, eager tourists who were out exploring. Thank goodness Drayton was escorting guests to tables with his usual cordiality and efficient aplomb.

"You do tend to plunge right in and sort through our local mysteries," murmured Tidwell. The corners of his mouth twitched ever so slightly.

"Not lately, I haven't," Theodosia protested.

Tidwell dropped his head and stared at her.

"Not for a while," she amended.

Now a smile fluttered across Tidwell's face. "You still seeing your two boyfriends?"

Theodosia's face flushed bright pink. "I don't have two boyfriends! I have a current

34

thing I could think of last night. I only played a small part in last night's tragedy."

"Tell me what you know about Jason Pritchard," said Tidwell.

"Daria's assistant?"

"Correct."

Theodosia thought for a few moments. "He always struck me as a nice enough fellow." She didn't know Pritchard well, since Daria had only hired Jason a few months ago. "Daria had been running her shop, building her map and document collection, pretty much doing it all herself," continued Theodosia. "Then she hired Jason and his presence seemed to allow a certain degree of breathing room for Daria." She glanced down at the table, rubbed an index finger over one of the deep scratches. "Gave her the luxury of dropping by here for lunch, taking days off, that sort of thing."

Tidwell gave a slight nod and his jowls sloshed from side to side. "So you knew this fellow Pritchard?"

"Not so much. Daria once told me he had a fairly good eye. I know for a fact that he was running all over the county, hitting auctions, digging through estate sales, to find various documents for the shop. Building the inventory, I guess you'd call it."

"And Pritchard wasn't present last night,"

31

said Tidwell.

"When you talked to the boyfriend . . . Joe Don Hunter?"

Tidwell gave a quick tilt of his head.

"Joe Don seemed to say that Daria had already sent Jason home for the evening," said Theodosia. "That she'd been ready to close up shop."

"So the story goes," said Tidwell.

"Do you know . . . where was the boyfriend when Daria was attacked?"

"Over at the Chowder Hound, getting take-out."

"And you know that for sure?" asked Theodosia.

"He dropped his order directly on my Thom McAn loafers when I told him how Daria was killed," said Tidwell. "Smelled like crab chowder to me."

"Hmm," said Theodosia.

"But enough questions for now," said Tidwell. His chubby hands gripped the table, ready to push himself out of the groaning captain's chair he occupied, which, luckily for everyone, had been constructed of sturdy Carolina pine.

"Actually," said Theodosia, "*I* have a few questions."

3

Tidwell's furry eyebrows raised high above his beady eyes, then waggled like two errant caterpillars. "Oh?" came his baritone voice, the tone slightly disapproving.

Theodosia plunged ahead. "Last night you speculated that the killer might have thought Daria was really me, given that we're about the same height and both have curly reddish hair. You implied that Daria's murder might have been a case of mistaken identity. Do you still believe that?"

Tidwell settled back in his chair, assuming a reluctant pose. "I suppose it will depend, Miss Browning, on what *engagements* you've had lately."

Theodosia thought for a moment. "Quite a few, actually. We catered the reception for the Symphony reception last week, hosted a tea for the Dorchester Club, and we're helping the Featherbed House participate in the annual Bed-and-Breakfast

boyfriend and a former boyfriend."

"Do they know that?" asked Tidwell. "Are they clear on the order of things? The order of the universe, *your* universe?"

"Of course, they are," Theodosia shot back. "Exactly what are you implying, Detective Tidwell?"

"Nothing, I'm just mildly curious."

"Surely you've heard the old . . ."

"Adage," responded Tidwell. "About curiosity killing the cat?"

"To say nothing of personal-bordering-on-rude questions," said Theodosia. "Certainly not very gentlemanly."

"Apologies," said Tidwell, a mischievous grin slashing his broad face.

Theodosia decided turnaround was fair play. She leaned in close to Tidwell and in a cozy, conspiratorial manner asked, "What was the weapon used to strangle Daria?"

Tidwell shook his head abruptly, as though a swarm of gnats was suddenly buzzing around him. "Can't say. Forensics lab will have to make that exact determination."

"Plastic cord? Wire? Something else?" she prompted.

"No idea," said Tidwell.

"Feels to me like you're stalling," said Theodosia.

"Not I," said Tidwell, sounding righteous

as he sprang from his chair. "In fact, I'm off to question the victim's shop neighbors. Just think of me as the shark that never sleeps, a predator that moves relentlessly forward." He bobbed his head with formality now. "Thank you for the morning repast of tea and scone."

"Scones," Theodosia said, putting a touch of sibilance on the final *s*.

"Now who's being rude?" muttered Tidwell, as he crossed the tea room, deftly dodging customers, then yanked open the door and disappeared down Church Street.

Drayton was at Theodosia's side in a heartbeat. "Not the font of information you'd hoped?"

"Tidwell's playing his cards extremely close to his vest," said Theodosia, thinking it was a mightily straining vest ready to pop a few buttons.

"The important thing," said Drayton, "is that he's working the case."

"I have to believe he'll do his best," said Theodosia. "He always has before."

"Ah," said Drayton, a slight gleam in his eye. "With your capable assistance, he has."

"I'm not getting involved," said Theodosia, glancing across the tea room to the front counter, where Haley had just snatched up the ringing phone.

"That's what you always say," said Drayton. "But you do possess certain investigative skills."

"That's right," said Theodosia. "I'm Charleston's own little Nancy Drew."

"No," said Drayton, following her across the tea room, "you're better."

Haley held out the phone, waggling it back and forth. "It's your aunt Libby," she told Theodosia. "And does she ever sound upset."

Theodosia grabbed the phone from Haley. She knew Aunt Libby was far too stoic to be upset, but she also knew that Aunt Libby would be deeply concerned. A delicate balance of yin and yang.

"Aunt Libby," said Theodosia.

"Theodosia," began Aunt Libby, "when Sophie Shand called me this morning, I couldn't quite believe it! Daria murdered? An absolute tragedy! And now I've got the Charleston *Post and Courier* spread out in front of me spilling the entire dreadful story in gruesome detail."

"Oh dear," said Theodosia. She hadn't looked at the paper yet. She could only imagine how sordid the murder sounded. The paper had a new police beat reporter, Nick Van Buren, who seemed to revel in true crime.

"And you were right there!" wailed Aunt Libby. "An actual eyewitness! I can't believe it, I don't want to believe it!" This was followed by a few genteel sniffs and a blowing of her nose. "Sorry," she said, finally.

"Nothing to be sorry about," Theodosia told Aunt Libby. "We're all feeling just awful here at the tea shop."

"You realize Sophie is one of my dearest friends," said Aunt Libby.

"I know that."

"To have her own daughter murdered . . ." Aunt Libby let loose a low sob, then struggled to clear her throat.

"I know you'll be there for Sophie," said Theodosia. "Give her a shoulder to cry on." Aunt Libby may be a tiny bird herself, but she was a tough one.

Aunt Libby seemed to gather her words as well as her emotions then. "I'll do more than that," she responded in a firm voice. "In fact, I've already assured Sophie that you'll stay as involved as possible in the investigation."

"I'm not sure I can do that," said Theodosia hedging. "Better to let the police handle things."

"No," said Aunt Libby, and now there was a certain, decisive *tone* in her voice. "You're a very smart girl and an outstanding amateur detective."

"The real detectives don't think so."

"What do they know?" shrilled Libby. "Anyway, I pretty much *promised* Sophie that you'd keep a careful watch of this whole dreadful thing. Especially since you already have a close working relationship with that particular detective. Tinkwell? Is that his name?"

"Tidwell," said Theodosia.

"Of course," said Aunt Libby, "Tidwell." She paused, allowed herself another small sniffle. "So . . . you'll help?"

"As much as I can," said Theodosia, somewhat reluctantly. *As much as I'm allowed,* she thought.

"Thank you, dear," said Aunt Libby. "I'm feeling better already. In fact, I'm going to call Sophie and tell her you're our own personal avenging angel who'll watch over the investigation."

Oh dear.

"I'll talk to you later, dear. All right?"

"Good-bye, Aunt Libby," said Theodosia.

"Oh," said Aunt Libby. "One other thing?"

"Yes?" said Theodosia, spinning on her heels as the bell over the front door let loose a merry jingle.

"See what you can find out about that Jason Pritchard who worked for Daria, will you?"

Theodosia stared at Jason Pritchard, who was standing in her doorway, and said, "Sure thing."

It took Theodosia a couple of seconds to switch gears. Then she said, "Jason . . . hello." Not because they were friends but because she was startled to see him.

"Miss Browning," Pritchard said, his face beginning to crumple.

"Call me Theodosia," she told him, plucking at his shirtsleeve. "And let's get you to a table. You look a little peaked."

"I feel a lot peaked," said Pritchard, once they were seated. Tall, blond, and slightly ethereal, Pritchard looked like he hadn't slept well. His navy polo shirt looked hastily ironed, his khaki slacks just plain rumpled.

"Drayton?" Theodosia lifted a hand and Drayton was beside her in two seconds flat.

"A pot of tea?" Drayton asked, taking in the situation with a single glance.

"Strong tea," said Theodosia. Then she turned back to Pritchard. "Are you okay?"

He shook his head. "Not really. Daria . . . I can't quite believe it!"

Drayton arrived with tea and an apple muffin, set it down discreetly, then hastily departed.

"Have you spoken to the police?" Theodosia asked him as she poured out a cup of tea. Nice, strong Ceylon tea, from the smell of it.

"Last night and again this morning," Pritchard told her. "They came to my apartment last night to tell me about Daria." He frowned and shook his head angrily. "Didn't show any respect for her at all, just jabbed away at me with a thousand different questions."

"What did they want to know?" asked Theodosia.

Pritchard hung his head in a defeated gesture. "They asked if I knew any reason why someone would want to kill Daria."

"Did you?" asked Theodosia.

"No!" Pritchard cried. "Daria was a neat lady. I *liked* working for her."

"What other questions did they ask?" prodded Theodosia.

Pritchard took a bite of muffin and chewed thoughtfully. "What time I left the map shop, what stops I made on the way home, what time I arrived home." He swallowed hard, then took a tiny sip of tea to wash it all down. "Tea," he said, as if noticing it for the first time. "Don't usually drink this stuff."

41

"It's pretty good."

Pritchard nodded. "It's okay."

"What else did they want to know?" Theodosia gently prodded.

"Oh," said Pritchard, wrinkling his nose. "They wanted to know who Daria was dating, who her friends were, was she having family problems, was the business solvent. That kind of stuff."

"And do you know, *were* there any problems in those areas?" asked Theodosia.

Pritchard shook his head. "Uh-uh. Not that I know of. I mean, I *worked* for Daria. We didn't exactly chitchat about our personal lives. We kept that stuff separate."

"A business relationship," said Theodosia. "And that's quite appropriate. But . . . I also get the feeling there's something you want to ask me. Or tell me. You didn't just show up here by chance today, did you?"

Pritchard gazed down at the table. "No."

"So, go ahead," said Theodosia. "I'm listening."

Pritchard lifted his eyes and gazed earnestly at Theodosia. "Daria talked about how smart you were," he said in a halting voice. "She really thought the world of you."

"Okay," said Theodosia. She settled back in her chair, giving the young man room to continue. He did.

"Daria said you were real cagey at figuring stuff out. That you helped solve a big kidnapping case last fall."

"Not really," said Theodosia. "I was only peripherally involved."

"That's not the way Daria told it," said Pritchard. "She was pretty impressed."

"I sense you still have a question pending," said Theodosia.

"More like a request," corrected Pritchard.

"Excuse me?"

"Request for help," said Pritchard. "Like I said, I was interviewed by the police again this morning."

"They're just doing their job," Theodosia told him. "Looking for little slivers of information that might shed some light on this whole sad mess."

"No," said Pritchard, "I get the feeling they want to pin Daria's murder on me."

"What?" said Theodosia. "Oh, I can't believe that."

"Here's the thing," said Pritchard, somewhat reluctantly. "I haven't always been the nicest guy in the world."

Theodosia gazed at him. Where was this going? What was Jason Pritchard about to reveal?

Pritchard drew a deep breath and seemed

to gather his courage. "Daria took a chance on me when she hired me. I did some stupid stuff when I was a kid." He gazed at her, smiled, and said, "You probably think I'm still a kid, since I'm only twenty-six."

"Some people are still kids at sixty-six," said Theodosia. "Maturity isn't always about numerical age."

"Thank you," said Pritchard. "But to get back to my . . . well, I guess you'd call it a sort of confession. The thing is . . . I have a police record."

Theodosia's gaze never wavered.

"I was an idiot. Committed felony crimes that would have sent me to Allendale for a few years, if I hadn't been under age. Drugs and other stuff. Anyway, I've been on my best behavior since, especially working for Daria. Taking history classes at the College of Charleston and trying hard to learn more about antiquities."

"Very commendable," said Theodosia.

Pritchard squinted at her. "So I was hoping you might run interference for me with the police. Because I'm . . . I'm innocent! Heck, I'm even gonna try to keep the shop going!"

"The family asked you to do so?"

Pritchard nodded vigorously. "The sister did, yeah."

"Okay," said Theodosia. "That's a good sign. It means they have faith in you, that they trust you. The fact that the police are eyeing you is another matter."

"That's why I need *your* help," said Pritchard. He gazed at Theodosia with such earnestness, it touched her heart.

"I'll do what I can," she told him. "But until Charleston Robbery-Homicide comes up with a solid suspect, they could be rough on you."

"But you'll see what you can do?"

"Yes. Of course."

"Thank you," Pritchard told her in a hoarse voice.

"I'm also doing this for Daria," responded Theodosia. "If she believed in you, then I believe in you."

Pritchard swiped at his eyes with the back of his hand, then struggled clumsily to his feet. "Daria always said you were kind. To people . . . as well as animals."

"Daria was a good friend," said Theodosia, her eyes suddenly glistening with tears.

"Got to get back to the shop now," said Pritchard. "Try to keep things going." He turned, gave a sad, slightly hopeful smile, then added a little wave.

"Jason," Theodosia called after him, "when

45

you said you were in trouble with drugs and other stuff . . ."

"Yeah?"

"What exactly was the other stuff?"

Pritchard's eyes slid away from her. "Forgery."

4

"Seafood quiche," said Haley. "Plus a mixed green salad, cheddar and chutney tea sandwiches, and tuna roll-ups." She stood at the massive industrial stove they'd shoehorned into the world's smallest kitchen, stirring an enormous, simmering pot of vegetable soup. "And my vagabond vegetable soup," she added.

"That's lunch," said Theodosia. "And it all sounds wonderful. What about afternoon tea?"

"Orange blossom bars and apple tea cake," said Haley. "Plus we still have cinnamon scones from this morning. Oh, and I'm going to whip up a batch of almond-flavored Devonshire cream. One of my new inspirations."

Theodosia laid out a series of floral bowls on the counter. "Don't forget, Drayton's friends from the Historian Club are coming at twelve thirty."

"That'll be a cinch," enthused Haley. "They get scones, soup, special ham and pear panini sandwiches, and cake for dessert."

"Did Drayton have a chance to mix up a pitcher of green tea sparkler?" asked Theodosia.

"I think he did," said Haley. "I hope he did . . . but you know Drayton."

"What about me?" asked Drayton, suddenly looming in the doorway. "What sin of omission am I guilty of now?"

"The sparkler?" asked Haley.

"Always jumping to conclusions," chided Drayton. "It's already brewed, mixed, and sparkling away in the cooler."

"Then we're all set," said Haley. "No *problema.*"

"There rarely is," intoned Drayton.

Lunch was busy, busy, busy with a half dozen reservations, a yellow horse-drawn jitney dropping off a tour group, and at least a dozen take-out orders. And just as everything seemed to reach critical mass, Drayton's friends from the Historian Club came pouring in. Five men whom he proudly seated at the large round table in the center of the room. Drayton was the sixth guest, but rarely would he connect with his chair,

so eager was he to impress.

Drayton, being Drayton, had set out the good Saint Dunstan by Tiffany silverware, Fraureuth porcelain dinnerware, and Heisey cut-crystal water goblets. He'd also appropriated a gold linen tablecloth and Theodosia's nicest floral arrangement to serve as the table's centerpiece.

Now, white tapers flickered, glasses clinked, and good cheer seemed to prevail. One of the club's members, Lyndel Woodruff, had just published a book titled *The Battle of Honey Hill,* so they jabbered excitedly about the new release as well as the upcoming book talk and signing event at the Heritage Society this Saturday night. Drayton had asked Theodosia to handle the catering, and she'd willingly agreed. Her current boyfriend, Parker Scully, proprietor and head chef at Solstice Bistro and Tapas Bar was out of town all week, attending a restaurant convention in Las Vegas, of all places. So, as far as her personal life went, Theodosia was free as a bird.

"A toast," proposed Drayton, hefting a glass. "To Lyndel and his newly published tome."

"A toast," intoned the others, also hoisting their glasses.

"Thank you all," said Woodruff, looking

49

enormously pleased. He was a tall, thin man with a nervous air and a perpetually florid face. But Woodruff was a true scholar and professor, having taught American history for more than thirty-six years at the College of Charleston, much to the delight of several generations of students. Now that he was retired, he'd been able to do research and finally write his book. "And I hope you all enjoy my talk this Saturday night." Woodruff glanced around, a trifle embarrassed, then added, "At least I *hope* you'll be coming."

"We wouldn't miss it," declared Drayton, circling the table, pouring refills of green tea sparkler.

"Understand you folks had some excitement around here last night," piped up Jack Brux. Brux was a pinched-face, narrow man who ran an antique shop down on Royal Street and was working on a book himself. "A rather nasty murder," Brux added.

Drayton blanched white. "Terrible thing," he said, shaking his head. "Daria was a great friend. Used to come in every afternoon at three on the dot. Order her favorite chamomile tea and the scone du jour."

Woodruff shook his head. "Pity about her shop being torn up like that."

"Very strange," agreed Brux.

Woodruff gazed across the table at Brux.

"You're a real map fanatic, Jack. What do you make of it?"

Brux grimaced. "Crazy person," he said. "Have to be crazy to strangle a defenseless woman, then trash a shop like that. All those valuable maps."

Theodosia set a plate of apple tea cake on the table. "I understand the Antiquarian Map Shop carried some extremely rare maps. One of a kind items."

"Indeed they did," agreed Woodruff. "A few pieces weren't even marked for sale." He gazed across the table at Jack Brux. "You tried to get her to sell you that Waccamaw Neck map, but she never would."

Brux bobbed his head. "That's right. Told me it was for display purposes only," he said in a petulant tone. "Even when I wanted to borrow it as reference material for my book. Now maybe I've got a chance. Depending on who takes over management of the shop."

Theodosia caught Drayton's eye and frowned. It worried her that Brux would talk like that.

"The estate, I suppose," said Drayton.

"Which is basically the owner's mother," said Brux. "And I don't imagine she's going to want to run the place."

"You never know," said Theodosia. "I

51

wouldn't rule anything out at this point."

Once lunch was finished, dribs and drabs of customers oozed their way in for afternoon tea. A few were locals, many were tourists who'd spent the morning and early afternoon tromping the historic district, gazing at the grand dowager homes that lined the Battery, wandering the cobblestone alleys and pathways that meandered past old cemeteries, churches, Charleston single houses, and quaint cottages.

"Excuse me?" said one newcomer. "The tea you have listed on your board as Earl Green? What is that?"

Theodosia straightened up from behind the counter, touched a knee to a box of tea lights, and shoved it back into the cupboard. "It's a blend of Chinese black tea and green tea, along with a touch of high quality silver tips and bergamot oil."

"It's good?" asked the woman. She was tall and thin, her dark hair worn in a blunt pageboy style. Silver Tiffany bracelets clanked on both wrists; a giant vintage starburst brooch, in shimmering tones of pink, orange, and amber, was pinned to the lapel of her tailored tweed suit.

"Earl Green is extremely mellow yet big on aroma," said Theodosia. "I think you'll enjoy it, but if it's not to your liking, I'll gladly fix something else."

"You're very kind," said the woman, "And I *do* want to try the Earl Green. A cup to go, please." She gave a perfunctory smile. "Since I'm here, I should probably introduce myself." She stuck a hand across the counter, her jewelry clanking once again. "Cinnamon St. John."

Theodosia smiled with surprise. "Oh my goodness, you own the new . . . shop. Down the street. Um . . . fragrance shop, am I right?"

"Jardin Perfumerie," said Cinnamon, a touch of pride in her voice. "Just a hop, skip, and a jump down Church Street." She wrinkled her nose, hunched her narrow shoulders, and gave a tight little shudder. "Right next to that dusty old map shop. Thank *goodness* we weren't open last night!"

"A tragedy," said Theodosia, not really wanting to go into detail.

"Now that we've finally met," said Cinnamon, "I'd love it if you dropped by for a visit. See what we're all about."

"I've actually heard a little about your shop," said Theodosia, pouring hot water into the single serving glass teapot, watching the tea leaves unfurl in their "agony of the leaves" dance. "Brooke, from Heart's Desire, mentioned it just last week."

"Oh sure," said Cinnamon, nodding, "I've met Brooke. Such a dear. She came in and bought scented candles. That poor map shop lady was in, too."

"I didn't realize your shop was officially open," said Theodosia.

"We're not," responded Cinnamon. "My aunt Kitty thought a quiet opening would be best. Let folks wander in while we're unpacking for a few quick, casual sales. Meet the neighbors, get our feet wet in the business, that type of thing."

Theodosia poured the cup of fresh-brewed Earl Green into an indigo blue cup and snapped on a white plastic lid. As she leaned forward and slid it across the counter, she inhaled sharply and wiggled her nose. For some reason, she'd just caught a whiff of the scent she thought she'd smelled last night.

How . . . strange.

"That's a rather, um, interesting scent you're wearing," said Theodosia, feeling a little flustered, trying to fight an unsettling sense of déjà vu. "I assume it's one of the fragrances you carry?"

Cinnamon gave a wide smile. "A custom scent, actually. Something my aunt Kitty and I concocted during one of our wilder moments. A blend of lavender, lime blossoms, and mint. I call it Chant du Cygne."

Theodosia instantly understood the translation. "Swan song," she said.

Sitting in her office, leafing through catalogs, Theodosia was supposed to be scribbling up any number of orders. They were low on tins of tea for their retail area. And she knew she should be ordering tea cozies, tea towels, and probably some more of those adorable miniature bone china teacups. The tiny cups had proved to be enormously popular. One customer had created a giant grapevine wreath for her sunporch and decorated it with silk flowers and more than a dozen of the miniature teacups.

But Theodosia, elbows on her desk, feet doing a tippy-tap on the floor, was having trouble focusing. Just couldn't seem to get it together. For one thing, Daria's murder hung heavy over her head. Her heart was sad, which made her brain feel fuzzy as well. She also hadn't slept very well. The closing on her cottage seemed to be creeping along at a snail's pace and she felt at odds with things. Maybe, she decided, if she went over to the cottage tonight to make a few quick sketches and take detailed measurements, it would give her the *illusion* of speeding things along.

Yes, she decided, that was probably a fine, constructive way to handle her case of ennui. Remain positive and keep looking forward instead of glancing back over your shoulder. Turn wishful thinking into reality.

"Theo?" Haley stood in the doorway, clutching a silver tray. "Do you have a minute?"

Theodosia pushed aside her catalogs. "Always. And I hope that cup of tea is for me."

Haley slid into the office and placed her tray on Theodosia's desk. "Drayton brewed you a cup of silvery tip pekoe and I added a few chocolate samples. For your . . . um . . . critical review, shall we say."

Theodosia took a quick, fortifying sip of tea, then said, "I take it these are your entries for tomorrow's Chocolatier Fest?" The Chocolatier Fest was an annual event held at Charleston's upscale Dorchester Club. Chefs, bakers, and candymakers from all over the area entered their finest truffles, trifles, candy, and cakes, hoping to take home the coveted Silver Cupcake Award. Haley had entered last year but only placed fourth with her green tea truffles. This year she'd definitely set her eyes on first prize.

More power to her.

"Okay," said Haley, plopping down on the cushy, brocade chair that sat wedged across from Theodosia's desk. "Here's the thing. Last year I was close but no cigar. This year I have a strategy."

"Bribe the judges?" said Theodosia, deadpan.

"Hah," said Haley. "Good one. But those guys are unbribeable. They're all snooty French pastry chefs from New York or Boston."

"Okay," said Theodosia. "Then plan B."

"Multiple entries," said Haley. "I checked and it's allowed. Up to four entries per person."

"Awful lot of work," said Theodosia. "Especially since you want everything to be as fresh as possible."

"Has to be done," said Haley. "In fact, I plan to stay here tonight and slave away like a mad scientist. Stay all night if I have to."

Theodosia took another sip of tea and glanced at Haley's tray. "Looks like you already did."

"Nah," said Haley, "these are just my prototypes. I'm conducting a highly unscientific taste test to see which ones are best."

"And you're asking Drayton and me for an opinion?"

"Sure," enthused Haley. "You're the most unscientific people I know."

"Thank you," said Theodosia, gazing at the tray. "I think." She reached out, inched the tray toward her, and eyed Haley's chocolates. Of course, everything looked superb. "So what do we have here?"

"First," said Haley, "truffles." She poked an index finger at a chocolate dollop dusted with ultra-fine cinnamon. "That one's a champagne truffle. The one next to it's a tea truffle."

"You entered tea truffles last year."

"I know, but this time I used a much better grade of tea."

"Let me guess," said Theodosia. "You pinched some of Drayton's expensive gyokuro? From the stash he keeps in his secret spot under the counter?"

Haley bobbed her head happily.

"Good girl."

"So take a nibble," urged Haley.

Theodosia took a tiny bite of the champagne truffle, nodded, then took a small nibble of the green tea truffle. "They're both great," she said, still chewing. "But the green tea truffle's better."

"That's what I think, too," said Haley. "Now try the chocolate bourbon ball."

Theodosia did. And loved it. As well as

Haley's white chocolate fleur-de-lis-shaped bonbon and a gooey chocolate praline that was so sticky it had the potential to rip out dental fillings.

"This nutty little blob here," said Haley, pointing at the final piece, "is a gopher. Similar to your standard chocolate, pecan, and caramel turtle, but made with black walnuts instead."

Theodosia took a nibble and let it melt in her mouth. "Wonderful. To die for."

"Wait," said Haley, looking pleased, but holding up a hand. "Gotta tell you about my final idea. I haven't exactly *made* it yet, but I've got a gem of a receipt that my granny gave me."

"What is it?" asked Theodosia, smiling. Receipt was the old southern term for recipe.

Haley assumed a beatific expression. "A bittersweet chocolate pavé."

"I'm intrigued," said Theodosia, not quite sure what a pavé really was.

"Here's the thing," said Haley. "Pavé is basically a rich, dense, mousselike chocolate dessert. I mean, we're talking triple decadent."

"Death by chocolate," said Theodosia.

"Almost," agreed Haley. "Once the pavé is cooked, coddled, and baked, it sets up all

59

nice and firm. Then it's sliced and topped with fresh berries or fruit puree."

"Good heavens, Haley!" exclaimed Theodosia. "And you want me to tell you which dessert to enter? Every one is fantastic!"

"I know," said Haley. "But you still have to pick four."

Theodosia thought for a minute. "Okay, then I cast votes for the green tea truffles, bourbon balls, gophers, and your granny's chocolate pavé. But only if you have time."

"Oh, I'll make time."

"You're going to end up owning your own patisserie," said Theodosia, meaning it.

Haley grinned back. "I already do. Kind of. You always give me free rein on everything that has to do with baking. Almost everything," she amended.

"It's called trust," said Theodosia.

"So . . ." said Haley, flushed with excitement, "you're still coming with me to the luncheon tomorrow, right? I mean, just in case I win I gotta have a cheering section."

"I'll be there to cheer even if you don't win. Count on it."

"I'm gonna make everything tonight," said Haley, half mumbling to herself, "then drop it off first thing . . ." She nodded to herself, then suddenly swiveled her head, frowned, and said, "What?"

Voices raised in discord suddenly drifted toward them. One distinctly Drayton's, the other . . . ?

"Oh no!" exclaimed Haley. She jumped up and headed for the door, arms akimbo.

Theodosia rose, too, a prickle of worry suddenly gnawing at her.

"Oh man!" said Haley, stopping abruptly in her tracks and taking a reluctant step backward.

Then Drayton's voice, tight with anger, said, "*Excuse* me, but I told you she was . . ."

And that's the exact moment Jory Davis, Theodosia's ex-boyfriend and rat fink extraordinaire, popped his head into her office and said, "Hi there."

5

Hi there. The words registered in Theodosia's brain, sounding bright and innocent. Even warm and friendly. The reality of the situation was considerably more complex. Jory Davis had been Theodosia's boyfriend for a number of years. Then, one day, he'd announced to Theodosia that he was up and moving to New York. Marriage was part of the package deal he extended to Theodosia, but so was dumping her tea shop.

Big decision for Theodosia? Heartrending to be sure. Better to dump the boyfriend.

Which she did.

But like trying to strike a deal on a used car, nothing was ever quite final. Jory had popped back into her life again for a few days last October. Then they'd been incommunicado. Until now. Until he poked his handsome, inquisitive face into her office, oblivious of a scowling Haley and a downright frosty Drayton.

Drayton didn't bother mincing words. "What are *you* doing back in town?" he asked in his brusque-bordering-on-oratorical tone. "I thought you were back at your law offices in New York, defending hedge-fund scoundrels and corporate raiders."

"I'm here to wrap up some business," said Jory, trying to brush off Drayton and edge his way over to Theodosia.

This time Haley picked up her tray and conveniently stepped in to block Jory's way. "Oops, sorry. Didn't mean to whack you with my tray."

"That's okay," said Jory, rubbing his arm. "But I would like a word with Theodosia, if you don't mind. In private."

"She's awfully busy," Haley told him. "Maybe you should come back another time."

"Or better yet," added Drayton, "call."

"Yeah," said Haley, giving Jory a cheesy, fake-bright smile. "A *quick* phone call would be even better."

"It's okay, Haley," said Theodosia. "Drayton?" She raised her brows at him, feeling like she was calling off Cerberus, the proverbial watchdog of hell.

"Thanks," said Jory, nodding at Drayton and Haley. "Thanks for your hospitality."

"You don't have to be sarcastic," said Theodosia, once the two of them were alone. "They're just watching out for me."

"Couple of tough gatekeepers you've got there." Jory grinned.

"Good friends," said Theodosia. "And Haley wasn't just making excuses, I am busy. So . . . what can I do for you?" Theodosia sat back down, stared at Jory across her desk. Tried to remain cool and confident in her own skin.

Jory plopped down on the chair Haley had recently vacated and crossed his legs, looking like he wanted to settle in for a while. "I heard you had some trouble here least night."

"Trouble," said Theodosia, her brows knitting for an instant. Then she was back to cucumber cool. "Is that what you call it? In that case, yes, we had some very nasty trouble last night."

"Theodosia," said Jory, "I didn't come here to fight, I came here to make sure you're okay."

"Not to worry," Theodosia said, lightly. "I can take care of myself."

"You sure about that?" Jory seemed bound and determined to elicit some sort of emotion from Theodosia, even though she remained reserved and slightly aloof.

"Quite confident," said Theodosia.

"I bet you're getting involved," needled Jory. "It's a murder mystery, after all. Isn't that your specialty?"

"Not really."

"I don't believe you," said Jory. Now his eyes sparkled with a hint of mischief.

Theodosia raised her shoulders an inch. "Believe whatever you want."

"Listen," said Jory. "I'm only in town for a couple of days. I was wondering if . . . well, are you still dating that restaurant guy?"

"Yes. Of course, I am," said Theodosia.

"Are you seeing him tonight?"

Theodosia fixed Jory with a polite but level gaze. "I'm sorry, that really isn't any of your business."

"Would you go out to dinner with me tonight?"

"No, thank you."

"Greetings again," said Drayton, bustling into Theodosia's office with a fresh pot of tea and a teacup for Jory. He made a perfunctory bow, handed Jory his cup and saucer, and said, "If you don't mind my asking, Mr. Davis, I was under the impression you were engaged to a certain young lady."

"Not anymore," said Jory, staring directly at Theodosia.

"How unfortunate," said Drayton, pouring a cup of tea for Jory. "Might I inquire as to what became of the young lady?"

"No, you may not," interjected Theodosia. She glanced at Drayton and gave a meaningful look.

Jory let loose a low chuckle. "It's okay. Drayton does have your best interests at heart." He took a sip of tea, then winced. "Puckery," he said.

"Brisk," intoned Drayton. "That particular tea is an acquired taste, I might add."

"Beth Ann and I broke up a few weeks ago," Jory explained to both of them.

"I'm sorry to hear that," said Theodosia, even though she was suddenly secretly relieved. She'd met Beth Ann at the Opera Society's Masked Ball last autumn, and the woman had seemed a little too brash, a little too coarse for Jory's taste. Of course, that was predicated on the fact that Jory's sensibilities hadn't changed in the few years he'd been gone.

"So unfortunate," murmured Drayton. "Just when we were hoping you two would stroll off into the sunset and live happily ever after." Smiling like a friendly barracuda, he glanced at Theodosia and added, "I'll be within shouting distance if you need me."

"Thank you," said Theodosia, as Drayton slipped away. Then she focused her full attention on Jory. "So it just wasn't in the cards."

"I guess not," said Jory. He peered across his teacup at Theodosia. "Does that change anything?"

Theodosia shook her head. "Not really."

For the first time, Jory looked thoughtful. "It's over, isn't it? I mean, with us?"

"It has been for a long time," said Theodosia.

"I worry about you," said Drayton. He stood holding a gray plastic tub of dirty dishes, looking fretful and a little forlorn. Only a few afternoon customers lingered in the tea room.

"Don't," said Theodosia. The afternoon sun was pouring through the leaded glass windows, bathing everything in a pure, white light. Making her heart feel lighter, too.

"Jory can be very . . . . persuasive," said Drayton.

"Trust me," said Theodosia. "Our relationship is over. Finished, *fini, finito.*"

"You're sure?" asked Drayton, doubt still clouding his face.

At which point Haley popped out of the

kitchen and joined the conversation. "You mean, like, capital O-V-E-R?" she asked.

"That's right," said Theodosia.

"Because," said Drayton, "and I realize I have no right to say this, but I'm just going to blurt it out anyway . . ."

"Blurt away!" enthused Haley.

Drayton pulled himself up to full height and said, "I don't believe Jory is good for you."

"It really isn't a case of good or bad," said Theodosia, "it's just a matter of moving on."

"Timing," pronounced Haley. "And the timing's so right for Parker."

"I think so," agreed Theodosia.

"You going to marry him?" asked Haley.

"Haley!" said Drayton. And then, in a small voice, asked, "Are you?"

"He hasn't asked," said Theodosia.

"We just springboarded into a whole new decade," said Haley with a laugh. "Maybe *you* should ask *him*."

"You know," said Theodosia, edging back to her office, "I would if I wanted to."

And drifting back to Theodosia were Drayton's whispered words to Haley: "Well, I guess we know where Theo stands on *that* particular subject."

Some twenty minutes later, Theodosia

headed down the block to the Antiquarian Map Shop. Aunt Libby's heartfelt plea and Jason Pritchard's earlier request had been swirling around in her head all day, like a wildly spinning centrifuge. She'd developed a mental itch where Daria's murder was concerned and was suddenly determined to scratch it.

But when she arrived at the map shop, Theodosia was surprised to find not only Pritchard but two other people there as well. A mopey-looking young woman with mousy brown hair who sported a most unflattering, gray shirtwaist dress. And the handsome but sad-looking Joe Don Hunter, the man she'd seen last night, wearing jeans, a white T-shirt, and a buckskin-colored suede jacket.

"Miss Browning!" said Pritchard, popping up from behind a glass counter where any number of priceless documents were on display.

"Theodosia," she said, stepping into the store. "Call me Theodosia."

"Oh my," said the woman, coming forward to greet her. "I'm Fallon, Daria's sister. Nice to finally meet you. Your aunt Libby is one of my mother's dearest friends."

"Of course," said Theodosia, taking Fallon's outstretched hand in both of hers.

"And my sincere condolences."

Fallon bobbed her head in acknowledgment. "And this is Joe Don Hunter. Joe is . . . was . . . Daria's boyfriend."

Theodosia shook Joe Don's hand, too. "Mr. Hunter, I briefly saw you last night and . . . well, I'm so very sorry about Daria."

"Thank you," said the boyfriend. His voice was low and gravely and he spoke with a catch in his throat. "And I'm just plain Joe Don."

"Theodosia's agreed to help us," piped up Pritchard. "Do some . . . I'd guess you'd call it freelance investigating."

Fallon and Joe Don both stared at Theodosia with puzzled looks.

"Oh, not really," said Theodosia. She held up a hand, scrubbed it in the air as if to erase Pritchard's remark.

But Pritchard seemed not to hear her. "Daria always told me that Theo could solve any kind of mystery there was. So I asked if she'd help us, and she very kindly agreed."

Fallon turned bleary, basset hound eyes on Theodosia. "Really?"

"The thing is," said Pritchard, jumping in again, "Theodosia was *here* last night."

"Must have been awful," said Fallon, touching a hand to her heart.

"Did you get a look at her attacker?" Joe

Don asked suddenly. "Do you think you could ID her killer?"

"I'm sorry," said Theodosia. "But it was awfully dark and . . ." She let her voice trail off.

Joe Don shook his head. "Doggone it. That would have given us *something* to go on."

Fallon seemed to be struggling to put her words together. Finally she said, "Your aunt Libby did tell my mother that you were a first-class amateur detective."

"Aunt Libby tends to brag a bit," said Theodosia.

"But she said you've helped in other instances," pressed Fallon, looking almost hopeful.

Theodosia gave a tight nod. "Yes, I suppose I have."

"So what can it hurt?" Pritchard asked the other two. "If we huddle up and try to give Theodosia a few details."

"I think it's a good idea," said Joe Don. "Better than sitting around waiting for the police to do something."

"I agree," said Fallon, wiping away a tear. "In fact, it's heartening that one of Daria's friends would step forward to help."

"We all loved her," said Theodosia. She didn't know what else to say.

"So," said Pritchard, "what can we tell you? What do you want to know?"

Theodosia edged up to the glass case, set her bag down, and pulled out a spiral notebook and her black Montblanc pen. It had been a departing gift from her marketing firm colleagues when she'd resigned her position as account exec to purchase a dusty little carriage house and venture into the land of entrepreneurship and free-market economics. Also known as the tea and catering business. "Tell me what was going on in Daria's life," said Theodosia.

Fallon's gaze fell on Pritchard. "Jason?" she asked. "You worked with Daria. You were here every day."

"She seemed fine," said Pritchard. "Business was a little slow, but she had some hot-shot collector in Savannah on the hook, a guy who was negotiating to buy at least a dozen maps."

"Has he purchased the maps yet?" asked Theodosia. "Put money down? Paid for them? Taken them into his possession?"

"Uh . . . not yet," said Pritchard. "I should probably call him," he added.

"You probably should," agreed Fallon.

"Anything else going on in Daria's life?" asked Theodosia. "Problems with money, issues with other customers?"

"Not that we can think of," said Joe Don. "Just before you got here, we were kind of noodling those kinds of ideas around. Didn't come up with much of anything."

"Tell me about last night," said Theodosia.

"The back-alley crawl," said Pritchard. "It was amazingly effective. We got a ton of people coming through here that ordinarily wouldn't venture into a store like this."

Lots of people, lots of suspects, thought Theodosia. Someone could have seen Daria, a woman who was not unattractive, and allowed a bizarre, murderous fantasy to caper through his or her twisted mind. Then what? Returned to fulfill that awful fantasy? Theodosia grimaced at her own dark thoughts.

"What time did you leave?" Theodosia asked Pritchard.

He scratched his head. "Probably . . . nine thirty?"

"And you went directly home?" said Theodosia.

Pritchard nodded. "Uh-huh. And that's where I was when the police came banging on my door."

"Okay," said Theodosia, putting together the time line in her head. "And Joe Don, you were here helping out, too?"

"Yes, ma'am," said Joe Don. "Until I went to grab some take-out from the Chowder

73

Hound."

"And that was around . . . ?" asked Theodosia.

"Nine forty-five," filled in Joe Don.

And I came wandering along about ten, Theodosia thought to herself.

"Still lots of folks on Church Street when I came back," added Joe Don.

"Wait just a minute," said Theodosia. She let her gaze wander about the store. Maps hung on all the walls; sepia-tone and hand-drawn maps were displayed in old-fashioned glass cases, as were vintage photos and ephemera such as old letters and papers. Three large wooden flat files held even more maps. A large library table stood in the center of the room, the perfect place for unfurled maps.

"When I spoke with Detective Tidwell," Theodosia continued, "he told me someone had completely trashed this place. And theorized that the struggle had probably started in here."

"It *was* an absolute wreck," agreed Pritchard. "But the crime scene guys took most of the ripped up maps along with them. Well, first they photographed everything, then they gathered it all up in big plastic garbage bags and carted it away."

"Interesting," said Theodosia, wondering

what Detective Tidwell hoped to glean from those shredded and tattered pieces. "So you cleaned up everything else?" she asked Pritchard.

Pritchard nodded. "Did my best. Plus Fallon came in around noon and helped."

Theodosia turned her attention on Joe Don Hunter. "And you just happened to drop by?"

Joe Don looked like he was ready to burst into tears. "I didn't know what else to do," he said in a strangled voice. He swiped at his eyes with the back of his hand, the strain of his girlfriend's murder definitely showing.

"As far as the shop goes," said Theodosia. "What do you think the future holds?"

"I'd like to keep it going," said Pritchard. "Maybe even . . . buy it?"

"Can you afford it?" asked Theodosia. She knew she was being blunt, but they'd asked her for help. Direct questions were part and parcel of any kind of investigation. Even her kind.

"Not really," said Pritchard, looking glum.

Theo turned to Fallon. "Did Daria leave a will, or did she have a partner we don't know about?"

Fallon gave a tight shake of her head. "I have no idea," she said in a squeaky voice.

And now tears were streaming down her face. "I just . . . don't know."

"My apologies," said Theodosia, "I didn't mean to push the boundaries of decency on this."

Fallon dabbed at her eyes with a Kleenex. "I'm just so . . . ah, dear . . . so *confused*."

"We all are," said Joe Don.

Theodosia asked a few more perfunctory questions, but nobody seemed to have any answers. Or offer any insight.

"I'm sure you all did your best," Theodosia told them. "Okay if I go out the back door and look around?"

Fallon looked stricken. "Just be careful," she said, her voice husky.

Theodosia slipped down a short hallway, past Daria's small office, and let herself out the back door. Thick and heavy, painted Williamsburg blue, it was a wooden door probably constructed of cedar or pine. Probably installed when the brick building had been constructed more than a hundred years ago.

Standing on the narrow cobblestone walkway that snaked along the back of the building, it was hard for Theodosia to believe this was the exact spot where she'd seen Daria struggling for her life. Now a cool, refreshing breeze wafted down the alley, riffling the leaves on a thick stand of palmettos.

Theodosia glanced down at the cobblestones, looking for something, anything, that might yield a clue. But saw nothing. Probably, if there'd been a button or fiber or something dropped during last night's struggle, the crime scene team had already pounced on it. So not much to go on.

Half closing her eyes, Theodosia slowly walked down the back alley, keenly aware of the dampness and the sound of her own footfalls. How was it no one had heard anything? How could no one have seen anything?

Then she was jolted back to the here and now, realizing *she'd* seen the struggle. She was the sole witness.

Too bad she couldn't keep that little nugget under wraps.

Circling back around the block to Church Street, Theodosia strolled along, thinking about Jason Pritchard and Joe Don Hunter. Both claimed to be close to Daria, both seemed heartbroken. And yet, each one of them had had considerable opportunity.

Ah, but the big doozy of a question was, did either have motive?

It didn't appear they did. Not yet, anyway.

Finding herself directly in front of Jardin

Perfumerie, Theodosia peered in the large front window. And was utterly delighted by a spectacular array of perfume bottles and crystal atomizers that glinted in the afternoon sun. One tall, obelisk-shaped bottle caught her eye. She leaned in closer, trying to read the label. ARISTOCRACY. Interesting.

Then, in a spur of the moment decision, Theodosia stepped to the front door, where a tiny CLOSED sign hung, and rapped her knuckles sharply against the glass. She fully expected Cinnamon St. John to come scurrying from the back, tug open the door, and welcome her with a big, neighborly howdy-do.

But none of that happened. So Theodosia pressed her face to the window and peered in. Saw only a dim light in the back of the store where shadowy figures glided back and forth. Seemingly ignoring her.

Strange.

6

Tucked among splendid historic district mansions, Theodosia's cottage was a dream come true. Built in the Cotswold style, the storybook English cottage featured a sharply pitched roof, gingerbread trim, leaded bow windows, and a corner turret on the top floor. Just the sort of thing you'd see in a Currier and Ives print or described in *Anne of Green Gables,* although that was supposedly set on Prince Edward Island.

"What do you think?" Theodosia asked Earl Grey as they paused on the sidewalk, staring at what would soon be their new home. The charming little place sat hunkered back from the street, shielded by a wrought-iron fence and overgrown shrubbery, with darkness wrapped around it. Theodosia smiled to herself, knowing that once her blue-and-white Chinese lamp glowed in the window, it would be a homey, welcoming beacon.

Earl Grey tilted his head and responded to Theodosia's question. "Grrrr." *Great.*

"Hazelhurst," whispered Theodosia. The little cottage even had a name. "Lovely, isn't it?" she asked Earl Grey. "I think we're going to be very happy here." Pushing open the wrought-iron gate, stepping briskly along the brick walkway, it *felt* like they were both going home. Felt warm and cozy and just right.

"There's even a backyard for you," Theodosia told Earl Grey, as she fumbled with the lock box combination. She spun the dial, didn't get it quite right, so she flipped the dial back to the top and started over. This time the little lock box gave a reassuring click and an old-fashioned skeleton key tumbled out.

"First order of business once we move in," said Theodosia, "is to install better locks. Honestly, anyone could get inside using this kind of key. I see huge entire rings of these old keys for sale in antique shops for, like, five dollars."

"Rarrr," said Earl Grey. *Right.*

Pushing open the arched door, Theodosia flipped on an overhead light and stepped across the threshold. "Well? This is it. Your first look-see. Sure hope you like it."

Earl Grey's toenails clicked against the

floor of the small brick foyer, then he wandered slowly across the polished wooden floor. He glanced around the empty room with watchful eyes, then walked over to inspect the brick fireplace that was set into a wall of beveled cypress panels. He stopped, touched the tip of his fine muzzle to the fireplace screen, then turned to stare at his beloved Theodosia. Earl Grey's limpid brown eyes shone like bright oil spots and his long tail swished eagerly. Then he tossed his head in a gesture that was part proprietary, part approval, and dashed off to explore the kitchen.

"Excellent," Theodosia murmured. "I think I've just been awarded the Canine Good House Seal of Approval." She dropped her suede hobo bag on the floor, slipped off her jacket, and went to work.

First order of business was to take accurate measurements. Theodosia had an inkling that her blue-and-persimmon Chinese rug would fit perfectly in the living room, but she wanted to know for sure. Ditto her chintz sofa, damask chair, and rosewood coffee table. She already knew the walls were more than adequate to display her small collection of oil paintings. In fact, there was enough wall space that, finances permitting, she could continue to indulge her passion for collecting with a few more pieces of early American art. She also had her eye on a Louis XVI–inspired fruitwood secretary that was on display in the Legacy Gallery down on Royal Street. She figured it would fit comfortably against one wall and more than adequately showcase some of the finer pieces in her antique teacup collection. The Royal Winton chintz teacup for sure. And the James Kent hydrangea pattern and the Crown Ducal peony chintz.

Theodosia spent a good thirty minutes pacing the rooms, spinning out her metal tape measure and jotting down room dimensions. She worked methodically, starting in the living room, moving on to the small but jewel-like dining room with its cove ceilings, Georgian paneling, and French doors, then moving upstairs.

Because of the pitch of the roof, there was one nice-sized bedroom upstairs along with two much smaller rooms. The bedroom had a cozy turret corner that would be perfect as a reading nook. Theodosia took measurements, figured that everything she had would fit quite well and then some, and decided to ignore the two other rooms. She already planned to turn one room into a small study and outfit the other as a walk-in closet. Never enough closet space, she told herself, no matter what size your house.

Just as Theodosia was measuring the turret window, dreaming about swags and valances and maybe even velvet portieres dusting the floor, Earl Grey came padding upstairs.

"Almost done," she told him, jotting a final number. "Then we'll go explore your little domain." As they walked downstairs together, Theodosia paused on the landing. A faded print that she'd passed off earlier as a run-of-the-mill birds and bees print hung on the wall. But now, upon closer inspection, she noted the grace of the drawing, the careful attention to detail. Could it be an Audubon print, left or forgotten by one of the former owners? Theodosia decided she'd have to look at her contract again, see if maybe that little item might be included.

Continuing down the stairs, she turned and went into the kitchen. The counters were junky, the cupboards not much better. Updates would have to be made, new appliances installed, but that could all unfold over time. No hurry. Better to settle in first and get a feel for things. Old houses had a way of whispering truths and history to their owners, of telling them what needed fixing and what parts were best left untouched, original, and charming.

"Cold in here," said Theodosia, snapping on the light over the sink, frowning as it buzzed and blinked, then cut out entirely. "Don't tell me . . ." She flipped the switch again, and this time the light came on and stayed on. For the time being.

That's when Theodosia noticed the open window.

"What on earth!" she cried, as Earl Grey stared solemnly at her. "Was this open when we came in?" Then she answered her own question. "Had to be. Nobody here but us guys, huh?"

Strange, she decided. Perhaps the owner had been airing out the place for some reason? Or maybe Maggie Twining, her Realtor, had been by?

Worry nagging at her, Theodosia stepped over to the window, pushed firmly on the sash, trying to slide it down. The window was old and warped and stuck obstinately in its track. Grunting and tugging, she struggled with it. And suddenly, amidst the squeaks and groans of the window, Theodosia heard a distinct thump in the backyard.

What?

Followed by a loud pop and a patter of footsteps. At which point every light in the place winked out.

Whoa. Now what's going on?

Abandoning the stuck window, Theodosia dashed for the back door, ready to careen out into the backyard. Until fear jabbed a talon in her and Theodosia decided maybe the best course of action *wasn't* to rush out quite so hastily.

Grabbing Earl Grey by the collar, Theodosia decided to enlist him as a first line of defense as well as a par excellence guard dog. Plus dogs had nocturnal vision, right? So Earl Grey should be able to see what was going on.

Hanging on to his collar, Theodosia stepped slowly out into the yard. Ordinarily, it was a perfect little Charleston garden, made even more picturesque with magnolia and dogwood trees, a tangle of vines crawling up the back wall, and a tiny fountain that pattered prettily into a small fish pond. Utterly idyllic. Except when things went bump in the night!

Creeping ahead stealthily, Theodosia and Earl Grey crossed the tiny postage stamp–sized patio, aware of the scent of plum blossoms and damp grass. Five, six, then seven footsteps in, they hit a muddy patch of garden. Theodosia pulled a foot from the sticky stuff, wondering why there was so much mud, then remembered how hard it had rained last night.

And just as Theodosia touched her fingertips to the wrought-iron back gate, she heard the distinct grating of shoes on cobblestones. Of someone coming up the dark alley. Heading directly for her!

Crouching into her best kung fu position, Theodosia improvised by landing a hard, sideways kick on the wrought-iron gate. The force of her kick weakened the rusty hinges, causing the gate to fly open and crash loudly against the brick wall. Quick as a wink, she dashed into the dark alley — and ran smack dab into Jack Brux!

"You?" she cried, while Earl Grey danced around Brux, making anxious doggy chuffing sounds and nipping at Brux's heels.

"Get that dog away from me!" Brux yelled. He was startled, angry.

"What are you *doing* out here?" Theodosia demanded. "Why are you skulking around in my alley?"

"*Excuse* me?" said Brux, his face contorting into a disapproving snarl.

"I asked what you were doing here," Theodosia repeated.

Brux stared at Theodosia, incredulous. "I live down the block," he rasped. "A better question might be what are *you* doing here?"

"I live here, too," responded Theodosia. "Well, I'm *going* to live here, in about two weeks. Look, there was just an intruder in my backyard."

"Not me," snapped Brux.

"Did you see anyone?" she asked.

"No," came his terse reply.

"Strange that you just happened to come bobbing along out of nowhere," said Theodosia, her blood still simmering. She wasn't a huge believer in coincidences.

"This isn't nowhere," Brux snarled at her again. "I just *told* you, I live down the block."

But he still wasn't getting through to Theodosia. "My lights went out. You know anything about that?"

"I suggest you call South Carolina Electric and Gas," said Brux, practically spitting his words at her.

"I'm actually thinking about calling the police," responded Theodosia.

"Not on me you're not," cried Brux. Illuminated from above by a flickering back-alley gas lamp, his face looked harsh and deeply lined. Even threatening. "And maybe you should put your dog on a leash," he added in a sniping tone. Jack Brux spun sharply to see what Earl Grey was up to now, and suddenly, in the space of about two seconds, his face morphed from angry pink to pale white. "Oh my heavens!" he suddenly breathed.

"Is . . . is something wrong?" Theodosia asked. Maybe she'd been too aggressive after all, maybe she'd unwittingly pushed Brux into some kind of cardiac arrhythmia!

But Jack Brux continued to stare at the gate leading to Theodosia's yard, where Earl Grey now stood. Brux's lips seemed to be moving, but he wasn't making meaningful sounds.

Puzzled, Theodosia turned to see what had caused Brux such palpable shock. And saw Earl Grey standing there, paws gobbed with sticky black mud, clutching a bone in his mouth. A rather large bone.

Theodosia took a quick step closer and peered at Earl Grey's find. That's when her face turned a few shades paler, as well. *Oh, sweet mother of pearl!*

No way was she a medical professional. In fact, she hadn't been a particularly astute student when it came to biology. But even to Theodosia's untrained eye, the bone Earl Grey held in his mouth looked hideously like a human femur!

"Give it to me, boy," Theodosia urged. "Come on, hand it over." Theodosia crept closer to Earl Grey.

Thinking they were playing some wonderful, new game, Earl Grey immediately dropped into pounce position. Head down, muddy paws outstretched and quivering, back end up in the air. Bone still firmly clenched between his jaws.

"C'mon, boy," said Theodosia, getting more and more flustered.

"Dumb dog," muttered Brux.

Theodosia spun around, held up a single index finger, and hissed to Brux, "Don't." Then she finally pulled it together and remembered the proper command she and her dog had been taught. "Drop it."

Earl Grey promptly dropped the bone. It clunked loudly and hollowly on the pavement and rolled a couple of inches toward her.

"That's a good boy," murmured Theodosia. "Let's take a look at what treasure you found." She moved closer and poked gingerly at the bone with the tip of her shoe. Ugh. It sure looked like a human bone.

"What are you gonna do?" asked Brux, peering nearsightedly. "Call the police after all?"

"Not sure," said Theodosia. She stared at the bone again, trying to recall the myriad of technical diagrams in her college biology book. The bone certainly *looked* like a femur. Or maybe it was a tibia. In any case, the bone appeared to be human remains. So that meant alerting the police.

Five minutes later, a black-and-white patrol car slid to a stop in the alley.

Two officers, both young and good-looking, one white, one African American, got out, hitching up their black leather utility belts as they exited.

"I found a bone," Theodosia told them in a tumble of words. "At least my dog did. Dug it up, I think."

The African American officer, whose name tag read Darby, spoke first. "Take it easy, ma'am, we get a lot of these calls."

Theodosia grimaced. She knew they were being polite, but the ma'am thing just made her feel old. Which she wasn't. At least she didn't think she was. If sixty was the new forty, what was mid-thirties? The new mid-twenties? Hardly.

"Ma'am?" Officer Darby said again. "We're gonna have to take that bone with us. You want to put your dog inside the house? He looks a little vicious."

"He's a therapy dog," Theodosia told them. "I take him to senior citizen homes."

"Still, what breed is he?" asked the other officer. Officer Lomax. "Maybe like . . . a Doberman?"

"Dalbrador," said Theodosia. "A cross between a Dalmatian and a Labrador. And he does have a name. Earl Grey."

"Cute," said Darby, relaxing some.

Lomax gazed at her and suddenly snapped his fingers. "I recognize you. You're that tea lady. I saw you on TV a couple of weeks ago."

"I did a demo for Channel Four," said Theodosia.

"And my girlfriend went to your shop," continued Lomax. "And now she's forever brewing tea and making me tiny sandwiches with the crusts cut off."

"Really?" asked Darby. He sounded like he wouldn't mind a sandwich with the crusts cut off. Or any kind of sandwich, for that matter.

"And you see your girlfriend's activities as a *good* thing?" asked Theodosia. She wasn't sure whether Lomax was pro–tea sandwich or anti–tea sandwich.

"Oh yes, ma'am," Lomax said earnestly. "I particularly like the sandwiches with chicken salad and chitney."

"Chutney," said Theodosia.

"Right," said Lomax.

Darby popped open the trunk and grabbed a pair of latex gloves along with a black garbage bag. "So," he said, "let's bag up that bone."

Jack Brux, who'd watched the whole exchange, asked in a peevish tone, "Can I *go* now?"

7

Come Wednesday morning, Haley, in particular, was stunned by Theodosia's story about the bone. "And you actually think it's a *human* bone?" she asked.

Theodosia nodded. She'd waited until they'd set all the tables for morning tea before breaking the somewhat bizarre news about Earl Grey's late-night find.

Haley jabbed an elbow at Drayton. "Pretty weird stuff, huh? Really creepy."

"The thing is," said Drayton, looking thoughtful and not one iota creeped out, "finding human bones around our neck of the woods really is quite commonplace."

"That's what the police told me," said Theodosia. Although the notion still unsettled her.

"Think about it," said Drayton. "The first English settlers arrived here, at what was dubbed Charles Towne, in 1670. Since then, our fair city has endured the Revolutionary

War, War of 1812, War Between the States, and various floods, periods of pestilence, and deadly hurricanes. It's no wonder this entire place isn't one big bone yard."

"Well, that's a happy thought," said Haley.

"Then let's change the subject to something more upbeat," said Theodosia, as she folded a linen napkin into a bishop's hat arrangement. "How did you fare with your chocolate endeavors last night?"

Haley brightened immediately. "Got 'em all made! Even the bittersweet chocolate pavé, which turned out to be quite spectacular if I do say so myself."

"Glad to hear it," said Theodosia.

"Anyway," said Haley, "I dropped everything off at the Dorchester Club early this morning and filled out my entry forms in triplicate." She gazed eagerly at Theodosia. "You're still coming with me to the luncheon, right? It starts at one o'clock."

"Wouldn't miss it for the world," said Theodosia.

Drayton cleared his throat. "Since you two are planning to be in absentia for a few hours, I assume Haley will have prepared a no-fuss lunch? Realize, of course, it will be up to dear Miss Dimple and myself to serve it."

"Haley?" said Theodosia.

"Three easy entrées," replied Haley. "Chicken salad in tomato tulips, spring pea cream soup, chilled and served with cornbread, and ham and Gruyère sandwiches. No muss, no fuss." She grinned a wicked grin. "Think of it as tea time for dummies."

"You don't have to phrase it quite so inelegantly." Drayton blanched. "We're not exactly neophytes at serving customers."

"Hey, all I did was figure out a few things I could make and prep beforehand, so you could focus on plating the food and being your charming selves," said Haley. "Sorry. Didn't mean to ruffle any feathers."

"Haley," said Theodosia, "you'll prep the tomatoes, as well?"

"Sure thing," she said, tossing back her long blond hair and giving Drayton another snarky look as she headed for the kitchen.

"I wish you could come along to the Chocolatier Fest," Theodosia said to Drayton. "I've got a good feeling about Haley's entries."

"How could you not?" responded Drayton. "Our entire kitchen smells as if a giant, chocolate neutron bomb had been detonated. Or perhaps it's the same aromatic, lingering scent that hangs over Hershey, Pennsylvania?" He leaned down, opened a cardboard box, and carefully lifted out a small glass jar.

"Your scent jars came," observed Theodosia.

Drayton turned the small apothecary jar in his hand, studying it. "Yes. Finally. Now we'll be able to give our customers the joy of sniffing our fresh loose-leaf teas before they make their selection."

"I think you had a wonderful idea," said Theodosia, as Drayton continued to line the jars on the second shelf of a mahogany highboy. "It's basically sampling, which makes the whole tea-buying experience highly interactive."

"Sniff, sniff," said Drayton, pleased that she was pleased.

"How many teas are you thinking of putting on display?" Theodosia asked.

"I ordered twenty-four jars, so I think we should put out a full complement of teas."

"What about labels?" asked Theodosia. "We'll have to have labels."

Drayton held up a hand. "Please."

"Oh," Theodosia said. "Really?" Drayton was a skilled calligrapher and often volunteered to do elaborate hand lettering for menus, place cards, and special invitations. "Because if you're pressed for time, I could whip something out on my computer."

"Better I do the labels," said Drayton.

"You are a stickler for quality control," allowed Theodosia, her lips twitching at the corners.

"Someone has to be," replied Drayton, in complete seriousness. "Makes for a far more ordered and pleasant world. Would you . . . ?" He tilted his head back, gazed down his nose, looking suddenly thoughtful.

"You want to fill the jars now?" asked Theodosia. "Before the morning rush?"

Drayton pushed up his left sleeve and peered at his antique Piaget watch, which perpetually ran a few minutes slow. "I think there's time. You think we have time?"

"We'll fill as many as we can in the time we have," said Theodosia.

"Always so practical," said Drayton.

"Someone has to be," grinned Theodosia.

Theodosia dashed to the front counter, gathered up as many tea tins as she could comfortably grasp, then carried them over to Drayton.

"Thank you," he said, sounding pleased and happy. Theodosia had noticed, more and more, that Drayton had evolved into a very task-oriented person. Give him a menu to hand letter in bâtarde alphabet or small tea jars to fill, and he was happy as a clam.

"Drayton," said Theodosia, watching him

pour Nilgiri tea leaves into a jar, enjoying a small contact high from the slightly sweet, almost fruity aroma. "What do you know about Jack Brux? Do you think he's an okay guy?"

Drayton tapped the tea tin against the jar, eyeing the amount he'd just poured in. "Brux has always been a hardworking champion for the Heritage Society," said Drayton. "If that's what you're asking."

"It is and it isn't," said Theodosia. "To your knowledge, does Brux have a nasty temper? Or even a violent streak?"

Drayton's head jerked back and he stared at her. "You think he killed someone and buried them in your backyard? That your dog unearthed one of his poor victims?" He sounded deadly serious, but his eyes twinkled merrily.

"No," said Theodosia. "It's just that Brux strikes me as being somewhat ill-tempered. At least he was last night, when I ran into him."

Drayton let loose a snicker. "He *can* be awfully salty. Brux once removed his shoe and banged it on the table at a Heritage Society committee meeting to protest the admittance of a new board member."

"What?" asked Haley, who'd just wandered over to inspect Drayton's lineup of jars. "He took off his shoe? Like that old story about Khrushchev at the UN?"

"That wasn't a story, dear girl," said Drayton. "It really happened."

"What was the fuss about, anyway?" asked Haley.

"Cold war," said Dayton.

"Cold war?" asked Haley, looking slightly puzzled.

"And I'm not talking Celsius or centigrade," said Drayton. "Back in the day, particularly during the fifties, we were all terrified the Russians were going to drop a bomb and blast the bejeebers out of us."

"Duck, roll, and hide, huh?" said Haley, giggling. "And throw a few cans of Spam in the old bomb bunker?"

"Bomb shelter," said Drayton. "And, believe me, Haley, you wouldn't find it all so amusingly anachronistic if you'd lived through that era."

"S'pose not," said Haley. "Hey, those scent jars are terrific. And look how you managed to pour equal amounts of tea into each jar. You know, Dayton, besides being a certified tea taster, you've got a heckuva fine eye."

And with Haley's final pronouncement still hanging in the air, the floodgates of commerce suddenly opened. A half dozen eager customers pushed their way into the Indigo Tea Shop, and just like that, the joint was jumping.

Then a familiar yellow horse-drawn jitney clip-clopped its way to the front door and disgorged another dozen or so passengers. So, in the space of about ten minutes, the tea room buzzed with customers.

"Busy," murmured Drayton as he strutted past Theodosia, clutching a teapot in each hand.

"Right behind you with the scones," said Theodosia. Popping into the kitchen, she slid six plates onto her silver platter, each plate holding a cream scone along with tiny glass dishes filled with Devonshire cream and strawberry jam.

A few minutes later, when Haley's pecan pie muffins came out of the oven, all gorgeous brown and smelling of cinnamon and toasted pecans, Theodosia delivered those to waiting customers as well.

When most of her customers were finally sipping tea and happily spooning extra helpings of sinful Devonshire cream onto their scones, Theodosia took a moment to gaze about her tea shop. This, of course, was the golden hour. When the rich aroma of Chinese black tea hung redolent in the air, tea kettles chirped merrily, and Drayton glided from table to table pouring refills and charming customers with amusing stories. This little picture of contentment always reassured Theodosia that she'd made the right choice in giving up a well-paying job in the hustle-bustle world of marketing.

"Theodosia?"

Theodosia pulled herself from her brief reverie and quickly turned toward the front door. "Brooke!" she exclaimed, at seeing the smiling face of one of her fellow shopkeepers from down the block. "I didn't hear you come in." Brooke Carter Crockett was in her mid-fifties and petite, with a sleek mane of silver-white hair. Since Brooke had taken up yoga, she also seemed more lithe and had an aura of contentment about her.

"You look great," said Theodosia. As sole proprietor of Heart's Desire jewelry shop, Brooke dealt in the purchase and sales of elegant estate jewelry and was also recognized as a craftsman of contemporary pieces in gold and silver.

"Thank you," said Brooke. "I had a little downtime this morning so I thought I'd drop by for a proper tea. Not just grab a cuppa to go." She glanced around. "Don't know if you have a table, though . . ."

"Over by the fireplace," said Theodosia. "See, that couple is just getting up to leave.

I'll turn it around in a heartbeat."

"Perfect," declared Brooke.

Drayton, on seeing Brooke come in, sped over to do the honors himself. Cleared away dirty dishes, wiped down the scarred wooden table, laid out a fresh placemat along with flatware, plate, teacup, and linen napkin.

"This is the life," said Brooke, settling in. "A handsome fellow to do my bidding." She winked at Drayton, giggled when he blushed slightly.

"I understand you paid a visit to the new perfumery down the block," said Theodosia, sliding into the captain's chair across from Brooke.

"Last week," said Brooke. "Then I had to fly to Atlanta for the big jewelry show. When I returned yesterday, it was the first I'd heard about Daria's murder." A faint line insinuated itself between her brows. "I pored through all the newspapers and got caught up." Brooke leaned forward, looking grim, and rapped her knuckles against the table. "Must have been awful for you. Since you were the one who witnessed the assault and can supposedly ID the killer."

"The only problem," Theodosia told her, "is that I really *didn't* get a good look at the attacker."

"That's not how the newspeople painted it," replied Brooke. "They made it sound like you were very much involved."

"An unfortunate overstatement," said Theodosia. "Journalistic puffery."

"Does that worry you?" asked Brooke. "That the killer *thinks* you might be able to identify him?"

"It does bother me a little," said Theodosia. "No, actually, it bothers me a lot."

Drayton was suddenly at the table with a cream scone and orange marmalade, as well as a freshly brewed pot of tea. "I have something new for you to try," he told Brooke. "A lovely tea from the Dooars region in India. Even though Dooars is the fourth most important tea-growing region, it's simply not as well known as the Assam Valley or the Darjeeling region." He lifted his teapot, a lovely pink-and-green bone china pot done in the shape of a cabbage. "But the tea they produce in Dooars is rich and slightly fruity, with just a tiny hint of malt." He poured out a steaming cup. "Try it. Enjoy it."

Brooke took a sip and nodded almost immediately. "Oh, I see what you mean. I can taste the fruit and there's also a tiny hint of astringency in the finish."

Drayton beamed. "You have a very refined

palette."

Brooke smiled back at him. "I had a very good teacher."

When Drayton finally moved on, Theodosia asked Brooke about her visit to the perfumery.

"Cute little place," Brooke told her. "Loads and loads of inventory, really amazing stuff. You'll have to drop by and meet the ladies."

"I already met one of them," said Theodosia. "Cinnamon stopped by yesterday. She seemed nice enough."

"Ah," said Brooke, "but the real power behind the throne is Miss Kitty, her aunt. Did you by chance meet her?"

"Haven't had the pleasure," said Theodosia.

"Oh, you'll cross paths," said Brooke. "And believe me, Miss Kitty's a real trip. Outspoken, high energy, a world-class talker and promoter. She's already asking me to craft some sterling silver perfume bottle charms to retail in her shop."

"Sounds like a cute idea," said Theodosia. Brooke was renowned for her Charleston-themed jewelry and had created more than a dozen or so tiny charms that were adorable on charm bracelets or could be linked on chains as pendants. Her more recent charms included miniature palm trees, pineapples, magnolia blossoms, wrought-iron gates, sailing ships, oysters, and churches.

Taking a bite of scone, Brooke chewed thoughtfully, then said, "So . . . are you going to get seriously involved?"

"In . . . ?"

"You know," said Brooke, studying her carefully. "The murder. Daria's murder."

"I think I'm already involved," said Theodosia.

"Your buddy Detective Tidwell is on the case?"

Theodosia nodded.

"Then you're already on the inside."

"Not really," said Theodosia.

"You know Tidwell's sweet on you," purred Brooke. "Not romantic sweet, but in a quiet, admiring way. I've seen how he looks at you."

"He watches me like a cat observes a mouse hole," said Theodosia. "It's discomforting."

"Still," said Brooke. "Tidwell is well aware how skillful you are at piecing together clues."

"Only if I can find a clue," said Theodosia, glancing up at Drayton, who had suddenly planted himself at her elbow. "Need help?"

she asked, starting to rise from her chair.

"There's a young man here," said Drayton. He gestured toward the front door, where a sandy-haired man, looking rather studious in horn-rimmed glasses, stood waiting patiently. He was young, maybe twenty-seven or twenty-eight, and was dressed in khaki slacks and a matching khaki shirt loaded with pockets and epaulets.

"And we're out of tables," said Theodosia.

"No," said Drayton, suddenly looking more than a little concerned. "He doesn't want a table. He says he want to talk to you about your bones."

Tred Pascal was from the State Archaeology Office, hence the Indiana Jones outfit. Turns out, Tred's boss had received a phone call this morning from the Charleston Police Department. So Tred had been duly assigned to deal with the bone. Theodosia's bone. All because the powers that be thought it should be examined for archaeological significance.

Tred explained all this to Theodosia while sitting across from her in her office, glancing sideways at dozens of ceramic and bone china teapots, a pile of grapevine wreaths decorated with ribbons, teacups, and silk flowers, and dozens of piled-up boxes with stacks of wide-brimmed straw hats teetering on top.

"Archaeological significance," said Theodosia. The words sounded stilted to her, especially when applied to a grubby old bone. And would probably come as a crushing disappointment to Earl Grey, who'd been counting on having his precious find returned to him.

"The thing is," said Tred, "folks uncover bones all the time. Digging up gardens, during excavations, that sort of thing. Most of the time they're simply animal bones, but once in a while they turn out to be historically important. Native Americans, early settlers, bones that date back to the Revolutionary War era, Civil War soldiers."

"So I've been told," said Theodosia.

Tred wrinkled his brow, looking concerned. "I did some quick, seat-of-the-pants research. There's a chance your cottage might have been built on the very spot where pirates were once hanged."

"I thought that all happened at White Point Gardens," said Theodosia. "The gallows and the pirate hangings, I mean." That's what she'd always been told. That's what most historic district tours underscored as well. All the ruffian pirates that had been caught plaguing the southeastern seaboard had been summarily hunted down, captured, and hung from a permanent gallows that had occupied a lonely, shell-scattered beach.

"But your place isn't that far away," Tred pointed out. "Maybe the condemned were executed at White Point Gardens, then buried somewhere else. Like in your yard."

"A happy thought," said Theodosia. Who wanted a potter's field in their backyard? Not her!

"What I'd like to do is set up a small archaeological dig," said Tred. "See if anything else turns up."

Theodosia shifted uncomfortably. "You're not serious."

"Even a small dig can yield stunning results," enthused Tred. "I was part of a dig last summer at the Topper Site —"

"Where?" interrupted Theodosia.

"On the Savannah River, over in Allendale County," said Tred, real excitement lighting his face. "The tools and stone implements we unearthed revealed that ancient humans had been present as far back as sixteen thousand years ago. That's three thousand years earlier than previously thought!"

"Wow," said Theodosia. She felt like she ought to be impressed, but her mind kept circling back to having her backyard dug up. Or should she think of it as prepping the soil for tomato plants? Or perhaps a lovely rose garden?

"Knock, knock," said Haley, suddenly looming in the doorway. "I'm gonna take off for the Dorchester Club now," she told Theodosia. Then she smiled shyly at Tred and gave a warm, "Hey there."

"Haley," said Theodosia, "this is Tred Pascal from the State Archaeology Office. He's here about the bone."

"Cool," said Haley, giving him another shy smile. "Where'd you go to school?"

Tred focused his attention on Haley. "I graduated from the University of South Carolina in Columbia. Department of Anthropology."

"Love the bwana outfit," Haley quipped, obviously feeling playful. "Was that part of the deal?"

Tred blushed.

Haley folded her arms and edged a little closer to him. "And now you get to run around digging up old bones and stuff?"

"Sometimes I do," said Tred. "Most of the time, we're in the laboratory analyzing them. Using carbon dating or electron microscopes." He swiveled his head toward Theodosia. "You still have the bone in question?" he asked.

"Oh, silly me," said Haley, with exaggerated earnestness. "I'm afraid I tossed it into the soup pot."

The look on Tred's face was priceless. "What!"

"Relax," said Theodosia. "Haley's just pulling your leg. She does that once in a while. It's her idea of sport."

"You two are quite a tag team," said Tred, looking a little unsettled.

"Actually," said Theodosia, "the police took the bone last night. Bagged it, tagged it, promised to do the whole CSI thing. Which, I guess, *you're* really going to do."

"So the bone's probably downtown at their lab," said Tred, nodding. "Okay."

"Okay," echoed Haley. "So . . . see you at the luncheon, Theo?"

Theodosia nodded.

Haley grinned at Tred. "Good luck and all. See you around."

"Maybe so." Tred smiled.

"Hope so," said Haley.

"When you said you wanted to set up a small archeological excavation," said Theodosia, getting back to the subject at hand, "what exactly did you have in mind?"

"First," said Tred, "we'd have to determine if your backyard really is worth exploring. According to state guidelines, an archaeological site is defined as an area yielding three or more historic or prehistoric artifacts within a thirty-meter radius."

"Okay," said Theodosia. "So first you'd have to find more bones."

"Or artifacts," said Tred. "Since a site can also be an area with visible or historically recognized cultural features, such as a cemetery, rock shelter, chimney fall, brick wall, or pier . . . well, you get the idea."

"It's really only a cottage," said Theodosia. "A former carriage house. And, technically, I don't even own the property yet. You'd have to get permission from the current owners."

"When were you supposed to close on the property?"

"I was hoping in about two weeks."

"That might not be possible," said Tred.

Theodosia rose in her chair. "Please don't say that. I already started packing. I have a sort of . . . schedule."

"Look," said Tred, "I'm going to do my best to fast-track this whole thing. Take a quick look-see in the next couple of days, then make a determination."

"Based on what you do or don't find," mused Theodosia. "Okay. Hopefully, nothing else will turn up."

"And I'm kind of hoping something does," Tred told her as they walked out of Theodosia's office. Ducking past the velvet celadon-green curtain that closed off the tea shop from the kitchen and back office, they headed for the front door.

Curious at all the hustle and bustle, Tred glanced around and asked, "What kind of food do you serve here, anyway?"

"We're a tea shop," Theodosia told him. "Today we're offering soup, salad, scones, and sandwiches. Plus we can brew pretty much any type of tea you have a taste for." She paused. "Why? Are you hungry?"

Tred nodded. "Famished. But I don't have time to eat right now. I'd like to come back sometime, though." His eyes twinkled. "Are you always here?"

He was flirting with her and she knew it. Funny, she thought he'd been seriously charmed by Haley.

"Most every day," said Theodosia, "since I'm the owner." She paused. "Tell you what. Why don't I package up a cup of tea and a couple of scones to go."

"Takeaway?" Tred looked positively jubilant. "You'd do that?"

"Give me a minute," said Theodosia. She slid over to the counter, poured a splash of Formosan oolong tea into a cup, and dropped two scones in an indigo blue bag. Then, on impulse, ran back into the kitchen and packaged up a nice ham and Gruyère sandwich.

"Tea party in a box," she told Tred, when she handed it to him.

113

His grin was wide and sincere. "Thank you so much. Once I pick up the bone, do a little lab work, and talk to my boss, I'll let you know, okay?"

"Sure," said Theodosia. "Come back anytime."

"Problems?" asked Drayton. He'd removed his long, black Parisian waiter's apron and slipped into a camel-hair jacket, the better to meet and greet luncheon customers. Today Drayton's bow tie was a red-and-green tartan, a veritable Celtic-looking butterfly that lent a striking contrast.

"No problems out of the ordinary," Theodosia told him. "Nothing I can't handle."

"Are we still attending the Blessing of the Fleet tonight?" Drayton asked her. The Blessing of the Fleet was a new event for Charleston. This first ever blessing was to be held at White Point Gardens, a lush strip of land right at the tip of the peninsula, where the Ashley and Cooper rivers surged past on each side. Yachts, sailboats from both the Charleston Yacht Club and the Compass Key Yacht Club, and even some oyster boats and shrimp trawlers were going to take part. It was an idea they'd basically pinched from Mt. Pleasant, who did a Blessing of the Fleet on their fishing boats every April.

"Yes," Theodosia told him. "And I'm really looking forward to seeing the sailboats." She knew that two entire fleets would be tacking past, their masts and sails outlined in tiny white lights. Scheduled for dusk tonight, with the crashing Atlantic as a backdrop, the decorated boats were sure to be an awe-inspiring sight.

Reaching past her, Drayton grabbed a cardboard box and plunked it carefully on the counter.

"Don't tell me you're putting out more scent jars?" said Theodosia.

Drayton peeled open the box with a smile. "That shipment of teacup candles you ordered finally arrived." He lifted one out gently. A teacup with a pink-and-cream rose motif, seamlessly epoxied to its saucer, was filled with what looked like pink tea but was really a scented candle and wick.

"These are even more adorable than they were in the catalog," exclaimed Theodosia. "If you put them on display today, they'll probably sell out."

"Then I shall do exactly that," said Drayton.

Theodosia lifted out another teacup candle and sniffed. "Mmm, this one's orange-scented."

"Our shipment should include mandarin, raspberry, lemon verbena, and teaberry," said Drayton.

"Teaberry," said Theodosia, frowning slightly.

"Hmm?" asked Drayton, absently. His tortoiseshell glasses slid halfway down his nose as he studied the design of one of the teacups. "This chintz pattern reminds me of a Shelley pattern."

"You know," said Theodosia, half to herself, half to Drayton, "I'm going to check on something. Satisfy my curiosity."

"Yes," said Drayton, setting his teacup down and giving a perfunctory smile. "Do have a lovely time at your event."

But Theodosia had fifteen minutes to spare before she had to leave for the Dorchester Club. So she headed down the street to Jardin Perfumerie. This time the little shop was open for business when she arrived at their front door. Perfect, she decided, stepping inside a little jewel of a shop that glittered and glowed and proved to be even more fragrant and spicy than when she was brewing a dozen different teas at her own shop.

Cinnamon was there, of course, standing behind a black marble counter that displayed a myriad of dazzling glass bottles. She was just packing up a fragrance for a customer and smiled warmly at Theodosia. A smile that also said, "I'll be right with you."

Theodosia took these few opportune moments to look around. Interestingly enough, Jardin Perfumerie reminded her of an upscale jewelry shop. Lovely glass cases filled with delicate bottles that sparkled like gems. Mirrored walls with glass shelves that held scented soaps, candles, and essential oils. She reached out, picked up a small votive candle in a brocade-decorated glass, and decided it reminded her of a stained-glass window from one of Charleston's fine old churches.

Once Cinnamon's customer had slipped out the door, she wasted no time plying Theodosia with a little soft sell. "I'll bet you'd like us to create a personal fragrance for you," she purred.

"Can you do that?" asked Theodosia. The notion struck her as fun and a trifle indulgent.

Cinnamon came a step closer, her long, midnight blue silk skirt rustling, her long pearl necklace clacking softly and set off beautifully by her white ruffled blouse. She was dressed like a lady of the Belle Époque and was doing her best to play the part. No Junior League suit today; this costume portrayed elegance, grace, and turn-of-the-century glamour.

"We've created hundreds of personal scents," Cinnamon told Theodosia, as she picked up a small glass bottle. Removing the stopper, Cinnamon tipped the bottle toward Theodosia. "Somehow I see you as a clean, woodsy scent. Along the lines of this."

Theodosia took a sniff. Scents of pine, cherry, and sandalwood tickled her nose. "I like it."

Cinnamon narrowed her eyes and cocked her head, as if deep in thought. Theodosia decided Cinnamon had her sales patina down perfectly.

"But maybe a touch more . . . sophistication?" Cinnamon mused. "And perhaps . . ." Now her fingertips danced across the tops of a dozen different bottles. "Perhaps something with a hint of mystery, as well." She selected a bottle, pulled out the stopper, and held it up. "This has lovely top notes."

Theodosia dutifully sniffed again. This time she thought she recognized vanilla. And maybe lavender.

"Vanilla and lavender?" she asked.

Cinnamon looked more than a little surprised. "Goodness but you have an educated nose. That's quite a rarity."

"I do own a tea shop," replied Theodosia. "And, of course, Drayton, Drayton Conneley, my master tea blender, has helped me tremendously when it comes to learning aromas, blending, and scents." Theodosia had the feeling she'd somehow blundered into Cinnamon's special world. Hadn't exactly one-upped her, but certainly demonstrated an equality of knowledge.

Cinnamon snatched the bottle back. "Perhaps you'd enjoy one of our proprietary scents instead. We have several and they're *very* popular." There was just a hint of coolness in her voice.

Theodosia decided to try to warm her up again. "Your shop is really quite amazing. I see you even sell scented drawer liners and room fragrances." She thought these might come in handy, once she moved into her new cottage.

Cinnamon smiled dreamily. "Soaps, candles, essential oils, and more than a thousand different fragrances. From such venerable fragrance and couture houses as Chanel, Bulgari, Tiffany, Dior, and Creed. This one . . ." she pointed at a pyramid-shaped crystal bottle . . . "is Poivre by Caron. A thousand dollars an ounce."

"And a lovely bottle, too," said Theodosia,

wondering who would spend that much for a fragrance.

"Baccarat crystal," said Cinnamon. She waved a hand airily. "I could go on and on."

"There's a scent I used to adore," said Theodosia. "Le Dix by Balenciaga? Hard to find though."

"We just happen to have it," chirped Cinnamon. "As well as several of the very popular pheromone-infused fragrances." She let loose a soft giggle. "Should you be looking to make a man fall in love with you, pheromones will do the trick!"

"Good to know," said Theodosia. She pointed at a square, matte black bottle that sat, looking sexy and a little evil, on an elevated glass pedestal. "One of your proprietary scents?"

Cinnamon nodded. "I call that one Requiem. A hint of black cherry with top notes of spicy ginger and amber."

"Unusual," said Theodosia.

"Unusual is our specialty," replied Cinnamon.

"What about a teaberry scent?" asked Theodosia. For some reason, the notion of teaberry had stuck in her mind ever since the night Daria had been murdered.

"A wonderful scent," enthused Cinnamon. "So minty and fresh. We have some around here as well as some essential teaberry oil on order. I'd have to check my inventory list for the exact date."

"And you've sold some?" asked Theodosia.

"Probably," said Cinnamon, smiling broadly. "But you simply *must* come back this afternoon when Miss Kitty is in. She's my aunt and the driving force behind Jardin Perfumerie. Miss Kitty worked for Fragonard in Paris at their shop in Saint-Germain-des-Prés. She's even visited Grasse in the Provence region of southern France during their May harvest of *Rosa centifolia* flowers."

"An impressive pedigree," said Theodosia.

"Miss Kitty is extremely well versed in the fragrance industry," said Cinnamon. "So you might want to reserve any questions for her."

"Just one question right now," said Theodosia.

Cinnamon raised her eyebrows in anticipation.

"Is your name really Cinnamon?"

That brought on a somewhat sheepish grin. "My given name is really Cynthia. But I thought Cinnamon sounded a little more . . . um . . . apropos."

9

"I'm so glad you made it!" Haley exclaimed to Theodosia, as they pushed their way through the buzzing crowd of people that had convened in the lobby of the Dorchester Club. "And with five minutes to spare."

Theodosia glanced around at the guests. It appeared to be a crazy-quilt mélange of chefs, bakers, foodies (particularly dessert freaks), ladies who lunch, and Charleston socialites, although Theodosia decided those last two categories were probably one and the same.

"Do we have time to peek at the Chocolatier Fest entries?" Theodosia asked.

In answer, Haley grabbed Theodosia's hand and quickly pulled her past a sea of faces into the Dorchester Club's wood-paneled Fireplace Room. There, a series of tables had been set up to showcase all the cake, chocolate, truffle, and trifle entries.

"Wow," Theodosia murmured, under her

breath, as she beheld the striking display. White linen tablecloths had been draped over dark brown silk table coverings. White- and cocoa-colored tapers flickered from tall silver candelabras. And against the back side of each display table were boundless bouquets of chocolate-colored day lilies, gingerbread-colored irises, maroon-brown pansies, and feathery brown and gold ornamental grasses. Some intrepid floral designer had gone all out to create chocolate-inspired floral offerings that coordinated perfectly with the entries.

And what amazing entries they were!

Chocolate truffles with ganache centers and buttercream zigzag decorations. Petit fours and chocolate raspberry cheesecake. Chili pepper chocolates and chocolate lace cookies. Chocolate gelato and chocolate walnut bread. Amazing miniature chocolate bowls that were hand painted to look exactly like porcelain. Champagne chocolate truffles. And a rich chocolate cake displayed in a small, round pillow-top hat box with a wildflower bouquet perched on top.

"I guess chocolate's not just for dessert anymore," joked Theodosia.

"That cake in the hat box?" said Haley, looking slightly in awe. "Over at the Yellow Bird Gift Shop it retails for a whopping one hundred and eighty dollars."

"Awfully steep," admitted Theodosia. Who would pay so much, she wondered, for a cake?

"And see over here?" said Haley, pointing. "A layered chocolate truffle made from seventy percent Criollo cocoa from Venezuela — the best in the world — layered with creamy ganache and infused with real truffle oil." She paused, as if a certain reality was sinking in. "I don't have a chance."

"Yes, you do!" enthused Theodosia. "Your entries hold their own beautifully."

"You think?" said Haley, a little wistfully.

"Look at it this way," said Theodosia. "You took fourth place last year; now it's your turn to move up the ladder."

"What if I slide down a few rungs?" asked Haley, as they headed for their table in the main dining room.

"There's no shame in trying," said Theodosia. "You've given it your best shot; now the decision rests in the hands of the judges." Suddenly catching sight of an overly animated woman in a bright yellow dress, Theodosia added, "Uh-oh, do you see who I see?"

"Huh?" asked Haley, head turning, hair swishing.

"I think Delaine is seated at our table."

"Oh, she is," said Haley. "I peeked at the place cards earlier."

"Delaine's probably going to be bubbling over about her fashion show this Friday. Ah well."

"You weren't planning to attend?" Haley asked.

"Not unless I get my arm twisted," murmured Theodosia.

Of course Delaine spotted them immediately.

"The-o-dosia!" Delaine called, in a frenetic, high-pitched voice. "Over heeeere!"

"Prepare to get twisted," murmured Haley, as Delaine Dish came speedballing at them, taking rapid-fire baby steps in four-inch stiletto heels.

"Long time no see! Long time no see!" cried Delaine, cooing little greetings and peppering them with air-kisses. With her lovely heart-shaped face, inquisitive violet eyes, and dark hair wound up into a psyche knot atop her head, Delaine was beauty with an attitude. A whirling dervish filled with energy, self-confidence, and boundless curiosity. She was also proprietor of Cotton Duck, one of Charleston's finest boutiques. Delaine's shop featured racks of elegant, airy cotton clothing that was perfectly suited to stand up to Charleston's high heat and humidity. She also stocked silk tunics, filmy tops, long evening dresses, scarves the weight of butterfly wings, strands of pearls, swishy skirts, and even a few racks of vintage clothes. Delaine's latest addition included several high-end lingerie lines, including La Perla, Cosabella, and Guia La Bruna from Italy.

"Looks like we're at your table," said Theodosia, trying to extricate herself from Delaine's firm grip. A grip that felt like it would leave talon marks on her arm.

Delaine wasn't having it. "I'm so *happy* I ran into you, sweetie," she gushed. "I wanted to *personally* invite you to my trunk show this Friday afternoon at Cotton Duck." She released Theodosia's arm only to place both hands on Theodosia's shoulders and exert another vicelike grip. "You're *coming,* aren't you? Please tell me you are!"

"If I had to take a wild guess," said Haley, trying hard to keep a straight face, "I'd say she's coming."

"Of course, I'll come," said Theodosia. It was like being captured by terrorists. She'd say anything to negotiate a release.

Delaine let Theodosia go and clasped her hands to her chest in joy. "Thank goodness! Where would I be without my very dearest friend!"

Dearest friend? thought Theodosia. *Lord love a duck, am I really Delaine's dearest friend?* Then she decided that, based on Delaine's over-the-top theatrics, she might be her only friend.

Delaine leaned in and whispered in Theodosia's ear, "Please don't bring up anything about that awful business that happened during the back-alley crawl, will you?"

Her words gob-smacked Theodosia right between the eyes. *Awful business? That's one way to categorize it. Another might be murder.*

"Come, come," Delaine cried brightly, as she shepherded Theodosia and Haley toward their table. "See who else is sitting with us! The ladies from Popple Hill Design!"

Theodosia and Haley slipped into their seats, grateful to be diverted from the slightly manic Delaine, and greeted warmly by Marianne Petigru and Hillary Retton, two lady decorators who, in the last five years, had managed to make Popple Hill one of the top interior design firms in Charleston. Marianne Petigru was tall and thin, with short, spiky blond hair. She was also old Charleston society and knew her way around the Heritage Society, Opera Society, Theater Guild, Art Institute, and the various parties and black-tie dinners that were part and parcel of Charleston society. Her business partner, Hillary Retton, was shorter, dark-haired, and, although she'd been residing in Charleston for a good ten years, was still considered somewhat of an outsider.

"How fortuitous we're all seated together!" exclaimed Delaine. "Our dear Theodosia just purchased that adorable little cottage down the block from the Featherbed House Bed and Breakfast, and she is in *dire* need of a decorating consult!"

"I heard you bought Hazelhurst," drawled Marianne, referring to the name that the cottage bore on Charleston's list of historic places. "A charming little abode." She herself owned an enormous 1850s Victorian mansion replete with multigabled roof, turrets, domed skylight, and all the requisite gingerbread trim. "I just hope your cottage is structurally sound," continued Marianne. "My place may be listed on the historic register, but it's still a futsy old albatross with a mind of its own. It's been seven years since we moved in, and we're still dealing with a bad foundation."

"That sinking feeling," quipped Hillary.

But Marianne just shook her head, almost to the point of fuming now. "You put money into the ground, you never see it again.

Nobody does. And the fees construction companies charge — positively criminal."

"I think my cottage is structurally okay," said Theodosia. "At least the building inspector gave it a passing grade."

"Thank your lucky stars," said Marianne.

"And it doesn't need that much decorating, does it?" asked Hillary. "As I recall, there's a small marble entryway and fairly decent wood flooring."

"The cottage is all very Old World," Theodosia told them. "And in fairly good condition. I'll probably need to install new draperies, but that's not such a big deal."

"We can surely help with that," Hillary told her.

"Think about slubbed silk with Parisian pleated sheers," suggested Marianne.

"And you're moving in two weeks?" asked Delaine. "Theo, dear, you really must take advantage of these two decorating geniuses."

"Two weeks will fly by . . ." Hillary snapped her fingers. "Like that."

"Actually," said Theodosia, "there's a slight problem."

"I'm sure it's nothing that can't be fixed," said Delaine in a self-assured tone of voice. "You can always slip an extra twenty to the . . ."

"The State Archaeology Office wants to

129

dig up the backyard," Theodosia told them.

Delaine, Marianne, and Hillary collectively inhaled, then exclaimed, in unison, "What!"

And so, over chilled strawberry and chocolate soup, goat cheese and pumpkin seed arugula salads accented with white chocolate bits, and chocolate chicken mole, Theodosia related to her rapt audience how Earl Grey had discovered the strange bone, why Tred Pascal had suggested a small dig, and how her long-awaited move might have to be postponed for a couple of weeks.

"That's the craziest thing I ever heard," said Delaine. "Bones." She gave a derisive snort. "Who gives a rat's backside about a bunch of old bones?"

"Obviously the State Archaeology Office," Haley quipped in a droll tone.

"And you don't want to mess with them," agreed Marianne, looking serious. "I know a woman who owns an old plantation house over in Georgetown County near the South Santee River. Last year her gardener was using a rototiller and unwittingly discovered some kind of primitive, stone-age tool made from a deer leg. Long story short, she had to abandon her tomato patch for the entire summer just so the State Archaeology Office could take a closer look."

Delaine made a face. "An old deer leg. Makes you want to rethink venison, doesn't it?"

"Or planting tomatoes," said Haley.

"They're only going to poke around in the backyard," said Theodosia. "It's not like they want to excavate five stories down or dismantle the entire house. I mean, how long can something like that take?"

Delaine rolled her eyes. "If I were you, sweetie, I'd put all your moving plans on hold."

"Please don't say that," murmured Theodosia. But Marianne only nodded sagely.

Keeping to the theme of Chocolatier Fest, the dessert the Dorchester Club served was a showstopping assortment of chocolate cakes, cookies, and candies. Waiters brought out three-tiered trays, similar to the ones Theodosia used at her tea shop, filled chockablock with the most delightful chocolate goodies.

"Is that a chocolate-covered orange peel?" asked Delaine, as a waiter placed their tray in the center of their table.

"*Agrumelli,*" said Haley. "Almond paste pillows stuffed with zest of lemon and orange. And that's a honeyed caramel. And it all looks very good." She glanced around, then let loose a nervous high-pitched sound, a cross between a giggle and a sigh.

"It won't be long now," Theodosia told Haley, who was starting to jitterbug in her seat.

"Theo, dear," said Delaine, as she pulled out her makeup kit and reapplied a slick of mauve lip gloss, "have you had a chance to visit that new Jardin Perfumerie that opened down the block from you?"

"Theodosia's not only been there," said Haley, looking slightly frazzled, "they even offered to create a personal fragrance for her."

Delaine snapped the cap back on her lip gloss and managed a surprised double take. "A *personal* fragrance? Really?"

"Might be fun," said Theodosia.

"Well, la-de-da," said Delaine, sounding positively jealous. "Aren't you the indulgent one."

A tap on Theodosia's shoulder was a welcome diversion from Delaine. But when Theodosia swiveled in her chair and saw who it was, she inwardly cringed.

Bill Glass, the publisher of *Shooting Star,* Charleston's local, glossy gossip tabloid, flashed a wide grin at her, along with lots of white, Chiclet-sized teeth.

"Glass," muttered Theodosia. Bill Glass,

with his slicked back hair and olive skin, wasn't a bad-looking man. But it was his condescending and cavalier attitude that constantly rubbed her the wrong way. Basically, Bill Glass was Charleston's local version of a paparazzo, a self-absorbed, self-indulgent photographer and publisher who adored rubbing elbows with society and loved it even more when they screwed up. Preferably in front of his camera.

"Some shindig, huh?" he asked Theodosia. "I thought skinny society-type ladies never indulged in dessert. In fact, I thought they only lived on air and water. 'Course, you're not all that skinny."

"What are you doing here?" Theodosia asked, with thinly disguised contempt.

Glass held up his Nikon camera. "Just grabbing a few quick shots. I live for the moment when some society babe tips back too many Cosmos or gets a sugar buzz and dives headfirst into a potted plant. But, hey, that ain't nuthin' compared to the excitement you guys had Monday night." He flashed another callous, careless grin. "Looks like your best-laid plans went awry, huh? Sorry I missed all the excitement."

"Excuse me?" said Theodosia in a cool voice. Glass, as editor of his own mini *Enquirer,* really was a scuzzball.

"The back-alley crawl was *your* idea, right?" Glass asked. "Obviously it backfired big time. Didn't count on capping off the event with a brutal murder, huh?"

"Could you please get away from our table?" snapped Delaine. "You're really quite boring." Even though Delaine was incredibly rude in her treatment of Glass, Theodosia practically applauded her. Served him right.

"Yeah, yeah," muttered Glass, fidgeting with his camera lens. "Maybe I'll run into some of you lovelies later on. Once this happy crap is over I'm gonna hit Church Street and grab a few interior shots of that new perfume joint." He smirked. "Don't mind too much 'cause that Cinnamon St. John babe is quite a looker." As if that wasn't bad enough, he added a nasty sound effect: "Grrrr."

Haley stared at Glass with narrowed eyes. "Do you really think your ridiculous, outdated machismo impresses women?"

"Honey, I know it does," boasted Glass.

"In that case," said Haley, "I think we just determined what type of woman you prefer."

"Shhhh!" hissed Delaine, as a man in a tuxedo stepped to the podium and tapped a finger against the microphone. "They're going to announce the winners." She shot a quick glance at Haley. "Honey, I just hope you're not too disappointed."

"Delaine!" said Theodosia, as Glass scuttled toward the podium. "Haley needs support, not pessimism." She turned to Haley and gave a hopeful, commiserating smile. "Whatever happens, you'll be just fine, Haley."

Haley clapped her hands over her ears and scrunched up her face. "You tell me what happens, Theo. I'm too nervous to listen!"

10

"You're back!" squealed Miss Dimple. Short, plump, with a perpetual grandmotherly expression on her apple-cheeked face, Miss Dimple was Theodosia's freelance accountant who also adored filling in at the tea shop.

"Not only are we back," cried a jubilant Haley, "but we've returned victorious!" Haley thrust her trophy, a pink-and-chocolate-colored enamel cupcake sprinkled with brilliant crystals, into the air for everyone to see. "Look! We brought home the Silver Cupcake Award!"

"Oh my goodness," exclaimed Miss Dimple, grabbing her hot-pink glasses from the beaded chain around her neck and popping them onto her nose. "Let me take a look at that."

"Well done!" chimed in Drayton as he joined the admiration society. "I never doubted you for a minute, Haley."

"Now that's a trophy!" declared Miss Dimple. "And I love that glittery pink!"

"Yes . . . it is a rather vivid strawberry pink," said Drayton.

"Pepto pink," declared Miss Dimple.

Drayton put an arm around Miss Dimple's shoulders. "I love how you think, my dear."

"I hope lunch went okay," said Haley, setting her trophy on the front counter and quickly checking the tea room where three tables of customers still lingered.

"Using the nomenclature of the day, it was a piece of cake," said Drayton. "Since you had everything so carefully prepared for us."

"We had a fine time," said Miss Dimple. "We served everyone tea and complimentary scones, then I plated in the kitchen, while Drayton delivered the orders."

"Like clockwork," said Drayton.

"But your watch is always slow," pointed out Haley.

Drayton pursed his lips. "Like I said, clockwork."

"So we didn't miss much," said Theodosia. She was relieved the lunch hour had gone so smoothly.

"Only a phone call from your newfound friend, Miss Cinnamon," said Drayton. "She called . . . perhaps ten minutes ago?

Apparently her aunt . . . a Miss Kitty . . . ?"

Theodosia nodded. "That's right."

"Ah, yes," continued Drayton. "This Miss Kitty is now in attendance at said perfumery and Miss Cinnamon has cordially extended an invitation for you to come meet her."

"Hello Kitty," giggled Haley, still riding high from her victory.

Drayton peered down his nose at Haley. "But who are we to question a person's name, when it's undoubtedly a pet name or term of endearment."

"I guess," said Haley.

"Huh," said Theodosia. She had a certain curiosity about Miss Kitty. "Okay, if there's nothing crushing for me to handle at the moment, maybe I'll take some tea and scones down to them." She threw a questioning look at Miss Dimple. "We have scones left?"

"Goodness yes, dear," said Miss Dimple. "Do you want me to pack some up for you?"

"I can do it," Theodosia told her, "but if you have time to step in the back office with me, I can give you the receipts for the last ten days."

"Back to reality," said Miss Dimple.

"Your day job," said Haley.

Miss Dimple gazed at Theodosia, Drayton, and Haley, with a beatific smile on her face. "You do realize that working here is my fantasy job, don't you?"

"Sometimes it feels like a fantasy to me, too," remarked Drayton.

"So you're Theodosia!" exclaimed Miss Kitty, in a tumble of words and a cloud of perfume. "Come in, dear, and let me get a good look at you. Cinnamon has told me so much about you!"

"All good, I hope," said Theodosia. She handed her indigo blue bag of tea and scones to Cinnamon and blinked as she beheld the rather amazing Miss Kitty. In her well-tailored purple suit, red silk blouse with a pussycat bow, and at least eight ginormous diamond rings twinkling from almost every finger, Miss Kitty looked like a cross between a saloon girl and a widow who'd run through three or four rich husbands. She weighed maybe ninety pounds soaking wet, with blue-tinted hair that was teased, swooped, and swirled into a creative bouffant hairdo worthy of a Motown singer from the sixties. Her lined countenance was rouged and powdered, her eyebrows plucked into thin apostrophes. And her eyes, dark, dark brown with tiny glints of green in the center of the irises, were the eyes of a magpie. Inquisitive and curious. Eyes that

139

probably wouldn't miss much, whatever happened to be going on.

"So lovely to finally meet you," said Theodosia, trying to reserve judgment on this animated, birdlike woman. "Cinnamon's told me so much about you, too." As the words sprang from her mouth, Theodosia realized that Cinnamon really hadn't told her much of anything. She'd mentioned that Miss Kitty was the doyenne of the shop and that she'd once worked in Paris. But those were fairly broad strokes. No, Theodosia decided, she really hadn't gleaned any definitive, concrete information about Miss Kitty at all, who, from her piercing, calculating stare, looked like she wasn't born yesterday.

Miss Kitty grasped Theodosia's hand with both of her tiny, bony hands. "Delighted to meet another Church Street neighbor," she purred. "Ya'll have made my niece and I feel so doggone welcome."

"You're from Charleston originally?" asked Theodosia.

Miss Kitty released Theodosia's hand and waved hers in an imperious gesture. In doing so, her rings caught the overhead pinpoint spotlights and sent a kaleidoscope of sparkles dancing across the tops of bottles. "I've lived here before, yes," said Miss Kitty.

"Lived lots of different places. Good for a person to move around, broadens their outlook on life."

"I don't know if Cinnamon told you," said Theodosia, deciding to play the whole encounter as straight as possible, "but I'm quite in love with your shop."

Miss Kitty gave a satisfied nod. "It's getting there. Of course, we still have merchandise pouring in."

"I can't imagine where you'll put it," said Theodosia. "Plus, you already carry a galaxy of amazing scents!"

"And I can't wait to add more," said Miss Kitty. She spun slightly, let her fingers fly lightly across the tops of several bottles as she spoke. "Look at this," she said picking up a tall bottle. "Hermès Vanille Galante."

"Very expensive," murmured Cinnamon.

Miss Kitty's apostrophes shot skyward. "Two hundred thirty-five dollars a bottle. And worth every drop." With a touch of pure drama, she swept a hand above a display table, like a hostess on *The Price Is Right*. "And over here, Miller Harris Fleurs de Bois, as well as Narciso Rodriguez Essence, and Badgley Mischka Couture. Which really *is* couture." She gave a self-satisfied smile. "You can't find these scents just anywhere."

141

"This is Shalini by Maurice Roucel," said Cinnamon, holding up a bottle. "Nine hundred dollars for two-point-two ounces."

"We also carry Eau d'Hadrien by Annick Goutal. Fifteen hundred dollars for three-point-four ounces. Sicilian lemons, grapefruit, and cypress."

"Very impressive," said Theodosia, trying to maintain her neutral stance.

"Of course, not everything is sky-high expensive," explained Cinnamon. "We also offer a fabulous line of French sachets and essences, as well as these handmade soaps in beaded organza lace bags. You see? The bags are studded with tiny seed pearls . . ."

"They're breathtaking," said Theodosia. Could she use something like that for her T-Bath products? Maybe. Something to look into. Amp up the razzle-dazzle factor, which was certainly in generous supply inside this shop.

"Show Theodosia our Egyptian perfume bottles," said Miss Kitty, self-consciously pausing to retie the bow on her blouse. Or was that posing, Theodosia wondered?

Cinnamon handed Theodosia a tall, elegant bottle topped with a fancy gold atomizer. "Leaded glass hand-etched by artisans. And the gold top is from Venice. Very difficult to obtain."

"We were lucky to get our hands on a dozen," said Miss Kitty.

"Our goal here," said Cinnamon, "is to be a veritable perfume emporium. Offer a far greater selection than even the finest department store."

"Like a Middle Eastern souk or bazaar," intoned Miss Kitty.

Theodosia's eyes bounced from glamorous display to elegant arrangement. There truly was a dazzling array of perfumes, apothecary bottles, French milled soaps, bath soap on a rope, scented candles, and couture cosmetics.

"We even offer a series of mix-and-match scents," said Miss Kitty. She picked up three small, colorful bottles. "You can wear these fragrances individually or layer two or three at a time."

"Seriously?" said Theodosia. She'd never heard of such a thing.

"Oh absolutely," said Cinnamon. "You could spray one on the nape of your neck, another on your wrists — well, you get the idea."

Theodosia had to admit she was enthralled. "And the scents are . . . ?"

"We carry spring orchid, red ginger, vanilla bean, champagne musk, and lavender," said Miss Kitty. "Did you know there are two hundred varieties of lavender?"

"I do now," said Theodosia.

Cinnamon smiled. "As I mentioned earlier, we'd be delighted to create a personal fragrance just for you."

"Mmm," said Miss Kitty, narrowing her eyes. "I'm thinking bergamot as a top note, jasmine for the heart note, and possibly sandalwood as a base note." She gave a tiny shrug and her tiny hands flew up. "A thousand ways to go, but the ultimate accessory, no?"

"It certainly would be," agreed Theodosia. "I was telling Cinnamon this morning that I always considered my tea shop to be a bouquet of scents, but your shop trumps it totally."

"Oh my, yes." Miss Kitty laughed. "And we do try to swoon regularly."

"We've experienced such an amazing rush of customers," said Cinnamon, "as well as so many mail orders, that we're already thinking about expanding."

"Our initial plan was to slowly grow a loyal customer base," explained Miss Kitty. "But now there's a good chance that old map shop next door will be available shortly, so I'm pushing my niece to begin negotiations with the landlord." She wrinkled her nose and added, "Sad about that poor girl who got killed, but it really is an awful place filled with dusty old maps."

Theodosia gazed at Miss Kitty and decided that she didn't seem one bit sad at all. More like . . . opportunistic.

"Of course, the map shop would require *tons* of cleaning," added Cinnamon.

"I've always found the Antiquarian Map Shop quite charming," said Theodosia.

Miss Kitty shrugged. "Probably is, dear, if you're in the proper frame of mind for such things. No doubt it's my learned nose that keeps me from appreciating the . . . shall we say *variances* . . . of the place."

"It's been amazing," said Theodosia, "learning about all your various perfumes. But I'm afraid we let the tea go cold."

"Not to worry," said Cinnamon. "We have a microwave in back."

Miss Kitty grabbed Theodosia's hand and patted it. "It's been lovely to make your acquaintance, dear. We keep hearing from everyone up and down Church Street how plugged in you are to the community and the historic district. And that you're socially conscious and involved in dozens of interesting events. I understand your little tea shop is even catering a book signing at the Heritage Society."

"This Saturday night," said Theodosia.

"It's going to be a smaller gathering. After the reading and audience questions, we'll have a candlelight reception out on the patio. Champagne, tea . . . an assortment of sweets and savories."

"Then you must let us donate the candles!" chirped Cinnamon.

"Maybe the Phoenicia cedar candles," said Miss Kitty. "They're so uplifting and warm. Or possibly soy candles or some lovely hand-dipped tapers." With a perplexed look, she turned to Theodosia and asked, "What do *you* think, dear?"

"I'm sure anything you select will be greatly appreciated," said Theodosia.

"The soy votive candles then," proclaimed Cinnamon. "Perfect for an outdoor tea. And here, take one of our silver candle lighters along with you."

Miss Kitty shuddered. "Absolutely *must* use a candle lighter. Matches are so déclassé!"

That was a trip and a half, Theodosia decided as she strolled back to her tea shop. Miss Kitty had been positively manic and Cinnamon also seemed swept up in a perfume delirium. Were they just two crazy ladies who were nuts over fragrance? Or was something more sinister at work here? They did, after all, seem more than ready to snatch up the lease on the Antiquarian Map Shop.

And if they did negotiate for that space, where would the maps go, Theodosia wondered? And who exactly would they go to? She supposed that Daria's mother would sell them at auction. Or would Jason Pritchard find his backer and somehow buy out the inventory? Of course, finding a backer, running a shop, and making enough money to cover a lease were all difficult undertakings. Handling one aspect was tricky enough, let alone all three.

As she stopped in front of the Cabbage Patch gift shop to gaze at a Fitz and Floyd rabbit teapot in their window, Theodosia noticed Burt Tidwell slowly strolling down Church Street. With his hands clasped behind his back, stomach protruding from between his tweed jacket, and beetled brows set in a scowl, Tidwell looked utterly lost in thought.

So of course Theodosia immediately accosted him.

"A return to the scene of the crime?" she asked Tidwell, then grimaced at her own words. She hadn't meant to come across so flippant.

Tidwell didn't seem a bit surprised to see

147

her. "I am, in a manner of speaking," he responded. "I've been conducting face-to-face interviews with various Church Street shopkeepers."

"Have you learned anything new?"

"Possibly," responded Tidwell. "Memory is a tricky thing. Some witnesses can recall *more* information after a couple of days have gone by."

"Any information you'd care to share with me?" Theodosia asked him.

Tidwell assumed a puckish expression. "Not unless you've suddenly passed the lieutenant's test with flying colors and been hired by the CPD."

Tidwell's words didn't dissuade Theodosia in the least. "Any word from your forensics lab yet? And I'm referencing the murder weapon, not the bone Earl Grey dug up."

Tidwell pursed his lips. "Yes, I heard about your bone."

"And the murder weapon?"

Tidwell set his face in a tolerant smile. "My, my, aren't we the eager little investigator."

"What do *you* think the killer used to strangle Daria?" Theodosia asked, plowing ahead. "Twine? Wire? A belt?" She drew a breath, blew it out slowly. "Take a wild flier here, Detective Tidwell. Stun me with your brilliant speculation."

"I don't speculate," Tidwell said in an icy tone. "I postulate."

"There's a difference?" Theodosia asked.

"There is to me."

Waggling her fingers at him, Theodosia said, "Okay, then postulate."

Tidwell sucked air in through his front teeth and rocked back on his heels, looking for all the world like a large Toby mug. "Possibly a cotton rope," he told her. "Something similar to a wash line."

"Just rope," said Theodosia, her voice tinged with disappointment. Somehow, her mind had conjured up something far more exotic. A leather strap that could be traced to a certain shop. Or perhaps an unusual type of chain.

"Garden-variety rope," repeated Tidwell. He seemed to take pleasure in deflating her.

"Okay," said Theodosia, changing course. "What do you know about Jack Brux?"

Tidwell lowered his head and glowered at her. "And why would you bring up his name?"

"Just because Brux seemed to have a beef with Daria. He tried to buy a particular map from her that she didn't want to sell. And then he was sort of lurking in the alley last night . . ."

"He lives nearby," said Tidwell.

"Still," said Theodosia, unwilling to let it go. "Brux has a nasty temper."

"Did it ever occur to you," said Tidwell, "that you might have badgered the man unduly?"

"Not really," said Theodosia.

"Why does your answer not surprise me," said Tidwell. He withdrew a black leather notebook from his pocket and made a few scribbles.

"Something I said?" asked Theodosia.

Tidwell's jowls sloshed. "Another matter entirely. There's been a rash of truck hijackings lately. Coffee, processed meats, frozen shrimp, fine wines — a trailer can be worth anywhere between twenty thousand and one million dollars these days. Anyway, a request has come down from on high to see if I might possibly put two and two together."

"You?" asked Theodosia.

"I do head the *Robbery*-Homicide division," he snapped. "And now, since I have a great deal of work . . ." He executed an amazingly quick spin for such a large man and lumbered off down the street.

"Hmm," said Theodosia, as she continued down Church Street, pondering the irascible Jack Brux, noodling Tidwell's remark about rope.

It wasn't until Theodosia had her hand on the front door of the Indigo Tea Shop that she remembered the display of soap on a rope at Jardin Perfumerie.

11

"What's he doing here?" Theodosia asked as she stepped inside the tea shop. She jerked her head toward the small table in the corner where Bill Glass sat nibbling a scone.

"He just showed up," said Drayton, looking like he didn't want any part of Theodosia's problem with Glass. "You didn't want me to be rude to the man, did you?"

"Turnabout is fair play," murmured Theodosia as she headed for Glass's table.

Glass saw her coming and favored her with a smarmy, too-broad smile. "Hello there, Miz Browning. We meet again."

"What are you doing here?" she asked him.

Bill Glass lifted his teacup, waggled it in midair, then set it back down. "Enjoying the lovely food and hospitality of your tea shop. At least I hope there's hospitality aplenty here." Then his voice hardened.

"Aren't you the sly one. Not telling me about the bone."

"There's nothing to tell," responded Theodosia.

Glass waved an index finger back and forth in an accusatory gesture. "That's not what I hear. It appears your happy new home may be the exact spot where captured pirates were summarily executed. Death by hanging, that sort of thing." He gave a quick but mirthless grin, his dark eyes drilling into her.

"Why would that interest you?" asked Theodosia. "You publish a glossy *gossip* rag. You speculate on which hostess feuded with which guest. What Charleston society lady is looking a trifle stretched across the cheekbones. Who wasn't invited back to serve as a board member. The really important news of the day."

"You make my job sound so glamorous," smirked Glass, reaching for his Nikon. "Still, pirates and old bones are exciting stuff. Imparts a certain *creep factor* that helps sell magazines." Aiming his camera directly at Theodosia, he clicked off a quick series of shots. "Right up there with sightings of Elvis and UFOs that have crash landed."

"Stop it!" cried Theodosia, holding up a

hand as if to ward off evil. "Please don't do that!"

"I can see the headline now," laughed Glass. "Haunted Hazelhurst."

"Don't you dare!" seethed Theodosia.

Theodosia was still fuming when Bill Glass picked up and left some five minutes later.

"Don't waste your energy on him," Drayton advised. "The man simply isn't worth it." He turned toward Haley, who'd crept out of the kitchen to catch the fireworks. "How was it you so aptly phrased it?"

"The man occupies so much space in your head, you oughta charge him rent," said Haley, grinning crookedly at Theodosia.

"Pithy verbiage, wouldn't you agree?" asked Drayton.

"Glass isn't inside my head," Theodosia told them, "he's stuck in my craw."

"Oh, that's entirely different," said Drayton, raising one quivering eyebrow.

"Theo," said Haley, "what if I gave you my award?"

That stopped Theodosia in her tracks. "Haley, what are you talking about?"

"You're one of the kindest, gentlest people I know," said Haley. "But you're working yourself into an absolute frizzle-frazzle over a guy who publishes a crappy tabloid. Think

154

about it."

Theodosia did. For about two seconds. "You're right," she told Haley. "The whole thing's ridiculous. Okay." Her hands fluttered about her head, as if to stir up any residual negative energy. "I hereby banish him from my thoughts."

"Banish who?" asked Miss Dimple, emerging from the kitchen, wiping her hands on an embroidered tea towel.

"I can't even remember," said Theodosia. At which point the bell over the front door tinkled and Angie Congdon strolled in.

"Oh my gosh!" exclaimed Theodosia, putting a hand to her mouth. "The Featherbed House. We're supposed to cater your open house tomorrow night!"

Angie suddenly looked nervous. "You didn't forget, did you?" she asked in a quavering voice. Angie Congdon was the proprietor of the Featherbed House B and B, one of the premier B and Bs in Charleston's historic district. Her short, curly blond hair set off a friendly oval face that flashed a perpetually welcoming smile. Guests loved Angie and passed out recommendations like jelly beans. As a result, Angie's website was filled with glowing customer testimonials.

"I didn't forget completely," said Theodosia. "I just relegated your event to the back burner. Apologies, Angie, now you're cooking like mad on my front burner."

"Mine, too," chimed in Haley.

"Glad to hear it," said Angie, "since I'm unable to stuff a cherry tomato or render a decent pinwheel sandwich if my life depended on it. Which puts me utterly at your mercy."

"Of course, we're doing your catering," Theodosia told her.

"Wait a minute," Haley said to Angie. "Back up. You always manage to lay out a lovely wine and cheese board every evening for your guests at the Featherbed House. *That* requires some culinary skill."

"No, it doesn't," said Angie. "That's just popping corks and cubing cheese."

"Tell you what," said Theodosia, "let's sit down and figure out a few nice appetizers for you to serve."

"Actually," said Angie, "I was hoping you'd serve them."

"No problem," said Theodosia. "Haley, are you up for an extra catering gig?"

"For Angie?" Haley grinned. "Sure. Anytime."

"Take the big table," said Drayton, "so you can spread out and noodle your ideas around. Haley, grab that Brown Betty teapot and help me with refills for our afternoon guests. Then I've got to study my feng shui book."

"How many B and Bs are taking part in the open house?" asked Theodosia.

Angie slid a colorful brochure across the table and said, "Eight tomorrow night, fourteen on Friday. Almost every one in the historic district."

"Wow," said Theodosia. "I didn't realize we had so many."

Angie grinned. "Tells you how popular our little sliver of Charleston is, doesn't it?

"The chamber of commerce estimates we get about four and a half million visitors a year," said Theodosia. "So I guess they have to stay somewhere."

"I'm hoping they'll start booking with me," said Angie. "Business has been a little slow lately."

"Lots of businesses feeling the pinch," said Theodosia. "So tell me about open house night. Who, what, when, where, and why?"

"The main thing," said Angie, "is that our Innkeeper's Association wants to really showcase the B and Bs. Get locals as well as visitors to do the walking tour and visit the B and Bs. Then, hopefully, stay with us or make favorable recommendations to friends and relatives. Also, since an awful lot of B and Bs are located in some of our finer old mansions, we want to tell visitors a little bit about the history of the different homes. Impart some fun, historical facts. You know, like who built the place, what's the architectural style, any resident ghosts walking the halls, that sort of thing."

"Your promotion sounds very well thought out," said Theodosia. In her former life as a marketing executive, she knew how important it was to create an event that was newsworthy, able to draw a crowd, and was also promotable.

"That's not all," said Angie. "We'll also be selling our *Historic District Innkeeper's Cookbook.*"

"Oh, you finally self-published," said Theodosia. "Good for you."

"Over a hundred pages," said Angie. "And, believe me, it wasn't easy pulling it all together. Innkeepers can be fairly dysfunctional when it comes to working together and meeting deadlines."

"Lot of that going around," said Theodosia. "Did Drayton give you one of his recipes for the cookbook?"

"Thank goodness, yes," said Angie. "He gave me his recipe for Charleston breakfast casserole. Mostly because I couldn't conjure up a single recipe on my own." She laughed and pushed a fluff of hair off her forehead. "There's a reason Mrs. Klingberg comes in every morning to cook breakfast for my guests. If I had to whip up eggs Benedict or French toast on my own, it would be a kitchen nightmare. Think egg yolks dripping from the chandelier and puddles of pancake syrup."

"Makes for sticky going," agreed Theodosia. "But what you lack in cooking skills you make up for with hospitality and amazing service. Most innkeepers don't go out of their way like you do with coffee and croissants midmorning, wine and cheese in the evening, handmade feather beds, a beautiful backyard patio garden, and arrangements for special walking tours."

"We try." Angie sighed.

"So we'll need finger food for tomorrow night," said Theodosia. "Along with . . . what? Tea? Wine? Cider? Champagne?"

"I think maybe tea and wine," said Angie. "And if you have an interesting tea idea up your sleeve, this might be the time to pull it out."

"I do," said Theodosia. "Or, rather, Drayton does. He discovered the most wonderful pomegranate oolong and everyone who's had a taste has gone gaga for it."

"Then that's our tea," said Angie. "To

serve with . . ."

Theodosia had her pen out and was jotting ideas. "How about pimento and walnut tea sandwiches, roast beef and cheddar tea sandwiches, and miniature apple-raisin scones?"

"Wow," declared Angie. "You make it sound so easy." She grinned. "Guess you've done this before."

"A few times," said Theodosia, as she opened the brochure Angie had given her and scanned it. "So your open house starts at seven?"

"Right," said Angie. She hesitated. "And you can bring teacups? I know I don't have nearly enough."

"Not a problem," said Theodosia, thinking about the boxes and boxes of teacups she had stashed in her upstairs apartment. Probably more one-of-a-kind teacups than a crazed tea tippler could go through in a lifetime. They were going along to the new house, so she'd have to locate some very gentle movers.

"Now I have to ask," said Angie, touching a hand to Theodosia's sleeve. "Have you heard anything more from the police? About Daria?" Angie had phoned Theodosia the morning after the murder to express her dismay. Now she, like most inhabitants of

160

the historic district, were waiting with bated breath for news the killer had been apprehended.

"I ran into Detective Tidwell about an hour ago," Theodosia told her. "Unfortunately, he was wearing his typical Easter Island face."

"So no information," said Angie. "But what exactly was the great detective detecting? Do you think he's seriously on the case?"

"He is as far as I can tell," said Theodosia. "And he did share one tiny shred of information with me."

"What's that?" asked Angie, her eyes going big.

"Tidwell said he thought Daria might have been strangled with rope. Basic ordinary clothesline is how he put it."

"Oh," said Angie, looking disappointed. "That could come from anywhere. Plus, isn't it difficult to trace something like that?" She glanced about the tea room and leaned forward, dropping her voice. "And how goes it with the backyard bones?"

Theodosia sat back in her chair. "You heard about that?"

"The rumor mill's been going crazy," admitted Angie. "Hard to keep something like that under wraps."

"Why don't they just run a big fat announcement in the *Post and Courier*?" murmured Theodosia.

Angie bit her lip. "Don't say that. They just might!"

12

"You're looking awfully tricked out for a beach party," Theodosia told Drayton as he clambered stiffly into the front seat of her Jeep. Tonight he'd varied his appearance only slightly, donning a navy blue sport coat, gray slacks, and pink bow tie. Very snappy. She, on the other hand was dressed in white slacks and a blue-and-white striped French sailor's T-shirt. *Tres* casual.

"It's not exactly a picnic," said Drayton. "There's a reason they call it the *Blessing* of the Fleet."

"Sure," said Theodosia, "but there's also going to be music, food booths, and probably goofy stuff like face painting and funnel cakes. And the event is being held at White Point Gardens, which is technically a park."

"Shoes," said Drayton, pointing to his loafers. "I made a concession to casual dressing with my choice of footwear."

"You're right," Theodosia chuckled, as she pulled away from the curb. "It's like you stepped out of a J.Crew catalog."

"Where's Earl Grey?" asked Drayton, adjusting his seat belt. "I thought for sure you'd bring him along. After all, this is one occasion where canine sidekicks are probably welcome."

"Cleo Hollander from Big Paw picked him up earlier and took him over to the Cranston Elder House on Sullivan's Island," said Theodosia. Earl Grey was a trained therapy dog, certified under the auspices of Big Paw, Charleston's very own service dog organization. As such, Earl Grey made regular visits to children's hospitals, senior citizens' homes, and hospices. Most of the time Theodosia accompanied him, taking tearful delight in the sight of a sick child grinning with glee as she cradled Earl Grey's furry head. Or watching an eighty-seven-year-old woman whoop with joy as she tossed a rubber ball down a hallway and Earl Grey came bounding back with the ball only to deposit it gently in her lap.

"Sounds like Earl Grey's enjoying his own social outing," said Drayton.

"He really loves it," said Theodosia. "And he's *good* at interacting with people." When she'd found Earl Grey in her back alley, he'd been a starving puppy huddled in a cardboard box, trying to get out of the rain. She'd worried that he'd never get over the trauma of abandonment, but gentle words and a loving home had more than brought Earl Grey out of his shell. And when he'd begun training as a therapy dog, he'd reveled in the attention and the feeling of being needed. Theodosia had a theory about that. It was almost as though Earl Grey realized what a lucky guy he was and wanted to help bring joy to others.

"You're right," said Drayton, as they meandered past stands of palmettos and live oak trees, then caught sight of the park with its booths, bands, and crowds. "It looks like a carnival swept into town. No dancing bears or sword swallowers, but still plenty of whoop-de-doo."

"A Blessing of the Fleet is supposed to be joyous," said Theodosia, "not a straightlaced, all-day Calvinist prayer meeting. A blessing can be fun, too, don't you think?"

"Of course," responded Drayton, "I just didn't realize it entailed people sipping alcoholic drinks."

"Just beer and wine," Theodosia told him. "See if you can go along with it, okay?"

"Hmph," said Drayton, but Theodosia

could detect a slight twinkle in his eyes.

White Point Gardens in Battery Park, the rolling green park that occupied the very tip of the peninsula, was rocking tonight. Musicians in the gazebo played jazz tunes interspersed with a little local folk rock. Red-and-yellow striped food booths featured roast oysters, she-crab soup, Frogmore stew, and country sausage sizzling on charcoal grills along with seared red and green peppers.

"Oh my goodness," declared Drayton, as they wandered through the park. "Frogmore stew. Doesn't that bring back memories."

"Then let's get some," suggested Theodosia, happy that Drayton seemed suddenly happy.

They stepped up to a wooden booth decorated with stars and bars bunting and ordered two plastic cups of the steaming stew.

"I haven't eaten this in years," said Drayton, digging his fork into the rich mixture and spearing a plump shrimp. "I hope the recipe's authentic."

Theodosia peered at Drayton as he nibbled, tasted, and pondered, his nose twitching like a dubious rabbit. "Well?" she asked. "Is it?"

"Fantastic!" roared Drayton. "Really delicious."

"Whew," said Theodosia. "You had me worried."

"I had myself worried," said Drayton, eagerly spooning up more stew. "Do you know that Frogmore stew is named after the tiny hamlet of Frogmore over on St. Helena Island?"

"I kind of guessed it might be," said Theodosia, enjoying the rich mélange of shrimp and sausage and corn.

"Used to be a booming terrapin business over there," added Drayton, as if he had a rousing story to tell.

"I'm not sure I want to know details," Theodosia told him as she bit into a shrimp. "Especially while I'm eating."

They strolled past booths selling sweetgrass baskets, pralines, and fried oysters, eating their stew, getting slightly messy from their small pieces of corn on the cob.

"Look who else is here," said Drayton, arcing his paper cup into a trash receptacle, then wiping his hands on a pristine hanky. "Timothy." Drayton waved a freshly wiped hand. "Timothy! Hello!"

As silver-haired patriarch of the Heritage Society, Timothy Neville stood tall in the community, though he was diminutive in stature. Timothy was descended from French Huguenots who'd come over from France in the late 1600s to escape religious persecution. His ancestors had been ship owners, bankers, and indigo planters. All good things in the South. Timothy himself lived in a huge Italianate mansion on Archdale Street, served on many civic committees, played violin with the Charleston Symphony, and was a decent watercolorist. A talented, well-connected Renaissance man of sorts.

Now Timothy Neville, head up, hooded eyes scanning the crowd, strolled casually over to greet them. He was an octogenarian who could pass for much younger and was a good friend of Drayton's. Like Drayton, Timothy was turned out in a double-breasted navy blazer and gray slacks.

"Did you two text message each other about what to wear?" Theodosia joked.

When they both stared blankly at her, she said, "Twitter?" When they continued to stare, she shrugged and dropped the subject. Oops. Different generation.

"Theodosia," said Timothy, crossing his arms and fixing her with a purposeful gaze. "I may be able to help shed some light on your mysterious bones."

"Bone," she said, frustration seeping into

her voice. "Does everyone know about that?"

"Yes . . . probably," answered Timothy. His smooth, tightly stretched brow twitched into a furrow. "Why? Is there a problem?"

"Only for me, I guess," Theodosia replied. She lifted her shoulders, exhaled slowly. "You were saying . . . ?"

"We have several old maps at the Heritage Society," said Timothy, "that accurately detail various parts of the historic district, including the location of your new home."

"An excellent idea," enthused Drayton, who loved nothing better than to pore over old maps. "Perhaps we'll uncover an important clue." Now he looked positively jubilant. "Maybe even determine that Theodosia's cottage is located on an early settler's graveyard."

"Hopefully not," said Theodosia. "I really wouldn't enjoy living atop the bones of our early residents."

"Oh no?" said Timothy, who also seemed enamored of the graveyard idea.

"But Timothy," continued Theodosia, "you bring up an excellent point about studying maps. Maybe the Antiquarian Map Shop would have something, too."

"They're a fine resource," allowed Timothy. "But . . . do we know who's going to

169

take over as proprietor? *Is* someone going to take over?"

"Probably still up in the air," said Theodosia. "Although Jason Pritchard expressed interest in keeping it going."

"But the direct heir would be the mother, correct?" said Timothy.

"I suppose so," said Theodosia. Then murmured, "Sophie," thinking about how heartbroken she must be. And feeling grateful, once again, that Aunt Libby was her close friend.

Timothy looked like he was clicking off rapid-fire calculations in his brain. "Perhaps Mrs. Shand would be interested in donating the existing inventory to the Heritage Society."

"Perhaps that question should wait until after her daughter's funeral tomorrow," said Theodosia.

"Let's wander over to the shore," suggested Theodosia, once Timothy had moved on. "The boats should be coming along anytime now." She turned to Drayton, saw he was staring blankly into the crowd, and said, "Earth to Drayton. Are you stargazing or just staring out to sea?"

Drayton turned to face her, a strange expression on his lined face. "You remember that young lady Jory Davis was dating? The one he brought to the masked Verdi ball last fall?"

"Beth Ann?" said Theodosia, her voice rising slightly. "How could I forget?" Beth Ann had been tipsy, overdressed, and overly possessive of Jory that night. Not that she'd had anything to worry about. Except maybe how much her head was going to hurt the next morning from all the wine she'd drank.

"I swear I just caught a glimpse of her," said Drayton, his face pulled into a full-on frown now.

"Couldn't have," said Theodosia, though she rose on her tiptoes and tried to peer over the undulating sea of people. "They broke up. When Jory stopped by yesterday, he made a point of mentioning it." *And he was also very interested in taking me out to dinner.*

"Granted, I just caught a glimpse," said Drayton, still looking befuddled. "But I had the distinct impression . . . the blond hair . . ." He waved a hand and said, "Ah, I must have been mistaken. So many people . . ."

"Oh, I'm pretty sure that whole Jory–Beth Ann relationship is kaput," said Theodosia. "And that Jory's here in Charleston by himself."

"Apologies then," said Drayton. "I didn't mean to give you a start."

"You didn't," said Theodosia.

"Theodosia! Miss Browning!" A man's voice was calling to her, fairly demanding her attention.

"Jack," said Drayton, turning, blinking, and homing in on the voice. "Good to see you."

But Jack Brux wasn't having any of Drayton's friendly greeting. He flapped his arms like an angry crow and got right in Theodosia's face. "What do you think you're *doing?*" Brux demanded.

"Ex*cuse* me?" said Theodosia, staring into his pinched, practically rabid face. At such close range, Theodosia saw that he'd gone completely florid. *Whoa,* she thought, *this guy's really on a tear. Not so healthy for the old ticker!*

"I'm not stupid!" snarled Brux. "I know what you're trying to do!"

"You do?" said Theodosia. What exactly was she trying to do?

"You're trying to pin that murder on me!" Brux shrieked.

Not one to cower when fired upon by a bully, Theodosia calmly stood her ground. *Doggone that Tidwell, he must have said something to Brux.* "Of course, I'm not," said

Theodosia. "But it's no secret that I've been asking around." *Looks like that cat's out of the bag.*

"More like trying to put a bug in that fat detective's ear!" snarled Brux.

"I'll be happy to share that with him, too, if you'd like," said Theodosia, still standing her ground.

Drayton held up a hand. "You're out of line, Jack." But Brux was too angry to listen to reason.

"Go pin your murder on some other poor donkey!" huffed Brux. "And leave me out of it!" Then he turned abruptly and stomped off into the crowd.

Drayton stared after him. "Did I mention that he has a bad temper?"

"The question is," said Theodosia. "Is Jack Brux crazy enough to kill?"

"Look!" exclaimed Drayton. "The boats." They gazed at the harbor where a parade of almost fifty boats, all lit up and sparkling like Christmas decorations, glimmered on the water.

"Beautiful," breathed Theodosia.

"Marvelous," echoed Drayton.

Enthralled by the shimmering vision, the crowd quieted down just as the orchestra struck up "Southern Star" by the group

173

Alabama.

> Oh, southern star, how I wish you would
>   shine
> And show me the way to get home

As the orchestra played softly and people hummed along, the boats drifted past like floats in a torchlight parade. Theodosia had read somewhere that courtiers at Versailles had constructed elaborate boats to amuse King Louis XVI and Marie Antoinette. She imagined they must have looked something like tonight's spectacle. Twinkling brightly, bathed in white, the waves reflecting the light in a million dazzling points.

A minister stepped up onto a makeshift reviewing stand and read a short prayer, then a high school marching band played a slow-moving version of "Dixie." It was all very lovely, very Old South, and probably a little bewildering to anyone who wasn't from here.

"That was really quite splendid," said Drayton, as they strolled back across the grass toward Theodosia's car.

"I loved the . . ." began Theodosia, then stopped abruptly. "Jory?" Her ex-boyfriend had suddenly stepped in front of her. This was an unexpected encounter. Or was it?

"Good evening," said Drayton, dropping into the cool, reserved mode he always used when dealing with Jory.

But Jory couldn't have cared less. He fixed Theodosia with an eager smile and said, "I was hoping I might run into you."

"We were just leaving," said Drayton, pretending to stifle a yawn, trying his best to nudge Theodosia onward.

But Theodosia planted solidly in her tracks. "Give me a moment, will you?" she asked Drayton.

Drayton hesitated for a few seconds, then his Charleston manners got the better of him. He managed an abrupt nod and said, "As you wish."

"What's up?" asked Theodosia, when the two of them were alone. Or as alone as they were going to be with a throng of revelers streaming past them.

"You look so cute," Jory told her, reaching out to touch a fluff of her auburn hair. "Like a French sailor."

"Jory . . ." said Theodosia. She really didn't want him to start something here. Or anywhere.

Jory seemed to pick up on her mood and nodded at the distant flotilla of sailboats that continued to bob and glow. "I was supposed to be out there with them tonight." He sounded almost wistful.

"So why weren't you?" Theodosia asked.

"I had my boat all ready to go," Jory told her. "Sails rigged, lights strung. Chuck Strom, the manager over at the Charleston Yacht Club, helped me get it all set up. Then I got a call from my assistant, like an hour ago. He tells me there's an emergency. Which means I have to fly back to New York."

"Too bad," said Theodosia. She knew how much Jory would have enjoyed sailing his J/22 in the regatta.

"I'm actually on my way to the airport now," said Jory. "I just stopped by for a couple of minutes to sort of drink in the spectacle."

And maybe see me, Theodosia thought to herself.

"The boats looked lovely," said Theodosia, not wanting to toss him too many leading questions.

"Didn't they?" said Jory, but he was gazing at Theodosia.

"You don't want to miss your plane," said Theodosia, taking a step backward. Then she gave him a slightly guarded look and added, "You're flying back alone? By yourself?"

"Sure," said Jory, edging toward her. "Who else would I be going with?"

"Just wondering," said Theodosia. She looked around for Drayton, finally spotted him. "Have a good flight," she bid Jory as she managed a hasty retreat.

13

"Did you have a good time?" Theodosia asked Earl Grey. He sat next to her in the front seat, his big head bobbing every time she hit a pothole, which seemed to be in abundance out here on Sullivan's Island.

She'd dropped Drayton off at his home some thirty minutes ago and then driven out here to pick up Earl Grey. Cleo Hollander had assured her that Earl Grey had been on his best behavior and that the residents of Cranston Elder House had enjoyed her dog's visit immensely.

"You're so grown up to come by yourself," Theodosia told him.

As if in response, Earl Grey turned serious brown eyes on her and said, "Grrrr?"

"Very grown up," she emphasized. "Now maybe you should lie down, since you're riding up front, which is kind of a no-no, and you're not wearing a seat belt, which would pretty much be impossible. Okay?"

Earl Grey made one quick circle on the front seat, whacked Theodosia in the head with his plumed tail, then curled up, nose to hind toes, looking tired but self-satisfied.

"Good boy," she praised him. Theodosia's right hand slipped off the steering wheel and cupped the soft dome of Earl Grey's head, then slid down to tickle a floppy ear. "You just rest your eyes and we'll be home in twenty minutes."

Cranking down the passenger-side window, Theodosia gazed out as they whooshed along Atlantic Avenue. The gentle *cusssh* of the waves sliding in, the salty breeze on her lips, stars twinkling overhead, made the place seem like a magical, enchanted island, far away from the hustle and bustle of the city.

Theodosia loved it out here on Sullivan's Island. It was quiet and residential, mostly a mix of old and new beach houses, with a few small shops and restaurants thrown in to give a cozy, small town atmosphere. Long, long stretches of beaches lent a romantic escapist feel, plus there were acres of undeveloped woods and marshland, as well as meandering little estuaries with names like Conch Creek, Crab Pond, and Narrows Creek.

Lots of history out here, too. In the early

years of the Revolutionary War, a makeshift fort had been constructed. Builders had used unseasoned palmetto logs, cut from the surrounding countryside, and fashioned into a kind of log cabin fortress. On June 29, 1776, that small fort had proved its mettle when Colonial forces withstood almost constant bombardment from Lord Cornwall's British forces.

Turns out, the palmetto logs used in the building process were so spongy and damp that they miraculously absorbed the impact of the British cannonballs!

To commemorate this Battle of Fort Moultrie, as it came to be known, a white palmetto tree was added to South Carolina's blue-and-white crescent moon state flag.

Flashing past Raven Drive, Theodosia was also reminded that poet and horror writer Edgar Allan Poe had been stationed here in the mid-1800s. As she slowed, made a turn onto Dibbo Lane, she veered close to Gold Bug Drive and Poe Avenue. Probably, she decided, Mr. Poe would have been pleased. This, after all, was where he'd tromped the rain-swept beaches and put quill pen to paper and composed "The Gold-Bug."

Now Theodosia sped past Woody's Clam Shack, a venerable old building with peeling yellow paint and a flickering pink sign in desperate need of a shot of neon. It looked like a dump, but inside, Woody's was cozy and tidy. The menu, painted on the wall and unchanged in years, included specialties such as fresh-caught blue crab, succulent Carolina oysters, and hot, salty sweet potato fries.

Gotta come back here and eat, Theodosia told herself as she glanced into the rearview mirror. A large, dark car seemed to be hanging right on her tail. She braked, as a kind of warning signal, then sped up and hung a left onto Ben Sawyer Drive.

Glancing in her side mirror, Theodosia saw that the same car had followed her into the turn and was, once again, creeping up behind her. A little too close for comfort. She frowned and sped up slightly. The car behind her sped up, too.

"Oh, that's helpful," she muttered. "Climb right on top of me and shine your brights. Thanks a lot."

Earl Grey, who'd been curled up beside Theodosia, snoozing, glanced up with a worried expression.

"Don't worry," Theodosia told him, "we'll lose this jerk as soon as we cross the bridge."

Up ahead was the Ben Sawyer Bridge. It was an old swing bridge, narrow and picturesque, that took a full fifteen minutes to

181

creak open when a sailboat hailed the bridge master and requested passage through the channel. The Ben Sawyer Bridge was slated to be updated soon, but was still sitting in limbo on the highway department's to-do list. Probably, lack of state funds had stalled the repairs, just like lots of other road and bridge projects across the country.

Theodosia felt the first flutter of fear just as she approached the bridge. It was fairly late now, with no streetlights to illuminate the road and not another soul in sight. She goosed her engine, determined to outrun the clown behind her. But just as her foot tapped the gas, the car tailing her slid even closer.

Glancing in her side mirror, Theodosia muttered an angry, "What on earth . . . ?" And was suddenly slammed from behind. Shocked beyond belief, she had only moments to comprehend what was happening as the nasty, crunching impact sent her Jeep careening across the center line and sliding wildly into the incoming lane.

Fighting hard to regain control, Theodosia jerked her steering wheel to the right and tried frantically to brake, even as Earl Grey was suddenly up on all fours and barking his head off.

"No, boy, get down!" she yelled, as a

second impact, harder still, caught her left rear fender. Now, the nasty combination of her overcorrection and the second hit sent her careening straight toward the old metal railing!

Bracing for impact, Theodosia hung on to the wheel, praying Earl Grey could brace and fend for himself. She tried to steer away at the very last second, to just graze the metal grillwork, maybe sideswipe it and lessen the impact. But she was traveling too fast and her speed was too great. Her Jeep hit hard with a metallic screech, shuddered mightily for a few seconds, then spun like a child's top into a sickening, heart-stopping one-hundred-and-eighty-degree turn.

Another grating thunk and the car behind zoomed past her, flying at an amazing speed now, this time clipping her front fender! As Theodosia continued to fight for control, Earl Grey was hurled against the dashboard like a rag doll. And all she could do was let loose a scream. A bloodcurdling "Noooooo!"

Silence. Then the sound of running feet slapping pavement and a man's gruff voice asking, "Are you okay in there? Hello?"

Theodosia sat up suddenly, certain she'd heard a far-off voice reverberating in her head. Then she caught sight of Earl Grey, cowering on the floor, squashed beneath the dashboard where he'd been thrown. Oh no! Her beloved dog was shaking like a leaf, looking both dazed and terrified.

"Ma'am?" came the gruff voice again. Creaking her head to the left, Theodosia peered out the side window. A man with a bushy gray beard, wearing a blue chambray shirt, stood beside her Jeep. Concern seemed to etch his face. "You want me to call somebody?" he asked. "Cops? Ambulance?"

Warily, Theodosia cranked down her window. "Did you see what happened?" she gasped. "Did you get the license plate number of the car that hit me?"

The man gave a vigorous shake of his head. "I only saw your car." He peered at her, a little doubtful she was tracking properly. "Looks like you hit the side of that bridge pretty hard. Let me call someone," he offered again, pulling his cell phone from his shirt pocket.

Earl Grey whimpered, then scrambled halfway onto the front seat. He seemed to be having trouble pulling himself up.

"No," Theodosia told the man. "I have to . . . um . . . get my dog to a vet."

Concern bloomed again on the man's

face. "You got a dog in there with you?"

Theodosia nodded.

"There's an emergency animal hospital up ahead in Mt. Pleasant," he told her. "Open most of the night, I think. If your car can make it."

Turning the key and restarting her engine, Theodosia didn't detect any discernible clank or knock in the engine. She inhaled shakily and asked, "Where?"

"Take the Coleman Boulevard exit."

"Thanks," she said.

Together, Theodosia and Earl Grey limped into the Loveland Emergency Veterinary Clinic. A vet tech in green scrubs met them at the door. "You two okay?" The vet tech was an African American woman with the name KEISHA embroidered on her top.

"Car crash," Theodosia rasped in a dry, hollow voice. "Gotta have my dog x-rayed. He . . ." The tears were starting to come now. "He hit the dashboard pretty hard, and he's limping badly."

"We can surely check him out," said Keisha. She had an aura of crisp efficiency mingled with compassion that helped calm both Theodosia and Earl Grey. "Let me fill out a quick chart on your boy. What's his name?"

"Earl Grey," said Theodosia, rubbing her shoulder.

"Maybe we should x-ray your shoulder, too," suggested Keisha.

"No, just take care of him," said Theodosia. "I'm okay. Really."

Turns out, Earl Grey was okay, too. The clinic did blood work, checked Earl Grey's heart and lungs, and shot hip and shoulder X-rays. A young veterinarian, Dr. Mark Felden, prodded Earl Grey gently, checking his legs, neck, and shoulders for range of motion, shone a flashlight into his still-worried eyes, and did all the tests a doctor can do with a patient who can't tell him where it hurts.

They left with a bottle of Deramaxx and paperwork on all the tests Dr. Felden had conducted. As well as good wishes from Keisha.

By the time Theodosia and Earl Grey arrived home, they were both exhausted. Earl Grey limped slowly upstairs and padded directly to his dog bed in Theodosia's bedroom.

Theodosia did something she rarely did. She sat down at her dining room table and poured a drab of brandy into a cut-crystal glass. And as she sipped the twenty-year-old

Napoleon brandy, a gift from Drayton some five years earlier, it tickled fiery and rough in the back of her throat. And served to stoke her inner furnace until she was good and mad.

Obviously, someone had intended to do her serious harm. And in their obnoxiously conceived hit-and-run, had brought harm to her dog! In the South, where canines were hunting buddies, beloved companions, and sometimes even accorded honors in family plots, attacking someone's dog was considered a heinous offense! A reason to fight back!

So, of course, the question that flickered and danced like a searing blue flame in Theodosia's mind was *who?*

Taking another small sip of brandy, Theodosia leaned back in her high-backed chair and gazed about her apartment. It was hard to believe she was going to pack up and leave here in a matter of weeks. She'd lived here, above the tea shop, ever since she'd first opened the place. And her apartment, decorated over the years with furniture, antiques, and paintings she'd managed to acquire from King Street and French Quarter antique shops, had evolved into a comfortable patois that bespoke both coziness and elegance. Moody seascape paintings hung over the fireplace. Her chintz sofa and chair were cushy and just right for cocooning. And a recently acquired highboy of fine Carolina pine held her collection of antique teacups, two Chinese blue-and-white bowls that dated back to the Ming dynasty, and a prized Staffordshire dog.

So . . . sitting here in the comfort and safety of the little home she'd built for herself, Theodosia let her mind plumb the depths of the unfathomable. Who on earth wanted her out of the picture? And why?

The reasonable answer was because she'd been asking questions about Daria's murder. Okay, maybe she had been on the prowl. But that still led directly back to the question — who wanted her out of the way? Or dead?

Was it Jack Brux? Was there a special map at the Antiquarian Map Shop that he was fiercely desperate to get his hands on? Was it Cinnamon or Miss Kitty, who were strange at best and perhaps even obsessive about expanding their shop? Or could it be Jason Pritchard, Daria's assistant. Was he not the trusted right-hand man she'd thought he was?

Or could there be someone else entirely? Someone she didn't even know about? Or hadn't suspected?

On the other hand, and this would be coming out of left field, the attack on her tonight might somehow be related to the mysterious bone Earl Grey had dug up in her backyard!

Theodosia's brain continued to ponder the possibilities, but like a Möbius strip that always led tantalizingly back to the beginning, she couldn't quite fathom a single concrete answer.

Theodosia pulled herself up from her chair and carried the brandy bottle to a small wooden sideboard she used as a bar and display area. Brain still in a whirl, she set the bottle down next to her collection of old hotel silver. A large silver pitcher engraved with HOTEL SHERMAN — CHICAGO. A sterling silver ice bucket engraved with MANSION HOUSE HOTEL, GREENVILLE, SC.

Hesitating, Theodosia reached out and let her fingertips run across the word RESERVED, spelled out in raised letters on a sterling silver table sign.

But no answers here.

The Aubusson carpet whispered beneath her feet as she shuffled around her apartment, turning out lights, checking window and door locks. Then she tiptoed quietly into her bedroom. Earl Grey was curled up tight, sleeping softly, making snuffly doggy snores.

Theodosia breathed her thank-you to the Lord that her pup was all right. And that she was, too. Inside her walk-in closet, she turned on an overhead light and rustled around for a few moments, searching for one particular outfit. When she finally found what she was looking for, Theodosia pulled her black suit from its plastic dry cleaner's bag and hung it on the door. After all, first thing tomorrow morning she had a funeral to attend.

Which, when all was said and done, was depressing at best.

14

The steeple of St. Philip's Church thrust boldly into the bright blue sky as pink and blue clouds scudded across the far horizon. St. Philip's was one of several dozen historic churches that dotted the cityscape and earned Charleston the moniker of "Holy City." St. Philip's was also a noted landmark, usually remembered as the strangely sited church that stuck halfway out into Church Street.

Theodosia glanced up at the tall, elegant steeple as she drove down Church Street, headed for Daria's funeral. In the late 1800s, a light beacon had been installed in the steeple to help guide ships into the safety of Charleston Harbor. Now, Theodosia was praying she herself might find safe harbor in the church. Or at least peace of mind, so she could hopefully figure out some much-needed answers.

Last night's hit-and-run or smash-and-dash, or whatever it had been, still weighed heavily on her mind as she entered the cool darkness of the church. An organist up in the balcony was playing Simon and Garfunkel's "Bridge Over Troubled Water" on the magnificent Casavant Frères organ, and the music flowed out smooth and pure. Walking slowly down the center aisle, under high, neoclassical arches, Theodosia was surprised at the large number of people that had turned out for this funeral. The huge showing indicated a heartfelt tribute to Daria, she decided, who'd practically been a fixture on Church Street and a friend to so many.

Midway down the aisle, Theodosia halted and slid into a wooden pew, still mentally running the words of the song through her head.

Like a bridge over trouble water
I will lay me down

Up ahead, sitting together in the first row, two white-haired ladies clutched each other in sorrow. Daria's mother, Sophie, and Theodosia's own aunt Libby.

Craning her head to the left, Theodosia saw the sister, Fallon, as well, looking tearful as she hung on the arm of Joe Don

Hunter, Daria's boyfriend. Joe Don's shoulders were slumped and his head bowed forward. He seemed beyond sorrowful, verging on catatonic.

And then the music gently shifted from the more contemporary Simon and Garfunkel into a slow-paced funereal version of Chopin's Prelude in C minor. A few seconds later, Daria's silver casket rolled slowly up the aisle, guided by the hands of a dark-suited funeral director. Her final visit to a church she had known and loved since childhood.

Theodosia watched it all with crystal clarity. The silver casket sliding by on gently clacking wheels. A heart-shaped spray of white lilies, roses, and baby's breath teetering on top of the casket. Mourners turning a sad gaze on the casket, then dipping their heads and wiping away tears. Tragic. All of it tragic.

Reverend Meader met Daria's casket as it slowly rolled to a stop. He put a hand on it, gazed out at the congregation, and began the service.

His words were comforting, eloquent, and uplifting. Still, even though it was deemed a celebration of life, Theodosia couldn't help thinking about Daria's death. If only she'd been a minute sooner. If only she'd screamed louder. If only . . .

Lost in her own thoughts, Theodosia was suddenly aware that the church organ had played a few opening chords and everyone was reaching for a hymnal. She grabbed a well-worn, leather-covered book that sat beside her and paged hastily through it, looking for the song "Just a Closer Walk with Thee."

There it was. She joined the voices already lifted in song and tried to focus on the words.

Just a closer walk with thee,
Grant it, Jesus, is my plea

The words were lovely and soothing. But still Theodosia felt restless. Like she was close to figuring something out, but that something was still unformed and slightly ethereal.

Well, of course it is, she told herself. *Because Daria's killer is a very clever person. And maybe someone who's closer to us than we suspect.* She gazed around the church, eyeing the various mourners, speculating. Still, nothing seemed to gel.

In closing the funeral service, Reverend Meader quoted from a poem by an unknown author.

Life is but a stopping place,
A pause in what's to be,
A resting place along the road,
To sweet eternity.
We all have different journeys,
Different paths along the way, .
We all were meant to learn some things,
But never meant to stay.

Then, all too soon it seemed, the casket was being wheeled back down the aisle, closely trailed by the grief-stricken family. Theodosia watched as Aunt Libby, her back straight, eyes dry, her tiny seventy-eight-year-old form seemingly filled with strength, beckoned for her to join them.

Me? She touched her thumb to her chest, unsure.

Aunt Libby gave a quick nod.

Theodosia joined the group and followed along down the aisle. In the vestibule, Aunt Libby gripped her hand tightly and said, "We need to talk."

"Of course," Theodosia whispered back, knowing in her heart what that talk would be about.

And she wasn't far off. Once Daria's casket had been loaded into the long black hearse, Sophie Shand, Daria's mother, turned to her and asked, "Can you help us?

Will you help us?"

"Honestly," said Theodosia, accepting Sophie's hand, "I'm doing everything I can."

"Because you were there," moaned Sophie. "You saw . . ." Her voice cracked and she put a hanky to her mouth, unable to continue.

"Take it slow, dear," said Aunt Libby.

"Unfortunately, I didn't see that much," said Theodosia, feeling like a failure. "I've been trying to remember more, and talking to . . ." Now she was the one who couldn't go on. The images in her head were of dark figures, swirling together, dancing a dance of death. But she couldn't pull the face of the attacker into focus.

Aunt Libby, bless her heart, stepped into the breach. "But our dear Theodosia is a smart lady," she told Sophie. "She's unraveled murder investigations before and I have all the faith in the world that she can help figure this one out."

Gulp, was Theodosia's sole thought.

Aunt Libby's eyes burned bright as she gazed at Theodosia. "You're already asking lots of questions, aren't you? You've already settled on a couple of suspects?"

"I have," Theodosia admitted. She didn't have to heart to tell Sophie Shand that's all she had.

"Bless you," said Sophie, staring at Theodosia with red-rimmed eyes. "You're an angel. Heaven sent."

"She'll be our avenging angel," murmured Aunt Libby.

"I don't know about that," said Theodosia. "But I'll try to stay in the loop with Detective Tidwell and keep pressuring him. And I will continue to ask questions." She hadn't realized how strong her conviction was until she spoke those words. *Yes, I will,* she thought. *I can do this. I can figure this out.*

Out of the corner of her mouth, Aunt Libby said, "Your detective friend is standing right over there."

Theodosia canted her head and saw that Detective Burt Tidwell was indeed among the crowd of mourners who had congregated on the sidewalk. In fact, he seemed to be offering condolences to Fallon and Joe Don Hunter. Well, kudos to him.

"Excellent," murmured Theodosia, "I need to talk to him anyway. This just makes things easier." After administering hugs to both Sophie and Aunt Libby, Theodosia dodged her way through the crowd and managed to nab Tidwell as he started to sidle away.

"Detective Tidwell!" Theodosia waved a hand at him, trying to catch him.

Tidwell heard Theodosia's voice and stopped. Didn't wave back, though. He held a rolled up newspaper in one hand and had his other hand jammed in his pocket, jingling random change.

"Who was the woman who sat three rows behind you and couldn't keep her eyes off you?" asked Tidwell, once Theodosia skidded to a stop in front of him.

"What!" Theodosia cried. "What are you talking about?" Whirling around, suddenly unnerved and gripped with fear, she quickly studied the people nearby, thinking maybe the person who'd run her off the road last night was among them. But she saw only a sober group of mourners, talking among themselves. And no one she recognized.

"What did the woman look like?" Theodosia asked Tidwell.

"Average," said Tidwell.

"What was she wearing?" asked Theodosia.

"Black jacket and skirt, like you," said Tidwell.

"You're a detective," shrilled Theodosia. "You're supposed to be hypersensitive to these things. You're supposed to *remember* details about suspects."

Tidwell seemed almost amused. "This woman is a suspect?"

"I wonder . . ." said Theodosia, fretting now. Could it have been Delaine sitting behind her? Or Cinnamon St. John? Would she even come to this funeral? Or was it someone else entirely? The someone who'd tried to do her harm last night?

"I have something to tell you," Theodosia said to Tidwell. When the detective squiggled his furry brows together, Theodosia plunged ahead. Choosing her words carefully, she told Tidwell about picking up Earl Grey last night on Sullivan's Island, being followed by the dark car, then being run off the road. Or rather, almost run off the bridge.

As she told her story, they walked slowly over to her Jeep. "You see," she said, "it's bashed in the back and on the side."

Tidwell took his time to study both gashes. "You were lucky," he said, finally. "It seems as though someone meant business."

"I'll say they did!" said Theodosia. "Earl Grey was even thrown to the floor."

"Were you able to get a look at the driver?" Tidwell asked. "Could you make a positive ID?"

Theodosia shook her head. "No. Not really."

Tidwell's slightly bulging eyes stared fixedly at her for a few moments. "But you harbor a suspicion." It wasn't a question.

Theodosia wrinkled her nose and grimaced. "I do, but I'm not sure I should say."

Tidwell pursed his lips and rocked back on his heels, another sprightly gesture for such an ungainly man. "Spare me your well-bred southern manners, Miss Browning, and just tell me flat out. This may dovetail with our ongoing investigation into Daria Shand's death."

"You think?" she asked.

"And spare me any sarcasm," growled Tidwell.

"Okay," said Theodosia, taking a deep breath. "There are quite a few people on my list that I'm not sure about."

Tidwell slapped the rolled up newspaper against his leg again and waggled his fingers. "Names please."

"Jason Pritchard strikes me as a person with motive," said Theodosia. "Cinnamon and Miss Kitty, who own the Jardin Perfumerie, talk a good game about being sad over Daria's death, but they're frantic to move into her space."

"You think Daria Shand was killed because of a real estate issue?" asked Tidwell.

Theodosia ignored him. Now who was being sarcastic? "And I'm not exactly in love with Jack Brux, our local map fanatic."

"And why," asked Tidwell, "would any of these persons have you in their sights?"

Theodosia stared at him. "Because they're all suspects in Daria's murder? And I've been asking questions about them?"

"Ah," said Tidwell, "we finally journey to the crux of the matter. You *do* ask a lot of questions. And capriciously jump to varying conclusions."

A wrinkle insinuated itself in the middle of Theodosia's forehead. "Wait a minute, are you telling me you have someone else in mind?"

"You might say my focus varies a degree or two from yours," replied Tidwell.

Theodosia was intrigued. "But . . . who?"

Tidwell raised his head and swiveled it like a periscope, his laser gaze scanning the crowd then landing squarely on Joe Don Hunter.

Theodosia followed his gaze. "The boyfriend?" she said, her voice rising in a squawk. "Are you serious?"

"I rarely make jokes when it relates to a homicide," responded Tidwell.

"But . . . why?" asked Theodosia. "Why him?" To her, Joe Don Hunter just seemed like a beaten, broken man.

Tidwell's beady eyes carried a gleam. The wild gleam he got when he was seriously on the hunt. "Why, you ask? Because the man is a treasure hunter."

The words seemed like such a non sequitur, they zipped past Theodosia's brain without registering. "Pardon?"

Tidwell assumed the look of a third-grade teacher who's been forced to repeat a simple recitation. "Did you ever hear of the Kipling Club?"

"Not that I can recall," said Theodosia.

Tidwell's gaze lasered over to Hunter again. Hunter was standing in a crowd of mourners, shaking hands and thanking people for coming. "The Kipling Club is a loosely organized group of about a dozen amateur treasure hunters who also engage in, shall we say, cowboy archaeology."

"What are you talking about?" Theodosia asked. "I mean, the cowboy part."

"Unauthorized," said Tidwell. "Clandestine. In other words, my dear Miss Browning, these gentlemen, and I use the term loosely, go out and about searching for relics from the past without any authorization whatsoever."

"Weird," said Theodosia, letting her brain wrap around the notion. "And his name's even Hunter," she murmured.

"Occuponomous, wouldn't you agree?" asked Tidwell.

Theodosia let Tidwell's words cycle through her brain for a few moments. "Kipling Club for Rudyard Kipling?" she asked.

"Bingo," said Tidwell. "Give that lady a fluffy, pink panda."

"And you think . . . what?" said Theodosia. "That Joe Don got cozy with Daria because of her dandy map collection? If you ask me, your reasoning strikes me as being awfully thin."

"Then how about this," proposed Tidwell. "Perhaps our Mr. Hunter was on to something. Perhaps he'd found a trove of Civil War relics or something relating to Native Americans or even pirate treasure?"

Theodosia digested Tidwell's statement. He hadn't veered completely off course. The area surrounding Charleston was a hotbed for treasure and treasure hunters. There were antiquities, military relics from Civil War time, and doubloons from pirates who'd plied Carolina waters. Interesting items were forever being discovered. Case in point, the bone in her own backyard.

"And you think Joe Don discovered something?" said Theodosia. "Or Daria didn't approve of his methodology?"

"Possible," said Tidwell. One corner of his mouth twitched. "I've asked Jack Brux to do some forensic work for me."

203

"What!" Theodosia exclaimed, in an injured tone of voice. Jack Brux? Working *with* the police?

Tidwell remained calm in the face of her turmoil. "We want to reconstruct some of the old documents that were found shredded on the floor of the Antiquarian Map Shop." He pursed his lips. "It was as if someone wanted to obliterate old maps and documents."

"Who would want to do that?" Theodosia wondered out loud. Then answered her own question. "The murderer."

"Granted, it's a long shot," said Tidwell, "but I have to examine all the angles. Even those that are somewhat oblique." He stared at her, looking a little tired, a little frazzled.

"I suppose," allowed Theodosia, still nervous about Brux.

"And I have other things on my plate, too," he told her.

"The hijackings?" she asked. "How's that going? Any leads?"

"Working on it," he told her. "Keeping an eye on our Interstate Ninety-five and Highway Seventeen corridors."

"You think it's local people?"

"Organized crime most likely," said Tidwell. "When we tightened our borders after 9/11, a lot of former narcotics smugglers turned to cargo crime. Breaking into distribution centers, grabbing trucks right off the highways. And these guys are smart. Once a truck's GPS is dismantled it's almost impossible to find."

"Wow," said Theodosia. "Sounds like big business, huh?"

"On both ends," said Tidwell. "Hijackers as well as the receivers of stolen goods."

"Well, good luck with that, too," she told him.

Tidwell gave an absent nod, then unfurled his newspaper and held it up for Theodosia to see. "Have you seen this?"

Squinting at a grainy black-and-white photo that bore an uncanny resemblance to her soon-to-be backyard, Theodosia hastily read the accompanying headline: Human Bone Discovered in Historic District Backyard. State Archaeology Office to Conduct Excavation.

"Oh dear," she murmured. This was the *last* thing she needed!

Theodosia was just about to pull away from the curb when she saw Jason Pritchard. She hit the brakes, threw her Jeep into park, and rolled down the window. "Jason," she called. "Over here."

Jason sauntered slowly toward her. "Tough

one," he said, when he got closer.

"Yeah," she said. "Tougher than most. How are you holding up?"

He shaded his eyes from the sun and peered into the dark of her car. "Hanging in there."

"You still thinking about buying the map shop?" Theodosia asked him.

"Maybe," said Jason. Where once he'd seemed anxious to keep it going, now he seemed slightly evasive.

"Did you find a partner?" Theodosia asked. "A backer?" She knew how tough it was to start a business, if not purchase one outright. You had to assume a lease, buy the inventory, and get the word out to existing customers. At which point you fought to transition them into becoming *your* customers. There were a million more things to do and a how-to manual didn't exist. You just had to gut it out on your own.

"I might have somebody," Pritchard allowed. "A guy in Savannah who'd be a sort of silent partner."

"The guy that was Daria's hotshot customer?" She remembered Pritchard's words exactly.

"Uh, yeah," said Pritchard. "But nothing's in writing yet. It's still in the planning stages."

"Good for you," said Theodosia. "What did you say his name was again?" Pritchard hadn't mentioned a name, but she was more than a little curious.

"Snelling," said Pritchard, looking unhappy. "Jud Snelling."

"I suppose you've been putting in some long hours at the map store," said Theodosia. "You were probably there last night, right?"

"Yes, I was," said Pritchard. "Why do you ask?"

"Was Fallon there with you? Going through inventory and stuff?"

Pritchard lifted his chin and narrowed his eyes. "Nope. Just me."

"Purchasing the shop means negotiating with Daria's mother," continued Theodosia. "Not easy to do. She'll be emotionally connected."

"I'm not too worried," said Pritchard. Then added, "I'm sure she'll set a fair price."

"Good luck to you then," said Theodosia. "Keep me posted."

Pritchard strolled away and Theodosia watched him. He seemed different now. Not the same guy who'd come into her tea shop, asking for her help. Now he seemed almost . . . opportunistic. Like he'd already dismissed Daria's death. Or maybe wasn't all that sorry.

Also, and this struck her as strange, Pritchard hadn't mentioned a thing about the dents in her car. So he'd either been nervous or self-absorbed.

Theodosia drummed her fingers on the steering wheel, thinking. Then she frowned into the rearview mirror, checked the street, ready to pull out into traffic. The mirror also reflected a sliver of old cemetery that wrapped around St. Philip's Church. A solemn, dark place that was filled with ancient, canted gravestones belonging to early settlers, original signers of the Declaration of Independence and U.S. Constitution, and a former vice president.

The cemetery was also reputed to be haunted. Ghost walk guides in fluttering, dark capes led eager tourists through the cemetery at night, armed with flickering torches and spooky stories. Glowing orbs had been reported as well as photographed. Ghosts of Civil War soldiers had materialized. Voices had cried and whispered.

Thinking about the cemetery made Theodosia assess her own backyard. Had it been a cemetery as well? Was her little cottage going to suddenly assume the reputation of being haunted? Was she going to have to deal with ghost walks and curious tourists and pranksters on Halloween?

And there was something else bugging her, too. Could Joe Don Hunter and his rogue Kipling Club have had their hand in Daria's murder?

15

"Hey!" Haley called from the kitchen as Theodosia slipped in the back door of the tea shop. "You made the paper."

Theodosia dumped her handbag on her desk and traded her tweedy black jacket for a long black apron. "I've already seen it."

"Not this one you haven't," said Drayton, taking up where Haley had left off. He held up a copy of the *Shooting Star*, pinching the corner between thumb and forefinger like it might be infected with bubonic plague. Front and center was a photo of a startled-looking Theodosia superimposed on what was supposed to be her backyard, but looked more like a full-scale archaeological excavation at Karnak.

Theodosia stared at the photo with a mixture of anger and disbelief. "Doggone Bill Glass," she muttered.

"Can you believe it?" asked Drayton. "The man has unmitigated gall. Half the story's a

210

complete fabrication." He scanned the article, pushed his glasses up his nose. "Actually, most of it is."

"Of course it is," said Theodosia. She knew that all Glass's stories were either made up, cobbled together with inaccuracies, or complete and total fluff pieces. Take your pick.

Haley popped her head out of the kitchen again. "Pretty crazy stuff, huh?" She, on the other hand, seemed amused by the whole thing.

"Excuse me," said Theodosia, who didn't come close to finding the situation hilarious, "but is anyone watching the tea shop?"

"Miss Dimple came in again," Drayton told her. "I asked her to work because we're booked to the rafters and she loves working here. Also, our customers seem to adore her mothering ways."

"It's a win-win situation," agreed Haley. She peered at Theodosia, suddenly sensing her prevailing mood. "Uh-oh, you look tired. How'd the funeral go?"

"Sad," said Theodosia. "And a little strange."

"It's a strange world," said Haley, hustling back into the kitchen, pulling open the oven door, and yelping, "Holy cats, these butterscotch scones have gotta come out now before this whole place goes up in a blue blaze!"

Theodosia followed Drayton into the tea room, where it did appear that the very capable Miss Dimple had everything under control. And thank goodness for that!

Drayton slid behind the front counter and grabbed a pot of tea. "Got a surprise for you," he told Theodosia.

"I'm not sure I can take another surprise," she told him. "Or even want one."

"No, no, this is a nice surprise," said Drayton, pouring steaming hot liquid into a pink, purple, and gold Gladstone teacup. "You were so intrigued with teaberry the other day that I went ahead and ordered a tin of teaberry-flavored tea." He slid the cup toward her, a shy smile on his face. "Try it. I think you'll find it an interesting blend of white tea, green tea, teaberry leaves, hibiscus, dried cranberries, and honey. A trifle on the minty side, but quite delicious."

Theodosia took a quick sip. "It is good. Who blended it?"

"Kent and Dinmore, one of our favorite tea purveyors."

"You're thinking of adding this to our tea menu?" They already had a list of more than one hundred fresh-brewed tea offerings, to say nothing of their infusions list and teatotalers menu of nontea beverages.

"I wouldn't mind," said Drayton. "Would you?"

"You're the master tea blender," said Theodosia. "I leave it up to you."

"But you're the boss lady." Drayton smiled, seeing her humor creep back.

Theodosia gave a chuckle. "Please don't call me that. At least not in public."

"Honey," asked Miss Dimple, scurrying up to them. "I have a table asking for an organic Darjeeling. Do we have that?"

"Is that honey me or honey Drayton?" asked Theodosia.

Miss Dimple grinned and waved a hand. "Honey meaning Drayton," she said. "Isn't he the big, important tea guy?"

"You see?" Theodosia said to Drayton.

"To answer your question," replied Drayton, "yes. And I shall be happy to brew a pot of Darjeeling, although it's going to be from the Ambootia Estate, since we're completely out of Makaibari Estate."

"Uh . . . no problem," said Miss Dimple, hurrying back to her customers.

Drayton reached up and grabbed a tin of tea from the huge array of tins, glass jars, and metal bins that occupied a warren of floor-to-ceiling wooden shelves. "You see? No problem."

"Maybe not with tea," said Theodosia in a low voice. "But more than a few other issues have cropped up."

"Hmm?" said Drayton, carefully measuring out scoops of loose tea leaves.

And so Theodosia quickly related her little episode of last night. Black car, nasty crash, injured dog. Then she filled him in concerning her earlier conversation with Detective Tidwell.

Drayton was stunned. "You've obviously struck a nerve!"

"The question is, whose nerve?" replied Theodosia. She reached for a teapot, pulled out a Staffordshire green spatterware teapot, and stared fixedly at it. Tempest in a teapot? she wondered. Or great big storm brewing?

"Okay, you guys," said Haley, corralling Theodosia and Drayton at the front counter. "I want to take a couple of minutes to go over today's menu."

"Busy day today," muttered Drayton, as he measured Assam tea into an antique Haviland teapot with gold and ivy trim. Besides their regular luncheon customers they had a group of Red Hat Ladies coming in at one o'clock and an afternoon tour group driving up from Beaufort.

"Butterscotch scones," said Haley. "Mediterranean salad, squares of spring vegetable quiche, and lemon tea bread."

"And the tea sandwiches?" asked Drayton, trying to hurry her along.

"Getting to that," said Haley, checking her notes. "Three different kinds today. Chicken salad with almonds, cucumber mint, and goat cheese with sun-dried tomatoes."

"Wonderful," breathed Theodosia.

"I don't know how well goat cheese and sun-dried tomatoes are going to go over," said Drayton.

"We'll just have to wait and see," said Haley, not allowing herself to get rattled. "And, to help you keep it all straight . . ." She reached into her apron pockets and pulled out small index cards. "Cheat sheets for everyone."

"So our customers can order any of the offerings in any combination," said Theodosia.

"Think of it as a free-for-all," quipped Haley.

"Perhaps a la carte might be a more genteel and accurate term," said Drayton.

"Perhaps we should tend to our customers," said Theodosia.

"Or I might do an assortment on three-tiered trays," said Haley.

"Whatever works," said Drayton.

■ ■ ■ ■

With a large silver tray propped against one hip, Theodosia was serving scones to a table of six when Delaine Dish came parading into the Indigo Tea Shop. She was wearing an exquisitely tailored tweed jacket and had another woman, not so finely dressed, in tow. Pausing at the front of the tea shop, Delaine let her sharp eyes skitter across each table until she finally spied Theodosia.

"Theodosia!" Delaine called in an authoritative voice that clearly rose above the noise and rustlings of the luncheon crowd. "A table, please."

Theodosia finished setting out the Devonshire cream and lemon curd, then hurried to head off Delaine. But Drayton arrived there first, bless his heart and soul.

Upon encountering Drayton, Delaine melted slightly, blowing air-kisses and gushing compliments. Wallowing in his even more lavish compliments, she finally remembered that she had her sister in tow.

"Y'all remember my sister, Nadine, don't you?" she said, giving an offhand wave and causing Nadine to blush.

"Of course," cooed Theodosia. She remembered Nadine quite well. Three years ago, when Nadine had first showed up in these parts, she'd been a practicing kleptomaniac. Had made off with silver teaspoons, a couple of necklaces, and some old coins. Theodosia could only hope that Nadine had long since sought therapy and had somehow overcome her little problem. Or at least reined it in.

"Lovely to see you again," said Drayton, giving Nadine a chaste peck on the cheek.

Not to be outdone, Delaine let loose her big pronouncement. "Nadine's come all the way from New York to help me with my big fashion show tomorrow." She smiled brightly at Theodosia and said, "You're still coming aren't you, dear?" There was an arch tone to her voice.

"I'll certainly try," said Theodosia. She led Delaine and Nadine to a hastily set table while Drayton hurried off to grab a pot of tea.

"No, no, no," said Delaine, plopping into a chair and suddenly raising an index finger in Theodosia's face. "Try isn't even in my vocabulary. I come from a place of *do*ing."

"You absolutely *must* come," said Nadine, grabbing Theodosia's hand. "Delaine's launching her new lingerie boutique."

"I'm calling it Méchante," said Delaine, trying to approximate a French accent.

"Which means naughty in French," said Nadine with a giggle.

"We're showing our new spring and summer fashions interspersed with the lingerie," Delaine rhapsodized. "The event is going to be truly delicious. In fact, I instructed my assistant Janine to twitch all my customers."

"Twitch?" said Theodosia.

"She means Tweet," corrected Nadine. "Delaine's into Twittering."

"All over town," said Delaine. "Just for my show!"

"In that case," said Theodosia with a smile, "I don't dare miss it."

Delaine gave a little shiver. "This is really shaping up to be a big weekend. My show Friday and Lyndel Woodruff's book reading at the Heritage Society on Saturday."

Drayton was suddenly at their table with a steaming pot of tea. "Oh," he said, trying to be pleasant, "you enjoy lectures on Civil War history?" Delaine was a crackerjack fund-raiser for the Heritage Society, but she'd never shown more than a passing interest in their lectures and book events.

"Can't say's I do," said Delaine. "But I try never to miss a nice social opportunity. Nothing like a good mingle."

Drayton raised his eyebrows but held his tongue as he poured tea into their teacups.

"This is Gingerbread Peach Tea," he told them. "One of my proprietary blends. Chinese black tea, ginger root, cinnamon, and citrus."

"Oh my goodness," said Nadine. "So . . . you made it yourself?"

"Blended it," said Drayton.

"Delicious," proclaimed Delaine, taking a quick sip.

Drayton looked pleased. "To quote the poet John Milton on tea, 'One sip of this will battle the drooping spirits in delight beyond the bliss of dreams.'"

"Who's drooping?" asked Delaine. At which point everyone broke into laughter and Drayton beat a hasty retreat.

"Delaine," said Theodosia, gazing at her friend's black-and-cobalt-blue tweed jacket, "do my eyes deceive me or is that yet another Chanel suit you're wearing?"

Delaine grinned a Cheshire cat grin, delighted to be called out for her expensive outfit.

"Of course, it is," she told Theodosia, shifting in her chair to best show off her jacket, basking in the recognition.

"Delaine positively adores Chanel," Nadine added, looking a little wistful, like maybe she *couldn't* afford to wear the double Cs.

"Delaine's going to have to join Chanel-anon pretty soon," joked Theodosia.

"I *love* it!" Nadine screeched, then proceeded to parody Delaine's slightly patronizing tone of voice. "Hello, my name is Delaine and I'm a Chanel addict."

"I'm not *that* addicted," protested Delaine, looking slightly sheepish.

"Oh yes, you are," Nadine insisted.

"No, dear," Delaine told her sister, a gravely firmness in her voice. "I adore Prada, Dior, and Cavalli just as much. You might even say I'm an equal opportunity clotheshorse."

"Enjoy your tea," said Theodosia, "while I grab you a selection of sandwiches."

Over at the counter, Theodosia whispered to Drayton, "Is Delaine and Nadine's table set with the good sterling silver?"

Drayton nodded. "The Gorham."

Theodosia snuck a peek at Nadine over her left shoulder, then said, "Keep an eye on it, will you?"

16

Twenty minutes later the Red Hat Ladies from Goose Creek came pouring into the Indigo Tea Shop. Calling their chapter the Goose Creek Gadabouts, they definitely seemed gabby and giddy.

Filling three tables, the Gadabouts proceeded to warm Drayton's heart by ordering pots of Lapsang souchong, a nice smoky Chinese tea, as well as a high grade of Earl Grey that was a blend of both Chinese and Ceylon tea along with natural oil of bergamot.

Drayton, of course, had set the three tables using Limoges china and cut-crystal water glasses and created special red-and-purple bouquets using lavender, purple irises, and roses.

And because the Gadabouts were so animated and fun, continually jumping up to look at the T-Bath products and antique teacups that were for sale, Haley decided to change up her serving style, too. Instead of serving separate courses, she pulled out her extra-large, three-tiered serving stands, which were always a showstopper. Scones were placed on top, of course. Three types of tea sandwiches were arranged on the middle tier. And the savories, quiche in this instance, went on the bottom tier. Haley added a few edible nasturtium flowers and the serving stands were ready to go.

Twenty-five minutes later, the bus tour from Beaufort arrived and they did it all over again.

"Haley," said Theodosia, "you didn't tell us your sandwiches were going to be so exotic." Haley had baked her own bread in narrow heart- and flower-shaped tubes, so when the bread was sliced thinly, the designs were readily apparent.

"Just something I decided at the last minute," said Haley, as they stood in the kitchen, arranging four more three-tiered trays.

"What am I going to do when some big fancy hotel offers you a job as the catering manager?" asked Theodosia. She grinned ruefully, then added, "I'll advise you to take it, of course. You're a very skilled chef and baker."

Haley wrinkled her nose as she carefully

arranged quiche squares on tiny silver doilies. "Don't be so sure I'm ready to scurry off. I really like it here. You and Drayton let me run my own show. Any other place there'd be management via helicopter."

Theodosia squinted. "Helicopter?"

"Hovering," explained Haley. "They'd be asking me to try this or telling me to add such and such dish to the menu. Or I'd do a lobster Cobb salad and some stick-in-the-mud bean counter would decide the ingredients were too expensive and tell me I should use canned tuna." She wiped her hands on her apron and stepped back to appraise her lavishly arranged tray. "Anyway, it wouldn't be my call anymore."

"I see your point," said Theodosia.

"Truth be told," grinned Haley, "I'm looking forward to moving into your upstairs apartment. Once you get the high sign to move into your cottage, that is."

"Haley," said Theodosia. "There's something I have to tell you. Something that could possibly affect our safety here. Yours, mine, and Drayton's."

Haley glanced up sharply. "Huh? What are you talking about?"

So Theodosia told Haley about last night. Gave her the 411 on what had happened to

223

Earl Grey and her.

Except for concern over Earl Grey, Haley wasn't all that fazed. "Somebody comes after me," she declared, "I'll give 'em a dose of pepper spray."

"Perhaps a better decision might be to turn and run," said Theodosia. "And scream very loud."

"Sometimes," said Haley, artfully tucking a half dozen ripe strawberries among her tea sandwiches, "you just have to take a stand and fight."

Theodosia didn't know it then, but those words would prove to be prophetic.

Once the tea trays were delivered, oohed and aahed over, and more tea was brewed and poured, Theodosia slipped away to her back office. For one thing, she wanted to see if she could find out a little more about Joe Don Hunter and the Kipling Club. She wasn't quite sure what she was looking for as she typed "Kipling Club" into Google, but she knew she needed more information.

Not much turned up. A couple of references in the Charleston *Post and Courier* about the Kipling Club holding an oyster roast out on Johns Island. Another note in a local shopper.

But wait, here was something that made

her perk up. A mention in the *Summerton Gazette* about a citation issued to two members of the Kipling Club, specifically Joe Don Hunter and a Ferris Allan, concerning unlawful use of a metal detector near the Santee Indian Mound and Fort Watson Site.

Theodosia leaned back in her chair and slid off her shoes. Rubbed her toes across the carpet, thought about what the two men might have been looking for. Surely not pocket change. Then . . . what? Civil War uniform buttons? Fossils and arrowheads? Old trade beads? Although those last couple of items wouldn't necessarily register a hit on a metal detector.

On the other hand, what if the so-called metal detector had really been a ground-penetrating radar device? Then Hunter and his buddy could have turned up all sorts of things. Pottery shards, old tools from the Colonial period, even . . . dinosaur bones. It was all out there, slumbering under layers of mud and muck, waiting to be found by anyone with half a brain and a penchant for digging.

Theodosia also knew that type of exploration would definitely be classified as an illegal dig.

So now what? Should I go ahead and con-

225

front Joe Don Hunter?

Theodosia spun that notion around in her brain for a minute. Decided that the problem, of course, was confront him about what? Participating in illegal digs? That fact had pretty much been established. Confront Hunter about strangling Daria Shand? That route took her into what could turn out to be either dangerous territory or false accusations.

Because, when all was said and done, good old boy Joe Don Hunter might be exactly what he appeared to be. A fellow whose girlfriend had been savagely murdered. Someone who was caught in the leg trap of hard grief. A person whose extracurricular activities led him into gray areas.

Theodosia's fingers tapped idly on her computer keyboard. So . . . what now? Or rather, who else bore a second look?

Like a cartoon bubble forming above her head, Jason Pritchard popped into her brain again. Which brought to mind the possible backer and new co-owner of the Antiquarian Map Shop.

"Jud Snelling," Theodosia said aloud. "Sounds like an old-timey name. So . . . maybe an older guy?"

Hmmm.

Another quick search brought up the

Silver Plume Antique Shop in Savannah, Georgia. Theodosia clicked on the website and found that Jud Snelling was listed as the proprietor and that the shop specialized in Civil War relics, American paintings, old glass and crockery, and fine antique furniture. Very interesting.

Clicking and scrolling through the website Theodosia found several pairs of Civil War–era spurs, a Jefferson Davis hat pin, antique glass ale bottles, and some nice paintings.

At the bottom of the page was the address and phone number for the Silver Plume. She squinted, thinking of a plausible reason to call Jud Snelling. Then, after a few moments of creative brainstorming, punched in the phone number.

Jud Snelling picked up on the second ring. "Silver Plume Antiques."

"Hello there," said Theodosia. "You don't know me, but I'm a friend of Daria Shand's. In fact, I own the Indigo Tea Shop just down the street from her place."

A long silence spun out and then Snelling said, "Oh my. I wanted so much to attend the funeral yesterday, but I couldn't get anyone to watch the shop. I'm so sorry I missed it."

Theodosia drew breath, thinking. Snelling sounded sincere. Then, again, so did Ted

Bundy when he worked the hotline at a women's crisis shelter.

She plunged ahead with her plan. "The reason I'm calling," she told Snelling, "is to invite you to an event this Saturday night."

"Oh?" Now Snelling sounded genuinely puzzled.

"Yes," said Theodosia. "A local author and historian by the name of Lyndel Woodruff is doing a book reading at the Heritage Society this Saturday night. He's written a book titled *The Battle of Honey Hill*? Anyway, there's going to be a cocktail party afterward and some of Daria's friends will be there." Crossing her fingers, Theodosia went on with her little white lie. "There'll be a sort of remembrance for Daria, too."

"I've met Woodruff," said Snelling. "And the reception afterward . . ." He hesitated.

Was he going for it? Theodosia wondered. Was that enough to bring Snelling up here so she could take a look at him? Quiz him. Maybe even get Tidwell to speak to him. Informally, of course.

"I'll try to make it," said Snelling.

"Excellent," breathed Theodosia.

"The Heritage Society you say?"

"That's right. You know where Gateway Walk is? The Heritage Society is located at the far end of it."

"Yes," said Snelling. "I've been there a number of times."

"I look forward to meeting you," said Theodosia.

Pleased and a little embarrassed with her ruse, Theodosia wiggled back into her shoes and headed into the tea shop.

The atmosphere out front, to put it mildly, was a love fest. The Gadabouts and the Beaufort tour ladies had seemingly merged into one large, gregarious group. Spirits were running high, tea and lemon tea bread were in constant demand, camera phones snapped playful poses and group photos, and Drayton, standing in the middle of the room, was just about to begin a recitation.

"He's a charmer," Miss Dimple said to Theodosia, as she stood in the doorway watching the proceedings. "Those ladies have been begging Drayton to recite one of his tea poems ever since they arrived."

"I doubt he needed much prodding," said Theodosia. Drayton, as parliamentarian and frequent lecturer at the Heritage Society, adored an appreciative audience. And this one was so warmed up, he could have read the phone directory and received a shower of applause.

"Look at him," said Miss Dimple. "He

loves it." And with that, Drayton stepped to the center of the room.

"Just a small piece," he told the group, "snipped from a lovely poem written by Minna Irving back in 1920 titled 'My Fragrant Cup of Tea.'"

I pour the steaming amber drink
In china thin and fine,
Gold banded, bordered daintily
With wild rose flower and vine,
Add cream and sugar or condensed,
And sipping slowly see
A film of far off scenes unroll,
The drama of the tea.

Applause rang out and Drayton, not one to loosen his grip on an audience, reached over and grabbed a pink-and-white tea cozy. "Thank you kindly," he told the women. "And now, I simply must show you a new tea cozy that the Indigo Tea Shop has added to our giftware section."

"He's really good," marveled Miss Dimple.

"Drayton could sell Ginsu knives at a state fair," responded Theodosia.

"This new wraparound tea cozy fits directly over your teapot and stays there," continued Drayton. "No more pulling your tea cozy off to pour." He popped the pink-and-white-gingham tea cozy onto a teapot, demonstrating for the crowd. "You see? Plop it on and simply pull the drawstring ribbon to snug the tea cozy tightly. Now only the teapot's handle and spout are left sticking out."

A woman in a froufrou red hat raised her hand. "You have other colors?"

"Of course," said Drayton. "Other patterns, too." He set the teapot down and adjusted his glasses. "Gingham, patchwork, and a lovely ticking stripe as well."

"And you sell loose tea?" asked another woman.

Drayton pointed toward the shelves and highboy that stood against the brick. "Thirty-seven different kinds of tea, with many available for sniffing thanks to my new scent jars. And, of course, we also have our T-Bath products, a selection of antique teacups, DuBose Bees Honey, and our wild grapevine wreaths decorated with miniature teacups."

Needless to say, more than a few tins of tea, wreaths, and jars of honey were sold that day.

"What a success," Drayton chortled some forty minutes later as they cleared the tables, loading dirty dishes into gray plastic tubs. "Even though it's more work, I adore having larger groups come in."

"Then you're in luck," Haley told him, with a mischievous grin. "Since we have another group coming in tomorrow."

Drayton let loose an inquisitive, "Oh?"

"That's right," continued Haley, looking even more impish than usual. "Tomorrow's our children's tea."

Drayton suddenly straightened up like a martinet called to attention. "Tell me it isn't so."

"No can do," said Haley with a laugh, "since it's really happening." She glanced over at Theodosia. "Right, Theo?"

Theodosia nodded. "It's been on our calendar for almost two months."

Now Drayton looked exasperated. "The event completely slipped my memory." He shook his head. "I seem to be having more and more lapses the older I get. Probably, I should stay home tomorrow and try to recover my . . ."

"No way." Haley laughed. "You're going to work this tea if it kills you."

"But . . ." said Drayton, sounding genuinely aghast, "there'll be *children* present. I don't generally deal well with children."

"This will be good for you," Haley assured

him. "Help you get reacquainted with your own inner child."

"Drayton doesn't have an inner child," Theodosia commented, as she picked up a Crown Dorset Chintz and Cameo teapot and wiped the outside with a dish towel. "He was born old."

"Thank you, Theodosia," said Drayton, looking slightly heartened. "Yes, I've always had an old soul. Although I believe the more appropriate term would be mature. Case in point, my great-uncle Edgar taught me how to play chess at the tender age of three and I'm pleased to say I never looked back."

"Wait a minute," said Haley, not quite buying Drayton's story. "You're telling me you never played cops and robbers? Or mumblety-peg? Or whatever it was people did back in the Dark Ages?"

"Not when I could be reading Dickens," said Drayton. "Or classics like *Moby-Dick* or *Treasure Island.*"

"Please!" Haley begged, "just spare me the anguish of recounting how many miles you trudged to school. Or how you had to haul wood to stoke the fireplace or something."

"No fireplace." Drayton smiled. "Central heating."

"Wow," said Haley, pretending to be amazed. "Modern stuff."

17

While Haley bustled around in the kitchen, prepping food for the open house that night at the Featherbed House B and B, Drayton fussed over a fern terrarium.

"That's a lovely arrangement," Theodosia told him. "I hope it's for display here at the tea shop." Drayton had taken a large glass bell jar, filled it with rich black dirt and bright green sphagnum moss, then planted an assortment of ferns. Southern lady fern, netted chain fern, even a cinnamon fern.

"It's actually a prototype," Drayton told her. "If this terrarium turns out nicely, I thought I'd make one for each table."

"Your arrangement is gorgeous," Theodosia told him. "In fact, it's so lush and elegant looking you could probably turn out a bunch and retail them." Indeed, she'd seen terrariums and other botanical arrangements selling for well over two hundred dollars at Floradora, the floral shop down the street.

"Making them via assembly line might take the fun out of it," said Drayton, as he picked up a final shoot of resurrection fern using his long silver bonsai tweezers and carefully transferred it into his terrarium.

"Suppose so," said Theodosia, looking at her watch. "You realize, we're supposed to meet Timothy Neville at four to finalize the food for Saturday night?"

"We've got time," murmured Drayton. He was judiciously placing a small rock into his grove of ferns. Interestingly enough, the addition of the rock suddenly gave the arrangement a sense of scale. Made it look like a believable landscape.

"Then I'm going to . . ." began Theodosia, just as a loud knock sounded on the front door.

She scurried over, thinking, *Must be stragglers. Tourists who don't know we're closed.* "I'm sorry," she called, putting her mouth to the door. "We're closed for the day." She peeked through the leaded glass window, gave a start as she suddenly recognized the straggler, and murmured, "Oh dear."

Turning the latch, Theodosia pulled open the door and let Fallon in.

Daria's sister didn't look much different than she had this morning. Sad, forlorn, a slightly defeated slump to her shoulders. Her black jacket was a little too large for her, her skirt a tad too long. The word *dowdy* bubbled up in Theodosia's mind, then she dismissed it as being mean-spirited.

"Apologies," Theodosia told Fallon as she lead her to a table. "I didn't realize it was you." She sat down across from her, then popped up from her chair. "Let me bring you a cup of tea."

Fallon smiled faintly. "That would be nice."

"Already have one for you," said Drayton, hustling toward them and setting a gleaming cup and saucer in front of their guest. "I hope you enjoy Assam tea?" he asked Fallon. "This one's nice and strong. Help perk you up from the difficult day you've had."

"Thank you," said Fallon, watching carefully as Drayton poured a hot, steamy stream of tea into her cup.

"My deepest sympathies," Drayton murmured to Fallon.

She made a sound in the back of her throat, acknowledging him.

Then Drayton said, "I'll leave you two alone." And melted away.

"This is so kind of you," said Fallon, staring at Theodosia. Her eyes were still red-rimmed and glistening and Theodosia hoped she hadn't been on a daylong crying jag.

"Try the tea," urged Theodosia.

Fallon picked up the cup and gingerly took a sip. "Mmm. Good." She took a longer, more satisfying sip, then placed her cup on the saucer with a tiny clink. Her troubled eyes met Theodosia's kind eyes. "You know why I'm here?" she asked.

"I have a fairly good idea," said Theodosia. "But why don't you tell me in your own words."

"I . . ." Fallon tried, but faltered badly.

Theodosia reached across the table and patted her hand. "Take your time."

Fallon worried her lower lip with her teeth for a while, then said, "Not to put pressure on you or anything, but do you have anything at all on Daria's killer?"

How to begin? Theodosia wondered. *And how much should I tell her?*

"Your aunt Libby was quite outspoken about how clever you are," said Fallon. "And how you've cracked cases before."

"Mostly I just ask questions," Theodosia responded.

"That's not what I've heard," said Fallon, doggedly. "I hear you're famously good at unraveling mysteries."

"Unraveling," murmured Theodosia. But

as she pondered Fallon's words, she decided that was a legitimate way to describe her investigatory style. She'd pick up a germ of an idea, tug on a string, and pull something into place. Of course, with more ideas and loose ends popping up, she generally ended up in a tangle and was forced to sort things out. Clues, people, events.

"The police still don't have any idea who strangled Daria," said Fallon. She hunched her shoulders forward and stared forcefully at Theodosia, as if willing her to take up the cause.

"The police, especially Detective Tidwell, who seems to be honchoing the investigation, are playing it close to the vest," Theodosia agreed. "But I doubt they're without ideas. Or suspects."

"After everything your aunt Libby told us," said Fallon, "I think I trust you more. And, of course, you . . ." She stopped. Her unspoken words, *you were there,* hung in the air between them.

"I understand what you're getting at," said Theodosia, any semblance of a smile slipping from her face. "And I'm still beating myself up about that. I mean, I should have reacted quicker. I should have given chase. I should have . . ." Theodosia drew a deep breath. "I should have done more."

Fallon brushed away a tear. "But you are now, aren't you? Asking questions and all?"

Theodosia nodded, tears forming in the corners of her eyes. "Honey, I'm going to give it my all."

Fallon stood up abruptly and came around the table. Slipped her thin arms around Theodosia and hugged her gratefully. "Thank you," she said, tears streaming down her face. "I don't even *know* you and I trust you. No wonder your aunt Libby says such wonderful things about you."

"Well," said Theodosia, sniffling and slightly embarrassed now. "She is my aunt."

"Bless her," said Fallon. "And bless you."

"Is she going to be okay?" Haley asked, once Fallon had left. "She seems to be in a real tailspin. You think she can pull herself out of it?"

"Eventually she will, yes," said Theodosia. Standing in the kitchen doorway, she watched as Haley mashed pimentos and walnuts into cream cheese. Filling for one of tonight's tea sandwiches.

"How about you?" asked Haley. "How are you doing?"

"I'm good," Theodosia assured her. "Don't worry about me."

"But you're going to keep at it, right?"

said Haley. "See if you can make sense out of things?"

"I'm going to do that," said Theodosia. "Yes."

"Want me to get you a can of mace?" asked Haley. "There's this really nasty stuff called Stop-Em-Dead. Kind of a cross between mace and pepper spray. I think cops even use it."

Theodosia shook her head and chuckled softly. "That's one of the strangest offers I've had, Haley. Thanks for your concern, but no, thanks. When I go out at night I'm going to put my trust in Earl Grey."

"And in me," said Drayton, coming up behind her. "Don't forget those kung fu lessons I took at Master Kwan's dojo." He suddenly jumped forward, knees bent, arms akimbo, assuming a martial arts pose. "Since I earned my black belt in under two years, these hands are deadly weapons registered in three states."

"What?" said Haley, looking startled. "Seriously?"

Drayton pointed a finger at Haley and winked. "Gotcha!"

"Oh you!" exclaimed Haley, searching for something to throw at him, finally coming up with a half-eaten scone.

"Watch it!" cried Drayton, ducking. "We

could sell that as half-price baked goods tomorrow."

"Not from my kitchen you won't," declared Haley.

But still Theodosia and Drayton couldn't get out the door. Because just as they were ready to leave, Tred Pascal showed up.

"Five minutes," said Drayton, looking dour and tapping his watch face. "That's it, then we have to leave."

"Right," said Theodosia, absently. People seemed to be popping up like errant mushrooms today and she was up to her elbows in events. She was starting to feel the frazzle and pictured herself dashing about like one of those old vaudeville performers spinning multiple plates on sticks. Because she *still* had to get to the Heritage Society, work out a menu with Timothy, dash back home to walk Earl Grey, then grab Haley and all the packed-up food so they could hustle over to the Featherbed House. Yikes.

"What's up?" Theodosia asked Tred as they stood by the front counter. She figured if they remained standing she might be able to hustle the meeting along. She was also strategically positioned so Haley could come sashaying out to flirt with the young archaeologist.

"We're going to go ahead and dig," Tred told her. "We talked to the owner of your property and he's granted us permission. Signed off on all the paperwork."

This didn't come zooming like a comet from the blue for Theodosia. "I figured that," she told Tred. "But please, tell me exactly what you'll be doing."

"Well," said Tred, "it's pretty much going to be a controlled dig."

"Controlled," said Theodosia. "Run that by me with a little more detail, will you?"

"We'll probably stake out a twelve-by-twelve-foot area," Tred explained, "since your backyard's not all that big. Then we'll divide it into three-by-three-foot squares and dig each square down about a foot or so. If we haven't encountered anything by that time, we dig down another foot."

"So," said Theodosia. "The digging down part. Exactly how far do you intend to go?"

"Maybe thirty feet down," said Tred.

"What!" shrieked Theodosia.

"Just kidding," said Tred, finally cracking a smile. "No, it'll be three or four feet max. We don't find anything at that depth, we let it go. No sense completely ripping up private property."

"An archaeologist with a heart," said Theodosia.

"No." Tred chuckled. "Just a limited budget."

"You'll be doing this yourself or bringing in students?"

"I'll jump-start things myself," said Tred, "then hand off to reinforcements. Archaeology and anthropology students mostly."

"Okay," said Theodosia. She couldn't launch much of a protest since she didn't technically own the property yet. And she didn't see that digging up the backyard was that big a deal. Frankly, it could serve as the basis for some landscaping of her own. Help make her backyard a little more pet friendly. She'd read a recent article about the importance of adding a doggy wood-chip area, planting shrubs to divert dogs from creating a "racetrack" in the yard, and giving them a few rocks to use as hidey spots.

"When do you start digging?" she asked.

"First thing tomorrow," said Tred. "You should be there. I've got a couple of papers that need your signature, too. Can you stop by?"

"I suppose."

Tred picked up a tin of Earl Green tea that was sitting on the counter and hefted it. "I really enjoyed the tea you fixed for me the other day."

"We'll turn you into a tea connoisseur yet," said Theodosia.

He took a step closer to her. "I think I already am."

"Theodosia?" called Haley.

One hand slowly parted the celadon-green velvet curtains, then Haley stepped out into the tea room. "Oh. I didn't realize we had company." Haley said it with such amazing innocence and guile that Theodosia couldn't help smiling.

"You remember Tred Pascal," said Theodosia. "From the State Archaeology Office."

"Of course," said Haley. She threw a warm smile at Tred, lifted her long blond hair off her neck, then let is cascade down over one shoulder. "Really nice to see you again." She put a tiny emphasis on *really.*

Tred colored slightly. "Great to see you, too."

"You coming to the Heritage Society Saturday night?" Haley asked him. "We're catering all the fixin's." Haley reached into her apron pocket and pulled out an invitation. "Oh look, I just happen to have an invitation." She handed it to Tred. "Lyndel Woodruff wrote a book on the Honey Hill battle," she added, as Tred scanned the invitation. "There's a reading and a reception afterward."

"Sounds neat," he told her. "Thanks. Maybe I'll drop by."

"Great," said Haley. "Maybe I'll see you then." She gave a little wave and disappeared between the curtains in a slightly mysterioso manner.

"Before you take off," said Theodosia, delighted that Haley had enjoyed her little moment, "there's something I want to ask."

"Shoot," said Tred, still clutching his invitation.

"You know anything about the Kipling Club?"

"Those idiots!" Tred spit out. "Yeah, I know *of* them."

"I take it they're persona non grata in the archaeology community," said Theodosia.

"They're not even *in* the archaeology community," said Tred. "They're just a pack of treasure hunters, interested in digging up arrowheads, pottery, and fossils so they can cash in."

"That's it?" said Theodosia. "They sell the stuff?"

"Like mercenaries," added Tred.

Theodosia nodded. "Lot of that going around."

The Heritage Society sat like a medieval castle at the far end of Gateway Walk, an enormous stone fortress that was the designated repository for the historical treasures of Charleston and its surrounding environs.

Hanging on its walls were early American oil paintings by such artists as Henry Benbridge, Jeremiah Theus, and John Wollaston. The cypress-paneled library held thousands of leather-bound volumes, a few of which dated back to Benjamin Franklin's own printing press. The Heritage Society's storage rooms contained thousands of paintings, prints, and maps, as well as early tradeware, artifacts from area rice and cotton plantations, firearms, antique uniforms, old silver, a fine collection of glass plate negatives, and a couple of prints by John James Audubon.

At the front desk, Camilla Hodges, the majordomo receptionist for the Heritage Society, greeted Theodosia and Drayton. She was sixty-something and petite, with a waft of white hair and the lingering scent of Arpège, or something equally old-fashioned.

"Good afternoon, Camilla," said Drayton. "Is Timothy available?"

Camilla grinned up at Drayton, who was quite obviously one of her favorite board members. "He is, and he's been waiting for you. Anxiously, I might add."

"We are a little late," admitted Theodosia.

"I hope it's not a problem."

"It probably is," said Camilla, "but that's because Timothy is tightly wired. But . . . we're used to making allowances for that here. After all, he is the heart and soul of the Heritage Society."

Theodosia giggled to herself as she and Drayton marched down a hallway carpeted with whisper-soft Chinese rugs. She could easily conjure up a few other excellent descriptors for Timothy.

"Look sharp," said Drayton, as they pushed their way into Timothy Neville's cavernous office, as if he knew what Theodosia had been thinking.

Turning his famously stern gaze on the two of them, Timothy half rose in his tufted red leather chair, then quietly lifted a hand, indicating for Theodosia and Drayton to be seated. They crossed a wide expanse of carpet and slid into the leather-and-hobnail club chairs that faced Timothy's massive wooden desk. And once again, Theodosia felt a hint of suspicion that the chairs had been purposely lowered to enable the diminutive Timothy to face them precisely at eye level.

"What have you there, Timothy?" asked Drayton. Timothy wore white gauze gloves on both hands and was obviously in the

248

middle of handling the small, framed oil painting that sat on his desk in front of him.

Theodosia pulled herself up straighter, the better to see.

"An early American oil painting attributed to Sir Godfrey Kneller," Timothy told them. It was a small painting, maybe twelve by fourteen inches including frame, of a lovely young woman wearing a pink gown. She was youthful but resolute-looking, with diamond earbobs and long, dark hair pinned up in a twist. The artist had seen to give her cheeks the same rosy glow as her gown.

"Lovely," said Theodosia. Though the oil paint was threaded with hairline cracks, the painting still had a strong presence.

"Only problem is," said Timothy, "Kneller wasn't really the artist."

"Is that so," said Drayton.

"Sir Godfrey Kneller enjoyed some repute as a sort of society artist," explained Timothy, "but most of his paintings were actually executed by Charles Bridges."

"So Bridges was a ghost painter," said Theodosia. "Along the lines of a ghost writer."

Timothy nodded. "Something like that, yes."

"Still," said Drayton. "An interesting piece for the Heritage Society. Since it is authentically old."

"I'm told it dates to 1750," said Timothy.

"Wow," said Theodosia. "And this was a recent gift?"

"Donation," said Timothy. "Someone discovered it in their attic. After it was dusted off, we became the lucky recipient."

"Remind me to check my attic again," said Drayton, who lived in a small, wooden, Civil War–era house.

"Good thing they didn't take it to *Antiques Roadshow*," said Theodosia. Then, focusing all her attention on Timothy, she said, "Have you by any chance located one of the maps you mentioned the other night? One that might shed some light on the location of my house and the . . . er . . . usage of the backyard?"

Timothy's normally tight brow furrowed. "I'm afraid I have not." He waved a hand, seemed to notice he was still wearing his gauze gloves, then pulled them off. "Been awfully busy. So much going on here." He gazed at her purposefully. "But I'll assign someone to look."

"Appreciate that," said Theodosia.

"So," said Timothy. "The menu for Saturday evening. More last-minute planning." He sighed heavily.

Drayton folded one leg over the other,

placed both hands loosely in his lap, and responded pleasantly. "Not really. Lyndel's reading is still a couple days away and we pride ourselves on speed and efficiency."

At that Timothy managed a faint smile. "Miss Browning?" he asked, raising his eyebrows in his tight, almost simian-looking face. "I presume, then, you've already prepared a menu?"

Theodosia hadn't, but she wasn't going to give Timothy the satisfaction of knowing she'd come unprepared. "Of course," Theodosia responded. "I was thinking of simple hors d'oeuvres. Shrimp and avocado kabobs, smoked salmon and goat cheese on baguette slices, and crab salad in puff pastries. Finger food."

Timothy steepled his fingers and nodded. "And you're assuming a full bar?"

"I think we should go simpler," said Theodosia. "Hot Russian caravan tea and flutes of champagne. Something top quality like Veuve Clicquot." She knew this was one of Timothy's favorites, since he stocked it by the case in his wine cellar. "And maybe, for a fun twist, some tea-tinis."

"Pray tell," said Timothy, his bright eyes betraying his interest, "what is a tea-tini?"

Theodosia turned her gaze calmly on Drayton. "Drayton?" She didn't have an actual tea-tini recipe in her head at the moment, but she knew she could count on Drayton.

"Glad you asked," said Drayton, leaning forward, never missing a beat. "Firefly Vodka, a local South Carolina distillery, makes Sweet Tea vodka, Raspberry Tea vodka, Mint Tea vodka, and several more."

"Hah!" said Timothy. "Intriguing. Served in martini glasses?"

"Of course," said Drayton.

Timothy mulled over their suggestions for a few moments, then said, abruptly, "I like everything you've proposed. Sophisticated but not overly fussy."

"That's us," said Drayton.

Theodosia nudged the toe of her shoe against Drayton's shin, then added, "We're thinking of serving a dessert, too."

"A sweet," said Drayton.

"Toll House cookie bars," said Timothy.

"Hmm?" said Drayton.

"I have a recipe," said Timothy, looking pleased. "Passed down from my great-grandmother. I'll have Camilla e-mail it to you immediately."

"I'm sure our Haley will adore your recipe," said Drayton, as Theodosia kicked him again.

18

Thursday night at the Featherbed House. Candles blazed, overstuffed couches and chairs beckoned, and an admiring crowd of tourists and locals drifted in and out of the sprawling lobby. Because the Featherbed House B and B didn't just look cozy, it was adorable bordering on splendid.

The geese, of course, were the focal point. Angie Congdon's Featherbed House was famous for its collection of handcrafted geese. There were giant white ceramic geese, calico geese, carved wooden geese, plush geese, needlepoint geese, and even colorful embroidered geese. All clustered in corners, perched on tables, cozied into chairs as pillows, and hung on walls. There were even geese motifs in the colorful rugs that graced the pegged wooden floors.

Theodosia and Haley had arrived at the Featherbed House just in the nick of time, just as the very first guests were starting to shuffle up the front walk for a guided tour. They set up hastily in the lobby, spreading everything out on a large, wooden trestle table set against a white board-and-batten wall. A window in the center of that wall afforded a view to the backyard garden. On either side of the window were geese paintings, trivets, and wall hangings.

"Holy smokes," said Haley, as they watched people pour in, "this Bed-and-Breakfast Tour is bigger than I thought it would be."

"I think there might be a lot of curious neighbors," said Theodosia. "Folks who are dying to get a look inside some of the grander old homes that were big enough to convert into B and Bs."

"You're probably right," said Haley, as she poured cups of pomegranate oolong tea and doled out pimento-walnut tea sandwiches as well as beef and cheddar tea sandwiches.

"Oof," said Theodosia, blowing a strand of hair from her face. "Warm in here."

"But your hair looks great," said Haley. "Really puffed up."

Theodosia patted her hair nervously. When the heat and humidity rose, which it tended to do in Charleston, her auburn hair, always full to begin with, expanded dramatically and formed an exotic halo about her head. "That's called frizz," said Theodosia, patting it again, wishing for some sort of control.

"Still," said Haley, "it's better than stick-straight hair like mine."

"I don't know about that," said Theodosia, sneaking a peek in the mirror, wishing she could somehow tame her mane.

"Anyway," said Haley. "You look great even though you're probably bushed. You've had a busy day and your meeting with Timothy ran long."

"Not so much running long as starting late," Theodosia told her. "But at least we got his menu figured out."

"And you're absolutely positive Timothy wants us to use his great-grandmother's cookie bar recipe?" asked Haley. She looked a little glum.

"Are you kidding?" said Theodosia. "He's already e-mailed it. I took a quick look and there's nothing too tricky, just your basic Toll House cookie recipe."

Haley wrinkled her nose. "I was hoping to make profiteroles and fill them with my homemade sour cream ice cream."

"Mmm," said Theodosia, then decided to pitch Haley on a compromise. "What if you whipped up ice cream cookie bar sandwiches instead?"

Caught off guard, Haley said, "What? Using Timothy's cookie bars?"

"Sure. Why not?"

"So my sour cream ice cream with Timothy's cookie bars," said Haley, mulling it over.

"Sounds delicious," said Theodosia, coaxing.

"I suppose," said Haley. "But . . . hey, are you going to run this idea past Timothy?"

Theodosia grinned. "Sure. And then we'll probably exchange banana bread recipes. What do *you* think?"

"Point taken," said Haley. "And surprises are fun. For most people anyway." She gazed out over the front parlor, blinked with recognition as she spotted two familiar faces in the crowd, and said, "Whoops, look what the kitty cat just dragged in. It's . . ."

"Delaine!" exclaimed Theodosia, as Delaine Dish elbowed her way toward them. "And Nadine. Nice to see you both." Delaine was a vision of sophistication in her hot-pink sheath dress with long, swishing strands of creamy white pearls. Nadine wore almost the same dress in canary yellow, only with black pearls.

"Isn't this an utter madhouse?" complained Delaine. "So many people. *Too* many people."

"It's an open house," said Haley, deadpan.

"Which I'm afraid is also an open invitation to the riffraff." Delaine sighed, fanning herself with her silver clutch purse and managing to look put-upon. "But I suppose this kind of crowd can't be helped."

"Duh. Angie wanted this crowd," said Haley.

"Are you ready for your big fashion show tomorrow?" Theodosia asked, hoping to steer the conversation in a more positive direction.

"More than ready," declared Delaine. "Cotton Duck is decorated to the nines, the chairs are arranged, runway installed, models have been fitted, and we're absolute stocked to the rafters with new merchandise."

"Now if our show attendees will just buy," put in Nadine.

"Of course, they'll buy," snapped Delaine. "They *always* buy."

Nadine looked puzzled. "But you said . . ."

"Never mind that," said Delaine, "let's take a look around and see if we can find Angie." She screwed her face into an exaggerated smile and waggled her fingers. "Bye-bye," she called to Theodosia and Haley.

"Byeeee," said Haley, rolling her eyes once she was sure Delaine was out of sight. "Are

257

you *really* going to her fashion show tomorrow?" she asked Theodosia.

"I told her I would," said Theodosia. "Why, do you want to come along? I'm sure it wouldn't be a problem."

"It would be for me." Haley laughed. " 'Cause her kind of glitz and glam is so not my style. Hey." She put a hand on Theodosia's shoulder. "I'm going to zip into the kitchen and grab a couple more trays of food, okay? We're going through tea sandwiches like jujubes at a Disney flick."

Theodosia straightened a stack of plates and was about to pop a miniature apple-raisin scone into her mouth when she heard a familiar whisper.

"Oh, tea lady. Tea lady . . ."

She knew that voice. It was . . . Theodosia turned to find Bill Glass looking at her, his expression halfway between a smirk and a leer. A smleer? Yeah, maybe.

"Don't you know it's rude to stare?" she told him.

"I'm lining up a shot," he said matter-of-factly, then hefted his Nikon to add credence to his statement.

"Well, please don't," she said. "In fact, I'm not even on speaking terms with you anymore. I saw the crappy article you wrote about me in your silly *Shooting Star* paper."

"But a cute picture of you, wouldn't you say?"

"There was nothing cute about it," said Theodosia, as Glass held his camera up and clicked off a couple of shots.

Theodosia threw up her hands. "Leave me alone," she pleaded. "*Please* leave me alone. Go take photos of Angie and the guests. Especially Angie. This place can use the press. Even bad press like yours."

"Come on," wheedled Glass. "You're lots more fun. I can always get a rise out of you. Besides, you look cute in that silvery dress."

Theodosia blushed, wishing she hadn't worn such a sporty T-shirt dress. "No," she said, deciding to treat Bill Glass like an unwelcome alley cat who'd come slumming around her back door looking for a handout. "No, you run along outside."

"Hey, babe, a couple more?" cajoled Glass. "What can it hurt?"

"Rats," Theodosia muttered, as she capitulated and posed with a pot of tea in one hand. That seemed to do it. Glass gave an approving nod, held up his camera, and took a few more pictures.

"Safeties," he told her.

"Fine," said Theodosia. "Done now?"

"I guarantee you're gonna love . . ." Glass studied the image on his small LCD monitor and scowled. "Huh."

"What's wrong now?" asked Theodosia. "You forget to remove your lens cap?"

Glass shook his head. "Nah, there's like a ghost image or something."

"Angie always told me this place was haunted," Theodosia joked.

"I'm serious," said Glass. "It almost looks like there was someone standing behind you." He looked up and gazed past her. "Funny. There really must have been someone." He gestured with his thumb. "Peering in that window."

Theodosia whirled around. There was a window there, all right, but no one was peering in. At least not now.

Glass was still thoughtful. "That's gotta be it," he muttered.

"Just delete the shot if you don't like it," Theodosia advised him. "In fact, I'd be delirious if you deleted *every* shot."

"Ha-ha," said Glass, giving a shrug, while still puzzling over the image. "I'll just count that as my artsy shot."

Angie Congdon was thrilled with both the food and the turnout. "I had no idea so many people would show up!" she gushed to Theodosia and Haley. "It's amazing what a few flyers can do."

"There were a couple of community event mentions on the radio, too," said Theodosia. "Which was nice since electronic media always garners attention."

"Oh," said Angie to Theodosia. "Did the person who was looking for you find you?"

"You mean Bill Glass?" asked Theodosia, as she hurriedly arranged more scones.

"No, there was a woman," said Angie. "Came in the back way, asked for you by name. I sent her over here . . ." Angie saw the look of concern that suddenly clouded Theodosia's face. "What? Something wrong?"

"Exactly what did this woman look like?" asked Theodosia.

Angie screwed up her face, trying to remember. "She was . . . uh . . . I don't know. Average height. Pleasant-looking." Angie waved a hand in front of her, fanning herself, looking flustered. "And . . . gosh I'm sorry to sound so ditzy and flaky, but there've been *so* many people through here tonight."

"That's okay," Theodosia told her. "Don't worry about it. Go charm your guests. Lead a tour or something."

"Is Angie okay?" asked Haley. "She seems kind of harried."

"Just lots going on," said Theodosia, still

wondering who'd come looking for her. Delaine coming back to harass her about tomorrow's fashion show? No, that wouldn't be right. Angie and Delaine knew each other.

"This is the last tray of sandwiches," said Haley. "Of both kinds. After that, we're out of luck."

"After that, we're out of here," responded Theodosia.

"This has been kind of fun, though," said Haley. "Kind of makes me want to go on tomorrow night's B and B tour. Check out some of the other places."

"That's what Drayton said, too," said Theodosia. "He's always wanted to poke his head inside the Rosewalk House B and B."

"Supposed to be fancy," said Haley. "With cool rose gardens and fountains out back. One of those hidden Charleston gardens."

Suddenly, Bill Glass was back and directly in their faces, looking cranky and a little panicked, too. "Did you guys see my camera?" he asked. "I set it down for one second and now it's gone!"

"Gone?" said Haley. She sounded disinterested veering toward bored. "What a shame."

"You don't have to be nasty about it," huffed Glass. "That camera cost me almost a grand." He threw a pleading look toward Theodosia. "Theo? You see anybody glom my camera?"

"Nope," said Theodosia, while all she could think was, *Rats, did Nadine get her sticky little fingers on Glass's camera?*

Forty minutes later the cupboard ran dry. They'd been cleaned out of sandwiches and scones and were down to the last dregs on tea.

Haley dragged the debris back into the kitchen, packed it all up in plastic bins, and together they toted it out to Theodosia's Jeep.

As Theodosia popped open the back hatch, Haley asked, "So when are you gonna get your fender and bumper ironed out?"

"Eventually," said Theodosia.

"You call your insurance agent?"

"That I did," said Theodosia.

"Make a police report?"

"Sort of," said Theodosia. "I talked to Tidwell."

"You think he's gonna bend over backward and file all the paperwork for you?" asked Haley. "Sheesh. He's probably forgotten about it."

"You're probably right," said Theodosia, drinking in the cool air and enjoying the darkness that wrapped around them like a soft, cashmere blanket. "Tell you what, Haley, you take the keys and drive back home. I'm going to walk."

"Really?"

"Sure," said Theodosia. "You head home and relax. Leave everything in back, we'll unload tomorrow."

"You going to wander down the block and take a look-see at your new place?" asked Haley.

"Maybe," said Theodosia. "Mostly I'm just going to enjoy a little quiet time."

"I hear you," said Haley, accepting the jingle of keys, then tossing them up and catching them. "But you take care, all right?"

"Will do," said Theodosia. She watched Haley climb into her Jeep, start the engine, then pull self-consciously away from the curb and proceed up the block. Taillights flared red and the turn signal clicked on, then Haley hung a left and disappeared from sight.

Theodosia exhaled slowly and turned back toward the Featherbed House. Guests still milled about on the front porch, every window blazed with lights. Gazing up at a second-story window, Theodosia noticed what was probably the last tour group going through the place, inspecting the high-ceilinged, elegant rooms that were painted a French palette of pale pink, ivory, and pale blue. They were probably marveling over the mounds of down comforters that graced each four-poster bed, too.

Better out here, Theodosia decided. The air was refreshing and the breeze fluttering in from the Atlantic carried a nip of salt and a dash of coolness. But not unpleasant. Theodosia tilted her head back and lifted a hand to massage her neck. Always the back of the neck. That's where she carried her tension. Probably time to hit the spa for a hot stone massage or some deep tissue work. Or maybe take a walk tonight, depending on how Earl Grey was feeling. It'd feel good to blow out the carbon and get some endorphins percolating.

Looking up at the sky, Theodosia saw puffy low clouds scudding along, with patches here and there where stars twinkled through. She tried to find a constellation, thought she might have spotted Cassiopeia, decided it was probably Orion. Then she let her mind wander, thinking about all the commercial fishermen who sailed the Carolina coast and sometimes ventured into the low-country bayous. How they probably depended on the stars for directional navigation. Or maybe they used GPS these days.

Who knew? Still, steering by the stars was a romantic notion.

Theodosia wandered back up the walkway, then followed a stone walkway around the side of the house and into the backyard where dozens of pillar candles sputtered low. It was a lovely yard, moody and evocative at night, replete with lush greenery, patio sitting area, and lovely little pond surrounded by judiciously placed boulders of blue granite that had been quarried and carted in from Winnsboro. She walked slowly to the free-form pond, hypnotically drawn by its dark, luminous reflection. Gazing down, Theodosia saw wriggling fish and something else shimmering at the bottom of the pond.

What was it? she wondered. Some sort of underwater light that wasn't working? Yeah, probably. Or, wait a minute, had someone haphazardly dropped one of Angie's good crystal glasses into the drink? Well, that wasn't good.

Getting down on her hands and knees, Theodosia placed her left hand on a large moss-covered rock for support and extended her right arm. She touched cool water, broke the surface with a minimum of ripples, and watched as tiny goldfish darted away from her intrusion. Reaching all the way down into the bottom of Angie's man-made pool, Theodosia's fingers grazed metal. She hesitated for a split second, then stretched her arm down a little deeper still, closing her hand around something that felt like it might be a transistor radio or cell phone.

And fished out what was left of Bill Glass's Nikon.

19

"You just missed seeing your seller," Tred Pascal told Theodosia. Standing atop a mound of dirt, wearing khaki shirt and slacks, he looked like he was ready to dig for the lost cities of Troy, rather than poke around Theodosia's backyard. But it was her yard all right. Birds tweeted and flitted from tree to bush, wondering what was going on. The sun burned down, golden and bright in an azure blue sky, promising another glorious early spring day.

"That's not really a problem," Theodosia told Tred. The seller, a somewhat surly lawyer by the name of Dougan Granville, wasn't exactly on her faves list. He was a little too slick for her taste, wore sharkskin suits, and, she suspected, might even have a bite worse than his bark.

"As you can see," said Tred, slightly effervescent now that they were actually starting work, "we're just staking out a grid."

"Just mind the magnolia tree, will you?" said Theodosia. "Take care with the root system." Drayton, who was a bonsai artist and gardening enthusiast, had once explained to her that the root system of a plant, any plant, mirrored below ground exactly what you saw above ground. And since the magnolia tree was large and bushy, Theodosia could only imagine that the root system was equally complex.

"We'll be careful," one of the student diggers assured her. "We've done this before."

"Okay," said Theodosia. "Thanks." She squinted at Tred. "You've got papers for me to sign?"

Back at the Indigo Tea Shop, Theodosia discovered that Drayton and Haley had already set up for morning tea.

"You don't need me," she told them. "You have morning prep down to a fine science. Tea Shop 101."

"Oh, we need you," said Drayton, as he popped a small pink tea candle into a glass teapot warmer. "When one thirty comes, you're going to be our point man."

Theodosia squinted at him, a crooked grin on her face. "What?"

"Point *woman*," Drayton corrected. "For

when, sigh, the *children* arrive."

"It's not only children that are coming," Theodosia told him. "Quite a few of the mothers will also be present. So there will be adult supervision."

"That's an enormous relief," was Drayton's snarky comment.

Theodosia reached out and gave him a conciliatory pat on the shoulder. "Don't worry," she said. "You'll do fine. Just be your own, immutable charming self."

"Are you kidding?" shrilled Haley, as she hurried in with a silver tray that held a dozen cut glass bowls filled with white poufs of Devonshire cream. "If Drayton really acts like himself, the self *we* deal with every day, he'll probably scare those kids to death."

"Thank you, Haley, for your kind and generous words of support," said Drayton, gazing at her with hooded eyes.

"On the other hand," said Haley, "maybe Drayton can lead by example and turn them all into proper little ladies and gentleman." At that she practically dropped to the floor, convulsed with laughter.

"I knew I should have confined myself to bed," muttered Drayton. "This entire day is going to be a veritable *trial.*"

"A tribulation," prompted Haley.

"No, it's not," said Theodosia, "but it will

270

be interesting. Think of this as another experience that will add to the fabric of our corporate culture." She glanced around the tea shop, glowing cozy and warm from the sun's morning rays that poured through the multipaned windows. The polished, pegged floor fairly gleamed, the tables sparkled with lead crystal glasses, pure white linens, and a mélange of bone china tea ware. The shelves and highboy that served as their gift area had been restocked with tins of tea, T-bath products, tea infusers, tea cozies, and tea timers. It was all so perfect that Theodosia was summarily stunned when her mind suddenly dredged up a vision of the Antiquarian Map Shop. The way it had looked the last time she visited seemed like a harsh contrast to her lovely shop.

Of course, the map shop was sadly without its owner now. And just as the sun shone brightly into the Indigo Tea Shop, gloominess had seemed to pervade the map shop.

But maybe, hopefully, she could do something to change that. Keep asking questions, continue to snoop around, try to find something that might point to Daria's killer. Somehow put into motion a *resolution*.

"Now what's on *his* mind?" muttered Drayton, gazing out one of the front windows, interrupting her thoughts.

"Who?" asked Theodosia.

Her question was answered almost immediately as the front door crashed open and Bill Glass stomped in.

"Oh," said Theodosia, touching a hand to her chest. "You got my message." Then she hurried across the floor to greet him.

Glass looked tired, cranky, and on edge. His photographer's vest hung on his frame and dark stubble shaded his face. "Yeah, I sure did," he told her. "Where is it?"

"You're welcome," said Theodosia, placing a hand on one hip and raising her eyebrows in a questioning gaze.

Glass bristled slightly, then said, "Yeah, okay. Thanks for pulling my camera out of the drink. Thanks for leaving a message with my answering service."

"You're welcome," Theodosia said again, this time much more graciously.

Drayton ducked behind the counter and grabbed the Nikon from the shelf where Theodosia had stashed it. "I was wondering whose camera this was. Figured it might be one of yours," he added as he handed it over to Glass. "Fine piece of equipment."

"Not if it's ruined," said Glass.

"What's the problem?" asked Drayton, who was a bit of a photography buff himself.

"Theo found it in the drink," explained Glass.

"The pond behind the Featherbed House," said Theodosia, translating.

"You don't say," said Drayton, surprised. He turned toward Glass. "Someone pinched it from you?"

"Guess so." Glass sighed. He peered at the Nikon speculatively, fiddled with the lens. "Doesn't look so good."

"See if you can revive it, will you?" asked Theodosia. "There's something I'd like to take a look at."

Both Glass and Drayton threw questioning glances at her.

"That photo you took last night," said Theodosia. "With the person looking through the window?"

Glass stared at her. "Yeah? What of it?"

"I think that might have been the person who stole your camera."

"What was that about?" asked Drayton, once Glass had stumped off. He stood at the counter, measuring spoonfuls of Sumatran black tea into a round floral teapot with a perky handle. Made by Meissen, the teapot had once been part of his private collection.

"Bill Glass snapped a photo of me last

273

night and happened to catch a kind of double image," said Theodosia. "I think someone was watching me through the back window."

"But it was an open house," said Drayton. "One that attracted a large crowd. So it could have been anyone."

"I don't think it was just anyone," said Theodosia. She'd pondered that notion the better part of the night and come to the conclusion that someone had been keeping tabs on her.

"So who do you think it was?" asked Drayton.

"If I could conjure a name and a face, I might get a bead on Daria's killer," said Theodosia.

"Now you're scaring me," said Drayton. He touched a hand to his blue-and-yellow-polka-dot bow tie and smoothed it nervously.

"Join the club," said Theodosia. "I've been jumpy ever since somebody tried to run me into that bridge embankment."

"So . . ." Drayton peered at her sharply. "You've made some assumptions as to the killer's identity?"

"Theodosia shook her head slowly. "That's what's so weird, because I really haven't. I mean, I've voiced a few minor suspicions to you and Haley . . . even to Tidwell . . . but nobody has popped up definitively on my radar screen."

"Maybe they have now," was Drayton's ominous response. "Only you have to figure out who it is."

"Not unless Glass can salvage that camera," said Theodosia. "Or I get a whole lot smarter."

"Guys," said Haley, clapping her hands together. "We've got a super busy day today, so I want to quickly go over the menu, okay?"

"As you wish, Haley," replied Drayton. He was standing behind the counter, arranging teapots, tea strainers, and tins of tea, off in his own fragrant and heady world of Assam, Darjeeling, Gunpowder Green, Yunnan, and Pouchong.

"For our breakfast cream tea," began Haley, "we have cherry scones and carrot cake muffins."

"And lunch?" asked Theodosia. "Early lunch, before the children's tea?"

"The Alice in Wonderland Tea," said Haley.

"Ooh," said Drayton, "the dreaded tea now has a theme. I think Haley's trying to intimidate me."

Haley ignored him. "Early lunch will be fruit salad with date nut bread, asparagus quiche, and chicken salad with chutney on cinnamon raisin bread. Each can be ordered as an entrée for seven ninety-five, or we can make up a kind of luncheon tasting plate consisting of all three for eight ninety-five."

"So we need to reserve the big table and try to get everyone out by one o'clock at the latest," said Theodosia.

"That's about the size of it," said Haley.

"I also have an announcement," said Drayton. "Concerning tea."

"Do tell," said Haley.

"Today we'll be brewing pots of American-grown tea," said Drayton. "American Classic black tea from the Charleston Tea Plantation here in our own backyard and a wonderful oolong from the Fairhope Tea Plantation in Fairhope, Alabama."

"Wonderful," said Theodosia. "I think our customers will enjoy those brews enormously."

Drayton pushed his half-glasses up with an index finger and gazed balefully at Haley. "And what is it you intend to serve at your so-called Alice in Wonderland tea?" he asked.

"That," said Haley, with a cock of her head and a twinkle in her eye, "is my little surprise."

Twenty minutes later they were buzzing with customers. Most of the tables were quickly occupied and Theodosia and Drayton began pouring tea and serving scones and muffins like crazy.

"Our customers are loving our home-grown teas," Drayton whispered to Theodosia as they swished past each other.

Of course they loved the teas, Theodosia thought to herself. Both teas had been grown on American soil, so a good deal of hard work and love had gone into the growing, pruning, and harvesting process. Plus, tea wasn't quite as natural a fit in this country as it was in places like China and India, where the tea-growing tradition had been handed down for several centuries.

Just as she was brewing a special-request single pot of lemon herbal tea, Theodosia glanced up to see Miss Kitty step through her front door. In her bright purple dress with a creamy yellow pashmina wrapped casually around her shoulders, there was no missing her. Drayton, unsuspecting soul, hurried over to greet Miss Kitty and was immediately swept up in her tidal wave of conversation.

"So excited to finally meet you," Miss Kitty burbled to Drayton as she grabbed onto his arm. "I've heard so much about you and your prodigious tea skills, but . . ." She stopped midsentence and gazed around, her bright eyes burning with curiosity. "What an adorable little shop! And so impressive that you brew such a huge variety of teas. Really amazing. And the aromas . . . all this time I thought my perfumery was rich with aromas, but this is over-the-rainbow heavenly, too!"

Since Drayton's face had acquired a slightly dazed expression, Theodosia hurried over to intercede. "Miss Kitty, hello."

Miss Kitty threw Theodosia a quick smile. "Hello, dear, I was just chatting with darling Drayton here and telling him what a lovely tea shop you folks have. Really darling, like something right out of the English Cotswolds." She hugged Drayton's arm possessively. "I'm assuming you have a table, dear fellow? It's just little old me this morning, but I simply can't wait to sample your tea and goodies."

"Drayton?" said Theodosia. "The table by the fireplace?" Theodosia figured they should put Miss Kitty where she'd be the least disruptive.

"Absolutely," agreed Drayton. He smiled down at Miss Kitty. "This way, madam."

Haley was suddenly at Theodosia's elbow.

"Who the heck is that?"

"That," said Theodosia in a low voice, "is the remarkable Miss Kitty. Cinnamon's aunt as well as the brains, and I assume money, behind Jardin Perfumerie."

"Brains, money, and brass," murmured Haley. "Miss Kitty looks like a lady who's used to getting her way."

"Strikes me that way, too," agreed Theodosia.

"And she's openly flirting with Drayton," added Haley. She sounded just this side of disapproving.

"Drayton can handle her," said Theodosia. "This isn't his first waltz around the dance floor."

Haley giggled. " 'Spose not."

"That's one crazy lady," Drayton whispered to Theodosia back at the counter. "It's like there's a cyclone whirring inside her head and random words just hurtle from her mouth."

Theodosia laughed silently, her shoulders shaking as she bent over a pot of tea.

"I mean it," said Drayton, chuckling a little himself. "And she wants to talk to you. Says it's of utmost importance."

"Me?" said Theodosia, straightening up. "I wonder what she wants?"

"Get over there," said Drayton, nudging

her. "Find out."

"Did Miss Kitty place an actual order?" asked Theodosia. "Or is she just here for conversation and general snoopiness?"

"Oh no, she ordered," said Drayton. "I'm putting together a plate for her now. So if you could be so kind as to deal with her . . ." Drayton hesitated. "And remain at her table until I deliver her tea and scone." He rolled his eyes. "Perhaps then she might be slightly less flirtatious."

But Miss Kitty wasn't a bit flirtatious when Theodosia approached her. In fact, she suddenly switched into tough-as-nails business mode.

"Exactly the person I need to talk to," said Miss Kitty, reaching a tiny birdlike hand across the table to firmly grasp Theodosia's arm.

"How can I be of help?" asked Theodosia, sliding into a chair, noting that Miss Kitty was surprisingly strong for her age and size.

"A favor," said Miss Kitty, her sharp eyes glittering.

"Ah," said Theodosia, relaxing. Miss Kitty was probably going to ask her to cater Jardin Perfumerie's upcoming grand opening, which shouldn't be a problem at all. Or perhaps ask her to serve tea and treats at a trunk show similar to the ones Delaine staged at Cotton Duck. Although she wasn't sure if perfumeries had actual trunk shows. Maybe . . . scent shows?

"It's about that map store next to me," said Miss Kitty, finally launching her conversational grenade. Her eyes were dead serious now, like a slumbering lizard that *appeared* to be in repose but was really itching to strike.

"The Antiquarian Map Store," said Theodosia. "Is that . . . a problem?"

"I want that space," Miss Kitty spat out. "And since you have a good relationship with the owner, I was hoping you might intercede for me."

Theodosia leaned back in her chair, trying to digest this request that had zoomed out of left field. "Unfortunately," she said, in a tight voice, "the owner is dead."

20

Miss Kitty waved an imperious hand, as if to brush off the insignificant fact of Daria's murder. "I know *that*. I meant the *new* owner. Whoever stands to inherit the place or is set to purchase it. You seem to know all the local denizens and stand in good stead with them, too. So I'd appreciate any help you can give me." She rapped her knuckles on the table as if to punctuate her sentence.

"I'm not sure what you're asking," said Theodosia, stalling. She knew exactly what Miss Kitty was asking, but her mind wasn't formulating a good response or even a decent-sounding excuse. Weasel words, as Haley would call them.

"For starters," said Miss Kitty, "you could help me negotiate a good price." She took a quick sip of tea and gave a wolfish grin. "The way I see it, that old place is distressed property now, so a sublease at a greatly reduced rate should be easy to negotiate." She pulled her napkin from her lap and touched it to her lips, leaving behind a smear of red. "Plus we're still in the middle of a tough economy, so . . ." She let her words trail off, but kept sharp eyes focused on Theodosia.

"You know," said Theodosia, turned off by Miss Kitty's rapacity, "you really should be talking to the building's owner about this. Or, better yet, enlist a commercial Realtor to determine if that space is even available, then have them handle all negotiations. Realtors take a commission, of course, but they often have the skills and know-how to strike a much more favorable deal."

"Oh, honey," said Miss Kitty, shaking her head in dismay, "I don't want to bother with commercial Realtors and paying commissions." She spat out the word *commissions* like it was cow manure. "I just want to do a little business deal. Keep it among friends, you know?"

Friends, thought Theodosia. *Really? Because it sure doesn't sound like friendship.* She was thinking of a few choice alternate descriptors, all plucked from the list of Seven Deadly Sins, when Drayton suddenly, blessedly, appeared at the table.

"I have a pot of cardamom tea, per your

request," Drayton told Miss Kitty. "Plus a fresh-baked scone with Devonshire cream and some lovely lemon curd." He set his tray down, then raised his eyebrows and stared fixedly at Theodosia. "And I certainly don't mean to interrupt, but, Theo, you do have an urgent phone call."

"Oh crap," said Missy Kitty, looking grumpy.

Saved by the bell, thought Theodosia as she quickly stood, murmured a hasty "excuse me," and dashed for her office.

Tred Pascal was on the line. "I have good news," he told her.

"You didn't find any more bones," said Theodosia. "You've finished and are packing up your tools of the trade, anxious to go home." *Wishful thinking on my part?* she wondered. *No, I'm pretty sure the whole bone ordeal is over. And thank heavens for that.*

"No!" exclaimed Tred, the line crackling with static. "We actually found a few more bones!"

"Please tell me you're joking," said Theodosia, her vision of a perfect end to the digging suddenly shattered. Sitting down hard in her desk chair, she stared at the new issue of *Tea: A Magazine* that lay on her desk. Wished with all her heart she could magically disappear into those pages and transport herself to some far-off, exotic tea plantation that was profiled inside.

"All in all, it's a rather exciting turn of events," enthused Tred.

"Sure it is," said Theodosia, without a single vestige of enthusiasm in her voice.

"Anyway," said Tred, "I just wanted to let you know. Looks like we'll be here for a while."

"Peachy," said Theodosia. "Just peachy."

"You don't look happy," said Drayton, when Theodosia finally emerged from her office.

Theodosia shook her head, as if shaking away a swarm of gnats. "The archaeologists found more bones."

Drayton grimaced. "Unfortunate."

"No kidding."

"Do they think it was an execution site?"

"Don't know," said Theodosia.

"So this means the archaeologists will continue digging?"

"For now," said Theodosia. "Yes."

"How long do you think it will take?"

Theodosia flapped her arms in frustration. "Who knows?" She wrinkled her nose, knowing she should try to relax, try to calm down. Getting upset wasn't going to help anything or anyone, least of all herself. She took a deep breath, hummed a quick

"Ommm," and asked, "So, how's Miss Kitty faring?"

Drayton peered over his tortoiseshell glasses with an owlish expression. "Bending the ear of everyone in her immediate vicinity. Whether they're interested in chitchatting with the old bat or not."

"She is a tough old girl," said Theodosia. Then thought, *But is there more to Miss Kitty than meets the eye?*

"Drayton," said Haley, flipping her straight blond hair back over her shoulders, "you've got to snap to and deliver checks. Try to move our customers out of here."

"They're paying customers," countered Drayton. "We can't just toss them out on their keesters. Besides, this is a tea shop. We're supposed to exude an air of genteel refinement — remember?"

"But I have to get ready for the children's tea," said Haley with a certain amount of stubbornness.

"*We* have to get ready," countered Drayton. "Which means we shall simply work around our good customers. That's really not a problem, is it? Or are you so obsessive-compulsive you need to have the tea room completely cleared?"

Haley thought for a few seconds. "Cleared

would be better."

"For you," said Drayton. "But not for everyone else. Now try to calm down and focus."

"Focus," repeated Haley, staring straight ahead with a glazed expression.

Drayton squinted at her. "That's right."

Haley continued to stared blankly.

"I'm not in the mood for games," said Drayton.

"But she is," said Theodosia, cruising past them with teapots in both hands. "Drayton, don't you know when Haley's putting you on?"

Haley blinked rapidly. "I am? I thought I was focusing."

"I know what you're trying to do," said Drayton, in a smooth voice. "You're trying to get me all discombobulated, right before the children arrive."

"Good call," shot back Haley.

"There will be payback for this," Drayton warned, a crafty expression stealing across his face. "You won't know when or how, but I intend to repay you in kind for all your craziness."

Haley faced Drayton with a lopsided grin. "Bring it on, big guy."

"Don't you have to check on the cakes, Haley?" asked Theodosia. "Drayton,

287

shouldn't you be setting up the large table?"

"I suppose I better get moving," said Haley. She stuck out her hand. "Sorry, Drayton. Friends?"

"You don't have a trick buzzer hidden in your palm, do you?" asked Drayton.

"Drayton!" exclaimed Haley. "Would I ever?"

"Yes!" exclaimed Theodosia and Drayton in unison.

"Oh my goodness!" said Theodosia, gazing at the carefully set tables. "This is simply amazing!" She'd just emerged from her office to do a final check on the tea room before the children and their moms arrived. "How did you . . . ?" she stammered. "When did you . . . ?" She looked from Drayton to Haley.

Drayton pointed at Haley. "She did it."

"You helped some," admitted Haley.

Theodosia pushed a fluff of auburn hair from her face and grinned from ear to ear. The four tables that had been set up were adorable beyond her wildest dreams. First off, everything carried an *Alice in Wonderland* theme. So there were oversized playing card placemats, little "drink me" bottles of fruit juice, and small white, fuzzy rabbits capering across the tablescape. Plus *Alice in*

Wonderland gift bags for all the children, and pink, purple, and green Mylar balloons bouncing everywhere.

"Where did you find the ceramic Cheshire cat centerpiece?" asked Theodosia, pointing at the fat and saucy grinning cat.

"Borrowed it from Leigh at the Cabbage Patch," said Drayton. "It's actually a cookie jar."

Theodosia turned to another table. "And the cake in the shape of a white rabbit with a fondant pocket watch . . . I know you made it, Haley, but did you decorate it, too?"

Haley executed a slight bow. "Indeed I did."

"And do I really see White Rabbit cups and saucers?" Theodosia asked.

"That's right," said Drayton. "Again, borrowed from our most generous neighbors."

"See?" said Haley. "Once Drayton put his mind to it, he went full steam ahead."

"Only because we made a commitment," said Drayton, holding up an index finger. "When you agree to host a tea party, no matter what the theme or circumstances, you're duty bound to do your best."

"And you most certainly did," said Theodosia.

"Now, if Drayton can only hang in there

for the actual party," added Haley.

But ten minutes later, when a dozen little girls and boys came scampering into the Indigo Tea Shop like a group of crazed space invaders, Drayton was the perfect gentlemen.

"That's right, take your seats," he told his youthful audience, as their mothers smiled on. "We have place cards at each setting, so find your name, then settle down."

Amidst giggling, scraping of chairs, and excited exclamations, all the young guests managed to get seated.

"Excellent," said Drayton. "And now, Miss Haley will come around and take your tea order. "Each of you has a bottle of apple juice in front of you, but we're also brewing hot cocoa as well as a very special tea. And I'm pleased to announce our first course will be gingerbread scones."

There were oohs and aahs, much like their adult customers, and then Drayton proceeded around the table with a Mad Hatter teapot.

"Is it really tea?" a young freckle-faced girl with braids asked him.

"A special tea today," Drayton told her. "Warm milk with a hint of vanilla bean and a dollop of tea."

"Will I like it?" she asked.

"My dear young lady," said Drayton, "if it does not please you I shall prepare something more to your liking."

"Thank you," she said in a small voice. "I'll try the tea."

"Good choice," said Drayton.

Then Haley appeared with a tray full of scones. "I hope you all like gingerbread scones," she said. "They're also stuffed with walnuts and apples and dusted with granulated pink sugar."

That brought a round of applause.

"Goodness," said Drayton, watching from the sidelines. "The little munchkins approve."

"You seem surprised," said Theodosia, who'd already had some experience with teddy bear teas and little princess teas.

"No," said Drayton, "I'm stunned."

While tea was being slurped and scones munched, Drayton stepped forward again. This time for an abbreviated lesson in etiquette.

"First point," he told them, "be sure you always settle your napkin into your lap." There were some surreptitious grabs for napkins, then all was quiet. "And when Miss Theodosia brings the tea trays out, be sure to say please and thank you," he reminded them. "Now, most of the foods we'll be serving today are finger foods, so it's perfectly acceptable to eat with your fingers. But, please. Take small bites. Even if a sandwich is small, kindly don't pop the entire thing into your mouth." He gazed around the table, noting the interested expressions. "Needless to say," he continued, "you never talk with your mouth full. And if you want something passed to you, just ask politely, instead of reaching." Firing a stiff glance at two boys who were smothering giggles, he added, "And never, ever, engage in rude discourse at the table — especially such things as a burping contest." He lasered his gaze at the boys. "That means you two fellows!"

Haley nudged Theodosia. "Never engage in rude discourse? He *is* trying to turn them into miniature Draytons."

"But it's working," said Theodosia. "Look, they're raising their hands and asking him questions. They think Drayton's the neatest thing since sliced bread."

"Go figure," said Haley, shaking her head.

Once the detritus from the scones had been cleared away, Drayton poured another round of "tea" and Theodosia and Haley brought out tea trays filled with sandwiches.

"Now you're in for a treat, children," said

Drayton. He smiled at Theodosia. "Miss Theodosia is going to tell us what Miss Haley has prepared for us today."

"I think you're going to enjoy it," said Theodosia. "We have peanut butter and jelly tea sandwiches, fruit kabobs, cream cheese and raisin triangle sandwiches, petite cheese tarts, and pretzels coated with honeyed yogurt."

Halfway through the tea, Drayton even did one of his famous recitations for the children. An abbreviated poem he'd picked up somewhere and modified.

Let's all sit down together and have a cup
    of tea — a nice warm cup of friendship
Brewed with love by me.

Dessert consisted of the white rabbit cake served with fudge ripple ice cream as well as sugar cookies in the shapes of teapots and clocks.

Afterward, during a rousing game of pin the tail on the white rabbit, when everyone was struggling to keep order, the phone rang.

"Hello?" said Theodosia, turning her back to the tea room. She could hardly hear above the din.

"Theodosia?" came a quiet voice. It was

Aunt Libby.

"Hang on, Aunt Libby," Theodosia told her. "I'm going to move into my office." She gestured for Haley to hang up once she'd grabbed the extension, then headed into her office.

"Okay, I'm back," said Theodosia, plopping down into her chair. "Can you hear me?"

"I can now," said Aunt Libby. "But what on earth have you got going there? It sounds like an awfully wild tea party!"

"You have no idea," murmured Theodosia, wondering how they were going to get the crunchy, pink sugar granules out from between the floorboards. Supersonic vacuum cleaner probably.

"I don't mean to put pressure on you, dear, but I was wondering if you'd made any progress," said Aunt Libby. "I was visiting Sophie this morning and she seemed so awfully down. Fallon was there, too. Poor girl isn't faring much better."

"You're such a good friend to Sophie," said Theodosia. "Fallon, too."

"I'm trying," said Aunt Libby. "But it's so difficult not *knowing.* The police tell Sophie they're working the case, but . . ."

"They are working it," said Theodosia. *Just not fast enough.*

"Made any inroads at all?" Aunt Libby inquired in a tentative voice.

"I'm still talking to people, asking around," said Theodosia. She really didn't want to tell Aunt Libby about the accident at the bridge a couple nights ago. It would only worry the poor dear.

"Well, you're a real champ to take this on," said Aunt Libby, encouragement in her voice.

"I haven't done that much," said Theodosia, feeling a tiny twinge of guilt.

"I have faith," said Aunt Libby. "I believe in justice and I believe in *you.*"

"Thank you," said Theodosia. She hesitated. "Still it might not hurt to say a prayer or two."

"I am praying, dear heart," said Aunt Libby. "I truly am."

21

The first thing Theodosia saw when she strolled into Cotton Duck was an elevated runway covered in white Mylar. The second thing she noticed was a knot of ultra-chic, beautifully coiffed women sipping flutes of champagne.

Theodosia had visited Cotton Duck millions of times, but this newly revamped Parisian-looking atelier looked nothing like the Cotton Duck of old. Besides the new earth-tone sisal carpeting, there were tons of green palm trees, low hanging, white-enameled chandeliers, and pinpoint spotlights that drew the eye to the various clothing racks and displays of accessories.

The clothes were the same fluttery evening gowns, featherlight silk tops, and cotton slacks and T-shirts Cotton Duck was know for. Plus new lines of designer pieces, couture handbags, giant status rings, and some very exotic-looking lingerie.

Then Theodosia spotted Delaine in her cadmium-blue-and-yellow short shift dress, flitting from group to group like an overcaffeinated bumblebee and noted that while her shop may have morphed into a cool, sophisticated boutique, Delaine still projected over-the-top enthusiasm.

Catching sight of Theodosia, Delaine threw back her head and screamed, "The-o-dosia!" Elevating the word to an eardrum-bursting pitch. She bulldozed her way through the crowd, grabbed Theodosia's arm in a viselike grip, and hissed, "You didn't dress up. I thought for sure you'd be more dressed up."

"I came from work," explained Theodosia, indulging in a little white lie. Actually, after the kids and moms had all gone home, after the tea shop had been cleared and readied for yet another day, she'd run upstairs and changed into what she'd deemed was a fashionable pair of pale yellow slacks paired with a cream-colored camisole and sporty, cream jacket. But even with the addition of long gold chains, her outfit apparently didn't pass muster with the fashion-conscious Delaine.

"There are serious *society* ladies here

today," Delaine told her emphatically. "Come to see my fashion show and view my expanded shop and new lingerie boutique." She pinched Theodosia's arm again. "There's a *reason* I'm outfitted head to toe in Yves Saint Laurent."

"A great-looking outfit," agreed Theodosia, surveying Delaine's lush silk dress. Forty gazillion silkworms had probably given their lives for it. "And I'm sure very expensive."

"You have no idea!" said Delaine.

"But on the plus side," added Theodosia, "you probably didn't have to pay retail."

"Uh . . ." said Delaine, amazingly at a loss for words. Then she said, "Oh *you*. But . . . you showed up, Theo. And that counts for a lot."

"Glad to hear it," drawled Theodosia. "I was beginning to worry."

"There's just a teensy little issue," began Delaine, looking serious now, her voice taking on the tenor of a surgeon addressing the family of a seriously ill patient. "A teensy, weensy problem."

"Okay," said Theodosia.

"One that I hope won't bother you."

"Try me," said Theodosia.

Delaine drew a deep breath. "Even though you are my dearest, bestest, closest friend,

I'm afraid we had to seat you in the second row."

"Oh no!" said Theodosia, pretending to be shocked.

Delaine nodded soberly. "I know, I know, Nadine and I hated to bump you, it practically *killed* us, but that's how the seating chart shook out. The thing of it is, it's critical we put the really important customers up front." She looked sorrowful, but firm. "Business, you know."

"I understand completely," said Theodosia, who really didn't care which row she was seated in. Who would have preferred to be elsewhere this afternoon.

"I *knew* you'd understand," Delaine gushed with relief. "I knew that you of all people wouldn't grouse and complain about being seated in the second tier."

"I can live with it," Theodosia told her, because it sure wasn't the worst thing that had happened to her this week.

"You're such a dear," said Delaine, administering a quick air-kiss. "Now you just toddle off and find your seat — your name's on a card somewhere — while I go make nice with the rest of my guests."

"Okaaaaay," Theodosia muttered as she gazed about Delaine's renovated shop. Which, she had to admit, did look rather spectacular.

"We meet again," a male voice murmured in Theodosia's ear.

Theodosia whirled around to find Bill Glass staring at her, a bemused expression on his face.

"What are you doing here?" Theodosia demanded.

Glass shrugged. "Playing photographer again," he said, touching the Canon that hung around his neck, a camera that Theodosia assumed must be his backup camera. Glass jerked his head at Delaine as she flitted about her shop. "*She* called me. Practically begged me to cover her fashion show."

"First the Chocolatier Fest, now this," said Theodosia. "Is this really in your line of work?"

"Nah," said Glass, "I just hang out to ogle all the great-looking women."

Theodosia raised an eyebrow.

"Hard to get the really hard-core, gritty stuff these days," admitted Glass. "Hard to be timely when everything's splattered all over the Internet within minutes." He sighed. "Seems like more and more I'm falling back on photos and articles about regular, old everyday events."

"That's not completely bad," Theodosia told him. "At least it's honest reporting."

"Just not as much fun," said Glass.

Theodosia reached a finger up and tapped the Canon slung around his neck. "How did your other camera, the Nikon, fare? Ever get it to work?"

Glass shook his head. "Nah. It's completely trashed."

"Couldn't get anything at all?" asked Theodosia. "I was really hoping you could pull up that double image thing from last night."

"Not gonna happen," said Glass. He stepped aside, let the hired DJ in his black leather jacket and matching chain bracelets push by them. "Classy event," he said to Theodosia, flashing a wicked grin.

"We should probably find our seats," suggested Theodosia.

Together they pushed their way through the crowd, eyed an ocean of white folding chairs that each had a name card tacked to the back, then finally located their respective seats. Theodosia's was in the middle of the second row; Glass was almost directly behind her.

Everyone else seemed to have the same idea, because suddenly there was a run on chairs. When the dust settled, a few unhappy guests were left standing, like a contentious game of musical chairs. Bill Glass, as exasperating as he usually was, suddenly scrounged a modicum of manners and offered up his chair.

Then the lights dimmed, a buzz of excitement filled the show room, and the pulsing beat of "Sweet Dreams" by the Eurythmics suddenly blasted from the speakers.

The first model burst onstage to huge applause. Wearing a short black dress with heroic shoulders, she clomped down the runway like she owned it, staring fiercely ahead.

The music pulsed louder.

Sweet dreams are made of this
Who am I to disagree?

The second model swished out in tight white slacks and a belly-grazing shirt, silver chains swinging, large bangle bracelets clanking.

Swinging hips and pouty lips, Theodosia decided. That seemed to be the MO for all these models. Still, they looked elegant yet breezy, showing off the clothes with great panache. Just the thing to intrigue the audience and maybe even stimulate sales.

Theodosia leaned back in her chair, enjoying the show. The music was thumping loud, the models were totally into it, and the guests seemed to be grooving, too.

Four minutes in and twelve outfits later, the DJ segued to a second tune. "Beautiful" by Moby. A little slower, a little more elegant, a little more haughty in atmosphere, but still amped at full volume.

Look at us, we're beautiful
All the people push and pull

Theodosia remembered that particular song from the soundtrack of *The Devil Wears Prada*. It had imparted a powerful statement. Still did for this show. Glancing around, she realized that many of the women around her were making little notes. Probably jotting down what they were going to purchase or special order later. Should she make notes, too? Maybe yes, especially since a swinging black jacket with a diagonal brass zipper had really caught her eye. But good.

Leaning forward, Theodosia reached into her cocoa-colored leather bag that rested in a puddle on the floor. As she did, she squiggled sideways in her chair and her eyes fell upon a woman sitting in the row ahead of her. A woman who looked strangely familiar.

Hmm?

As Theodosia continued to peer down the row, curious, she tried to dredge up a name to go along with that face.

She squinted again and was suddenly gob-smacked with a jolt of recognition.

Oh no, it can't be . . . can it?

Was it Beth Ann? Jory's Beth Ann? The wacked-out girlfriend he'd been previously engaged to? The one Jory claimed was no longer part of his life?

Clearly Beth Ann still was in his life! Because she was here! Sitting front and center at Delaine's spring fashion show. In Charleston. Not Beth Ann's ghost or even a reasonable facsimile thereof, but Beth Ann in the flesh.

The question was . . . why? What was she doing here?

As Theodosia stared with burning curiosity, a million questions zoomed through her brain like chase lights on a movie marquee. Then Beth Ann turned slightly in her seat, twisted her head, and in the dim light, with colored strobes flashing, suddenly met Theodosia's gaze full on.

Startled, caught in the act of staring, Theodosia's initial instinct was to be polite. A smile flickered at her lips and then . . . *ka-pow!* She was knocked back by Beth Ann's cold, icy glare!

What? Why is she . . . ? I mean . . . what is her problem anyway?

Straightening up in her chair, eyes riveted on the runway now, Theodosia fought to compose herself. Not an easy task when someone's shooting chilly daggers at you with their eyes. Or staring at you like they wished you were dead.

Let it go, Theodosia told herself. *Don't worry about Beth Ann.*

But she did worry. In fact, the longer Theodosia sat there, staring at the kaleidoscope of models and colored lights, letting throbbing music wash across her but not really hearing it, the more nervous she became.

Nerves have a curious way of running rampant, of jangling all sorts of emotions and what-ifs. And suddenly Theodosia found herself terrified.

For one thing, since it was quite obvious Beth Ann was camped somewhere in Charleston, then maybe Drayton really had seen her at the Blessing of the Fleet Wednesday night.

And if Beth Ann was still consumed with anger about losing Jory, then maybe Beth Ann was the crazy person who bashed in her Jeep and tried to run her and Earl Grey off the road!

Oh man, this isn't good.

Theodosia jiggled her leg, cleared her throat, and squirmed in her seat as her mind raced crazily.

Could it have been Beth Ann who was peeping in the window last night? Could Beth Ann have stolen Bill Glass's camera because . . . because she was afraid her image had been captured? Yeah, maybe.

Standing abruptly, Theodosia scurried down her row of chairs, in the opposite direction from Beth Ann, bumping knees and whispering "excuse me" all the way. She came out near the end of the runway, ducked behind a stand of klieg lights and then behind a three-panel screen with a trompe l'oeil design of the Champs-Elysées painted on it.

Putting up a hand to still her rapidly beating heart, Theodosia once again asked herself the all-important question, *What's going on?*

Because, just for openers, this had been one wacked-out week. Daria Shand murdered, strange bones turning up in her backyard, her Jeep run off the road by some nutcase, a stalker at the Featherbed House.

Was everything connected or just some of it? If so, how to put the pieces together? The pieces that counted.

Okay, Theodosia thought to herself, let's start with Daria's murder, the night of the back-alley crawl. Detective Burt Tidwell had made the astonishing remark that maybe she'd been the killer's intended victim.

She'd blown it off with a certain amount of anger and angst, but hadn't really taken him seriously.

Until now.

If Tidwell, smart ex-FBI guy and homicide detective that he was, had seen that as a possible angle, then maybe it *was* a legitimate angle. Maybe Tidwell's words had been prophetic; maybe he'd picked up a vibe that she'd missed completely.

Did that mean Beth Ann had murdered Daria Shand? Theodosia wondered. *Fully thinking that Daria was really her?* Possible. But not entirely probable unless . . . unless Beth Ann had been turned into a crazed stalker-killer because Jory jilted her!

Yowza. Got to talk to somebody about this. Have to talk to . . .

"Theodosia!" came a loud whisper. "Why are you crouching back here? Who are you hiding from?" Delaine had slipped up behind her and was peering with great suspicion, as if she'd just caught her in the act of shoplifting. "More important, why aren't you watching the show?"

307

"I . . . something startled me," said Theo-dosia, fumbling for words.

"In the show?" hissed Delaine, her voice tinged with disbelief. "On stage?"

"No," said Theodosia clutching Delaine's arm. "Someone here. A guest. A woman who scares the bejeebers out of me."

Delaine cocked her head. "What are you talking about? *Who* are you talking about? I'm sorry, Theo, you're not making sense at all."

"I'll show you," said Theodosia, plucking at Delaine's sleeve and peering around the screen. "*That* woman."

Delaine squinted into the somewhat rau-cous crowd of fashionistas who were clap-ping and responding to Rocky, the DJ, on stage. "Can you be a little more specific?"

"Front row, sixth from the end," said Theodosia, waggling a thumb at Beth Ann. "That one."

"Oh," said Delaine, stepping back behind the screen, keeping her voice low. "She's a new customer. But a very good customer I might add. She's already preordered almost two thousand dollars' worth of designer clothing."

"You can't be serious," said Theodosia. Beth Ann had money? She didn't strike Theodosia as having a good deal of disposable income at all.

"Just be careful," Theodosia warned, a cold tingle running up her spine. "That woman is scary-weird."

"Define scary-weird," said Delaine, bunching her perfectly arched eyebrows together. "You mean like she might be over the limit on her charge card or something?"

"No, I mean she's a stalker!"

"Oh," said Delaine, visibly relaxing. "You had me scared for a minute."

"Delaine!" said Theodosia. "Did you just hear what I said?"

"Yes, dear, that the young lady's a stalker." She glanced at her watch, a fancy, jewel-encrusted Chopard. "Now *please* keep your voice down. My grand finale's set to begin in less than two minutes! Just think, fifteen models strutting down the runway in one glorious burst of glitz and glam!" She hugged herself with glee. "And Rocky's going to play the opening track from *Sex and the City*."

"You're incorrigible, Delaine."

Delaine peered at her. "That's a good thing, right?"

"Sure," said Theodosia.

"Theodosia," hissed Delaine. "In case you haven't noticed, I have a major event taking place! Society women are present! Along with a scattering of trophy wives and wives of millionaires! Do you have any idea how critical these women are to my business? I'm sorry, but it can't always be about you!"

As Theodosia turned in frustration, her eyes fell upon Bill Glass. He'd hurried to the end of the runway, undoubtedly getting ready to line up a key shot. Theodosia hissed and waved a hand at him.

Glass turned, saw her, did a double-take, and touched a finger to his chest. Me?

Theodosia nodded vehemently. Yes, you.

Glass shuffled back to where she was semi-hiding. "What's up?"

"You see that woman sitting there?" whispered Theodosia. "The blond in the front row wearing the red suit?"

Bill Glass peered at Beth Ann, said, "Yeah."

"I want you to take her picture."

Glass made a rude, dismissive sound. "She's nothing special."

"I need to e-mail a photo of her to Detective Burt Tidwell," Theodosia told him. "So please stop being a lunkhead and just do what I ask."

"Why?" asked Glass, challenging her.

"Because I think she might be the one who stole your camera last night," said Theodosia. *And could be responsible for other strange goings on as well.*

Fumbling for his Canon, Glass sputtered, "Holy shi—"

"Shhh," warned Theodosia, putting a finger to her mouth. "Don't make a big deal about it. Please just *do* it."

22

While Bill Glass dodged his way around Cotton Duck, hopefully getting a few good shots of Beth Ann, Theodosia made her way to the front door and stepped out onto the street. With a bright Charleston sun shimmering down through rustling palm fronds and gently dappling her shoulders, she plucked her cell phone from her bag and dialed Jory's number.

When Jory came on the line, she said in a clipped tone of voice, "This is Theodosia. Where are you?"

Jory was both startled and befuddled. "Excuse me?" he responded. "What? *Theo?*"

"Yes, it's me," said Theodosia, "and I'm waiting, rather impatiently I might add, for you to tell me exactly where you are!"

Now Jory sounded even more flustered. "I'm in New York. At my office. Why? Where are you?"

"I'm in Charleston where I've always

been. Where I will continue to be. But I have a major news flash for you, my friend." She hesitated, letting her outrage build into a nice head of steam. "Are you sitting down?"

"Yes," said Jory. "What's this all about? I have to run to a meeting in about two minutes."

"You might want to cancel it," Theodosia told him. "Because while you are sitting fat and sassy in your high-rent law office somewhere on the island of Manhattan, your crazy girlfriend is perched ten chairs away from me at a fashion show!"

"What?" exclaimed Jory. Papers rustled, something clunked loudly — a chair going over backward? — and he said, "What?" for the second time.

"You heard me," said Theodosia. She knew she was gritting her teeth and fought to stop before she gave herself a permanent case of TMJ. "Beth Ann is here. In Charleston."

"Doggone," muttered Jory. He sounded confused, maybe even a little outraged. Theodosia was expecting some sort of commiseration, apology, or at least a stumbling explanation, but instead, his next words stunned her. "I knew something like this was bound to happen."

"What!" cried Theodosia, her heart suddenly beating out of her chest. "What are you talking about?" She gripped her cell phone tighter, aware her knuckles had turned white. Wished Jory were standing in front of her right now so she could bonk him on the head. "I want an explanation and it better be good. No, let me rephrase that. It better be stellar." She walked a few paces, moved out into the street where she could scream at Jory without upstaging Delaine's grand finale. Without being stared at by local fashion mavens.

"Beth Ann has been staying at my apartment over on Ashley Street," explained Jory, sounding high-pitched and nervous now. "And I can't seem to get her to leave."

"Excuse me?" said Theodosia. *What on earth is he talking about? And, did I hear correctly? He kept his apartment? Or did he get a new one? Was I really in love with this clown?*

Jory let loose an audible sigh. "It's a long story."

"Please," said Theodosia, biting off her words. "I have time."

"Beth Ann and I were planning to be married," Jory explained hastily, "and then we unplanned it. But Beth Ann never seemed to comprehend or completely accept the

314

breakup part. And this last time I came down to Charleston on business, she flew down to be with me."

"To be with you," said Theodosia.

"Yes," said Jory. "To try to patch things up, talk me into taking her back."

"And that's when she moved into your apartment," said Theodosia.

"Not really moved in," said Jory. "More like planted herself, like a solid, immovable object."

"Uh . . . did you try asking her to leave?"

"I tried *telling* her to leave," said Jory. "I tried to physically shove her out the door. But I didn't have any luck."

"You should have given her the old heave-ho," said Theodosia. "Like you gave me."

"That's so unfair," moaned Jory.

"Deal with it," snapped Theodosia. She drew breath, let it out slowly, watched a tour bus drive by with a sign on the side panel that said, SEE HAUNTED CHARLESTON BY NIGHT! Maybe there should also be a sign that said, SEE THEODOSIA GO POSTAL! She tried to pull her thoughts together then and regroup. "So . . . you honestly couldn't get rid of Beth Ann?"

"I tried everything," said Jory. "But she stuck like a burr. Still is, I guess."

"Listen to me, Jory," said Theodosia, "this

isn't just a case of puppy love gone awry. Or star-crossed lovers. There's a good chance this whole Beth Ann thing has morphed into something more serious. For one thing, I'm pretty sure she's been stalking me."

"I can't believe Beth Ann would do that," replied Jory.

"She would and she is," said Theodosia. *Is he not listening to me?*

"Oh man," moaned Jory.

"The really bad news," Theodosia went on, "is that there's a possibility Beth Ann is involved in a major crime."

"Like what? Give me some facts!"

"I need to speak to Detective Tidwell first," said Theodosia. "But, trust me, I will get back to you."

"You can't leave me like this . . ." said Jory.

But Theodosia thumbed the Off button on her phone before Jory could finish his sentence, then dropped the phone into her bag. She needed more information — and maybe even police cooperation — before she leveled any charges against Beth Ann. But once she talked to Tidwell, pointed him in the right direction, maybe all the components would fall into place. Maybe justice would finally be served.

Stepping back inside the door of Cotton Duck, Theodosia saw that the show had ended and the ensuing party was pretty much a madhouse. Models mingled with customers, clothes were flying everywhere, and Rocky was still up on stage spinning music. Delaine and her assistant, Janine, were nowhere to be seen. Neither was Beth Ann.

And that was good, Theodosia decided. Even though she felt fairly secure, surrounded by gobs of people, she didn't want to mess with Beth Ann. Not at this juncture.

But Theodosia did bump into Bill Glass.

"Did you get the photo?" she asked him.

Glass nodded. "Quite a few. That's what you wanted, right?"

"Perfect," breathed Theodosia. "Now I want you to e-mail them to Detective Burt Tidwell. You know who he is?"

Glass nodded.

Digging in her bag, Theodosia found her wallet and pulled out Tidwell's business card. "Here."

Glass glanced at the e-mail address and said, "Okay. I can remember that."

"Excellent," said Theodosia.

Glass peered at her expectantly. "This is about more than just my camera, isn't it?"

"Yes, it really is," admitted Theodosia.

"You gonna give me the full story?"

"When I unravel the full story," said Theodosia, as someone tapped her on the shoulder, "you'll be the first to know." She spun around, bracing for a face-to-face confrontation with Beth Ann, but it was Delaine's nutty sister, Nadine, who stood there grinning like a manic windup toy.

"Theodosia," enthused Nadine, "what did you think of the show? Wasn't it fantastic? Almost as good as Fashion Week in New York!"

"Really wonderful," said Theodosia.

"You don't sound very enthusiastic," said Nadine, managing a little pout.

"Probably because I'm still too stunned for words," said Theodosia.

"Any piece in particular catch your eye?" Nadine prodded. Theodosia saw that Nadine was holding a small notebook. "Because I get twenty percent commission on any orders placed today."

"I'm kind of in a hurry, Nadine," said Theodosia, starting to back out of the store.

Nadine's pout was back with a vengeance. "It won't take but a second," Nadine told her, sticking like glue.

"No," said Theodosia, and this time she put some backbone into it. "Not now, not today."

Out the door for the second time, Theodosia walked hurriedly to her car. She climbed in, locked the doors, glanced back over her shoulder. She didn't relish the notion of Beth Ann following her out, trying to engage her in conversation. Some phony little chitchat about bumping into each other, about Jory, about some imagined problem or betrayal. Then — *bap* — just like that, Beth Ann might do something nutty. Or murderous.

But there was no sign of Beth Ann.

Theodosia drove slowly down Church Street, checking her rearview mirror a couple of times, then headed into the heart of the historic district, finally ending up in front of her soon-to-be home.

Sitting in her car, gazing at a riot of green plants tumbling down the brick walkway that led to her front door, studying the wrought-iron fence that pushed up against a tangle of wild dogwood and crepe myrtle, she called Burt Tidwell.

It took a Herculean effort to go through the various gatekeepers and get Tidwell on the phone, but finally she had his ear. Quickly backgrounding Tidwell on Beth Ann, she told him about running into her today, the possible photo of her from last night, then voiced the very suggestion he'd put forth the night of the murder: "What if I really was the intended victim? What if someone mistook Daria, with her curly red hair and gray wool cloak, for me?"

Suddenly, Theodosia had his undivided attention.

"And this woman, Beth Ann, has been in town how long?" Tidwell asked, his voice a low growl.

"A week, ten days," said Theodosia. "Which gave her plenty of time to stew about Jory, lurk in the alley behind my tea shop, and maybe even decide to kill me."

"And end up strangling Daria Shand by mistake," said Tidwell. He said it slowly, as though he wasn't quite convinced now, merely chewing on the words.

"Yes," said Theodosia. "It's all possible, isn't it? I mean, you were the one who came up with that theory from the get-go."

"But now we find ourselves with additional suspects," said Tidwell.

"Well, I know that," countered Theodosia. "Any of which could be the guilty party. Still, I'm putting my money on Beth Ann."

"It doesn't quite work that way," said Tidwell.

"But you'll look into it, won't you?" Theodosia asked, suddenly gripped with a rising tide of panic. "You'll talk to her? Interrogate her?"

"You want me to beat her with a rubber hose, too?" asked Tidwell.

"I want you to *investigate,*" said Theodosia. "Do what you do best."

Once again Theodosia thumbed the Off button on her phone, feeling angry, frustrated, and a little bereft. She sat in her Jeep, watching the sunlight seep away, noticing how dark and unoccupied her cottage looked in the muted green of the late afternoon.

Going to change all that, she told herself. Once she moved in there'd be Tiffany lamps glowing, the aroma of fresh-baked scones, and real warmth in the house.

Tromping up the front walk, Theodosia parted a large bush and headed around to the back side of the house.

Tred and another young archaeologist, a young woman, were just packing up their tools for the day.

"Hey," Tred said, when he saw her. "I was wondering if you'd swing by again."

"How's it going?" Theodosia asked.

"Good," said the young woman. "Great." She was tall and skinny with tightly curled brown hair and the unbridled enthusiasm of a twenty-two-year-old.

Tred, more reserved, shrugged his shoulders. "We went down a couple more feet — nothing."

"That's good news, right?" said Theodosia.

"Maybe for you," said Tred.

23

"Look at the quality of these pieces," marveled Drayton. "A bombé Louis XV commode along with a fine Italian marquetry desk. Both quite distinguished."

They were standing in the library of the Rosewalk House, one of the B and Bs that had thrown open its doors to the public this Friday evening.

"I'm in love with that bronze-and-crystal candelabra," Theodosia told him.

"The collection of leather-bound books isn't bad, either," said Drayton, perusing the floor-to-ceiling shelves. "What does this place charge per night?" he wondered. "Everything is so Old World and elegant."

"What I want to know," said Theodosia, "is who do they get to guard all these goodies?" She glanced at the colorful brochure she'd been handed at the front door, then turned her attention to Drayton. Just as they'd planned, they'd met here some ten minutes ago. Of course, Theodosia hadn't wasted any time filling Drayton in about seeing Beth Ann at the fashion show. Breathlessly, she'd told him about calling Jory, then finding out that Beth Ann, his former fiancée, was ensconced in Jory's Charleston apartment.

Drayton was still mulling over this strange news as he eyed the various antiquities. "Nice rose medallion pitcher," he muttered, then asked, "Are you quite sure Jory was referring to the same woman?"

Theodosia nodded.

"The blond lady he was engaged to?" continued Drayton. "The one who overimbibed in Pinot Grigio at the Masked Ball?"

"Same girl," said Theodosia. "Beth Ann. Specifically mentioned her by name."

"Huh," said Drayton. "Same one. So maybe I did see her that night."

"Maybe so," said Theodosia. "You'll be happy to know she's still as charming as a rattlesnake." *And maybe just as dangerous.*

"And she's holed up in Jory's apartment."

"So he claims," said Theodosia.

"Like some kind of squatter," said Drayton, making it sound slightly sordid.

"Something like that," agreed Theodosia.

"I take it you called Detective Burt Tidwell immediately?" asked Drayton. "Expressed your deep concern? Explained that per-haps . . ."

"First thing I did," said Theodosia. "Right after I got off the phone with Jory."

"What was Tidwell's response?"

"He said he'd look into it," said Theo-dosia.

Drayton was taken aback. "That's it? That's all?"

"That's it," said Theodosia. "Disappoint-ing, no?"

"Disappointing, yes," agreed Drayton. "If there's a possibility this Beth Ann person is completely unhinged, she shouldn't be wandering around Charleston. Shouldn't be stalking people." He held Theodosia's eyes for a long moment, the subtext being, *she could be stalking you.*

"Exactly," said Theodosia. "Because the very real possibility does exist that she confused me with Daria."

"And murdered the wrong woman," said Drayton. "Just like Tidwell suggested at the very beginning."

"Chilling," said Theodosia.

"If this Beth Ann person is somehow involved in Daria's murder, then she should be cooling her heels in a jail cell. Dreaming up excuses to tell her attorney," sniped Drayton.

"I think," said Theodosia, "that most attorneys are fairly skilled at coming up with excuses on their own."

They wandered through the dining room, which was dramatic and elegant, the walls painted a deep emerald green, tall windows covered in gold damask draperies. A long dining table had a dozen Chippendale ladder-back chairs parked at it.

"How'd you like to eat your toast and jammy here?" asked Drayton.

"It's awfully formal," said Theodosia. Though Theodosia was no stranger to fine dining or elegant surroundings, she preferred the coziness of a smaller space. Still, this was a grand old dowager mansion that had been converted to a bed-and-breakfast, and the guests who stayed here were probably charmed to pieces.

"You want to take the upstairs tour?" asked Drayton, peering at her with slightly hooded eyes that conveyed his disinterest.

"Not if you don't," said Theodosia.

"Good," said Drayton. "Then let's push our way through this crowd and follow the hallway out to the back garden. That's what I'm most curious about."

"The rose garden," said Theodosia, as they descended curved, wide brick steps and saw the beautifully cultivated rose garden spread out before them. "Wonderful." Lights, luminaries actually, marked the edges of the patio and various paths. Rose bushes of all different species and colors were arranged in a large, pie-shaped pattern with brick walkways between them. An imposing brick wall at the rear of the property was a jungly jumble of small, pink climbing roses. White Greek statuary — modern, not old — had been installed throughout the garden.

"Isn't this grand?" remarked Drayton. "Sometimes I think about selling all my bonsai trees and starting over with roses. Dig up my backyard and cultivate exotic varieties. Perhaps Multiflora or Cherokee roses, all wild and overgrown like you see growing among tumbled-down ruins of an old abbey."

"Have you been reading Bram Stoker again?" Theodosia asked.

Drayton gave a wry smile as they headed for a black wrought-iron table and chairs. "But the thing is, I adore my bonsai, especially the tiny forests and windswept trees. And I enjoy the Zen-like feeling they impart. Hence my new fascination with feng shui."

"Why not grow both?" proposed Theodosia as she slid into one of the wrought-iron chairs. "Yin and yang? Look at my yard. I have a garden, a pond, and an archaeological dig."

"Say," said Drayton, leaning forward. "How's that going?"

"I stopped by earlier and they hadn't unearthed a single T-Rex bone or velociraptor tooth."

"Is that good news or bad news?"

"Good for me, I guess, bad for them," said Theodosia. "I think they were hoping to find a whole trove of bones." She glanced at the rose garden, said, "Those are fairly mature plants, aren't they?"

"Been here a while," said Drayton, studying the brochure he'd been given. "Several dozen years of pruning and cultivating. Of course, new plants are probably being added every year since new rose varieties are constantly being developed." He glanced up at her. "You know anything about the language of roses?"

"What do you mean?" asked Theodosia.

"During the Victorian era," said Drayton, "the use of rose symbolism was extremely popular. It became a subtle form of communication."

"Like text messaging today," said Theodosia.

"Not exactly," said Drayton. "For example, red and white roses mixed together in a bouquet stood for unity. While dark crimson roses symbolized mourning."

"I had no idea," said Theodosia, charmed. Was there nothing Drayton didn't know? "What else?"

"Yellow roses were used to convey jealously. Of course, now they express friendship and joy."

Theodosia pointed to the small bouquet of tea roses on their table. "What about tea roses?"

"Ah," said Drayton. "Tea roses mean remembrance. So they're most appropriate when you have old friends in for tea."

"Ma'am?" said a white-coated waiter, who'd suddenly materialized at Theodosia's elbow. "Care for any refreshments here?"

"What's on the menu?" Theodosia asked.

"Sweet tea, lemonade, coffee, and white wine," said the waiter.

"How about a lemonade–white wine spritzer?" asked Theodosia. "Mixed together in equal parts, shaken not stirred."

"I can do that," said the waiter. He glanced at Drayton. "And you, sir?"

"Same," said Drayton. "Please."

Theodosia smiled at Drayton and said, "What about red . . . ?" as her words were suddenly drowned out by a nearby burst of riotous laughter. Both she and Drayton swung sideways in their chairs, wondering who the noisy guests were, only to find Miss Kitty and Cinnamon swiftly descending upon them.

"Look who's here!" gushed Cinnamon. "Our new neighbors!"

"Why it's Miss Theodosia and Mr. Drayton!" cried Miss Kitty, taking up the cry.

"Please," said Drayton, scrambling to his feet, "join us."

Theodosia hesitated for a moment, hating to spoil the calm of the evening, then said. "Of course."

But luckily, thankfully, Miss Kitty and Cinnamon demurred.

"We're doing this Bed-and-Breakfast Tour on the fly," Cinnamon told her.

"Our own crash course on the historic district." Miss Kitty laughed. "Since this is our new home and we certainly want to cater to its more posh residents."

"I'm sure you do," murmured Drayton.

"We're still planning to come to the Heritage Society tomorrow night," added Cinnamon, shaking a finger at them. "Hoping you'll introduce us to all your friends."

"Oh," said Miss Kitty, lightly touching Theodosia's shoulder. "We dropped the candles off at your shop this afternoon. Since you weren't around, we entrusted them to dear Drayton." She laughed airily as if she'd just made the most wonderful bon mot.

"They're tucked away safely," Drayton assured her.

"Ta-ta!" said Miss Kitty, waving wildly as she grabbed Cinnamon's arm and pulled her away.

"Those two women are genuine characters," said Drayton, watching them scurry across the patio. "An interesting addition to our Church Street merchants."

"I suppose," said Theodosia, watching them go. "I hate to say this, because I can't quite put my finger on it, but it feels like there's something *off* about them."

"They can be a little *too* friendly," allowed Drayton.

"As well as overly gushy and enthusiastic," agreed Theodosia. "But . . ." She stopped, shook her head, murmured, "Something."

"Of course you're put off by them," said Drayton, dropping his voice. "They're also on your suspect list for Daria's murder."

"Not completely," said Theodosia. "There's no real evidence I can pin to them. Just the fact that Miss Kitty, especially, is hot to trot about taking over the map shop space."

"One of them could have argued with

Daria?" proposed Drayton. "Things turned ugly? Led to an unfortunate accident?"

"I don't think looping a hank of rope around someone's neck is particularly accidental," said Theodosia.

"Point well taken," said Drayton.

Their drinks arrived, and they sipped them slowly, enjoying the warm, dark evening as sputtering candles illuminated the garden, imparting a dark and moody splendor.

"Do you still see Jason Pritchard as a suspect?" asked Drayton. "Even though Beth Ann is now on the scene?"

Theodosia nodded. "It could be him. It could be Joe Don, the boyfriend, too. Or even Jack Brux."

"I don't think Jack . . ." began Drayton.

"If he wanted to get his hands on a particular map?" asked Theodosia. "And Daria didn't want him to for whatever reason?"

"Brux does have a nasty temper," said Drayton.

"As you said before. An argument . . . things turned ugly?"

"Possible," said Drayton. He glanced at his antique Piaget watch, said, "Do we still want to ankle over to the Magnolia Inn?"

"I don't know," said Theodosia. "Do we?" Talking about Daria's murder, analyzing suspects had left her in a bit of a funk.

"It's only a block away, just off Gateway Walk," said Drayton. "Come on, what's the harm? They're supposed to have a lot of lovely, detailed carvings."

"As if that matters to me," muttered Theodosia.

"It matters to me," said Drayton.

"Then we should go," said Theodosia. "And I apologize. I have no right to drag down your evening because I'm suddenly introspective."

"No," said Drayton, "I'd say you're rather *per*ceptive. I wouldn't be surprised if you figured this out yet."

The Magnolia Inn B and B was smaller than the Rosewalk House, but just as lovely. The front parlor featured hand-carved cornices, medallions, and plaster work along with a black marble fireplace and large gilt mirror. Aubusson carpets covered wood-planked floors and the four upstairs rooms, furnished with antiques, all featured canopy beds.

"It's a little jewel," declared Drayton. "And just the right size, too."

"Cozy," agreed Theodosia. It was a place where a weary traveler could relax and really snuggle in. Enjoy morning tea on the back balcony, evening wine and cheese in the parlor.

Apparently everyone else thought it was adorable, too, because every time Theodosia and Drayton ventured into another room, they had to deal with the crush of crowds.

"Because it's located so close to the Battery," said Drayton. "This is the historic district hot spot. Everyone wants to visit these homes and play 'let's pretend I live here.'"

"Plus it's got that neat porte cochere on the side of the house," said Theodosia, "that leads to a little cobblestone back alley." She said it with enthusiasm, then was immediately reminded of the back-alley crawl. Thought about how badly that had ended.

Drayton saw the look on Theodosia's face and said, "Come on, time to go. We've seen most of the house and you're introspective edging toward maudlin. You're thinking you might have saved Daria that night, when you really couldn't."

"Don't say that," said Theodosia, as Drayton led her outside. "Please don't say that."

"You're a good person, Theodosia," Drayton told her, as they stepped outside onto the front verandah. "You do charity work, garner media coverage for the Spoleto Festival, and take Earl Grey on visiting rounds at countless hospitals and senior citizen residences. And you've made quite a name for yourself with the Indigo Tea Shop. But as talented as you are, you're not a superwoman. There was nothing you could have done."

"But there's something I can do now," Theodosia said, quietly. "I can keep snooping around and asking questions. And maybe, just maybe, figure out who killed Daria."

"It's what you're good at," Drayton agreed. "Just . . . please, be careful."

"I always am," said Theodosia.

He looked at her askance, not believing her for a minute, but was too polite to say so. Instead, Drayton said, "Here. Let's follow the alley to Gateway Walk. Take the scenic tour."

24

Gateway Walk was a hidden, four-block city walk that consisted of lush gardens, ancient slate graves, and a famous pair of wrought-iron gates. It began at Archdale Street, rambled its way past the Library Society, Gibbes Museum of Art, and four different churches, ending in the graveyard behind St. Philip's Church. It was quiet, contemplative, and dripping with flora and fauna. It was also reputed to be haunted.

Old legends spoke of hair that had turned to Spanish moss and now beckoned spookily to unsuspecting visitors. Countless folk had claimed to see a headless torso in a Confederate uniform, aimlessly wandering the serene gardens and secret cul-de-sacs. Glowing blue orbs had been photographed but never explained.

None of that mattered to Theodosia and Drayton right now, as they strolled past the stately Library Society building, heading for the Governor Aiken Gates.

"Lovely here," mused Drayton, their footfalls echoing hollowly on the narrow stone footpath. Flowering white dogwoods brushed their shoulders and the occasional coo of a dove punctuated the silence.

"Maybe the most peaceful place on earth," agreed Theodosia.

"I've always thought," said Drayton, "that I wouldn't mind being buried here."

"Please don't talk like that," said Theodosia. "Don't talk old."

"I don't intend to leave my corporal body for a very long time," chuckled Drayton, "but when I do, I wouldn't mind being in the company of several centuries of Charleston history."

"I suppose you're right," said Theodosia. "The hidden gardens, all the old plaques and tombs . . . very peaceful."

"You know what would be interesting?" said Drayton.

"What?" asked Theodosia.

"If we swung by your cottage to see how the big dig is progressing."

"Not much to see," said Theodosia.

"Still," said Drayton, "I've never seen an actual archaeological excavation."

"Then you're on," said Theodosia. They walked past the Gibbes Museum, crossed

Meeting Street, continued past the Circular Congregational Church.

"When we get to St. Philip's," said Theodosia, "let's cut left and . . ." She hesitated and cast a glance over her shoulder.

Drayton picked up her vibe immediately. "What?"

"Someone behind us?" said Theodosia in a low voice.

They continued walking as Drayton took a quick check as well. "I think you might be right," he said quietly.

"Following us?"

"Maybe," said Drayton.

"Maybe not so good," said Theodosia. She grabbed hold of Drayton's arm and, together, they picked up their pace. She knew it might be smart to gain some distance on whoever was behind them. Get to St. Philip's graveyard where they could duck behind one of the larger tombs and figure out what to do — if there was anything to do. Sit tight, hide, or make a dash for it?

Just past a cluster of slate markers that dated to the 1600s was a large marble tomb. They scurried around it, ducked down, and waited, their breathing coming in measured gasps.

They waited fifteen seconds, then thirty.

Drayton finally poked his head up, like a

gopher taking a careful look.

"What?" Theodosia whispered.

"Something," he whispered back.

"Something or someone?" she asked, but Drayton just shook his head. Theodosia took a deep breath, then peered around the side of the marble tomb. Her eyes scanned the darkness, flitting across an old gravestone decorated with a skull and crossbones, a stand of magnolias, a statue of a winged angel, its face upturned, its hands almost melted away from the ravages of time.

Finally, she saw something. What looked like a person just standing alone in a copse of dogwood. Not moving, but maybe . . . muttering to himself?

Theodosia nudged Drayton. "Somebody's standing over there," she said in a low voice.

"You think they're dangerous?" he asked.

"I don't think it's Beth Ann, if that's what you're asking," said Theodosia.

"So, what do you want to do?" whispered Drayton.

"What I don't want to do is crouch here all night," Theodosia responded. "Or even just skulk away. It would seem kind of . . . I don't know . . . cowardly."

"Then what do you say we call that fellow's bluff," said Drayton, standing up abruptly. Theodosia followed suit and together they slipped out from behind the marble tomb and tiptoed back down the walk, retracing their steps.

"Careful," whispered Drayton as they drew closer.

Then Theodosia put a hand up, pushed back an overhanging hank of Spanish moss, and did a double take. "Joe Don?" she said, her voice rising in an off-pitch squawk.

Joe Don Hunter jumped as if touched by an electric wire, then rubbed his eyes and stared at them in disbelief. "You?" he breathed.

"What's going on!" Drayton demanded, using his Heritage Society call-to-order voice.

"What are you two doing here?" Joe Don Hunter asked in a quavering tone. He seemed more startled than they were.

"You were following us!" said Theodosia, jumping on him hard. "You were dogging our footsteps!"

Joe Don swiped at his forelock nervously. "No, ma'am," he declared. "Truth be told, I didn't even know you were here."

"You have to have known," said Drayton. "You're not deaf or blind, you knew we were walking ahead of you. What were you planning to do?" Theodosia had to hand it to Drayton, he was definitely keeping the pressure on.

"Following us is fairly suspicious," said Theodosia, adopting Drayton's harsh tone. "Especially in light of the fact I've been looking into your girlfriend's death."

Joe Don's face fell like he'd been thunderstruck. His mouth started to work, but no sound came out. Finally a tear rolled down his face, glistening in the low light, and he finally said, "That's what you think? That I was going to harm you?" He seemed to be in shock. "That I'm the one who killed Daria?"

"You're on the suspect list, yes," Drayton told him, putting both hands on his hips.

Joe Don extended his arms in a pleading gesture. "I wouldn't . . ." he said. "I couldn't . . ."

"Then what are you doing here?" demanded Theodosia. "We'd like an answer."

Sniffling loudly, Joe Don said, "I . . . I haven't been myself these last few days. The police haven't figured anything out about Daria's murder and I feel completely alone and helpless. Confused and . . . what would you call it? Bereft."

"Bereft," snorted Drayton, as if he hardly believed Joe Don knew the meaning of the word.

"I wander around aimlessly," Joe Don

confessed. "Just . . . trying to figure things out."

"And this is one of your aimless rambles?" Theodosia asked him. "Down Gateway Walk?" She wasn't sure if Joe Don Hunter was genuinely distraught or if he deserved an Academy Award.

Joe Don gazed around as if unaware of his surroundings. "Yeah, I guess so. I guess that's where I am."

Theodosia and Drayton exchanged glances, then Drayton suggested, not unkindly, "Perhaps you might benefit from some grief counseling."

"Yeah . . . maybe," said Joe Don.

But Theodosia wasn't willing to let him off so easy. She took a step closer to him and said, "Are you still participating in the Kipling Club?"

Joe Don stared at her.

"That's right," said Theodosia. "We know you're in a group of local treasure hunters."

"I am," said Joe Don, grudgingly. "So what?"

"I hope you're not digging up precious Civil War battlegrounds or Native American cultural sites," said Drayton.

"We're not like that," protested Hunter.

But Theodosia knew they were.

■ ■ ■ ■

Five minutes later, Theodosia and Drayton walked past the Featherbed House, where lights blazed but no crowds had gathered. Just lit up for the sake of the overnight guests, Theodosia figured.

"Did you believe Joe Don?" Drayton asked. "Do you think he's so distraught that he just wanders around aimlessly at night?"

"He did seem confused," admitted Theodosia. "And a little bit lost inside himself."

"I don't know," said Drayton. "Something about him seems fishy to me."

"Maybe Joe Don seems fishy because we're fishing for suspects," said Theodosia. "You realize we still haven't stumbled on one concrete shred of evidence. Against him or anyone else."

"You know," said Drayton, "Beth Ann being in town might be the best evidence of all."

"You like her for the murder," said Theodosia.

"From what I know about Beth Ann," said Drayton, "she strikes me as being cold, calculating, and a trifle unhinged. And the more you talk about her, the more I tend to suspect her."

"Which means I'm probably unduly influencing you," said Theodosia.

"Then again, you always do," said Drayton. They were standing on the sidewalk directly in front of Theodosia's cottage. A thin, silver crescent moon shone overhead, casting faint shadows and icing the landscape with its glow. Hunkered fifteen feet back from the sidewalk, the little cottage was a darkened curiosity, like something you might stumble upon in a forest.

"Can we go inside?" asked Drayton. "Do you have a key?"

"No key," said Theodosia, "but my Realtor gave me the lock box combination. I've been using that to scoot in and out."

"Unbeknownst to the owner?" asked Drayton.

"I think it's well knownst now," chuckled Theodosia.

They strolled quietly up the walk, Theodosia went through her usual fumbling with the dial on the lock box, and then they were inside. She hit the wall switch, bathing the front room in soft light.

"Say now," said Drayton, talking a few steps in, "this is even more lovely than I remembered."

"You think?" asked Theodosia. Lately she'd had the sinking feeling she might never move in. All sorts of problems seemed to conspire against her, barriers to closing on the house, barriers to her actually moving in.

"I really love it," said Drayton. "And I don't say that lightly."

"You do have a critical eye," said Theodosia.

"But this place . . ." Drayton strolled over to the fireplace, ran a hand across the cypress paneling. "This place has good bones. Architecturally speaking."

"That's what I think, too," said Theodosia. She was secretly thrilled that Drayton approved of her new home, humble though it might be. "And I can't wait to start decorating."

"Probably need to purchase a couple more pieces of furniture," mused Drayton.

"That's what I think, too," agreed Theodosia. "Maybe check out some of the shops on King Street." King Street was Charleston's acknowledged antiques district, where redbrick shops with white-washed windowsills stood shoulder to shoulder, bursting with English silver, old family crystal and china, estate jewelry, and antique furniture. Even browsing there became a joyful history lesson of sorts.

"And these window treatments have seen

better days," said Drayton. He reached out and gave a tentative tug on a long velvet drapery that had faded from maroon to off-pink.

"You don't have to be coy," said Theodosia. "I know they're tattered. So, yes, I'm definitely going to need new draperies."

"But you can make do for a while," said Drayton, who prided himself on being practical as well as frugal. "Best not to go overboard and buy everything at once. Better to . . . select a few choice pieces."

Theodosia agreed. She had friends who'd moved into new houses and did all their decorating in one fell swoop, ending up with Country French or Mediterranean or something that screamed mega-mansion. But that wasn't going to happen to her. Theodosia was a big believer in thinking big but taking smaller steps. That was how she'd settled into her tea business; that was how she'd settle into her new home.

Drayton was still peeking and probing, opening closets and nosing around. "And this dining room . . . it looks out over the back garden?" He cleared his throat. "On your archaeology dig?"

"I think at night," said Theodosia, "with a small amount of outdoor lighting, it could be quite spectacular."

"Mmm," said Drayton, frowning. "Outdoor lighting."

"Not tiki torches or anything like that," Theodosia hastily assured him. "I was thinking more like small, solar-powered lamps. Something tasteful and discreet."

"Might work," said Drayton. "And the kitchen?"

"Through there," said Theodosia, indicating an archway.

Drayton ducked through, batting his hand around, searching for a light switch, then finally found it. "This is a decent size, too, but you're —" He stopped suddenly and stared pointedly at the back door. "Did you know you have a broken window?" he asked.

Theodosia was beside him in two seconds, staring at her missing window pane. One of a dozen beveled into the back door. "What on earth!" She leaned forward, put her index finger where the missing glass should have been. Touched only . . . air. "This wasn't here when —"

A loud crash sounded from the backyard.

"Someone's outside!" said Theodosia, fumbling with the door lock. She pulled, rattled the doorknob, finally bullied the door open.

Now the sound of running footsteps echoed down the back alley.

"C'mon!" she yelled at Drayton, then took off in a mad dash. Skittering across muddy patio stones, Theodosia made a giant sideways leap, avoiding a wide, muddy pit, careened around a clump of magnolias, hopped over a low string, and then was out the back gate and into the alley.

"Stop!" she called. "Stop or I'll call the police!" She paused for a few moments, her heart thudding in her chest, waiting for Drayton to catch up to her.

He finally did. "Did you see anybody?" he asked, breathing heavily.

"No, but at the risk of sounding like a B movie, they went thataway."

The two of them continued down the alley, Theodosia walking briskly, then breaking into a jog, Drayton lagging behind. From behind a tall, wooden fence, a dog barked. A high-pitched, rapid-fire, upset-dog bark.

Then, as the cobblestone alley curved around to the left and plunged into darkness, Theodosia gave a little squeal and ran forward. Right ahead of her, like a crumpled heap of rags, lay a body!

"Theo, don't!" warned Drayton.

But Theodosia was already leaning over the man who was groaning and fighting to sit up. "Drayton! Over here!" she called to him.

Drayton approached with caution.

"It's Jack Brux!" Theodosia told him. "He's hurt!"

"Jack?" said Drayton, hurrying now. "What on earth?" He stared down into the angry, contorted face of Jack Brux.

"This is like a bad second act," murmured Theodosia, grabbing for Brux's arm, but unable to move him. His head, she noted, had a nasty cut and blood, shiny and dark in the moonlight, trickled down the side of his face.

Drayton immediately took an offensive posture. "What are you doing here?" he demanded of Brux.

Brux turned on him like a snarling wolverine. "What am I *doing* here? Excuse me, but I *live* here. Some idiot pushed me from behind and practically trampled me!"

"Are you okay?" asked Theodosia.

"Do I look okay?" snapped Brux. "Because I'm certainly not. My knee is throbbing like crazy and I cracked my head hard on the cobblestones. Does that sound okay to you?"

Theodosia thought Brux sounded pretty much like he always did. Feisty, cranky, and perturbed. But she was willing to give him the benefit of the doubt, especially since he was bleeding profusely. "Ambulance," she murmured to Drayton and pulled out her cell phone.

Drayton knelt down, his knees making little popping sounds. He got an arm around Brux and tried to help him to his feet. "Can you tell us what happened?" he asked in a kindlier tone.

Brux staggered a bit but finally made it to his feet. Now that he was upright, Brux seemed groggy and slower and less sharp-tongued. "I was taking my evening constitutional," he moaned, "when I heard somebody running, coming up fast behind me. I didn't think much of it — joggers come barreling down this alley all the time — rude buggers, all of them, even though I don't know why anyone in their right mind would want to run on cobblestones, but —"

"What happened exactly?" asked Theodosia. She really did want to cut to the chase without too much editorializing from Brux.

"Like I said," said Brux, "I was attacked from behind. Someone slammed me on the head and I . . . I went down." He put a hand to his head, felt the blood, said, "Oh man."

Four minutes later, the ambulance showed

up. The EMTs sat Brux on the back step of their rig, checked him for injuries, and shone a penlight in his eyes. All the while Brux managed to keep up a constant barrage of complaints.

"I think he's feeling better," said Drayton, deadpan.

Five minutes after that, a burgundy Crown Victoria came prowling down the alley and rolled to a stop. Theodosia wasn't all that surprised when the passenger door opened and Burt Tidwell hauled his bulk from the vehicle.

"Just what I needed on what was supposed to be a leisurely Friday evening," began Tidwell, lumbering toward them. "A callout because the two of you are involved in yet another problematic situation." He sighed mightily and stared at Theodosia and Drayton with an expression of supreme disapproval.

"We had no idea —" began Theodosia.

"Of course, you didn't," sang Tidwell. "You never do."

"But you were up late," said Drayton, trying to help the situation and failing.

"I certainly was not," muttered Tidwell. "And if you must pry into my personal habits, I was lying in bed reading *Ulysses*."

"A fine book," noted Drayton, still trying

to inject some note of normalcy.

"Is it?" said Tidwell. "I've been interrupted so many times I've barely made it through the first three chapters."

"Maybe you should think about retirement," piped up Tidwell's driver. He was a young, uniformed officer with surfer-boy blond hair who offered his remark in a lighthearted manner. Theodosia figured he'd soon learn not to attempt jokes with Tidwell.

Tidwell swiveled his giant head like the periscope of a German U-boat seeking out a nice tasty convoy to attack in the north Atlantic. Then his steely gray eyes bore directly into the young man, like a drill bit chewing rock.

"I didn't mean . . ." said the young officer. "Not that I . . ."

Tidwell's lips pursed, his jaw tightened. Theodosia almost expected to see steam come pouring out of his ears.

"Sorry," the officer finally muttered contritely. Definitely a fast learner.

"Harh," grunted Tidwell.

They watched as the EMTs put a couple of butterfly bandages on Brux's forehead, then placed an oxygen cannula under his nose.

Drayton cleared his throat, then said, "Do

you think this is related to the murder?"

Tidwell turned and stared at Drayton, almost daring him to continue.

"I mean," said Drayton, "what with Theodosia warning you about this Beth Ann person and Jack being a kind of, er, emotional fellow . . ."

"Don't know," said Tidwell. He looked like he was turning all the facts over in his mind, like a rock polisher sanding away on a few choice agates.

"Drayton and I have been talking all evening," said Theodosia. "And we think it's very possible Beth Ann was the killer."

"You were the one person who saw Daria Shand struggling with her assailant," said Tidwell, in an almost accusatory tone. "Did it look like this Beth Ann person to you?"

"I don't know," said Theodosia, feeling guilty again. "I wasn't close enough to really see."

Tidwell blew out a glut of air.

"What about the documents that were shredded in Daria's shop?" Theodosia asked. She glanced over at Jack Brux, who was being loaded onto a gurney now. "Do you know . . . did Brux ever come up with anything?"

"I spoke to Brux early this afternoon and he mentioned that he might have a couple of things figured out," said Tidwell. He gazed at the ambulance, as an EMT scrambled inside and pulled the back door shut. "But now . . ."

Drayton picked up on Tidwell's thought. "Let's hope that knock on his head didn't . . ."

"Erase his hard drive," finished Theodosia.

25

Theodosia was tired, bordering on cranky this Saturday morning. She hadn't gotten home until eleven last night, then she'd spent some time walking Earl Grey. Even after she finally crawled into bed, she hadn't been able to fall sleep right away, so she'd puttered around her apartment, murder on her mind. Not such a good thing.

Her sleep quota not being met, Theodosia was feeling decidedly depleted. And more than a little frustrated by Daria's murder and the slow-moving Robbery-Homicide Division of the Charleston PD. She was filled with dread every time the phone rang, thinking it was Aunt Libby calling or maybe even Sophie, Daria's mother.

Did she have any news for them? No. Could she impart any comfort by telling them she'd unraveled a clue or stumbled upon a nugget of information? Again, nothing. Basically, Theodosia had bupkes.

It also didn't help that Haley was wandering around this morning, redoing table settings and restless as a kid waiting for the recess bell to ring. Of course, Drayton hadn't wasted any time in filling Haley in on last night's strange doings. Relating tidbits about Joe Don's mysterious ramble in Gateway Walk and Jack Brux getting assaulted. So now Haley was postulating her own slightly wild theories.

"Maybe," said Haley, grabbing tulips and sprigs of dogwood to arrange in large ceramic crocks, "maybe last night's bump and run in your back alley was intended for you, Theo."

"Maybe it was meant for Jack Brux," said Theodosia. "The man's not exactly Mr. Warmth. He's not big into winning friends and influencing people."

"Or maybe it really was an unrelated accident," offered Drayton. "A clumsy jogger, smacking into Brux on his late-night run."

"No," said Haley, "from the way you guys have been telling it, the incident *feels* intentional. Brux was in the alley behind Theodosia's cottage, so I think his assault somehow relates to that cottage."

"There was that broken window," said Drayton, glancing at Theodosia.

"Did you ever think," said Haley, "that

your new place . . . what do they call it? Hazelhurst? That it might be haunted?" She gazed at Theodosia with saucer eyes. "What if the ghosts of all the pirates that were strung up there have come back to seek revenge?"

"A chilling supposition," agreed Theodosia. "But awfully far afield, since we don't know if a pirate's gallows ever really stood there. And, frankly, I'm beginning to have my doubts."

"About the spirit world?" asked Haley.

"I believe in all things spiritual," said Theodosia. "I'm just not sure deceased pirates have the innate ability to come back and annoy us." Theodosia was anxious to nip any sort of pirate or ghost legend in the bud. If that sort of tale started to spread, it could take on the dimensions of an urban myth and really lead to problems.

Drayton swiped the back of his hand across his cheek and asked, "Do you think it had something to do with the work Jack Brux was doing? Piecing together the shredded records? Assisting the police?"

Theodosia shrugged. "Possibly. Or maybe Jack Brux was in the wrong place at the wrong time." She hesitated. "Or maybe it was Beth Ann."

"Maybe," said Drayton.

"It's as if someone is stalking us," said Haley.

"Excuse me?" said Drayton. "Us?"

"Folks from the historic district," said Haley. "Think about it. First Daria, then Theo in her car, then Jack Brux last night."

"And the camera," pointed out Drayton. "Somebody did grab Bill Glass's camera."

"And Joe Don was following you guys last night," said Haley. "And Beth Ann turned up at the fashion show."

Theodosia set an antique Minton teacup into its matching saucer. "I hadn't thought of it that way." She reached back, pulled the ties of her black apron snugly around her waist. "Interesting."

"A pattern," said Haley.

They stood for a while, the three of them exchanging worried glances.

Then Drayton swallowed hard and said, "But who exactly is the stalker?"

They got busy then, propping open the front door to let the warm breezes from the Ashley and Cooper rivers swoop in, welcoming guests to the Indigo Tea Shop.

"It's almost warm enough to set up the outside tables," said Drayton.

"But let's not," said Theodosia. "If we do that we'll be deluged with customers who'll want to linger and sip. And we want to close a little early this afternoon."

"Right," agreed Drayton. "Get prepped for our catering gig at the Heritage Society tonight."

"I thought you didn't like the term *catering gig*," said Theodosia.

Drayton shrugged. "What can I do? Haley uses it almost constantly so it's part of my lexicon now."

"What can you do?" agreed Theodosia.

She delivered prune and date scones to a couple of tables, then grabbed a pot of black jasmine tea and made the rounds. As the delicious scent of jasmine filtered up through clouds of steam, Theodosia relaxed. And started feeling a little better. She'd already shrugged off her tiredness, although that could be accounted for by the two cups of Viennese Earl Grey she'd sipped earlier. Nothing like a little caffeine and a hint of bergamot to rev a person's brain and metabolism!

By the time Haley popped out of the kitchen to deliver small plates of French crepes stuffed with chicken and mushrooms in cream sauce, Theodosia was back to her old self.

"You're suddenly so peppy," Drayton commented. "Must be looking forward to tonight."

"You know," said Theodosia, "I am. Everything is so well planned I'm positive it'll go off without a hitch."

"Agreed," said Drayton. "I just hope we get a good crowd."

"Theo!" called Haley. She was standing at the front counter, holding up the phone, looking perturbed.

"What?" asked Theodosia, setting down her tray and grabbing a glass bowl filled with Devonshire cream. "A late reservation? A cancellation?"

"We should be so lucky," said Haley, rolling her eyes.

"Tidwell?" asked Theodosia, searching for a small silver spoon. Maybe he'd discovered something new.

"You're not going to believe this," said Haley.

"Delaine?" said Theodosia, tucking a napkin onto the tray.

Haley shook her head. "Nope. Jory."

"Seriously?" said Theodosia, accepting the phone gingerly, like it might contain spores of the deadly Ebola virus.

"Ayup," said Haley, squirting away.

Theodosia put the phone to her ear and said, "Now what?"

"Theodosia, hello," said Jory, in his best

hail-hearty, upbeat voice. "I'm still in New York, but if you don't believe me, you can call my office and check."

"I believe you," said Theodosia, sounding just this side of bored.

"The reason I called," said Jory, talking faster, "is because I need a small favor from you."

"What?" yelped Theodosia. Was he kidding? Or was this his idea of a bad joke?

"Here's the deal," said Jory, starting to sound chattery and a little panicked. "I just got a phone call from Chuck Strom, the manager at the Charleston Yacht Club . . . you know, the marina where I keep my boat?"

She said nothing.

"Anyway, the Coast Guard called Chuck early this morning and said they spotted my sailboat over at Castle Pinckney. They read him the registration number and it's my boat, all right." Silence spun out. "Chuck checked my boat slip and, sure enough, my sailboat's not there."

"That's great they found it," said Theodosia. *Is that what Jory wants? For me to commiserate with him? Because, really, I don't have time for this.*

"It's a lucky break," Jory continued, "but now I have . . . well, I have a problem. And a huge favor to ask of you."

No, no, no, thought Theodosia, closing her eyes and gritting her teeth.

So, of course, Jory voiced the words Theodosia was dreading to hear.

"Is there any way you can you go over to Castle Pinckney and bring my boat back to the yacht club?" he asked.

"You're not serious," breathed Theodosia. Castle Pinckney was a small island in the middle of Charleston Harbor. Basically an abandoned old fort.

Jory plunged on ahead. "I already set it up with Chuck. He's got his Chris-Craft Corsair all gassed and ready to go. He'll take you over and drop you."

"Excuse me," said Theodosia, annoyed beyond belief and letting Jory know it. "But why doesn't your pal Chuck just motor over and tow the boat back himself? Why don't you offer him a big, fat tip or reward or something?"

"Because Chuck doesn't have time to do all that," said Jory. "His cousin's getting married today. Over in Goose Creek. He can make the run over, but he can't mess around with setting up a tow line and hauling it back. Take too long."

"And you couldn't find another soul?" asked Theodosia. "Out of all the members at the yacht club? All those guys who run around in captain's hats and deck shoes with cute little tassels?"

"Nobody I can trust," said Jory. And now his voice turned pleading. "Theodosia, you've sailed my boat dozens of times. You *know* that boat. And I trust you implicitly."

Theodosia exhaled loudly and slowly into the phone. "Well, shoot. This isn't the conversation I thought we'd be having."

"Why did you think I called?"

"Oh, I don't know," said Theodosia. "Let me make a wild and crazy guess. Uh . . . maybe I hoped you pulled your freaky ex-fiancée, Beth Ann, off my case? Or how about this? You called to apologize."

"In that case, I apologize," said Jory. "In fact, I fervently extend a blanket apology for every caddish thing I've ever said or done. Past, present, and future."

"Oh jeez," groaned Theodosia. "You don't . . ." She stopped, shook her head to clear it, thought, *Why me?* "Jory, you know I'd help you if . . ."

"Does that mean you'll do it?" Jory asked in a semi-hopeful tone of voice.

"I suppose I could," Theodosia said slowly. Glancing at her watch, a classic Cartier tank watch from the fifties that had belonged to her mother, she tried to work out the timing on a few things. "Okay, I'm going to have to really book it, though."

"Wait," said Jory. "There's more."

"Don't tell me!" groaned Theodosia. Now her dismay was palpable. And she didn't care if Jory thought she was being rude or not.

"I think Beth Ann might have cut the sailboat's line on purpose," said Jory. "I think she's been stalking me, too. In New York and then flying back and forth, even before she sort of crash-landed in my apartment."

"Why didn't you tell me all this," Theodosia demanded, "when I talked to you yesterday?"

"I don't know," said Jory. "I suppose because I didn't want to assign it too much importance. I thought maybe she'd just . . . go away. Now I really feel terrible. About everything."

"You're crazy, you know that?" said Theodosia.

A long silence spun out and then Jory said, "I'm still crazy about you."

"Don't be," said Theodosia, as she hung up the phone.

Theodosia was still fuming as she motored out from the Charleston Yacht Club with

Chuck Strom. This was going to be her last contact with Jory, she decided. They were over, done, kaput. To keep flogging their broken relationship just made it sad and difficult for both of them.

So . . . the thing to do now was concentrate on the job at hand. Get Jory's sailboat rigged, sail it back across Charleston Harbor, then turn her attention to the book signing tonight.

As Theodosia adjusted her sunglasses and leaned back in the Corsair's bucket seat, she had to admit this was an almost perfect day for a sail. There was a fair amount of wind, about twenty knots, just enough to put a chop on the water and make things interesting. And the sun blazed bright in a parfait sky where wispy layers of yellow and pink clouds swirled on the breeze.

Rounding the tip of the peninsula, Theodosia swiveled in her seat, taking in a fine view of the Battery to her left. The green of White Point Gardens looked like a velvet carpet while just beyond it, the enormous Georgian, Italianate, and Victorian mansions stood like grand old matriarchs, sentinels of the harbor.

Straight ahead was Castle Pinckney, a brick and mortar fort that had been constructed in Charleston Harbor, on a large marshy island known as Shutes Folly, just prior to the War of 1812. Castle Pinckney had been occupied by soldiers over the years and had once been home to a lighthouse. Now the lighthouse and buildings were just piles of crumbling ruins, owned by the South Carolina Ports Authority. Boosters of the old fort had high hopes of converting it into some type of park, but funding never seemed to materialize.

Theodosia gazed at Castle Pinckney, then her eyes focused on another island in the distance. Fort Sumter. If they bypassed Castle Pinckney, then shot past Fort Sumter, they'd end up in the surging waters of the Atlantic. Probably no place for a boat this size. Or Jory's sailboat, either.

Strom was shouting something at her. She leaned toward him, listening over the roar of the engine.

". . . Beach over there," Strom was saying. He gestured toward a stretch of shimmering white sand. Theodosia homed in on it, tracked right for about fifty yards, and saw Jory's sailboat, his J/22. It had been washed into a small cove and now its foredeck nosed the beach, while the aft part of the boat bobbed gently, like a cork in the water.

"Okay," she said. Theodosia climbed from her bucket seat, glad she'd changed from her silk blouse and crop pants into boat shoes, red T-shirt, and navy shorts. Using the side rails for support, she made her way to the back of Strom's boat, ready to climb onto the rear swim platform.

Strom waved a hand at her, indicating he was going to back in. Then the boat bucked slightly and they swung into a one-hundred-and-eighty-degree turn, engines churning like crazy as Strom reversed toward the beach.

When they were fairly close, Theodosia nodded, then jumped down onto the swim platform. She counted to three, took a giant leap, and landed in about six inches of water. One heroic stride brought her to the beach, where shale and shells crumbled underfoot.

"You gonna be okay?" Strom called to her. He seemed concerned but anxious to get going at the same time.

She gave an exaggerated nod of her head. "I'll be fine," she called back over the roar of the motor. Strom seemed to hesitate for a few moments, then powered up his engine and swung around. Theodosia watched his boat, with its midnight-blue hull, take off like a joyful dolphin skimming the waves.

Okay, Theodosia thought, as she slogged toward Jory's sailboat. *Now we put my seamanship to the test. How long will it take to rig this boat? How long will it take to sail back to the Charleston Yacht Club?* She stood on the deserted beach, hands on hips, letting the wind whip her hair while she inhaled the salty breeze. Overhead, white gulls cawed noisily, floating on thermals, their wingtips curled expertly upward.

She wondered if the Coast Guard might send a cutter along to check if someone had indeed come to fetch Jory's boat, since they were the ones who'd first noticed it.

Interesting, she thought, that the J/22 had made it here seemingly of its own volition. On the other hand, the wind and water currents had probably just worked in concert with each other. And Pinckney Island wasn't that far from shore.

Standing alone now, motorboats droning in the distance, Theodosia did a quick scan of Pinckney Island.

Interestingly enough, she'd never set foot here before. Theodosia had sailed past it, read newspaper blurbs about how Civil War reenactors had used the place for special weekend events, but she'd never experienced the island up close until now. And like most folks, Theodosia was more than a little curious. Castle Pinckney was, after all, a piece of Charleston history. And Charleston was a town fueled by history.

So, Theodosia decided, wasn't this as good a time as any to take a look around? Wouldn't Drayton, history buff that he was, ply her with a myriad of questions? That said, shouldn't she make a quick reconnoiter before the Coast Guard shouted warnings at her via bullhorn? Before the Ports Authority got wind of her intrusion and tried to have her arrested?

Theodosia worried her lower lip with her teeth and thought for a moment. Ahead and to her right, where Jory's boat was hung up, stretched a large patch of tall marsh grass, green and yellow-gold, dancing in the wind. To her left stood the crumbling brick walls of the old fort, leafy green treetops bouncing and peeking up behind them. Really, what was the harm in taking a look at this so-called "forgotten fort?" She thought for a few moments. Probably no harm at all.

Crunching her way across the beach, Theodosia scrambled up a hill, mindful of sand burrs pecking at her ankles, and approached the crumbling brick wall. It was maybe six feet high, covered with tangled vines, and more than a little intriguing. Following along the wall, Theodosia touched a hand to the old bricks. Pitted and pocked with age, most were loose and unstable, barely held in place by small dabs of earthen mortar. Probably, she decided, a strong wind could blow these walls over. Probably most of these walls *had* blown over when Hurricane Hugo ripped through here in '89.

Still, Theodosia found the place fascinating. This little bit of history and mystery sat so close to a modern thriving Charleston, yet was clearly a throwback to the 1800s.

What could be inside, she wondered, as she ducked into a low, rounded passageway? She'd heard that most of the buildings were rubble. Still, there could be something . . .

Keeping her head low as she scrabbled through the ancient passageway, Theodosia put a hand on each side of the doorway as she emerged slowly into bright sunlight. A low, round stone artifact, possibly a well or cistern, sat directly to her left, while to her right was . . . holy cow! The biggest rattlesnake she'd ever seen!

Oh no! That thing is . . .

26

. . . A monster!

Theodosia gasped as she practically felt sharp fangs sinking into flesh, flinched in anticipation of hot venom searing through her veins.

But none of that happened. Just as her terrified brain registered the somewhat somnolent reptile and chattered warnings of imminent danger to her front cortex, she dove left, then skittered a good twenty paces. The mad dash, along with her body's own shot of adrenaline, had her heart pumping furiously. Pausing near a thicket of dogwood to catch her breath and reconnoiter, barely conscious of the low stir and whir of katydids, Theodosia shot a furtive glance over her shoulder. Much to her relief, no six-foot rattler had launched itself in hot pursuit. In fact, chances were good that the snake had been just as startled as she was. Still, Theodosia knew she'd have to be a whole lot more careful. Oh yeah.

Reaching up, Theodosia pulled hard on a sapling, twisted the leafy branch low, then snapped it off and quickly shucked sticky, green leaves. From now on, she'd prod the long grasses ahead of her to alert and dislodge any type of critter that might be hunkered there, no matter what. Even if it proved to be a harmless marsh hen or slow-moving terrapin.

Pushing through underbrush, probing her stick like a professional beater trying to flush a tiger from the bush, Theodosia carefully moved on, finally emerging in a packed earth circle that didn't offer much. Piles of bricks, crusted metal — maybe part of an old cannon? — and a few crumbled buildings. There wasn't even anything left of the old lighthouse, except remnants of the foundation.

Theodosia stood there, feeling like she'd stumbled upon the ruins of some ancient civilization, some secret place where people hadn't trod for a hundred years. Then she realized that was the legacy of Castle Pinckney. An old fort, abandoned for decades, left to molder and die a slow death.

So kind of fascinating, after all, she decided.

Poking her stick out ahead of her, Theodosia moved forward. Creeping along slowly, she still hoped to discover some small vestige of the old fort. Some sort of testament to the War of 1812 or even the Civil War. She stepped over bricks, rocks, and crumbling foundations. But there seemed to be nothing of any real significance.

She wondered if the Kipling Club had ever made its way out here. Maybe they had. Possibly, unbeknownst to the Ports Authority, they'd plundered anything of value.

Theodosia continued to wander. An entire forest of trees had grown up and thrived here, obscuring foundations and making it difficult to determine where buildings and barracks had once stood. As she rounded a clump of magnolias, poking and prodding with her stick, she discovered a sort of wall with narrow rifle slits built into it.

This had to be part of the old fort!

Bending forward, peering through the stone slit, Theodosia wondered what it had been like to see an entire fleet of British warships hurtling down upon you, Union Jacks flying, cannons pounding, sails billowing. Exciting, to be sure. And terrifying.

She stood for a moment, trying to sear that vision into her brain so she could tell

Drayton. Then, amidst the solitude of the ghostly ruins, Theodosia heard the smallest of sounds. A kind of *tink-clink,* like a pebble falling onto damp cement.

Theodosia froze. The notion that someone else might be here suddenly unnerved her. But who? Other clandestine explorers like herself?

Or maybe — and now her brain was working overtime — what if Jory's sailboat hadn't drifted haphazardly and beached itself here? What if a cool hand on the tiller had purposely steered the boat here?

But whose cool hand?

Beth Ann? Someone else? Someone who might be observing her right now?

Quick as a fox, Theodosia darted past the wall and plunged into a sea of tall grasses. Casting an eye toward the sun as she plodded through shifting sands, she adjusted her course and determined she was probably, hopefully, headed in the approximate direction of the beach. And she was right. Three minutes later, she emerged from the weeds and reeds onto the beach, close to where Jory's J/22 sat rocking listlessly.

Time to skedaddle, Theodosia decided. She kicked off her shoes and tossed them into the boat. Then she bent forward, grasped the prow of the boat, and shoved hard.

Nothing.

Digging her bare feet deeper into the sand, Theodosia braced a shoulder against the boat and pushed with all her might. And this time was rewarded with a sudden whoosh, as the boat heaved free of the sandbar.

Okay, she decided, *now we're cooking.*

Pulling herself aboard, Theodosia quickly apprised the situation. If someone had, in fact, sailed the J/22 over to Castle Pinckney, then they'd done a masterful job of stowing away the sails. Which probably hadn't happened.

With that calming thought, Theodosia pulled open the hatch, climbed into the fore cabin, and muscled the sails onto the deck. Then she quickly set about rigging them. Snapping clips to her mainsail and spinnaker, working as fast as she could. When everything was ready, she gave a sharp tug on the line and the mainsail ripped up the mast, catching air and billowing like crazy the higher it rode. Tying off the line, Theodosia scrambled back to the cockpit and grabbed the till. From there it was a simple matter of maneuvering the J/22.

Five minutes later, Theodosia was skimming across Charleston Harbor. Wind rattled the halyards against the aluminum mast, sails whumped and thumped while other, speedier, motorized boats zipped past her. Gazing down toward Fort Sumter, she could see one of the tour boats making its thrice-a-day jaunt around the harbor.

Trimming her sail, checking her speed slightly, Theodosia rounded the tip of the peninsula, close enough now to see actual Frisbee players lobbing orange discs at each other. She heeled over slightly, completing her turn, and then it wasn't long before she was easing the J/22 into Jory's slip at the Charleston Yacht Club.

Taking down the sails and stowing them was the easy part. She'd done it dozens of times, in happier times, on this boat, and could pretty much do it in her sleep.

With the sails folded and stored, Theodosia tossed her orange life vest down the hatch, then leaned down and coiled the last of the line.

Jory's joke had always been that when you bought line instead of rope, the decimal point moved over a couple of notches. But as Theodosia handled this line, her brain suddenly recalled the cotton rope that had strangled Daria.

Could it have been line from this very

boat? Cut by Beth Ann's own hand? Was Beth Ann the missing link in all of this? Was Beth Ann a zonked-out, crazy-lady killer?

Theodosia let the possibility trickle through her brain again as she walked the length of the dock back to her car and decided it might be a real possibility.

So what now? she wondered.

Popping the locks on her car, Theodosia leaned across the front seat, dug into her shoulder bag, and pulled out her cell phone. Tidwell didn't answer; instead she got his voice mail. But she left what she thought was a fairly tantalizing message. Along with an urgent request to meet her tonight — at the Heritage Society.

Haley was finishing up in the kitchen when Theodosia returned.

"You found the boat?" she asked, wiping her hands on a tea towel.

"Yup," said Theodosia.

"Get it back to the marina okay?"

"No problem," Theodosia told her. She wandered over to the small counter, helped herself to a plump, pink shrimp.

"Well," commented Haley. "I don't know how you're going to take this, but you look like you had a wonderful time."

Surprised, Theodosia quickly swallowed

her bite. "Really?"

"Oh yeah," said Haley, peering at her. "Your eyes look bright and your complexion's all glowy. Like you just had an oxygen facial or some other kind of spendy spa treatment."

"A wind-and-sea-salt scrub." Theodosia laughed. "Which I highly recommend."

Haley looked askance. "So you're not mad at Jory?"

"I didn't say that," Theodosia responded. "I'm still furious beyond belief, but I've decided not to let my personal dealings with him compromise activities that I enjoy. Case in point, sailing."

"Okay," said Haley, "I get it. I think."

Theodosia hastily changed the subject. "Looks like you've got everything ready for tonight."

Haley shook her hair back behind her shoulders. "Almost. Got to pack up the avocados and baguettes yet, but other than that we're good to go."

"I take it Drayton helped?"

"Enormously," said Haley.

"Okay then," said Theodosia. "I'm gonna scram upstairs and take a shower and try to get presentable."

"Which means I can load most of this stuff in your Jeep now," said Haley. "Right?"

"Right," said Theodosia, digging into her pocket and tossing Haley a jingle of keys.

But once Theodosia retreated upstairs, once she stepped into the shower and let hot water pound her head, back, and shoulders, once she shampooed her hair and let it air-dry, she couldn't make up her mind about what to wear that night.

Theodosia Browning, being a decisive, organized, and fairly low-maintenance person, always seemed slightly befuddled when it came to dressing up. Probably because she preferred to dress down. Enjoyed wearing comfy crop pants, a slinky T-shirt, and comfy sandals versus a dress and tottering high heels. Not that she didn't love dresses and high heels; it's just that they were so . . . dressy.

Digging in her closet, she pulled out a black cocktail dress and a short, sea-green silk shift with a hand-painted iris on it. Held them up in front of her, checked the mirror, still wasn't sure. Decided maybe she should solicit an unbiased opinion from the pup with the poshest taste around.

"What do you think, fella?" she asked, showing Earl Grey both dresses.

Earl Grey studied the two choices with solemn brown eyes. "Gwrrr," he finally told her.

"The green one?" she asked.

"Rwrrr." Right.

Theodosia studied the green dress again, said, "Maybe we should call Delaine. You think?"

Earl Grey laid down, placed his soft muzzle atop his front paws, and rolled his eyes.

"Just a quick check," she told him, reaching for her phone. "After all, she is a professional."

"What?" screeched Delaine, sounding harried.

"My green dress," said Theodosia. "The one with the hand-painted iris."

"Hmmm?" said Delaine.

"You think it's good for tonight?"

"Gosh, I don't know, Theodosia," replied Delaine. "Do you want to look positively smashing or like a little brown wren?"

"When you put it that way . . ." said Theodosia.

"Wear the green!" shrilled Delaine. "It's perfect. Besides, you bought it at my shop. Remember? The trunk show last summer?"

"How could I forget," said Theodosia. *Why did I call her? Why did I open myself up for such a direct hit?*

"And wear your silver Prada heels," Delaine added, then hung up abruptly.

Theodosia turned and gazed at Earl Grey, who regarded her with placid, unrelenting, doggy scrutiny. "I know, I know, I should have listened to you in the first place."

Earl Grey twitched an ear and sighed deeply. *Humans. Unpredictable creatures.*

27

"Excuse me, excuse me," murmured Haley as she and Theodosia, clutching large plastic bins, elbowed their way through the well-dressed throng of Charleston socialites. Hung with dark oil paintings of long-dead South Carolina residents and defunct rice and indigo plantations, the wide hallway as gallery was the perfect place to hobnob. Edging into the lecture hall, Theodosia and Haley encountered yet another scrum of buzzing people who were chatting and air-kissing. Finally, they made it into the small service kitchen at the back.

"Lots of people here tonight," said Theodosia, depositing her load on the aluminum kitchen counter. She was surprised so many folks had turned out for Lyndel Woodruff's lecture. Then again, Timothy Neville was a master at drawing a crowd and Drayton had been politicking nonstop to alert friends, members, and donors.

"It's hard to imagine so many folks are interested in hearing a lecture on a Civil War battle," said Haley, starting to unpack the food. "I even saw Bill Glass out there."

"Great," said Theodosia.

Haley hesitated. "Or do you think everyone's just here for the social part?"

"Probably a little of both," said Theodosia. Heritage Society events were a place to see and be seen. And Lyndel Woodruff's lecture just happened to fall right between the end of opera season and the beginning of the symphony's three-month run. Which meant that a lot of socially prominent people were on the prowl for a night out. And Timothy did have a way of twisting arms.

"Think we brought enough food?" asked Haley.

"If we run out, then everyone will just focus on drinking," said Theodosia.

"And hobnobbing," said Haley. "These people are really world-class hobnobbers. Hey, do you think that archaeology guy is gonna show?" She draped a black apron over her head, glanced about the small but serviceable catering kitchen.

"Tred Pascal?" said Theodosia. "He will if he knows what's good for him." She smiled at Haley. "Since he knows *you're* going to be here."

"Hah," said Haley. "We'll see how interested he really is."

"I'm going to be on the lookout for Jud Snelling," said Theodosia. "He's that fellow I told you about from Savannah who might be interested in becoming a silent partner in the Antiquarian Map Shop."

"You suspicious of him?" asked Haley.

"Maybe. A little."

"So you're doing some investigating," said Haley. "Besides the catering."

"You could say that."

"What's the plan?" asked Haley. "Do we have a timeline?"

Theodosia checked her watch. "Lyndel's lecture is scheduled to begin in ten minutes or so and, according to Drayton, should run about thirty minutes. Tacking on another fifteen minutes for audience questions, I'd say we need to have our food and tea on the patio no later than eight thirty."

"In that case," said Haley, "we've got oodles of time." She pointed to a metal door. "I can squiggle out that way to the patio?"

"Yes," said Theodosia. "And as soon as Lyndel's done answering questions, Drayton and I will open all the French doors so guests can stroll out."

"And then we do our thing," said Haley.

"Got it."

"What can I help you with?" asked Theodosia.

Haley held up a hand. "Absolutely nothing. You just go out and mingle. Have fun. Do your mystery-solving thing. Find the killer."

Theodosia's face assumed a slightly stricken look.

"Oh jeez," said Haley, trying to backpedal. "Apologies. I didn't mean to sound so flippant. Really. I just . . ."

"I know," said Theodosia, "we're all on edge over what's happened this past week."

Haley still looked pained. "Hey, I really am sorry. I know you and Daria were good friends."

"As are we," said Theodosia, giving Haley a quick hug.

Cinnamon and Miss Kitty accosted Theodosia the minute she emerged into the crowded hallway.

"Hello, dear!" squealed Miss Kitty. "Wonderful to see you!"

"This is so much fun!" gushed Cinnamon. "So many nice neighbors in attendance. Can you tell us, do most of these folks reside in the larger, fancier homes?"

Theodosia decided to remain noncommittal, since Miss Kitty and Cinnamon both seemed desperate to cultivate only customers with money. "The Heritage Society stages dozens of lectures and gallery shows throughout the year," Theodosia told them. "Perhaps you'll take a few more in and become members." *And perhaps I sound like the mission statement in their annual report,* she thought. *Oh well.*

"Maybe," said Cinnamon, glancing around, her eyes roving across those women who sported the real bling-bling diamond bracelets and matching earrings.

"Or you might even become donors," added Theodosia. At which point the two women went completely mute. Theodosia gave a sly smile, murmured, "Excuse me," and slipped away. She'd spotted someone else she very much wanted to talk to.

"See you later," called a subdued Miss Kitty.

"Fallon?" said Theodosia, hurrying over to a display of maps, daggers, and antique pistols. "I had no idea you'd be here tonight."

Daria's sister, Fallon, turned from where she was hanging a large map to greet Theodosia. "Theo, hello," she said smiling. "I wasn't planning to come, but then Timothy called about borrowing this map for display." She smoothed the sepia-tone map carefully with one hand. "Jason was going to come at first and then I thought, why don't I come instead?"

"Do you good to get out," said Theodosia. Dressed in a shiny black tank top and a slightly puffed short skirt, Fallon looked less mousey than usual. Quite presentable, in fact.

"I thought coming here tonight would do me some good," said Fallon. Her eyes assumed a slightly haunted look, then she asked, "How are you doing?" She dropped her voice to an even lower register. "I mean . . . with your undercover — or should I call it insider — investigation?"

Theodosia hesitated for a moment, then said, "I think I might be making progress."

Fallon's eyes widened and she leaned in closer. "Seriously?"

Theodosia put a hand on Fallon's shoulder. "Please don't get your hopes up. I need to speak with Detective Tidwell and untangle a couple of things yet."

"He's here?" asked Fallon.

"No, but I'm assuming he'll show up," said Theodosia. "I left a voice mail telling him it was fairly urgent that we meet."

"You really are on to something!" breathed Fallon. "Oh, you are such a love."

"No, no," said Theodosia. "Please hold any and all thanks until we have Daria's killer locked securely behind bars. But do understand that I haven't given up on this, okay?"

"Thank you," said Fallon, her eyes filling with tears. She reached in her small shoulder bag, dug past lipstick, mascara, and an atomizer, and grabbed a tissue.

"Theodosia," came a commanding voice.

Theodosia whirled to find Timothy Neville standing there, looking typically serious and a trifle imperious. "Timothy, hello. Great turnout tonight."

Timothy nodded in agreement to Theodosia, then said to Fallon, "That looks perfect, my dear. Many thanks for the loan of your map. Along with our display, it's a wonderful adjunct to Lyndel's lecture."

"You're welcome," said Fallon, ducking her head, looking pleased.

"And if I might have a word with you," said Timothy, grasping Theodosia's upper arm and pulling her aside.

"A problem?" Theodosia asked.

"No," said Timothy. "Fact is, I believe I've been able to shed considerable light on your backyard mystery."

"Uh-oh," said Theodosia, as they moved down the hallway together. "What's up? Did you discover a long-lost cemetery beneath my cottage? Or worse yet . . . catacombs?"

"Nothing so dire," said Timothy, reaching into the pocket of his snappy houndstooth jacket and pulling out several folded papers. "I had one of our interns do a bit of digging in our library. Studying old newspapers and documents, that sort of thing. Here." He thrust the papers at Theodosia. "See for yourself."

Theodosia unfolded Xerox copies of old newspaper accounts and scanned them as Timothy continued to talk.

"It seems the mansion next door to you was used as a temporary hospital in the final year of the Civil War," Timothy told her. "And your little cottage, Hazelhurst as it's now known, served as the chief surgeon's residence."

"Oh," said Theodosia, glancing up. "A residence?" She frowned. "I was under the impression it was an old carriage house."

"Might have been." Timothy chuckled. "I didn't say the doctor lived in a *first-class* residence. For all we know, it could have been falling down back then." He cleared his throat, still looking pleased. "Anyway, I'd be willing to bet that the bone or bones are probably the result of some poor soul who passed away while under the good doctor's care. Or are, perhaps, remnants from an old surgery or autopsy."

"Did you tell her?" asked Drayton, rushing up. He turned a serious gaze on Theodosia. "He told you?"

"About the doctor's quarters, yes," said Theodosia.

"Good news, wouldn't you say?" asked Drayton. He also looked scrubbed and slick in a navy-blue jacket and dove-gray slacks.

"Will this information get the archeologists to stop digging?" Theodosia murmured, almost to herself.

"We think so," said Timothy. "And you know I'll be happy to intercede any way I can."

"I'll take you up on that," said Theodosia, knowing Timothy's tremendous clout in the community. "And I owe you one."

Timothy gave a breezy wave. "All I ask is that our cocktail party go off without a hitch."

"That I can do," said Theodosia. "Our theme tonight is lovely and low-key."

"In that case," grinned Drayton, "I'd better run out and feng shui the patio. Make sure that we achieve harmonic balance to draw positive energy."

"Couldn't hurt," said Theodosia. She wasn't a big believer in charms, totems, and palm readers, but she was willing to give anything a try once. Well, maybe not *anything.*

Strolling back through the lecture hall, Theodosia noticed that people were beginning to gather in earnest now. She pushed her way back into the kitchen and found Haley arranging shrimp and avocado kabobs on three-tiered trays mounded with crushed ice. "Those look absolutely delicious," she told Haley.

Haley wiped her hands on the front of her apron. "Thanks. I'm gonna stick 'em in the cooler, though, until we need to take 'em out." She smiled. "Plus, I've got smoked salmon and goat cheese generously lathered on baguette slices and . . . what else? Oh, I have to spoon crab salad into puff pastries."

"I can help with that," said Theodosia.

"Okay," agreed Haley. "If you insist. I brought along some of our teeny gold teaspoons so we can add just the right amount . . ." Hearing a sudden whack, she turned toward the kitchen door as it blasted open.

Drayton came steamrolling in, looking unhappy. "There's a huge problem!" he wailed.

"Certainly not with the food," shot back Haley.

"Beverage service?" inquired Theodosia. Although she'd seen an efficient-looking bartender with his ice chests and multiple cases of champagne stacked outside.

"Worse!" wailed Drayton. "You know those marvelous Civil War–era weapons Timothy arranged in the display case in the front hallway? It seems someone's pried open the cabinet door and made off with a knife!"

"That's it?" said Haley. "You had me worried for a second."

"A theft *is* most certainly cause to worry," replied Drayton. He cast a meaningful glance at Theodosia. "Theo . . . ?"

"You think Theo took the knife?" asked Haley, slightly horrified.

"No," said Theodosia. "Drayton's asking in a roundabout way about someone else."

Haley's mouth opened, then closed without making a sound. Finally she said, "Holy shamoly, you mean Delaine's sister?"

"Nadine," said Drayton, sotto voce.

"Don't tell me she's still a practicing klepto," said Haley, almost amused now.

Drayton pounced on Haley. "You think Mrs. Wentworth from the History Club has sticky fingers? Or Philippe Dupree from the Civil War Reenactors Society?"

Or a crazy person from the Kipling Club?

Theodosia wondered to herself.

"Uh, I'm guessing the millionaires didn't do it," said Haley.

"I prefer to think of them as significant donors to Charleston's various arts and civic organizations," said Drayton.

"Fat cats," declared Haley.

"Whatever the case," said Theodosia, stepping in, "maybe we should pull Nadine aside and do some oh-so-gentle probing."

"Timothy's having an absolute hissy fit," said Drayton, "so I don't think we should be particularly gentle with Nadine."

"Then just probe her," snorted Haley.

Theodosia took off her apron and tossed it on a ladder-back chair. "I'll go talk to Delaine and Nadine right now. See if I can shed a little light."

"Thank you!" said Drayton.

Theodosia hustled out into the lecture hall where most of the guests had taken their seats by now, scanned the crowd for familiar faces, but didn't see either Delaine or Nadine. She slipped down the aisle and out into the main hallway, where only a few folks, latecomers and concerned-looking Heritage Society staff, still milled about.

Maybe one of the side galleries?

The Heritage Society had a half dozen

small galleries where oil paintings, photography, old silver, and antique pottery were displayed. But as Theodosia dashed from gallery to gallery, she could find no one.

So where?

Was it possible Timothy Neville had spotted Nadine with the missing object and was already grilling her? Or stalling her until the police showed up? Maybe he was holding her in the reception area or in his office behind closed doors where a certain amount of discretion could be maintained? Maybe.

Theodosia flew down another hallway and emerged in the reception area. But it was dark, silent, and unoccupied. Two upholstered armchairs were but dim lumps, a single, green glass shade glowed on Camilla Hodge's reception desk.

A slight noise, a whisper really, like footsteps on a carpet, caused Theodosia to whirl about and peer down the narrow hallway that led past Timothy's office. And did her eyes detect a slight movement at the end of that corridor? In the low light, had she maybe caught . . . a brief flash of pink?

Without hesitation, Theodosia hurried down that dim hallway. She paused at the doorway to Timothy's office, put her hand on the brass doorknob, and turned it. Nothing. His office was locked tight as a drum.

Continuing down to the end of the hallway, Theodosia paused, her hand caressing the worn knob of a wooden banister. This stairway led downstairs to the storage rooms.

Should she? Is this where the person she saw — or thought she saw — disappeared to?

Plunging downstairs, Theodosia almost tripped on the narrow, wooden stairs. Steadying herself, she clambered to the bottom only to be faced with another choice. Two corridors led off into darkness, with only twenty-watt bulbs glowing at the far end. Not much charm down here, she decided. Cement floor, cinder-block walls, a couple of locked doors complete with keypads and blinking lights. Obviously, a security system armed against possible intruders.

So if this person she'd been following, supposedly Nadine, had come down here, where had she gone? How had she disappeared like a wisp of smoke?

Edging down one corridor, Theodosia felt both nervous and a little silly. Because, probably, no one was prowling around down here after all. She was just chasing light and shadows, figments of her imagination.

Okay, enough said. Theodosia hurried

back upstairs and headed for the lecture hall.

She found Delaine, lounging in an aisle seat, chatting away with Hillary Retton, as the last of the guests filed into the hall.

"Where's your sister?" Theodosia murmured in Delaine's ear.

Delaine turned, frowned, and waved a hand. "I don't know. Socializing, I imagine."

"Socializing where?"

"Wherever," said Delaine, sounding peeved. "Last I saw Nadine she was talking to that adorable man, Barton Palmer. Have you met him? He owns Bubbles, that new wine and champagne bar."

"Okay, let me ask you this," said Theodosia. "What's Nadine wearing tonight? Is it a pink jacket and skirt?"

Delaine tilted her head back and seemed to ponder the question. "I'd say the color was more of a blush rose. Of course, under the absolute right lighting conditions it could be mistaken for primrose."

"Delaine . . . please!" said Theodosia. "We're not picking paint chips at Home Depot, just answer the question. It's important!"

Shrugging her shoulders in an I-don't-know gesture, Delaine hissed, "Shhh, Theo, the lecture's starting."

Glancing around, Theodosia saw that Delaine was right. Everyone had settled into chairs as the grand overhead chandeliers slowly dimmed. Then a bright key light fell upon Lyndel Woodruff as he took long, loping strides to the podium.

Stepping back into the hallway, Theodosia silently closed the door behind her and slumped against the deeply grained wood. She drew a breath and decided to take a look at the pilfered display case. Spinning quickly, she found herself gazing into angry, blazing eyes set into a hardened, female face.

Theodosia cringed even as she reflexively threw up a hand and cried, "Beth Ann!"

28

"Beth Ann," Theodosia choked out again, staring at Jory's ex-fiancée, regarding her almost as if she were some hostile spirit who'd magically materialized from the great beyond. "What are *you* doing here?"

Beth Ann lifted her chin in an imperious manner and gazed at Theodosia, hatred blazing in her eyes. "I came to see you, Theodosia. It's time we had it out." She spat out these last words, then took a step forward, doing her best to intimidate Theodosia by invading her personal space.

"Had it out?" said Theodosia, not yielding an inch. "Had *what* out?"

"As if you didn't know. The issue of Jory Davis, of course!"

Theodosia put her hands on her hips. "I don't have an issue with Jory Davis."

"You're trying to *steal* him back," said Beth Ann, seething with molten anger.

"No, I'm not," said Theodosia. "Fact is, I

haven't wanted Jory back for a long time."

"Liar!" snapped Beth Ann. Her nostrils flared; red blotches blazed high on her cheeks. Beth Ann was clearly overwrought and looked like she was ready to do battle.

Theodosia shook her head as if to clear away this nightmare encounter. "Listen to me," she said, biting off each word. "I don't want Jory. You can *have* him."

Beth Ann's eyes widened in shock and her resolve seemed to waver. "What?"

"Read my lips," said Theodosia. "You're welcome to Jory Davis. He's yours. End of story."

"I don't believe you," Beth Ann hissed. "You're just saying that to get rid of me."

"No," Theodosia muttered, "there's a better way to be rid of you." She squared her shoulders, turned away, took a few steps . . . then hesitated. Running through her brain was the notion that if Beth Ann was crazy enough to zoom around like the Wicked Witch of the East, spewing venom and nastiness, she might be crazy enough to engineer other things, too. Turning back toward her, Theodosia focused on Beth Ann and asked in a gravelly voice, "What are you doing here?"

Frustration manifested itself on Beth Ann's face. "Talking to you!"

"No," said Theodosia. "I meant here, geographically. In Charleston. Why are you here?"

Beth Ann huffed out an enormous sigh. "Typical of Jory not to mention it, but I've relocated permanently to Charleston. There's a good chance he and I will be married soon."

"Sorry, Beth Ann, that's not the story I heard."

"Don't say that!" screamed Beth Ann. "You're just jealous!"

"Uh, Beth Ann, could you please dial it down?"

"What?"

"Question number two," said Theodosia. "Do you have a car?"

Beth Ann stared at her, hatred radiating from her eyes like a demon possessed. "Of course I have a car," she spat out. "A rental. How else do you think I'm going to learn my way around these crazy, stupid streets?"

"What color is it?" asked Theodosia.

Beth Ann tilted her head to one side and folded her hands across her chest in a confrontational gesture. "I don't know. What do you care?"

"Please just answer the question," said Theodosia. When push came to shove, Theodosia could be just as stubborn.

Beth Ann let loose another deep sigh, as if coughing up an answer was a supreme imposition. "Dark. Navy. Black, maybe. I don't know."

"Okay," said Theodosia. "Now we're making some forward progress." The car that had tried to run her into the bridge embankment three nights ago had been black, so checking out Beth Ann's car was going to be a serious litmus test. If Beth Ann had a bash in her car or a dented front fender, then it stood to reason she'd been the one on the Ben Sawyer Bridge that night.

"What I need to do," said Theodosia, "is take a look at your car."

"What?" said Beth Ann again. "Why?"

"Indulge me," said Theodosia.

"You're crazy, you know that?" said Beth Ann. "No wonder Jory left you."

"Can we just . . . go outside for a minute?"

Reluctantly, Beth Ann followed Theodosia out onto the patio.

"Drayton," Theodosia called. "Could you come here for a moment?"

Drayton strolled over from where he'd been buzzing about, arranging napkins, silverware, and teacups on the tables. "Hmm?" Then his eyes widened in surprise when he recognized Beth Ann.

"Drayton," said Theodosia, "you remember Beth Ann, don't you? We're all going to go take a peek at her car."

"I say . . ." said Drayton.

Cocking her head toward Beth Ann, Theodosia said, "The bridge . . ."

Drayton picked up on her meaning. "Ah . . ."

"What's wrong with you people?" demanded Beth Ann. "Don't you talk in full sentences?"

"It's a southern thing," Theodosia told her. "Kind of a code you're going to have to learn if you intend to live here."

"You people really are crazy," muttered Beth Ann.

Beth Ann's rental was a shiny black Nissan Sentra. No bashes or mashes marred its sleek countenance. Hence, probably no recent bridge crashes.

"Happy now?" asked Beth Ann. She stood off to the side, fingering her electronic key fob. "You want to tell me what this is all about?"

"Not particularly," said Theodosia. She stared down the dark street parked solid with cars. Gaslights shimmered in the mist that had drifted in from the harbor, live oaks arched and whispered overhead.

"Definitely not the one," said Drayton.

"So we keep . . ." said Theodosia.

"Indeed," replied Drayton.

"You're doing it again!" screeched Beth Ann. "Talking in stupid riddles."

"It's just . . ." said Drayton.

"Oh, forget it," Beth Ann blurted in a sour voice. "I'm out of here." She extended her arm and punched the key fob, sounding a tiny electronic beep. Pulling open the door, she scrambled into her car, still railing at them, just this side of hysterical. "I really can't *stand* this place, you know? You people literally drive me crazy!"

Theodosia smiled faintly as Beth Ann gunned the engine all the while muttering to herself and making futile gestures. "She really is off the hook, isn't she?" They watched as Beth Ann slammed her car into gear and screeched wildly away from the curb.

"Now what?" asked Drayton.

"Not sure," said Theodosia. "But I think we just eliminated one suspect."

"So a bit of an upside," allowed Drayton.

They stood there talking for a good ten minutes. About Beth Ann, wondering where Nadine had run off to, and about Joe Don Hunter.

"What if he grabbed the dagger?" asked

403

Theodosia. "So he could turn around and sell it."

"Could have," said Drayton, "though I didn't see him prowling around."

"Still," said Theodosia, "Joe Don had to know about this evening." She thought for a few moments. "Maybe Fallon mentioned it to him."

"Maybe," said Drayton.

They chatted for a few more minutes, then strolled back through the darkness, down a gravel path lined with tall, whispering bamboo plants, and onto the Heritage Society's outdoor patio. With its exotic, almost Balinese feel, the patio was dark, deep, and secluded. Ground-level spotlights tucked into thick stands of bamboo, magnolias, and crepe myrtle cast shadows and heightened the feeling of wandering through an exotic land. A free-form pond brimmed with silver-white Japanese koi while water trickled down strategically placed rocks, emitting a hypnotic, melodious sound.

Wrought-iron tables and chairs were set around the patio; two larger buffet tables covered in white linen tablecloths had been arranged to hold appetizers, tea, and champagne.

All they had to do now was carry out food trays and teapots and alert the bartender,

Theodosia decided, since it was just a matter of time before their guests would come streaming out.

"Ye gadz," squeaked Drayton, glimpsing the lecture hall through the French double doors, "I think Lyndel's almost done with his lecture."

"Let's dash in and catch the tail end," suggested Theodosia.

They slipped through the back door and into the kitchen, where Haley and the bartender were locked in bantering conversation, then emerged in the back of the lecture hall.

"He is finished," Drayton whispered. Lyndel Woodruff was gazing out at his audience, looking pleased with the talk he'd just delivered. Looking a little relieved, too.

"What I'd like to do now," said Lyndel, "is open this up to all of you who were so kind to come here tonight." He spread his arms in a magnanimous gesture to the audience, then leaned forward and grasped the podium.

Off to his left, the hallway door suddenly slammed open and two troopers from the South Carolina Highway Patrol strode noisily into the room, boot heels drumming against old oak floorboards. Dressed in full regalia with insignia and guns, they appeared to have business on their mind. Then, as the overhead lights flashed on, Lyndel Woodruff seemed to falter and wilt at the podium, his face going blush red. A few members of the audience stood up to see what was going on, a loud buzz rose from the crowd.

Not sure what to make of this rude intrusion or how to soldier on with his program, Lyndel Woodruff asked in a quavering voice, "Are there any questions?"

The taller of the two officers, a man with a modified handlebar mustache and grizzled gray hair sticking out from under his Smokey Bear hat, strode to the podium, bent toward the microphone and barked out, "Are Cinnamon St. John and Kitty Devlin present?"

An even louder buzz erupted from the audience as heads twisted and the curious audience scanned the room for the two women in question.

"What's this about?" muttered a stunned Drayton.

His question was promptly answered as Detective Burt Tidwell, flanked by two uniformed police officers, entered the room at a brisk trot.

"You heard the state patrol officers," Tidwell snapped out, his jowls sloshing, his beady eyes roving the crowd.

Seated in the center of the room, Miss Kitty suddenly stood up, followed by a reluctant Cinnamon. A man next to them proclaimed, "This is an outrage!"

"No," said Tidwell, addressing the audience with all the aplomb of a trained Shakespearean actor, "this is an arrest."

"What are the charges?" wondered Theodosia, as she watched the two women being taken into custody by the contingent of officers. Had Tidwell somehow linked them to Daria's murder?

"This is so cool," exclaimed Haley, who'd rushed out to catch the fireworks. "I never saw anyone get arrested before."

"Isn't pageantry exciting?" asked Drayton, rolling his eyes.

"Tidwell must have discovered some sort of evidence against them," Theodosia murmured as the spectacle continued.

Actual handcuffs were produced and placed around the wrists of the two women.

One of the state patrol officers pulled a small, laminated card from the pocket of his khaki shirt and began to read. "Under sovereign authority entrusted to me by of the State of South Carolina, I hereby place you under arrest. You have the right to remain . . ."

With the entire crowd goggle-eyed and standing on its feet now, Theodosia edged up the aisle toward Detective Tidwell. He flashed a single glance at her, but kept his focus on Miss Kitty and Cinnamon. Finally, when the two troopers escorted the two women out, Tidwell lifted a single eyebrow and gazed at Theodosia.

She was beside him in a second. "Why were they arrested?" she asked. "Was it because of Daria's murder?"

Tidwell stared at her, looking almost confused. "No, that's not it."

"Then what?" demanded Theodosia.

Tidwell shook his head as if to dismiss Theodosia's previous statement. "Receiving stolen goods," he told her, as Drayton suddenly flew past them, then veered toward the podium.

"You mean . . . *perfume?*" sputtered Theodosia. "You're telling me Cinnamon and Miss Kitty were involved in the hijacking case you were working on? You *knew* they were receiving stolen goods?"

"I wish I could take credit for such amazing skill and deductive reasoning," said Tidwell. "In fact, we weren't having much luck at all until a disgruntled wholesaler in Miami finally placed a GPS transponder *inside* his last shipment. Guess where we traced it to?"

"Uh, a certain shop on Church Street?" said Theodosia, sounding disgruntled.

"Interesting, yes?" said Tidwell.

But it was disappointment that registered on Theodosia's face.

"Excuse me!" Drayton's cultured voice suddenly boomed from the microphone. "Will you all take your seats please?" He paused. "Thank you, thank you, everyone." As conversation began to die down and people actually took their seats, Drayton continued. "As a Heritage Society board member, I wish to apologize for this unusual and rather inconvenient interruption. However, our guest lecturer, Mr. Lyndel Woodruff, is far from finished." He mustered an enthusiastic grin for Lyndel. "Mr. Woodruff is now ready for the question-and-answer portion of the evening."

A spatter of applause broke out, then pretty soon the entire audience was caught up in the applause.

Drayton stepped back, relinquishing the podium to Lyndel. "Lyndel?"

With renewed energy, Lyndel Woodruff, began to accept questions from the audience.

Drayton rushed to the back of the lecture

hall where Theodosia and Haley whispered together. "They were really arrested?"

"Apparently," said Theodosia. She stared out into the front hallway where Tidwell was deep in conversation with Timothy. For some reason, she fervently hoped Timothy wasn't bothering him about the missing dagger.

"Because . . . ?" asked Drayton.

"Receiving stolen goods," said Theodosia. "But I think . . ."

"They had something to do with Daria's death, too?" Drayton asked breathlessly as they slipped back into the kitchen.

Theodosia exhaled slowly, suddenly feeling like the crack in the case hadn't cracked open that much. As if the bad dream might continue. "Building a murder case against them is up to Tidwell now. But if you ask me . . ."

"If you ask me," cut in Haley, "the case is closed. Cinnamon and Miss Kitty murdered Daria." She stared at them mournfully. "The sordid details will all come out eventually."

Drayton looked thoughtful. "But what possible motive did they have?"

"Perhaps," said Theodosia, venturing a guess, "Daria may have *seen* something?"

"Like a delivery!" said Drayton, pouncing

on the idea.

"It's possible," said Theodosia, piecing people and events together as she went on. "And then Daria put two and two together," said Theodosia. She paused. "Does that make sense?"

"Makes perfect sense to me," said Drayton.

"Wow," echoed Haley. "Who would have thought a couple of hoity-toity dames who sold bottles of perfume were really serious criminals?"

"You never know what lurks deep within someone's heart," said Drayton. He cocked his head, as if deep in thought, then said, "What about the candles and lighter those women donated for tonight? You suppose those are stolen goods as well?"

"Let's not worry about candles right now," said Theodosia, still trying to cobble together a murder scenario.

"Our little secret," Haley added with a wink.

"If you say so," said Drayton. "But I for one don't care to get busted."

"Busted?" Haley hooted. "Over donated candles? Gimme a break."

"Okay, guys," said Theodosia, knowing they'd better focus squarely on the cocktail party, "let's get back on track. You two double-check appetizer platters while I run out and take a final look at the patio. Once I give the high sign, we'll ferry everything out."

"Got it," said Haley.

Bustling about the patio, Theodosia didn't have to do much to make it any more gorgeous than it already was. The romantic lighting, the pond with its tinkling waterfall, the dense foliage that swayed slightly in the warm evening breeze set a magical scene.

Each of the round, wrought-iron tables also looked perfect, adorned with centerpieces of white roses, sweet peas, and lily of the valley arranged in crystal vases. Tiny white votive candles twinkled in silver julep cups. On the main tables, teacups and crystal champagne flutes were arranged just so, bottles of champagne rested in large silver ice buckets.

Theodosia felt lighter and, strangely enough, more hopeful, knowing it hadn't been Beth Ann who'd tried to force her off the bridge.

So maybe it had just been a crazy person that night? Or a drunk driver in an all-fired hurry? Or perhaps it had been Cinnamon and Miss Kitty after all. They seemed to be the crazy ones in this whole mess. They were the ones who'd been arrested and hauled off in handcuffs.

But were they murderers? Drayton's words rang so true — it was impossible to peer into someone's heart, to understand their motivation, the greed, or the demons that drove them.

Gazing at the main table, Theodosia decided she had to let this murder mystery go for the time being, release it like so many fluttering night moths. Better to light the candelabra, bring out the food, and signal the start of the festivities.

Drayton had generously brought along what he'd dubbed his Phantom of the Opera candelabra. It was an antique sterling silver piece that held a half dozen tall cream-colored tapers and looked absolutely stunning on the food table.

Now, if Theodosia could just find her lighter. She glanced around, trying to recall where she'd put it, momentarily delighted by the flickering white candles she'd positioned on the large rocks that outlined the small pond. Theodosia wandered across the patio, still absorbed. Maybe she'd left the lighter on one of the tables? Scanning the table nearest the door, her senses were suddenly tickled into awareness by a vaguely familiar scent. Something woodsy, like cut

413

grass or cedar?

Only at the very last second was she cognizant of the teaberry scent and someone coming up behind her. Sensing danger before she saw it, Theodosia spun quickly just as Fallon lunged from the darkness like a bloodthirsty vampire!

dosia tried to feint to one side, but stumbled and lost her balance.

Fast as a snapping turtle, Fallon was on top of Theodosia, shoving her backward into the pond, pushing her head underwater.

Struggling frantically, Theodosia opened her mouth and screamed an underwater protest. Bubbles streamed from her nose and mouth, her cry echoed hollowly.

Still no one came.

Gazing up through thrashing water, Theodosia saw Fallon's arm raised high above her head, ready to bring the knife down in a final coup de grâce. Realizing she was still clinging to the candelabra, she thrust it once again at Fallon! This time she made contact with a dull clunk, causing the blade to tumble from Fallon's hand.

Still peering up through the water, Theodosia was stunned to see the knife zip past her, then tumble harmlessly to the murky bottom of the pool.

Fallon had lost her weapon, but she was still driven for vengeance. As Theodosia bobbed up for air, Fallon wrapped both hands around her throat, squeezing hard, shoving her below the surface again in an attempt to strangle her!

Dropping the candelabra, Theodosia's hands flew up to pry Fallon's hands from

29

Shrieking like a banshee, brandishing a knife above her head, Fallon grinned malevolently as she rushed at Theodosia, poised to strike!

"Wha—" said Theodosia, stunned, terrified out of her mind, and backpedaling like crazy as she tried desperately to scramble from Fallon's reach. "You!"

"Yes, me," breathed Fallon in a hoarse, harsh voice as she swung her knife at Theodosia.

Theodosia jumped back again, caught her heel in a jagged crack, kicked out of her shoes, then backed away slowly. As if retreating from a rabid animal.

But Fallon was out for blood. She darted forward, swinging her knife back and forth in a wide arc.

"Stop it," said Theodosia, gasping for breath. "You don't have to do this."

"But I do." Fallon grinned. All reason and logic had seemingly evaporated from her brain. Now she was just a stone-cold killer.

Backing across the patio, extending her hands in a pleading gesture, Theodosia felt her hip touch the back of a wrought-iron chair. Scurrying around the table, she tried to put some sort of barrier between her and Fallon.

"Why?" asked Theodosia. "Why your sister?" If she could keep Fallon talking, maybe she could also attract someone's attention.

"Not sister," spat out Fallon. "Not even blood. I was the adopted one. Never pretty enough, never good enough, never smart enough."

"You know that's not true!" said Theodosia.

"I saw the pity on their faces," cried Fallon.

"Not pity, love," said Theodosia.

"And they never even *told* me," shrieked Fallon. "Everyone keeping the big, bad secret."

"I'm sure no one wanted to intentionally hurt you," said Theodosia.

"Never fitting in," spat Fallon, lunging around the table.

Theodosia skittered away, desperately hoping to seek refuge inside, but Fallon doggedly stalked her in a darkly comic

416

duck-and-hide ballet that took them ing and dashing around the entire pa

"Help!" Theodosia shrieked. "Som help me! Police! Fire!" she called out. ing and dodging, she pleaded for help never seemed to materialize. Backed against the large food table now, not r room to maneuver, Theodosia reached and snatched Drayton's candelabra. Ch pagne flutes wobbled, then crashed on ment, shards flying everywhere as Theodc thrust her makeshift weapon at Fallon, t ing bravely to deflect her jabs. But t candelabra was heavy and clumsy, and Theodosia could achieve were a few wea parries against Fallon's deadly blade.

"Nobody's going to help you," crooned Fallon in a low, strangled voice. "You're mine now, you meddling pest!"

"That's what you think," grunted Theodosia. Gathering her strength, she swung the candelabra with all her might, connecting hard with both the knife and Fallon's hand.

"Oww!" howled Fallon. But she was still crazy and quick. Charging Theodosia in an all-out push, she thrust and jabbed and threatened, finally backing her up against the edge of the pond. No place to go.

Knowing she was in serious danger, Theo-

417

her neck. But, caught in a murderous fervor, Fallon maintained her deathlike grip!

Arching her back, Theodosia fought harder as she realized her air supply was running out.

Not good, this is not good! Gotta make something happen!

But Fallon was crazed and crazed people often possess superhuman strength.

Theodosia's lungs burned like fire and her arms flailed helplessly, batting against the rocky edge of the pool, scraping nails and fingertips.

If only she could get a better grip! Grab onto the rocks and heave herself upward!

Fighting with renewed energy, Theodosia twisted and turned and struggled to get her legs under her, then fought to push up. It worked. Sort of. Theodosia gasped a tiny sip of air as she floundered mightily, her left hand scrabbling across rock again. And just as she was pushed under a third time, her fingers touched . . . metal.

Metal? My misplaced lighter? Has to be.

Keeping that thought as a homing beacon, Theodosia struggled harder, straining to grab the lighter. But even though her fingers touched cool metal again, she couldn't grab hold. It was just out of reach!

Thrashing and wrenching her head to the

left, Theodosia made slight contact with Fallon's right wrist.

Should I? Has to be done.

And bit down hard.

She heard Fallon's shriek, felt the woman's grip loosen just slightly. And made a final effort to grab the lighter.

Got it!

And just as everything faded black before Theodosia's eyes, just as her ears pounded like a million cannons firing, her index finger pushed down on the lighter's button.

She felt the click rather than heard it. But just knowing she had a weapon renewed Theodosia's resolve.

Taking a wild guess, what might be her only guess, Theodosia jabbed the flaming lighter at Fallon. Hoping, praying, she'd somehow make contact.

Staring upward, as if in a dream, Theodosia saw the lighter with its small, wavering flame and what appeared to be her disembodied hand.

Then slowly, amazingly, a ring of fire seemed to dance and grow and shimmer above her. And Theodosia suddenly realized she'd set Fallon's skirt on fire!

A bloodcurdling scream rent the air. Fallon's hands clenched reflexively around

Theodosia's neck, then slipped blessedly off.

Driving herself upward with the aid of her legs, drawing in blessed deep gluts of air, Theodosia flew out of the water like a seal heaving itself onto a rocky beach.

And beheld a scene as bizarre as any from Dante's *Inferno*.

Fallon, her skirt a flaming pinwheel, whirled and twirled her way across the patio like a drunken fire dancer. Frantic and frenzied, batting at the flames, high-pitched screams roiled from her in a death cry.

As Fallon's shrieks rent the air, curious, horrified guests cautiously opened the French doors to poke their heads out and see what was happening!

Theodosia, still gasping, pulled herself upright and watched in shock. Like a whirling dervish, Fallon crashed from one table to another, knocking over candles, setting white linen tablecloths on fire.

Dear lord, thought Theodosia, *this whole place might go up in flames!*

"Call the fire department!" yelped Drayton, as he ran out, balancing a tray of hors d'oeuvres.

"Somebody help her!" screamed Haley, standing stock-still, gripping a large silver teapot.

Theodosia sprinted for Haley, ripped the teapot from her hands, and lunged at Fallon. Splashing her head to toe with Russian Caravan tea, she managed to douse the flames.

30

So much for the party on the patio.

Poor Drayton had to pull himself together and deliver yet another speech. This one was considerably more somber and apologetic than the first, but carefully diffused the situation. The upshot of his words were — there'd been an unfortunate fire on the patio. No one was seriously injured, but could you all kindly exit via the main hallway so the fire department, ambulance workers, and police officers could do their job. So sorry the cocktail party had to be called off.

Once Drayton and Timothy Neville had managed to beat back all the curious guests and send them packing, they collapsed in heaps at one of the tables.

"The woman . . ." said Timothy, looking grim. "Fallon."

"Dispatched in an ambulance," said Tidwell, who had somehow found his way back to the Heritage Society and was now seated next to Theodosia, watching her carefully. "With police guard."

"Is she okay?" asked Theodosia.

"Medics thought so," replied Tidwell.

"Are *you* okay?" Drayton asked Theodosia, peering across the table at her. She was thoroughly drenched and had accepted Tidwell's jacket to wear. It billowed around her like a circus tent.

"I think so," Theodosia murmured. But she was searching for answers, too. "Any idea on Fallon's backstory?" she asked Tidwell. "What might have turned her into such a raving maniac?"

"Best as we can determine," said Tidwell, "Fallon's been having trouble all her life. Trouble in school, in and out of a couple of private clinics, taking serious doses of antidepressants."

"Even though she had a loving family," murmured Theodosia.

"It wasn't until Jack Brux called me a couple of hours ago that I strung it all together," said Tidwell.

"Strung what together?" asked Drayton.

"Fallon was adopted," said Theodosia.

"What!" exclaimed Drayton. "I never knew that!"

"Brux finally pieced a couple of those

documents together," said Tidwell. "The ones that had been ripped to shreds."

"Family records?" guessed Theodosia. She was beginning to get a clearer picture.

Tidwell nodded. "Obviously they were records where not a single mention of her was made."

"Fallon could have harbored feelings of anger and frustration that festered for years," said Drayton. "And seeing her non-heritage in black and white tipped her over the edge."

"Poor Sophie," said Theodosia.

Drayton nodded. "In a way she lost two daughters."

Theodosia turned toward Tidwell, suddenly angry. "But you *knew* about Fallon's mental state. And you'd just found out about the documents! So why didn't you warn me about her?"

"Because I had no idea she'd *be* here!" Tidwell shouted back. "After we picked up the crazy perfume ladies, I was going to issue a warrant for Fallon's arrest. Show up at her house, take her into custody quietly."

"But she was here," said Drayton.

"Mmm," said Theodosia, her anger starting to retreat. "And then I had to open my big mouth and tell her how close we were to catching Daria's killer."

"Because we were," put in Haley. "Weren't we?"

"But I set Fallon off," said Theodosia. "Maybe she would have gone quietly with Tidwell if I hadn't suggested I was hot on the trail. Maybe she would have confessed of her own volition, helped put things right."

Timothy Neville suddenly put his head in his hands. "No, this was my fault. I almost got you killed, dear lady," he said mournfully to Theodosia. "Calling the shop. Borrowing that map."

"Don't lose too much sleep over it," Tidwell told him. "Truth be told, Theodosia enjoys plunking herself in the middle of a crisis. Any crisis."

"Don't say that," said Drayton, rushing to defend her. "Theodosia was only trying to help."

"And now things are a mess," said a glum Timothy Neville. He looked around the patio. "This place is a mess."

"Look at the bright side," suggested Haley. "Daria's killer has been caught. And this has to have been one of the craziest, most memorable evenings the Heritage Society ever had. I'll bet this helps pull in new members like crazy."

"You really think so?" asked Timothy, in disbelief.

Haley winked at Drayton. "Oh sure. Wouldn't you agree, Drayton?"

"I'm sure there'll be fascinating stories making the rounds," allowed Drayton.

"Huh," said Timothy, noticing the food trays Drayton and Haley had brought out. "So what are we going to do with all this food?"

"And champagne," said Drayton. "Don't forget all those cases of champagne."

A sudden pop sounded directly behind them. They all turned and were startled to see Bill Glass holding up a large green bottle. White froth gushed from it, spilling onto the patio. "Did I miss the party?" he asked. Delaine's sister, Nadine, hung on his arm, staring up with love in her eyes.

"I'd say you *are* the party," murmured Drayton.

Jumping up, Haley grabbed champagne flutes for everyone and quickly passed them around. Bill Glass, already in an effusive mood, followed her around the table, happily filling each person's glass with the bubbling amber liquid.

"How about a toast?" proposed Haley.

"Do you think it's appropriate?" asked Drayton.

Theodosia thought for a minute, then smiled. "I have one that might be." They all lifted their glasses high and clinked them together as she recited: "Lord, grant us all a good long life for you are surely knowing, that earth has angels all too few while heaven's overflowing."/

FAVORITE RECIPES FROM THE INDIGO TEA SHOP

HALEY'S VAGABOND VEGETABLE SOUP

2 Tbsp. olive oil
1 cup onion, chopped
1/4 cup celery, chopped
1/4 cup pepper (green or red), chopped
1 cup sweet potatoes, diced and peeled
1 tsp. paprika
1 tsp. dried basil
1 tsp. salt
1/2 tsp. pepper
1 bay leaf
1 1/2 cups chicken stock
1 tomato, chopped
3/4 cup cooked garbanzo beans

HEAT olive oil in skillet, then sauté onion, celery, pepper, and sweet potatoes for 4 to 5 minutes. Add paprika, basil, salt, pepper, and bay leaf, then mix. Add in chicken stock, cover, and simmer over low heat for 20 minutes. Add tomato and garbanzo beans to the soup and simmer for an additional 10 minutes. Makes 4 to 5 servings.

PECAN PIE MUFFINS

1 cup brown sugar, packed
1/2 cup flour
1 cup pecans, chopped
1/4 tsp. cinnamon
2 eggs
1/2 cup butter, melted

COMBINE brown sugar, flour, pecans, and cinnamon in mixing bowl. Beat eggs well, then stir in melted butter. Add egg and butter mixture to dry mixture, stirring until moistened. Spoon batter into foil baking cups that have been greased, filling about 2/3 full. Bake at 350 degrees for 20 to 25 minutes or until done. Remove from pan and cool on wire rack. Yields about 8 or 9 muffins.

HAWAIIAN TEA SANDWICHES

1 cup sugar
2 cups crushed pineapple, drained
1 cup walnuts or pecans, chopped
1 pkg. cream cheese (8 oz.) softened
2 to 3 Tbsp. cream
Bread, very thinly sliced

COMBINE sugar and pineapple in saucepan and bring to a boil, stirring constantly. Cool, then stir in nuts. Mash cream cheese with fork and add enough cream to create a good spreading consistency. Combine cream cheese with pineapple mixture. Spread mixture on thin bread and top with another slice. Trim off crusts and cut into triangles or finger sandwiches. Serve immediately.

SMOKED SALMON FLORETS

Toast rounds
Chive cream cheese
6 strips smoked salmon (lox, the cold smoked variety)

SPREAD toast rounds with cream cheese. Trim smoked salmon into narrow strips and roll until it resembles a flower. Perch atop toast round and add a snip or two of fresh chive.

ALMOND DEVONSHIRE CREAM

4 ounces cream cheese, softened
1/4 cup sour cream
2 Tbsp. sugar
1/2 tsp. almond extract

MIX all ingredients together until smooth and creamy.

TIMOTHY'S TOLL HOUSE COOKIE BARS

1 cup butter
1/2 cup brown sugar, packed
1/2 cup sugar, granulated
1 egg yolk
1 tsp. vanilla
2 cups flour
10 oz. chocolate chips
1 cup walnuts, chopped

CREAM butter, both sugars, egg yolk, and vanilla. Stir in flour and mix well. Spread mixture on greased cookie sheet, forming a thin layer of cookie.

Bake at 350 degrees for 15 to 20 minutes. Melt chocolate chips in double boiler or microwave and spread gently over sheet of warm cookies. Sprinkle walnuts on and press them in firmly. Cut into bars while still warm. Serve when chocolate is hard.

CHUTNEY AND CHEDDAR TEA SANDWICHES

1/2 cup chutney
2 cups sharp cheddar, grated coarsely
1/2 cup sour cream
3 oz. cream cheese, softened
Salt and pepper to taste
12 slices bread, very thin-sliced

STIR together chutney, cheddar cheese, sour cream, and cream cheese. Add salt and pepper to taste. Spread filling on bread to make 6 full sandwiches, then cut into small sandwich rounds — or trim off crusts and cut into triangles.

PIMENTO AND WALNUT TEA SANDWICHES

1/2 cup pimentos, chopped
1/2 cup walnuts, chopped
4 oz. cream cheese
1/2 cup mayonnaise

MIX together and add salt and pepper to taste. Makes enough filling for 12 tea sandwiches.

CHARLESTON BREAKFAST CASSEROLE

1 1/2 cups croutons
1/4 cup butter, melted
1 cup cheddar cheese, grated
3 eggs
1 cup milk
1/4 cup red pepper, diced
2 tsp. prepared mustard
6 slices bacon, fried

GREASE 8-inch-by-8-inch baking dish and fill with croutons. Drizzle with melted butter, then sprinkle with cheddar cheese. Crack eggs into bowl and whisk, breaking up yolks. Add milk, red peppers, and mustard, then beat until well combined. Pour over crouton mixture and sprinkle with crumbled bacon. Bake in 325 degree oven for 40 minutes. Let stand 10 minutes before serving. Serves 4.

FROGMORE STEW

1 gallon water
1 1/2 Tbsp. Old Bay Seasoning (or other prepared seafood seasoning)
1 lb. spicy link sausage, cut into 2-inch pieces
1 onion, medium size, chopped
6 ears sweet corn, broken into smaller pieces
2 lbs. raw shrimp

BOIL water in large stockpot and add seasoning. Add sausage and onion and boil for 5 minutes. Toss in the corn and boil for another 5 minutes. Now add the shrimp and boil for an additional 3 minutes. Drain and serve immediately with chunks of hearty bread. Serves 4 to 5.

BUTTERSCOTCH SCONES

2 cups all-purpose flour
1/3 cup brown sugar, packed

1 Tbsp. baking powder
1/2 tsp. salt
1/2 cup butter, cut into pieces
1/2 cup cream, very cold
1 egg
1 cup butterscotch chips

SIFT flour, brown sugar, baking powder, and salt into medium bowl. Add in butter and stir or rub with fingers until consistency of coarse meal. Whisk together cream and egg, then add to butter/flour mixture and stir with fork. Add butterscotch chips. Drop dough onto lightly greased baking sheet. Bake at 400 degrees for 20 minutes or until scones are golden brown.

TEA TIME TIPS FROM LAURA CHILDS

SILVER SCREEN TEA

Dig out your movie magazines and dress like your favorite silver screen star!

Set your table with white roses in silver vases, your best silver and china, tall candles, and a killer cake displayed on a cake stand. Serve crab salad sandwiches on tiny baguette slices and cream cheese and watercress tea sandwiches. Entertain guests with a classic black-and-white movie — *Casablanca* anyone? Serve a flavorful, full bodied Assam.

CROQUET TEA

When warm weather rolls around, dust off your croquet set and invite the ladies outside for tea. Wear your white dresses or white polo shirts and skirts. Serve finger sandwiches of crab salad, shredded carrot and cheddar cheese, and pineapple cream cheese. Iced sweet tea would be perfect, but think outside the box (or teabag) with iced raspberry or sweet plum tea.

MAD HATTER TEA

Encourage all your tea guests to bring their favorite beads, feathers, ribbon, vintage pins, etc. Then you provide some wide-brimmed straw hats from the craft store to decorate. Of course, you'll also have to have some extra ribbons, feathers, glue, and doo-dads available, along with plenty of tea time treats. Think mushroom quiche, cream scones, and Earl Grey tea.

TEA IN THE COTSWOLDS

Turn your kitchen or dining room into a storybook English cottage. Set your table with a blue-and-white-checkered tablecloth, then add white crocks of flowers or lavender. Serve asparagus spears rolled up in ham, cream cheese with English chutney, and fresh-baked scones in wicker baskets. Make sure you have plenty of lemon curd and Devonshire cream on hand. Serve English breakfast tea or tippy Yunnan in extra-large cups.

SPRINGTIME TEA

Choose plates, cups, and saucers with a floral or vine motif. Carry on the theme with a floral tablecloth and buckets of flowers. Serve sliced strawberries and cream cheese on nut bread, cucumber sandwiches with cream cheese and chives, and a salad of mixed greens with edible flowers.

Delight your guests with pitchers of sweet tea, steaming pots of Darjeeling, and classical music, such as Mozart's *The Magic Flute.*

ROMANCE NOVEL TEA

If your friends enjoy a good bodice buster now and again, why not entertain them with a Romance Novel Tea! Make your table as romantic as possible with crystal vases filled with roses, candles, and cushy pillows in chairs that are draped in afghans. Stack romance novels in the center of the table and make Xerox copies of covers of romance novels for place mats. Serve ham and apricot pinwheels, popovers stuffed with chicken salad, biscotti, and pound cake with raspberry sauce. Serve a tea reminiscent of romance, too, like passion fruit, lemon verbena, or Egyptian chamomile.

Low-Carb Tea

If your friends are counting carbs, that's no reason to skimp on the tea goodies. Think ham roll-ups spread with light cream cheese and apricot preserves, deviled eggs, chicken salad on low-carb bread, crab salad in lettuce cups, and chocolate-dipped strawberries. Splurge on the tea with lemon Gunpowder or a fancy Formosan oolong.

TEA CRAFTING

Teacup Candles

It's simple to make your own teacup candles. Start by selecting a pretty teacup and saucer, then epoxy them together. Add a wick, pour in melted wax, add a few drops of scented oil, and let stand until your wax hardens.

Make Your Own Rose-Flavored Tea

Strip rose petals from a rose bouquet or from rosebushes in your own garden, then dry the petals very well. When they are dry and crumbly, simply add a few petals to your favorite tin of black tea. After a few days, the rose petals will impart a rosy flavor and fragrance.

TEA RESOURCES

Tea Publications

Tea: A Magazine — Quarterly magazine about tea as a beverage and its cultural significance in the arts and society. (www.teamag.com)

Tea Poetry — Book compiled and published by Pearl Dexter, editor of *Tea: A Magazine.* (www.teamag.com)

Tea Time — Luscious magazine profiling tea and tea lore. Filled with glossy photos and wonderful recipes. (www.teatime magazine.com)

Southern Lady — From the publishers of *Tea Time* with a focus on people and places in the South as well as wonderful tea time recipes. (www.southernlady magazine.com)

The Tea House Times — Go to www.teahousetimes.com for subscription information and dozens of links to tea shops, purveyors of tea, gift shops, and tea events.

441

Victoria — Articles and pictorials on homes, home design, and tea. (www.victoriamag .com)

The Gilded Lily — Publication from the Ladies Tea Guild. (www.glily.com)

Tea in Texas — Highlighting Texas tea rooms and tea events. (www.teaintexas .com)

Fresh Cup Magazine — For tea and coffee professionals. (www.freshcup.com)

Tea Websites and Blogs

Teamap.com — Directory of hundreds of tea shops in the U.S. and Canada.

GreatTearoomsofAmerica.com — Excellent tea shop guide.

TeaRadio.com — Listen to guests share personal tea journeys.

Cookingwithideas.typepad.com — Recipes and book reviews for the bibliochef.

Cuppatea4sheri.blogspot.com — Amazing recipes.

Theladiestea.com — Networking platform for women.

Jennybakes.com — Fabulous recipes from a real made-from-scratch baker.

Bigelowtea.com — Website for the Charleston Tea Plantation, the oldest tea plantation in the United States. Order their fine black tea, too!

Teanmystery.com — Tea shop, books, gifts, and gift baskets.

Allteapots.com — Teapots from around the world.

Thechurchmouse.com — Gift shop that carries tea produced by the Fairhope Tea Plantation in Fairhope, Alabama.

Fireflyvodka.com — South Carolina purveyors of Sweet Tea vodka, Raspberry Tea vodka, Peach Tea vodka and more. Just visiting this website is a trip in itself!

Teasquared.blogspot.com — Fun blog about tea, tea shops, tea musing.

Bernideensteatimeblog.blogspot.com — Tea, baking, decorations, and gardening.

Tealoversroom.com — California tea rooms, Teacasts, links.

Teapages.blogspot.com — All things tea.

Big Island Tea — Organic artisan tea from Hawaii. (www.bigislandtea.com)

Sakuma Brothers Farm — This tea garden just outside Burlington, WA, has been growing white and green tea for ten years. (www.sakumamarket.com)

Baking.about.com — Carroll Pellegrinelli writes a terrific baking blog complete with recipes and photo instructions.

Purveyors of Fine Tea

Adagio.com
Harney.com
Stashtea.com
Republicoftea.com
Bigelowtea.com
Teasource.com
Celestialseasonings.com
Goldenmoontea.com
Uptontea.com
Oliverstea.com

We hope you have enjoyed this Large Print book. Other Thorndike, Wheeler, Kennebec, and Chivers Press Large Print books are available at your library or directly from the publishers.

For information about current and upcoming titles, please call or write, without obligation, to:

Publisher
Thorndike Press
295 Kennedy Memorial Drive
Waterville, ME 04901
Tel. (800) 223-1244

or visit our Web site at:

http://gale.cengage.com/thorndike

OR

Chivers Large Print
published by BBC Audiobooks Ltd
St James House, The Square
Lower Bristol Road
Bath BA2 3SB
England
Tel. +44(0) 800 136919
email: bbcaudiobooks@bbc.co.uk
www.bbcaudiobooks.co.uk

All our Large Print titles are designed for easy reading, and all our books are made to last.